Perpetrators, Accomplices and Victims in Twentieth-Century Politics

These studies examine the ways in which succeeding democratic regimes have dealt with, or have ignored (and in several cases sugar-coated) an authoritarian or totalitarian past from 1943 to the present. They treat the relationship with democratization and the different ways in which collective memory is formed and dealt with, or ignored and suppressed. Previous books have examined only restricted sets of countries, such as western or eastern Europe, or Latin America. The present volume treats a broader range of cases than any preceding account, and also a much broader time-span, investigating diverse historical and cultural contexts, and the role of national identity and nationalism, studying the aftermath of both fascist and communist regimes in both Europe and Asia in an interdisciplinary framework, while the conclusion provides a more complete comparative perspective than will be found in any other work.

The book will be of interest to historians and political scientists, and to those interested in fascism, communism, legacies of war, democratization, collective memory and transitional justice.

This book was previously published as a special issue of *Totalitarian Movements and Political Religions*.

Anatoly M. Khazanov is Ernest Gellner Professor of Anthropology Emeritus at the University of Wisconsin-Madison.

Stanley G. Payne is Hilldale-Jaume Vicens Vives Professor of History Emeritus at the University of Wisconsin-Madison.

T0314726

Totalitarian Movements and Political Religions
Series Editors: **Matthew Feldman,** University of Northampton, **Roger Griffin,** Oxford Brookes University and **Robert Mallett**, University of Birmingham.

This innovative new book series will scrutinise all attempts to totally refashion mankind and society, whether these hailed from the Left or the Right, which, unusually, will receive equal consideration. Although its primary focus will be on the authoritarian and totalitarian politics of the twentieth century, the series will also provide a forum for the wider discussion of the politics of faith and salvation in general, together with an examination of their inexorably catastrophic consequences. There are no chronological or geographical limitations to the books that may be included, and the series will include reprints of classic works and translations, as well as monographs and collections of essays.

International Fascism, 1919-45
Edited by **Gert Sorensen**, University of Copenhagen and **Robert Mallett**, University of Birmingham

Totalitarian Democracy and After
International Colloquium in Memory of Jacob Talmon
Edited by **Yehoshua Arieli** and **Nathan Rotenstreich**

Religion, Politics and Ideology in the Third Reich
Selected Essays
Uriel Tal, with In Memoriam by **Saul Friedländer**

The Seizure of Power
Fascism in Italy 1919-1929
Adrian Lyttelton

The French and Italian Communist Parties
Comrades and Culture
Cyrille Guiat, Herriott-Watt University, Edinburgh
Foreword by **David Bell**

The Lesser Evil
Moral Approaches to Genocide Practices

Edited by **Helmut Dubiel** and **Gabriel Motzkin**

Fascism as a Totalitarian Movement
Roger Griffin

The Italian Road to Totalitarianism
Emilio Gentile
Translated by **Robert Mallett**

Religion, Politics and Ideology in the Third Reich
Selected Essays
Uriel Tal, with *in memoriam* by **Saul Friedländer**

Totalitarianism and Political Religions, Volume 1
Concepts for the Comparison of Dictatorships
Edited by **Hans Maier**

Stalinism at the Turn of the Milennium:
Russian and Western Views
John Keep and **Alter Litvin**

Totalitarianism and Political Religions, Volume II
Concepts for the Comparison of Dictatorships
Edited by **Hans Maier** / **Michael Schäfer**
Translated by **Jodi Bruhn**

Totalitarianism and Political Religions, Volume III
Concepts for the Comparison of Dictatorships - Theory and History of Interpretation
Edited by **Hans Maier**
Translated by **Jodi Bruhn**

The Independent State of Croatia 1941-45
Edited by **Sabrina P. Ramet**

Clerical Fascism in Interwar Europe
Edited by **Matthew Feldman** and **Marius Turda** with **Tudor Georgescu**

Perpetrators, Accomplices and Victims in Twentieth-Century Politics
Reckoning with the Past
Edited by **Anatoly M. Khazanov** and **Stanley Payne**

Perpetrators, Accomplices and Victims in Twentieth-Century Politics

Reckoning with the Past

Edited by Anatoly M. Khazanov and Stanley Payne

Routledge
Taylor & Francis Group

LONDON AND NEW YORK

First published 2009 by Routledge
2 Park Square, Milton Park, Abingdon, Oxon, OX14 4RN

Simultaneously published in the USA and Canada
by Routledge
711 Third Avenue, New York, NY 10017

Routledge is an imprint of the Taylor & Francis Group, an informa business

Typeset in Times by Value Chain, India

British Library Cataloguing in Publication Data
A catalogue record for this book is available from the British Library

ISBN13: 978-0-415-48625-5 (hbk)
ISBN13: 978-0-415-85024-7 (pbk)

Contents

Notes on Contributors

Laird Boswell is Professor of History at the University of Wisconsin-Madison. He is the author of *Rural Communism in France, 1920–1939* (1998) and has recently published "L'historiographie du communisme français est-elle dans une impasse?", [Has the Historiography of French communism reached a dead end?], *Revue française de science politique* 55 (2005). He is completing a book that uses the case of Alsace and Lorraine to examine the tense relationship between borderlands and national identity in twentieth century France.

David Chandler is Emeritus Professor of History at Monash University in Melbourne, Australia. His books include *A History of Cambodia* (4th edn, 2007); *The Tragedy of Cambodian History* (1991); *Brother Number One: A Political Biography of Pol Pot* (2nd edn, 1999); *Facing the Candia Past: Selected Essays 1972–1994* (1996) and *Voices from S-21: Terror and History in Pol Pot's Secret Prison* (1999). He has held visiting positions at Cornell University, Georgetown University, the University of Paris, the University of Michigan and the University of Wisconsin.

Ignacio Fernández de Mata is Associate Professor in Social Anthropology, Faculty of Humanities, University of Burgos, Vice-Dean of Humanities and Audiovisual Comunication. His present research project is related to the slaughter at the beginning of the Spanish Civil War in the francoist zone. This research is about traumatic events and social memory, using anthropological and historical methods. Before this topic he published several works on the origins of the medieval Castile, the identity of the Castilian people, the daily life of peasants during the nineteenth and twentieth centuries, the rise of ethnology in Castile and the memory of the excluded people from history after 1939.

Edward Friedman is a Professor in the Department of Political Science at the University of Wisconsin-Madison where he specialises in Chinese politics. His most recent books include *Political Transitions in Dominant Party Systems: Learning to Lose; Revolution, Resistance and Reform in Village China; China's Rise, Taiwan's Dilemmas and International Peace; Regional Cooperation in Northeast Asian and Its Enemies;* and *What if China doesn't democratize? Implications for war and peace.*

Milan Hauner is the author and co-editor of ten books and more than 100 scholarly articles on the modern history of India, Central Asia, Czechoslovakia, Germany, and Russia. He grew up in Prague where he studied history at Charles University and completed his Ph.D. Leaving at the time of the Soviet invasion in 1968 he settled in England, studying for his second Ph.D. in Cambridge. He then joined St. Antony's College in Oxford and lived in London from 1974, working in the Research Dept. of Amnesty International. Two years later he joined the

German Historical Inst. in London, before leaving for the United States in 1980 to join his family. Thereafter he has been affiliated with the University of Wisconsin-Madison, where his wife is Professor of African languages and Associate Dean of humanities. He has taught and done research at various universities in England (Warwick, L.S.E., Open U.), Germany (Freiburg, Leipzig – as a visiting Fullbright professor) and America (Philadelphia, Berkeley, Hoover Inst., Stanford, Georgetown, Chicago, Columbia, US Naval War College) – and after 1990 again in Eastern Europe. Recently he edited several unpublished manuscripts of the former Czechoslovak president Edvard Beneš, and reconstructed President Beneš's wartime Memoirs 1938–45 in three volumes, published in 2007.

Jeffrey Herf is Professor of Modern European and German History at the University of Maryland, College Park, USA. He received his B.A. from the University of Wisconsin, Madison in 1969, and his doctorate from Brandeis University in 1981. He has taught at Harvard and Ohio universities and lectured widely in the United States, Europe and Israel. His publications include: *The Jewish Enemy: Nazi Propaganda During World War II and the Holocaust* (2006); *Divided Memory: The Nazi Past in the Two Germanys* (1997); *War by Other Means: Soviet Power, West German Resistance and the Battle of the Euromissiles* (1991); and *Reactionary Modernism: Technology, Culture and Politics in Weimar and the Third Reich* (1984). He is currently writing a history of Nazi Germany's radio and print propaganda aimed at the Middle East during World War II and the Holocaust.

Christopher Kaplonski is a Senior Research Associate at the Mongolia and Inner Asia Studies Unit/Department of Social Anthropology, University of Cambridge, where he is Project Manager for The Oral History of Twentieth Century Mongolia. He is a political anthropologist who has carried out research in Mongolia since the early 1990s, specialising on memory, narrative and identity. His current research deals with political violence in the 1930s as well as representations of violence in postsocialist Mongolia.

Anatoly M. Khazanov is Ernest Gellner Professor of Anthropology Emeritus at the University of Wisconsin-Madison. He is a fellow of the British Academy and an honorary member of the Central Eurasian Society. He is an author and editor of some sixteen books and about two hundred papers. His current research interests include nationalism, post-communist countries, and transitions from the totalitarian rule.

Eva Kovacs is Senior Researcher at the Institute of Sociology, Hungarian Academy of Sciences, and Professor at the Department of Communication and Media Studies, University of Pécs. She has a Ph.D. in sociology (1994). She is member of the International Advisory Bord of the Commisson for Culture Studies and History of Theatre (Austrian Academy of Sciences). Her areas of research include: socialist and post-socialist monuments and museums in Hungary; oral history of World War II; historical anthropology of the Austro-Hungarian Monarchy; community studies; ethnic studies and discourse analysis. Eva Kovacs was co-curator of the Exhibition 'Political Iconography – Myths of the Nations – Struggle of Memories, Deutsches Historisches Museum, Berlin' (2004), and 'Roma & Sinti. Representation of 'Gypsies' in the Modern Age' (2006). She was co-ordinator of several international researches (Mauthausen Survivors Memorial Project; Documentation Project of Slave and Forced Laborers; etc.). Her publications include three monographs, a number of articles in international journals and edited volumes.

János Mátyás Kovács has worked as a Permanent Fellow at the Institute for Human Sciences (IWM), Vienna since 1991. He is also member of the Institute of Economics, Hungarian Academy of Sciences, Budapest, and serves as an editor of *Transit* (Vienna) and *2000* (Budapest). His fields of research include the history of economic and political thought in Eastern Europe, history of communist economies and politics, political economy of post-communist transformation, and economic cultures in Eastern Europe. His latest publications include: "Little America. Eastern European Economic Cultures in the EU", in Ivan Krastev and Alan McPherson, *The Anti-American Century* (2007); "Worte zu Schwertern. Wie in Ostmitteleuropa Wohlfahrtsreformen gezimmert werden", *Transit* 32 (2007); "Narcissism of Small Differences. Looking Back on 'Reform Economics' in Hungary", in Christoph Boyer (Hg.), *Zur Physiognomie sozialistischer Wirtschaftsreformen* (2007); "Between Resentment and Indifference. Narratives of Solidarity in the Enlarging Union", in Krzysztof Michalski (ed.), *What Holds Europe Together?* (2006); "Which Past Matters? Culture and Economic Development in Eastern Europe after 1989", in Lawrence E. Harrison and Peter L. Berger (eds), *Developing Cultures* (2006).

Luca La Rovere received his MA from the Ecole des Hautes Etudes en Sciences Sociales, his Ph.D. from the University of "Roma Tre" and his Post-doctorate from the Hebrew University of Jerusalem. He has taught History as visiting professor at the University of Rome 'La Sapienza'. He currently teaches Contemporary History at the University of Perugia (Italy). He is the author of books and articles on the formation of young intellectuals in the fascist regime. His book about the transition of the Italian intellectuals to postfascism is forthcoming.

Stanley G. Payne is Hilldale–Jaume Vicens Vives Professor of History Emeritus at the University of Wisconsin–Madison. He is the author of 16 books, mainly dealing with the history of Spain, the Spanish Republic and Civil War, the Franco regime and the history of fascism. The most recent is *Franco and Hitler: Spain, Germany and World War II* (2008).

António Costa Pinto is a Professor of Modern European History and Politics at Lisbon University's Institute of Social Science. He holds a Ph.D. from the European University Institute, Florence (1992). He is the author of *The Blue Shirts. Portuguese Fascism in Interwar Europe* (2000) and the editor of *Contemporary Portugal* (2005) and recently co-edited *Southern Europe and the Making of the European Union* (2002), *Who Governs Southern Europe? Regime Change and Ministerial Recruitment* (2003) and *Charisma and Fascism in Interwar Europe* (2007).

Franziska Seraphim teaches modern and early modern Japanese history at Boston College, where she is also involved in developing the global history curriculum. She published *War Memory and Social Politics in Japan, 1945–2005* with Harvard University Asia Center Press in 2006 and is currently working on a comparative social history of reintegration in the 1950s focusing on the release and rehabilitation of convicted war criminals in Japan and Germany.

Introduction

The impact of the totalitarian regimes of the twentieth century was so catastrophic that the costs and consequences are still being sorted out during the
twenty-first century. The legacies of communism, fascism and Nazism, together
with those of their satellite or kindred regimes, are still with us, and in some
respects have not been fully overcome, despite the achievements of recent
decades. Such legacies have been treated differently in various countries, and the
manner in which this has been done – or relatively ignored – has been an important factor in defining the future for some of them. An honest reckoning with the
past is almost always difficult, and all the more so in view of the complexities and
complicities of these regimes, combined with the extent of the trauma which they
inflicted.

Previous research on these problems has tended to focus on specific sets of
countries, such as western Europe after 1945, eastern Europe after communism or
the later South American cases. The studies in this book were originally prepared
for a conference convened at the University of Wisconsin–Madison in April 2006.[1]
The goal of that meeting was two-fold: one objective was to treat all the principal
European cases – both post-fascist and post-communist – in broader perspective,
while also including the leading case in East Asia – Japan – as well as those of two
post-communist countries in Asia – Kampuchea and Mongolia. The second goal
was to go one step further and to examine how the task of reckoning with the past
may have influenced the subsequent process of democratisation or, in the Russian
case, the limits thereof. In this regard it also seemed worthwhile to include an
examination of China, the principal post-totalitarian regime which has refused to
democratise.

The contribution of these studies is to analyse the ways in which a totalitarian
or authoritarian past has been dealt with in the leading European and Asian
cases, and also to illuminate the roles such efforts have or have not played in
attempting to move toward a more democratic future.

Anatoly M. Khazanov and Stanley G. Payne

1. The conference was made possible by generous assistance from the Anonymous Fund and the
   Mosse Program in History, both of the University of Wisconsin–Madison.

Post-Totalitarian Narratives in Germany: Reflections on Two Dictatorships after 1945 and 1989[1]

JEFFREY HERF

While large numbers of countries have experienced dictatorships of the Right and the Left, twentieth-century Germany has the dubious distinction of being among the few that experienced both varieties. In this paper I want to compare and contrast the 'post-totalitarian narratives' that after 1945 addressed the Nazi past, and after 1989/90 that of communist East Germany. The history of both of these retrospective confrontations draws attention to the impact of present politics on views of the past, as well as to issues of double standards and/or political consistency in dealing with past dictatorships of the Right and Left. During the Cold War, within and outside West and East Germany, controversy swirled around the concept of totalitarianism. Communists and Marxists bristled at Hannah Arendt's assertions that Stalin and Hitler had been totalitarian dictators. Historians of the Nazi regime argued that the concept presented a picture of a more unified and smoothly functioning dictatorship than the reality of competing and overlapping fiefdoms justified. Some claimed that the concept underestimated the active participation of the mass publics in favour of the seeming omnipotence of leaders, while others insisted that the opposite was the case and that there was far less popular support for regime extremism. Left-of-centre critics in particular suggested that the concept's focus on leaders diverted attention from the complicity of broad elites, white-washed the role of big business and lent moral legitimacy to, in their view, an unpalatable anti-communism.

One of the most striking features of these Cold War debates about totalitarianism is how rarely they did justice to the complexity and subtlety of Hannah Arendt's formulations in *The Origins of Totalitarianism*. So it is important at the outset to recall that, for her, and for Karl Bracher, the primary advocate of the value of the concept in West German studies of the Nazi regime, totalitarianism referred to a regime guided by an extremist ideology that became increasingly removed from actual events, which used terror as well as ideology to enforce its rule, crushed all political opponents and solidified central power precisely by fostering fragmentation and competition among an often chaotic set of government offices. Given that totalitarian regimes were said to be guided by ideological absolutes, Arendt and Bracher and their successors criticised those who tended to view totalitarian ideology as an instrument for other purposes. Applied to the Nazi dictatorship, the concept of totalitarianism thus placed radical anti-Semitism at the centre of its concerns. Hence, rather than being primarily a form of conservative apologia as its leftist critics suggested, the concept of totalitarianism drew attention to the most criminal, that is, genocidal dimensions of the Nazi regime which postwar conservatives often were reluctant to address in any consequential manner.[2]

During the Cold War in both West and East Germany, the public memory of the Nazi regime, World War II and the Holocaust was divided on political lines.[3] Arendt's *Origins of Totalitarianism* was one effort, written in the United States, that sought to surmount the Left–Right divide and to foster what Richard Lowenthal called an 'anti-totalitarian consensus'. In West Germany in the first postwar years, the willingness to apply the charged term 'totalitarianism' to both the Nazi past as well as the then existing communist dictatorship, was a feature of both the West German conservatism of Konrad Adenauer as well as West German Social Democracy as articulated by Kurt Schumacher, Ernst Reuter and the young Willy Brandt, among others.[4] Such a willingness was never part of East German 'anti-fascism' which completely rejected the slightest hint that its own regime had anything at all in common with the previous dictatorship.[5]

The combined impact of the political culture of détente as well as the revival of varieties of Marxism in the West German new Left in the 1960s produced an assault on the validity of the concept of totalitarianism, applied either to the Nazi past or communist present. Since the founding of the two German states in 1949, the memory of World War II and the Holocaust had been divided and fragmented along the fault lines of the Cold War. The fault lines of Right and Left in West Germany's 1950s deepened considerably in the era of ideological polarisation in the 1960s and 1970s. The postwar 'anti-totalitarian consensus' gave way to passions focused on one or the other kind of regime, and to many episodes of double standards applied to one regime or another. It was the case that much of the West German political, intellectual and scholarly establishment did not anticipate – and some were not particularly enthusiastic about – the East

German revolution of 1989, nor did it display much previous interest in or knowledge of the East German dictatorship. The issue of post-totalitarian narratives after 1989/90 after the Cold War ended in western victory raised the issue of whether, and if so in what way, the divided and binary memory of the past gave way to a willingness to look critically at both the communist as well as the Nazi dictatorships. Indeed, what the Germans called *Diktaturvergleich* or 'comparison of dictatorship' became a primary issue in the German reckoning of the 1990s.

The controversies surrounding confrontation with the communist past after 1989 took place in the shadow of long-standing debates about how both German states avoided and faced the Nazi past after 1949. In my history of public reflection and policies, *Divided Memory: The Nazi Past in the Two Germanys*, I posed the following questions: first, given the degree of support for the Nazi regime up to its very end, why was there any memory of the Holocaust and justice for its perpetrators, rather than none at all? Why after it emerged as a minority tradition in West Germany, did it expand in later years? Why after memory of the Holocaust emerged in the Soviet occupation zone and then in East Germany was it marginalised and its advocates repressed? After all, despite horrendous numbers of battlefield deaths – 1.5 million from January to May 1945 alone – the German armies fought to the bitter end.[6] No one would have been surprised if memory and justice in West Germany after Nazism had replicated the pattern of complete silence and outright distortion that we associate with the American South after the Civil War and slavery, or Japan after World War II. Yet, despite a broad climate of selective memory, premature amnesty and failure to bring many perpetrators to justice, memory of the Holocaust in West Germany emerged among a few political leaders and intellectuals in the Occupation era, and then expanded over time in the Federal Republic of Germany.

The West German reckoning amid the larger silence and premature amnesty was due to a conjuncture of the following causes. First, Allied unconditional victory during the war destroyed the Nazi party and left its ideology of racial supremacy in shambles. The totality of Nazism's military defeat was the obvious, yet too often taken for granted, precondition for the scope of reckoning with the past that took place. Second, Allied occupation policies assured that Nazism would not revive as a major political force. The postwar trials for war crimes and crimes against humanity in Nuremberg and elsewhere brought the essential facts about the crimes of the Nazi regime to the attention of a mass public, and did so largely on the basis of the regime's own documents and on testimony from key high-ranking officials. Third, the occupying powers facilitated what I called 'multiple restorations' of previously defeated anti- and non-Nazi traditions of German politics. Because modern Germany had major traditions of democratic politics before 1933 and because anti-Nazi political leaders of the Weimar era survived the Third Reich in foreign or 'inner' exile, they were able to revive these previously existing political traditions after 1945. These re-emerging political leaders played a central role in founding a postwar tradition of memory. Fourth, West Germany's need to restore good relations with the many countries in Europe that Nazi Germany had invaded, to become a member in good standing of the Western Alliance, and later to establish diplomatic relations with the states of Eastern Europe and the Soviet Union, pushed West German leaders to attempt to convince the world that a new and different Germany had emerged. The same was the case in the development of West German relations with Israel.[7] And fifth, over time, early arguments that silence and avoidance were essential to democratic stability and electoral success gave way to the contrary conviction that the credibility and stability of West German democracy needed to rest, instead, on clear memory and an honest confrontation with the crimes of the Nazi dictatorship. West German democracy displayed both the tendency of post-dictatorial societies to forget and avoid a difficult past, as well as liberal democratic institutions and the freedoms associated with them which facilitated a learning process about the Holocaust and other crimes of the Nazi regime.

There is no other case in modern history in which these five factors have co-existed to foster memory and justice about the past. However inadequate the West German record was, it remains the exception that proves a rule: following most of the episodes of modern dictatorship, injustice and genocide in Europe and elsewhere, there has been less public memory or trial and punishment than was the case in postwar West Germany.[8] Despite its anti-fascist declarations, the ability of East Germany to repress and then marginalise discussion of the Holocaust, and to place itself quickly among history's victims, has been more typical than the West German tradition of *Vergangenheitsbewältigung*.

In the year after the end of the war, the Allies arrested and interned approximately 100,000 Germans on suspicion of involvement in war crimes and crimes against humanity. In the year after the defeat of Nazi Germany, the most important still living Nazi leaders (many committed suicide after the end of the war) and many second-rank figures as well were on trial, in prison, in hiding, fleeing from the country or keeping their Nazi convictions to themselves. Between 1945 and 1949 in the three western zones of occupation, Allied occupation trials found 5025 people guilty of war crimes and crimes against humanity. Some 806 others were condemned to death, and 486 of the death sentences were carried out. Although the great majority avoided more serious punishment, these years of judicial reckoning with the criminal past of the occupation era was unprecedented in its scope.

A few prominent anti-Nazi politicians began to make speeches urging the sullen and bitter nation to reflect on past crimes as path to a better future. By 1947, Kurt Schumacher, the political leader of the Social Democratic Party, was calling for financial restitution for Jewish survivors of Nazi criminality. His conservative counterpart, Konrad Adenauer, offered gloomy retrospectives on how widespread support for National Socialism had been, and the future President of the Federal Republic, Theodor Heuss, the leader of Germany's liberals and the future *Bundespräsident*, urged his fellow citizens to remember the crimes of the past in order to establish a democracy on a foundation of truth.[9] In 1951, the West German government agreed to pay financial restitution to the state of Israel and to Jewish survivors around the world. In November 1952, standing at a memorial in Bergen-Belsen, Heuss stood next to Nahum Goldmann, the president of the World Jewish Congress, and reflecting on the crimes of the Nazi era, declared that 'no one will lift this shame from us'.

Moreover, the Nazi Party was banned and Nazism did not re-emerge as a major political force in West German politics. Of course, the 8 million members of the Nazi Party as of May 1945 did not disappear, nor did they change their ideas overnight. The Allies prevented neo-Nazis from attaining national prominence in the occupation years. A new variant of Nazi anti-Semitic legislation was not installed, nor was violence against Jews tolerated or encouraged by government authorities. During the four years of occupation in the western zones, the Allied powers balanced a desire for a revival of German politics with a bias in favour of German politicians with clear anti- or at least non-Nazi credentials. Finally, the trials of the occupation era presented the basic facts about the criminal actions of the Nazi regime. Thereafter anyone who sought to call them into question was immediately recognised as a Nazi sympathiser and thus consigned either to no, or a marginal, role in German politics. Many postwar West German politicians were loathe to discuss Nazi era crimes or declared a variety of premature amnesties. Yet after the Nuremberg and successor trials, no one in the mainstream of West German politics denied that such crimes had taken place and were committed by the Nazi regime. Even the most vigorous challenge to the West German tradition of memory during the *Historikersstreit* of the mid 1980s did not involve claims of Holocaust denial, but rather that such crimes were not unique to Germany. Such efforts to diminish or relativise the burden of guilt, however misguided, did not usually extend to disputing the well established facts of Nazi era crimes.

The postwar decades will be rightfully remembered for the reintegration of former Nazis into West German society, for its broad silence about the past and the absence of official West German zeal in efforts to bring perpetrators to justice. Yet a distinctive tradition of memory also began, rooted in indigenous, previously repressed political currents of the democratic Left, most importantly German Social Democracy. Kurt Schumacher, who was released in poor health from a Nazi concentration camp in 1944, represented 'the other Germany' which had opposed Nazism. Until his death in 1952, he was, along with Konrad Adenauer, the leader of West German Christian Democracy, the dominant political figure of the immediate postwar era. Schumacher speeches of the postwar months and years were the beginnings of West German critical reflection on the Nazi past. Speaking to the second National Party Congress of the Social Democratic Party in Nuremberg on 29 June 1947, he became the first of Germany's postwar leaders to publicly support German financial restitution to Jewish survivors.

> Comrades, we are astounded to see that today the part of humanity which was most persecuted by the Third Reich receives so little help and understanding from the world outside. I don't want to talk about the political fighters against the Third Reich. Rather, let's talk for once about the part of humanity which, due to the frightfulness of the blows it received, became the symbol of all of the suffering [inflicted by the Nazis.] Let us talk for once about the Jews in Germany and the world.

He concluded that it was 'the task of the Social Democratic Party in Germany to speak out and to state that the Third Reich made the attempt to exterminate Jewish life in Europe. *The German people are obligated to make restitution and compensation*'.[10]

The second founder of West Germany's traditions of public reckoning with the Nazi past was the liberal journalist, politician and then President of the Federal Republic, Theodor Heuss. The national and international resonance of Heuss's speeches from 1949 to 1959 stemmed from the peculiar office he occupied in the West German political system, that of the Federal President. Elected by parliament, not the popular vote, the Federal President (*Bundespräsident*) had no direct political power. Rather, the impact of the office lay in whatever moral authority its occupant could establish in public speeches and ceremonies deemed above the partisan fray. Heuss seized the opportunity offered by this platform to urge his fellow West Germans, especially the younger generation, to remember the crimes of the Nazi past. Before the founding of the Federal Republic and thus before he became *Bundespräsident*, Heuss worked as an editor of the *Rhein Neckar-Zeitung*. In his editorials he stressed that after 1945 there would be no second 'stab in the back legend' as had emerged after World War I, and that the Germans had no one but the Nazis to blame for the disaster that had enveloped, along with the military leadership, those who went along with them. In eloquent speeches at German universities he appealed to students to redefine the meaning of courage and patriotism to refer to the willingness to face the truth about a criminal past. The younger generation, he said, had a patriotic responsibility to find out the truth about the past and convey it, and not to focus only on the future or forget the past. A new democracy had to be based on honest confrontation of past misdeeds. As critical as he could be on occasion, Heuss refrained from examining how the rest of German society responded to the Nazi leadership.

In November 1952 Heuss participated in a memorial ceremony at Bergen-Belsen with Nahum Goldman. Merely appearing in such a public forum with a leader of a major Jewish organisation amounted to a dissonant statement. Heuss listened as Goldmann recalled in great detail 'the millions who found their tragic end in Auschwitz, Treblinka, Dachau and in Warsaw and Vilna and Bialystok and in countless other places'.[11] Goldmann brought the memory of the Holocaust into a postwar German national commemorative ceremony with unprecedented clarity. While the Germans might want to forget the past, the Jews would not and could not forget. Goldmann broke the constraints of Cold War thinking by pointing to the geography of German crime in what was then 'behind the iron curtain' in Eastern Europe. Attention to German crimes on the Eastern Front during World War II was becoming unusual as West Germans focused on the threat *from* the Soviet Union or dwelt on their own suffering at the hands of the Red Army.[12]

Heuss's speech in Bergen-Belsen, published with the title, "No one will lift this shame from us", was the most extensive public reflection to come from a leading official of the West German government about the crimes of the Nazi era in the 1950s. It was broadcast on radio, reported in the press and reprinted by the government's press office. 'Whoever speaks here as a German', he said, 'must have the inner freedom to face the full horror of the crimes that Germans committed here. Whoever would seek to gloss over, make little of, or diminish the depth of these crimes, or even to justify them with reference to any sort of use of so-called reason of state would only be insolent and impudent'. Whatever the Germans might do, 'the Jews will never forget, they cannot ever forget, what was done to them. The Germans must not and cannot ever forget what human beings from their own people did in these years so rich in shame'. He said that an 'honorable feeling for one's country' which requires that 'everyone place himself or herself in its history' was not composed of comforting myths or efforts to change the subject by pointing to the misdeeds of others or simple denial. The shame for these events would never be lifted above all because the Germans themselves understood that Nazism was a departure from the civilised morality that was also a part of German history. The moral imperative to recall the crimes of the Nazi era was not a burden imposed by occupiers and victors, but one that flowed from the better traditions of a once more existing 'other Germany'.[13] Though eloquent, Heuss was a cautious man. As *Bundespräsident*, Heuss did not push for a renewal of trials for Nazi era crimes in the decade when it would have done the most good, namely the 1950s when memories were fresh, many eyewitnesses were alive and unpunished perpetrators were living free in more or less comfortable obscurity. The initiative for the trials that did take place in Frankfurt/Main and elsewhere came, on the contrary, from local and state district attorneys.[14] Heuss was a civilised, eloquent and distinctly minority voice of an era that was marked more by a mixture of financial restitution to survivors, premature amnesty, widespread silence about the past and a paucity of judicial reckoning.

While Heuss argued that successful democratisation required a hard look at the past, the dominant political figure of the first decades of West German democracy took a different view. The postwar political career of Konrad Adenauer, the West German Chancellor from 1949 to 1963, illustrated tensions between rapid democratisation, memory and justice. The Nazis drove him out of the Mayor's office in Cologne in 1933. He spent the Nazi years in 'inner immigration', supported by wealthy friends and a Catholic monastery. He was briefly arrested by the Gestapo in 1944 but avoided direct contact with anti-Nazi resistance groups. In his speeches of the occupation era, Adenauer delivered sharp denunciations of the Nazi regime, which he called a totalitarian dictatorship. He believed Nazism had deep roots in German authoritarian traditions. The Germans had to return to 'the West', to its religious faith, belief in individual rights and to friendship with France, the United States and Britain. His benign view of Christianity and view of Nazism as a form of atheism and paganism led him to call for a religious revival but also to denounce anti-Semitism. Adenauer's conservatism encompassed a pessimistic view of human nature. He also had a low opinion of the political and moral judgments of his fellow Germans during the Nazi period. Adenauer's pessimism about the Germans reinforced his inclination to say as little as possible about the crimes of the Nazi era. His focus was firmly on the present and future and on avoiding raising issues that would cause the voting base of former and hopefully disillusioned Nazis from abandoning the Christian Democratic Union. His own inclinations to put the past behind merged with the desires of these voters. His voters voted for his anti-communism, his support for integration with the West, advocacy of traditional values of faith and family, along with a mixture of capitalism and the welfare state. These were the dominant issues that facilitated a succession of national electoral victories over the Social Democrats whose Marxism he denounced, and whose opposition to West German rearmament he condemned. His Christian Democratic base included voters who opted for him and the CDU because they trusted that he would 'leave the past behind', support amnesty measures for those who had fallen afoul of Allied de-Nazification policies and would not press for timely trial and punishment of those Nazi perpetrators who had managed to escape notice during the years of Allied occupation.

The pressure for amnesty, reintegration and forgetting also came from places normally thought to be the source of a moral compass, that is, the Christian churches. In the early 1950s, leaders of the Catholic and Protestant churches urged American High Commissioner John J. McCloy to pardon or offer amnesty to people who had been convicted of war crimes and crimes against humanity by Allied courts after the war. Their pleas for mercy and forgiveness led a disgusted and exasperated McCloy to write that such requests ignored the horrendous crimes of which the defendants had been convicted.[15] As the West German historian Norbert Frei has pointed out, the pressure to grant amnesty affected all political parties. In May 1951, the West German parliament, with support from the Social Democrats as well, passed Article 131. It stipulated that 150,000 persons who had been members of the armed forces and civil service at the end of World War II, but had lost their positions during the Allied occupation, were again legally entitled to pensions and possible re-employment in their former jobs. The parliament also ended investigations of former Nazis in government bureaucracies and supported re-hiring those who had been excluded from jobs in the public sector due to de-Nazification proceedings during the occupation era. Politicians and journalists spoke of 'the right to political error' and extended it to former officials of the Nazi regime who were either disillusioned, opportunists or both.[16]

The result was a predictable set of scandals, the most prominent and long-running of which was the fact that Adenauer insisted on choosing Hans Globke as his Chief of Staff in the Chancellor's office. Globke had been a high-ranking official in the Interior Ministry of Nazi Germany and had placed his legal expertise in the service of writing parts of the Nuremberg race laws. His presence in close proximity to the Chancellor sent a message to other former Nazi officials that if they changed their political colours and voiced support for Bonn's democratic institutions, there was a place for them in the new democracy, assuming that they had not been directly implicated the past regimes crimes. As early as 1951, the reintegration of former Nazi officials in the Foreign Ministry became a major scandal. In September of that year, the French High Commissioner reported that 62 of the 100 members of the diplomatic corps, the institution which sought to convince foreigners that a new and different Germany had emerged, had received ratings of complicity from de-Nazification courts. Forty-three were former members of the SS, and 17 were former officials of the *Sicherheitsdienst* or the Gestapo.[17] Faced with a parliamentary investigation led by the Social Democrats, Adenauer argued that the expertise of these former officials of the Third Reich was indispensable for rebuilding the Foreign Office. His Social Democratic opponents pointed out that such compromised persons in these offices damaged West Germany's efforts to foster trust and confidence abroad. Adenauer was not swayed. He feared that all this 'sniffing around for Nazis' would only stoke the fires of nationalist indignation and resentment, foster the emergence of one or more anti-democratic parties to the right of the Christian Democrats, perhaps push Germany out of its much needed anchor in the Western Alliance and frighten the rest of Europe with the spectre of a Nazi revival. His fully realistic and pessimistic view of the extent of support for the Nazi regime before 1945 led him to conclude that it was best not to investigate the past too carefully for, surely, much would be found that would anger his potential voting base.[18] The argument regarding expertise needed for the new state and society merged well with the popular mentality of drawing a line underneath the Nazi past.

In Adenauer's disillusioned view, reckoning with the crimes of the Nazi past meant first and foremost establishing a democracy firmly integrated into the Western Alliance and creating the conditions for economic recovery. Democratisation, the rule of law and preservation of political freedom should be the practical results of a post-totalitarian narrative. In addition, it should include payment of financial restitution to Jewish survivors of the Holocaust and to the state of Israel.[19] West Germany's relationship with Israel, which began under Adenauer, became one of the constants of West German and then German foreign policy. In view of West German dependence on Arab oil, this 'special relationship' had critics in West German business circles. Yet Adenauer and his protégé, Helmut Kohl, as well as every Social Democratic Chancellor, and foreign ministers from the Free Democratic as well as Green parties (such as Hans Dietrich Genscher and

Joschka Fischer) continued the policy of support for the Jewish state. Historians have often noted that Adenauer transformed conservatism in Germany from its anti-western, anti-French past to its post-1949 Atlanticist and Francophile policy. The transformation of the democratic right away from the anti-Zionism of the Nazi regime was no less remarkable.[20] Both before and after 1989/90, under governments of the centre-Right and centre-Left, the Federal Republic has been consistently supportive of Israel. Despite a growth in criticism of Israel in recent years, the Federal Republic's leaders have repeatedly spoken in favour of a compromise peace based on a two-state solution that ensures Israel's right to exist in peace and security. As the extermination of European Jewry was at the core of Nazi policy, West Germany's special relationship with Israel was another chapter of its post-totalitarian narrative.[21]

In 1959, in his essay, "What does coming to terms with the past mean?", the philosopher and social theorist Theodor Adorno drew a critical balance of the lost opportunities of the past decade.[22] The silences, he thought, had more to do with the evasive efforts of an 'all too wide awake' consciousness than with the much discussed supposed forgetfulness. The capture of Adolf Eichmann in Argentina by Israeli agents and then his trial in Jerusalem drew additional attention to the scope and large numbers of officials involved in the Holocaust.[23] State and local officials such as Fritz Bauer, the attorney general in the state of Hessen who prepared the trial of officials at the Auschwitz-Birkenau death camp, took the initiative in bringing indictments for Nazi era crimes, an initiative sorely lacking in the national ministry of justice in Bonn.[24] In 1960, the West German parliament, faced with the discomforting fact that many criminals had gone unpunished, held the first four major debates (1960, 1965, 1969, 1979). In 1979, it finally abolished it, thereby permitting continuing investigations and prosecutions.[25]

The new Left in the 1960s offered an ambivalent stance toward the crimes of the Nazi era. On the one hand, it challenged an older generation to face the truth about the Nazi past. On the other, the resurgence of Marxism within its ranks was accompanied by an attack on the concept of totalitarianism, a revival of discussion of the links between capitalism and fascism and thus a diminished interest in the specifics of Nazi anti-Semitism and the extermination of Europe's Jews.[26] The new Left produced both a critique of the shortcomings of the West German confrontation with the Nazi past, a Marxist analysis which spoke far more about capitalism and far less about the Holocaust, as well as a lunatic fringe of anti-Israeli terrorists.[27] Yet over the course of the 1970s and 1980s, the theme of the Holocaust and the totalitarian nature of the Nazi regime found firmer foundations in both scholarly and public discussion in West Germany. Following President Reagan's and Chancellor Kohl's ill-fated visit to the military cemetery in Bitburg, *Bundespräsident* Richard von Weizäcker, reaffirmed, elaborated on and further developed the German obligation to remember the crimes of the Nazi regime, the obligation which Heuss had articulated in the 1950s. In the 1990s, accompanied by vigorous debate and opposition, the Bundestag agreed to build a memorial to the murdered Jews of Europe in the centre of the government district in Berlin. The memorial opened in spring 2005.[28]

As I have written an account of the tragic history of the repression of 'the Jewish question' in East Germany, a country of official anti-fascism, the following summary will suffice.[29] Two currents of thought contended within the communist emigration after the Nazis were 'leveraged into power' in 1933.[30] The dominant view found a home in Moscow and was led by Walter Ulbricht and

Wilhelm Pieck. A peripheral tradition emerged in wartime Mexico City. Paul Merker, another member of the Communist Party's (KPD) Politburo, was its leading exponent. Ulbricht and his comrades repeated Comintern orthodoxy that the primary victims of National Socialism, which they called 'German fascism', were the German Communist Party, the German working class and, after 1941, above all the Soviet Union. Those who most deserved to be honoured and remembered were less the 'passive' victims, such as the Jews, but rather the presumably heroic and active members of the German communist resistance as well as the soldiers of the Red Army.[31] While the Jews suffered, so too did many other nations and groups. The orthodox communist, post-fascist narrative refused to attribute anything distinctive to the fate of the Jews that would distinguish them from that of Nazism's millions of other victims.

This was not the case among some of the German communists who fled into exile in wartime Mexico City. There a minority communist tradition emerged in which priority of attention and then memory was accorded to the Nazi extermination of Europe's Jews. Distance from Moscow, as well as the political desire to respond to the anguish of European Jewish emigrés, produced a distinctive communist focus on the Nazi persecution and extermination policies aimed at Europe's Jews. In what became a much discussed essay entitled 'Anti-Semitism and Us' published in the communist Mexico-based journal *Freies Deutschland*, Merker criticized the KPD for its failure to grasp the centrality of the Jewish question for the Nazi regime. The Jews, he wrote, were being killed because of who they were, not what they had done, yet the communists had not spoken out clearly about the issue. Merker also published a remarkably detailed and acute two-volume study of the Nazi regime, *Deutschland: Sein oder Nicht-Sein*, in which he argued that radical anti-Semitism and policies of extermination of the Jews were central to Nazi ideology and policy.[32] When he returned to East Berlin after the war, Merker and several other communist leaders returning from Mexico City made the case at the top levels of the newly formed Socialist Unity Party (SED) for financial restitution to Jewish survivors, support for a Jewish state in Palestine and for giving prominence to the memory of the murder of the Jews in East German anti-fascist commemorations.

The communists returning to East Berlin from Mexico City helped to establish the political dictatorship to which they soon fell victim. All of the German communists were of two minds about the Germans. On the one hand, they repeated slogans about how a minority of Nazis, capitalists and militarists oppressed the German working class and the vast majority of the German people. On the other hand, and probably more in keeping with their actual sentiments, they denounced the majority of Germans for rejecting communists in the elections of the Weimar years, voting instead in significant numbers for the Nazis, supporting Hitler in the 1930s and fighting for the Nazi regime to the bitter end. In their radio broadcasts from wartime Moscow and early statements to the Germans in the postwar months, the communist leaders made clear their profound distrust of the majority of Germans. The two made use of communist ideology as well as wartime experience to justify in their minds the imposition of a second German dictatorship. As Marxist–Leninists, they advocated imposition of an 'anti-fascist' dictatorship of the proletariat that would transform a society enmeshed in the false consciousness produced by Nazi propaganda. Yet they were also *German* communists and thus had a particularly deep mistrust of their compatriots in light of significant popular support for the Nazi regime. Communist memory of the Nazi era was a memory of political defeats and rejections, invasion of the homeland of the revolution and a home front that was unwilling and/or unable to respond to communist appeals and overthrow the Nazi dictatorship. Ironically, like Adenauer, they too had a most jaundiced view of the real sentiments of the Germans, but unlike him and the western Allies, neither the Soviet leaders nor the German communists were willing to risk a second German democracy.

Both Leninist and Stalinist ideology and communist memory, so strikingly expressed in their 'Appeal' to the Germans of 13 June 1945, reinforced their inclination to impose a second German dictatorship on a people they regarded with suspicion.[33] The more the communists remembered Nazi Germany and World War II, the more they concluded that imposition of a second German dictatorship was its logical consequence. Democracy was not the logical endpoint of their 'post-fascist' narrative. Ironically, though the communists furiously attacked the concept of totalitarianism as 'cold war ideology', their political practice implied that the hated theory captured a truth, namely that the Nazi regime had succeeded in attracting a discomforting degree of mass support. If the theory of totalitarianism was so horribly mistaken, then why not take a chance on a second German democracy. The vehemence of their attack on the very idea suggested that the communists thought there was something to it. In any case, for them a clear and vivid memory of the crimes of the Nazi regime as they understood them made imposition of a second German dictatorship a matter of ideological consistency, elementary common sense and necessary political didacticism. This mixture of propaganda about the marvels of 'socialist democracy', that is, one-party rule combined with deep and abiding mistrust of the Germans, characterised the East German regime throughout its history. It accounts, in part, for the vast growth and pervasiveness of the *Stasi*, the State Security Services. However, the imposition of a dictatorship froze political learning about the Nazi era in the ideological frameworks of the Comintern in the 1920s and of wartime anti-fascism. Germany during the Nazi years had suffered less from dictatorship *per se* but from the wrong kind of dictatorship. A different dictatorship, one of the Left, was required to undo the damage of its right-wing predecessor.

The breakdown of the anti-Hitler coalition and the emergence of the Cold War was accompanied by what the Soviets called the 'anti-cosmopolitan campaigns' of the early 1950s. In 1950 in the first of a set of purges of communists who had found exile in the West, Merker and Leo Zuckermann, another high-ranking communist and associate of Merker's, were dismissed from their political positions in the Socialist Unity Party (the *SED*) and in the East German government. In December 1952, Merker was arrested and charged with being the German counterpart of 'the Slansky conspiracy center' and thus part of an international, Zionist, American capitalist plot to overthrow communism in Europe. The leader of the East German 'central party control commission', Herman Matern, denounced 'the criminal activity of Zionist organization' in league with 'American agents' who were trying to destroy the peoples' democracies of Eastern Europe. Anticipating charges of anti-Semitism, Matern said that the Slansky trial showed that, 'a method of these criminals included efforts to discredit vigilant, progressive comrades by charging them with anti-Semitism'. Yet, he continued, 'the Zionist movement has nothing in common with the goals of humanity. It is dominated, directed and organized by USA imperialism and exclusively serves its interests and the interests of Jewish capitalists'. In Mexico City, Merker had 'called for indemnification of Jewish property only to facilitate the penetration of

USA finance capital into Germany. This is the true origin of his Zionism'. Matern described Merker's arguments in Mexico as serving the interests of 'Jewish monopoly capitalists', and dismissed the idea that the Nazis had singled out the Jews as victims. Matern's denunciation turned the memory of the past into a zero sum game in which recognition of Jewish suffering was interpreted to be non-recognition of the suffering of the Soviet Union.[34]

Following his arrest, Merker was held in prison and interrogated in preparation for a secret trial in the East German Supreme Court. The trial was held in March 1955. With opening of the East German archives after 1989/90, the transcripts of the court's verdict as well as of pre-trial interrogations held in the *Stasi* files became available. I made some use of them in the *Vierteljahreshefte für Zeitgeschichte* and later in *Divided Memory*.[35] The court found Merker guilty of violating Article 6 of the East German constitution and Allied Control Law 10 of 20 December 1945 and sentenced him to eight years in prison. In other words, this leading communist was convicted of violating a law designed to thwart a revival of Nazism in postwar Germany. The court found his writings about the Jews and support for restitution to be evidence of his connection to powerful Jews abroad who sought to undermine communism in Germany. The verdict found Merker guilty of seeking political support 'not in the political but in the racial emigration'. It attributed Merker's efforts to place the Jewish catastrophe at the centre of communist anti-fascist politics to be the result of his corruption by Jewish capitalists and the intrigues of western intelligence services.

Following Soviet Prime Minister Nikita Khruschev's secret speech in 1956 to the Twentieth Congress of the Communist Party of the Soviet Union, Merker was released from prison but never regained a leading position in the East German hierarchy. On 1 June 1956, in an unsuccessful effort to attain political rehabilitation, he submitted a remarkable 38-page statement of his 'position on the Jewish question'. He noted that his interrogators could not understand why he, a non-Jewish German communist, had been so outspoken about the Jewish question unless he had been an agent of American imperialism, Zionists or Jewish capitalists. His explanation was as follows.

> I am neither Jewish nor a Zionist, though it would be no crime to be either. I have never had the intent to flee to Palestine. I have not support the efforts of Zionism … I have occasionally said that, after having been plundered by Hitler fascism, most deeply humiliated, driven from their homelands, and millions of them murdered only because they were Jews, the feeling of a deepest bond and the desire for their own Jewish country emerged among Jews of different countries. This feeling was the expression of those most deeply harmed and outraged. Moreover, Hitler fascism emerged among us [Germans]. We did not succeed through the actions of the working masses, in preventing the establishment of its rule and hence the commission of its crimes. Therefore, we Germans especially must not and ought not ignore or fight against what I call this strengthening of Jewish national feeling.[36]

Zionism, he continued, was not, as the SED claimed in 1953, an agency of American imperialism but a movement of the Jews responding to their persecution in Europe. Merker recalled Soviet support for the foundation of the Jewish state. With bitter sarcasm of a man accustomed to speaking frankly to his equals, he told the politburo members that 'no one will want to claim that the Soviet government was an 'agent of American imperialism'. He insisted that German communists, no less than non-communist Germans, stood within the continuities and burdens of German history. Yet Merker's argument that communist anti-fascism should lead to support for memory of the Jewish catastrophe and for the new Jewish state fell on deaf ears. As of winter 1952/53 the debate about the place of the memory of the murder of the Jews of Europe came to an end in East Germany. With some modifications at the edges, the orthodoxy enshrined in the Matern denunciation of 1952 remained intact until the regime's end. This margin-alisation was the logical consequence of the communist's post-fascist, not post-totalitarian, narrative.

Subsequently, East German leaders placed Israel in the camp of western impe-rialism and denounced West Germany for its close ties with the Jewish state. The narrative of anti-fascism and anti-imperialism placed East Germany outside the burdens left by Nazi Germany. Bristling with revolutionary virtue, it situated itself with pride on the side of the Arab states in their struggles against western imperialism and 'Zionist aggressors'. Ulbricht denounced West Germany's resti-tution payments as a cynical tool of western imperialism. During the Six Day War of 1967, he attacked 'Israeli aggression', while politburo member Albert Norden compared Israel's actions to Hitler's invasion of the Soviet Union on 22 June 1941. In 1969, East Germany opened diplomatic relations with Egypt, Iraq, Sudan, Syria and South Yemen. In 1971, Yassir Arafat visited East Berlin and in August 1973, the Palestine Liberation Organisation opened a consular office there, the first in the Soviet bloc. East German arms, supplies and medical treatment for PLO wounded and orphans followed. In 1975, the East German delegation at the UN voted in favour of the resolution equating Zionism with racism. In 1980, it raised the status of the PLO consulate in East Berlin to the level of an Embassy, and denounced the Camp David accords as 'an imperialist separate peace'. In the 1980s, *Neues Deutschland* reported on meetings of 'military delegations' of the PLO with East German leaders. In 1982, following the massacre of Palestinian by Christian militia in Lebanon, the East German representative to the United Nations declared before the General Assembly that 'state terrorism and criminal genocide were the firm components of Israeli policy', and that 'the genocide of the Palestinian people' was the method by which Israel's 'ruling circles' had chosen to solve the Palestinian problem'. East Germany remained the only country in the Soviet bloc which, up to 1989, had no diplomatic relations with the state of Israel. Conversely, its support for Israel's armed adversaries never wavered.[37]

Hannah Arendt described totalitarian ideology as an offense against common sense. The ability of East German communists to speak of Israel in this way, to give arms to those attempting to kill Israelis and to do all of this with a good conscience as if they were fighting a noble and just fight against oppression and injustice, was an example of the way *their* totalitarian discourse offered the great psychological benefit of lifting the regime and the population out of the burdens left behind by the Holocaust. As I wrote in *Divided Memory*: 'The East German argument that anti-fascism should logically lead to helping the armed adversaries of the Jewish state indicated how a totalitarian ideology had substituted fantasy for common sense and theories of universal liberation for the burdens of local knowledge and memory'.[38]

The first public challenge to the communists' post-fascist narrative in East Germany since the Merker case came from dissidents in the Protestant churches on 8 May 1985. Markus Meckel and Martin Gutzeit wrote that 'the guilt of the others, even of the fathers, is not alien to us'. They argued that the German Democratic Republic [East Germany] had failed to reflect on its own responsibility. While many communists had fought in the anti-Nazi resistance, most of those who became citizens of the GDR had helped to support the Nazi regime with 'their passivity and silence'. Moreover, 'National Socialist ideas also remained intact and unworked through' among many East Germans. Coming to terms with the Nazi past, they continued, meant opposing injustice and the misuse of power in the GDR and respecting 'the rights and dignity of all human beings' regardless of their world view. In other words, coming to terms with the past did not justify imposition of a second dictatorship over a dangerous people. On the contrary, it meant rejecting a second dictatorship and respecting human rights and democracy. Meckel and Gutzeit turned the discourse of coming to terms with the past against communist ideology and practice.

The marginalisation of the memory of the Holocaust was a chapter in the history of the consolidation of the East German dictatorship. Its move to centre stage was an equally important moment in the emergence of democratic institutions in the post-dictatorial East. On 12 April 1990, the first act of East Germany's first democratically elected government was to end four decades of communist denial and evasion regarding the Holocaust and its consequences. It voted 379 to 0 with 21 abstentions in favour of a resolution which accepted joint responsibility for Nazi crimes, and expressed a willingness to pay reparations and seek diplomatic ties with Israel. The resolution admitted

> joint responsibility on behalf of the people for the humiliation, expulsion, and murder of Jewish women, men and children. We feel sad and ashamed and acknowledge this burden of German history. We ask the Jews of the world to forgive us for the hypocrisy and hostility of East German policies toward Israel and also for the persecution and degradation of Jewish citizens after 1945 in our country. We declare our willingness to contribute as much as possible to the healing of mental and physical sufferings of survivors and to provide just compensation for material losses.[39]

The Volksammer statement marked the public end of East German communism's post-fascist narrative. Over the course of the summer and autumn of 1990, Markus Meckel, East Germany's last Foreign Minister and Hans Modrow, its last Prime Minister, agreed to revise East German textbooks, enter negotiations about restitution to Jewish survivors and end the training of Palestinians or others engaged in armed conflict with Israel. German re-unification in the autumn of 1990 made these decisions moot. The key point to note is that the emergence of the memory of the Holocaust was bound up with the shift from dictatorship to democracy and rejection of dictatorship in the past and present. Some observers feared that nationalist euphoria accompanying German re-unification would lead to a new era of amnesia about the Holocaust. Yet the end of official East German anti-fascism had the opposite result. The memory of the Holocaust became a part of the German political calendar. The 27 January, the day the Red Army liberated Auschwitz, was declared a national day of Holocaust remembrance in Germany.[40] Although in the 1990s the Nazi past remained a contentious matter, in 1999, the Bundestag agreed to build a memorial to the murdered Jews of Europe in Berlin.

Following the East German revolution, the collapse of communism in East Germany and in Europe and German unification, the issue of a post-totalitarian narrative regarding the German Democratic Republic came to the fore. Many of the same issues that had emerged concerning the Nazi regime, among them the validity of the concept of totalitarianism, again became prominent. Following the end of the GDR, there was a widespread determination to avoid the silence and avoidance regarding the Nazi era during the first postwar decades in both West and East Germany. On 12 March 1992 the German parliament established a commission for 'the examination of the history and consequences of the SED dictatorship'. It was called the Enquete-Kommission Aufarbeitung von Geschichte und Folgen der SED-Diktatur in Deutschland (Investigating Commission for the Examination of the History and Consequences of the Socialist Unity Party Dictatorship in Germany).[41] From spring 1992 to summer 1994, the commission took testimony from 327 eyewitnesses and scholars in 42 public hearings. It met an additional 150 times to write its final report. In 1995 its 19 volumes were published by Suhrkamp Verlag, one of the Federal Republic's leading left-liberal publishers.[42]

The language of the parliamentary resolution that established the commission referred bluntly to the 'SED dictatorship'. For many advocates of détente, the proper term of reference for the German Democratic Republic was 'security partner', and the proper policy to ensure peace in Europe was to enhance, not undermine the stability of the East German government.[43] Now, however, the parliament declared that examination of this *dictatorship* was 'a common task of all Germans... . The experiences of injustice and persecution, humiliation and depression live on'. The word 'dictatorship' was uttered as if it was the most ordinary thing to do, and as if the demobilisation of sharp criticism of the East German regime had not taken place in West German political culture since the 1970s.[44]

The published reports covered the structures of power and decision-making in the East German dictatorship; the role of ideology and modes of integration in state and society; law, justice and the police; the German question; German–German relations and their international dimensions; the role of the Churches; forms of dissent, resistance and opposition; the revolution of 1989; German unification and the aftereffects of the structures of dictatorship; the ministry of state security (the *Stasi*); and a final volume on 'forms and goals of the debate over the two dictatorships in Germany'.[45] On 31 May 1994, the Enquete-Kommission issued its 600 page report covering all of the above mentioned themes.

Rainer Eppelman, the Commission's Chair and a veteran of the East German opposition, mentioned five goals of the report about a regime which he labelled as totalitarian. First, 'political coming to terms with the totalitarian past' entailed a 'precise analysis of the totalitarian structures of domination of the SED dictatorship'. Such an effort should ensure that 'those powers in the GDR that played an important role in organising the oppression of the people should never again have a political chance in a re-unified Germany'.[46] Second, though explanation of the 'unjust character' of the SED regime would have only a limited impact on judicial or material compensation, presenting the truth in public would offer some measure of 'historical justice'. Third, it would contribute to an 'inner unification' of the Germans by showing how the 'SED dictatorship ... deformed' the lives of individuals in the GDR but also 'had a deep impact on West German society and politics'. Fourth, in so doing, it would deepen a consensus in support of democracy in unified Germany. Fifth, the commission would offer suggestions for legislation aimed at overcoming the consequences of the SED dictatorship.

Eppelmann's references to the GDR as a totalitarian regime was jarring for much of the German political and intellectual establishment, and especially for those left of centre whose focus had been on coming to terms with the Nazi past. In defending this sharp reckoning with the communist past, Eppelmann referred to the following sentence from the famous speech about facing the Nazi past by *Bundespräsident* Richard von Weizsäcker of 8 May 1985: 'He who closes his eyes to the past will ultimately be blind in the present'. The Commission dealt extensively with the issue of the similarities and differences between the Nazi regime and East German communist regime. By invoking von Weizsäcker, Eppelmann stressed that confronting the communist past would not come at the expense of memory of the Nazi past. He sought a consistent democratic reckoning with past dictatorships of the Right and Left.

The Commission critically described East German anti-fascism as 'the most effective factor of ideological integration' for the SED system.[47] It argued that anti-fascism in East Germany, following its origins in the communist anti-fascism of the 1920s and 1930s, was an 'undifferentiated political weapon used against all political and social currents' which did not support Soviet policy. Further, the SED used 'the widespread rejection of the National Socialist regime and its atrocities' in order to legitimate itself. 'Confrontation with the NS-heritage, de-Nazification and anti-fascist, democratic construction as well as the establishment of a dictatorship were all closely connected'.[48] East German anti-fascism offered material for 'a quasi-religious state cult, for a secular religion' with cults of martyrs, heroes, rituals and educational materials. It stirred 'idealism and engagement in broad sections of the population' which resulted 'above all from the rejection of the NS dictatorship' that was supposed to stabilize SED rule. Anti-fascism took aim not only at fascists and Nazis but at anyone who opposed the communists from the Federal Republic as well as domestic opponents. Indeed, the SED called the Berlin Wall 'the anti-fascist protective wall'.[49] 'The instrumentalisation of anti-fascism also repressed the shared burden of the eastern part of Germany for the National Socialist era. A certain feeling of moral superiority vis à vis the Federal Republic resulted from the criticism that the West had not decisively broken with fascism'. Official anti-fascism, the report continued, made a substantial contribution to identification with the SED, especially for intellectuals who, 'failed to grasp the real essence of the GDR-regime and therefore minimized its repressive aspects'.[50] In contrast to East German claims, the task of coming to terms with the Nazi past had never been only a problem for West Germany. After 1989, the Commission reiterated that coming to terms with the Nazi past and honouring Nazism's victims was 'a constitutive component of the democratic awareness of the history of united Germany. Therefore the explanation of this [Nazi, JH] epoch must remain an essential task of historical–political educational work'.

In view of the enormous amount of effort put into the Enquete-Kommission, the vast array of subjects it covered and remarkable number and variety of experts it consulted about domestic and international affairs, it is regrettable that the only comment about the East German regime's memory of the Holocaust, its treatment of Jews after 1945 and stance toward Israel was 'a short remark' on only one of its 601 pages. The Commission authors unconvincingly wrote that they were unable to deal with 'the problem of the Jews and the Jewish community ...

due to time limits'.[51] That said, the report did mention that the Jews in East Germany were not granted any restitution simply by virtue of having been Jewish. It noted the presence of 'anti-Jewish measures' during the Stalinist purges. It recalled East Germany's denunciations of Israel as the 'tip of the spear of American imperialism in the Middle East', that Jews could receive social welfare provisions provided they did not cultivate their Jewish identity or have contacts with anyone in Israel, and that the Jews appeared only on the margins of the communist memorials to victims of fascism. However, the Commission did not devote much effort to examining the three decades of diplomatic, economic and military assistance to the Arab states and a PLO at war with Israel, East Germany's support for the UN resolution of 1975 denouncing 'Zionism as racism', or the dimensions of anti-Semitic themes that emerged in the anti-cosmopolitan campaigns of the early 1950s.[52]

In summer 1994, when the Commission issued its report, *Die Zeit* published my essay on the secret trial of Paul Merker. The editors noted that 'an American historian discovered in the *Stasi* archives one of the most shameful episodes of East German history'.[53] The German political scientist and historian, Sigrid Meuschel, had laid out the broad outlines of the anti-cosmopolitan purges in her important work in 1992, *Legitimation und Parteiherrschaft in der DDR*. Although Meuschel was called as an expert witness before the Commission, her work on this issue did not have the impact it should have had on the Commission's report.[54] The Commission received 152 essays from scholars and experts dealing with every imaginable aspect of East German politics: Marxism–Leninism, German–German politics, the *Stasi*, churches, the Berlin Wall, sports, education, peace movements, the West German political parties and détente, oppositional writers and alternative culture, law and justice, radio and television as instruments of domination, the events of 1989–90 and many more. None of these essays dealt with East German foreign policy in the Middle East, the GDR's active hostility to Israel or its involvement in the 1975 UN resolution denouncing Zionism as a form of racism.

Its final report did include an important segment about comparisons of the Nazi and the communist dictatorships. Indeed '*Diktaturvergleich*' or 'comparison of dictatorships' became a new word in German political language. It was clear that the Commission was determined to avoid the blunders of the *Historikersstreit*. Comparison, the authors noted, does not mean equation. They rejected equating the two dictatorships because doing so 'makes light of the crimes of the National Socialist regime'. Efforts to compare the two dictatorships could lead to the mistaken impression that the Nazi regime was not fundamentally worse than the GDR. 'In order to prevent such a falsification of history and clouding of consciousness, it is an urgent requirement that we always energetically oppose such efforts at comparison with those goals'.[55] For the same reasons it was not appropriate to speak of any 'continuity of dictatorship' (*Diktaturkontinuität*) given the ruptures following the end of World War II, as well as the 'social contradictions' between the Nazi regime and that of the GDR.

The Commission thought the term 'totalitarianism' applied to the East German dictatorship because of the persecution of any opposition and the indoctrination of the population. However, 'the differences between the NS regime and the GDR are so significant that there is no common conception and no theoretical approach that can grasp these respective social structures under one concept'.[56] Those who focus on the similarities between the Nazi and communist regimes stressed: rule by a party or dictator that claims a monopoly of power; the subordination of the state into an instrument for rule by the party; denial of the separation of powers and prevention of any controls over the exercise of power; the claim to a monopoly on truth based on the world view of the leading party and the rejection of pluralism in state and society; the intrusion of the state and political party into the private lives of individuals.[57] Yet, the report continued, those who focus on such comparisons 'forget or minimize … the grave differences between dictatorships of fascist and state socialist form' and thus tend to equate them.

The Commission was concerned to draw out similarities and differences between Nazi Germany and the GDR. Yet some of its comments about the GDR were surprisingly mild. It recalled that 'German fascism' unleashed World War II and made mass murder state policy during the Holocaust. The GDR, on the other hand, advocated a peace policy and arms control measures. Rather surprisingly, given East Germany's participation in Soviet 'peace offensives' of the tense debate over medium range nuclear weapons, the Commission oddly claimed that the East German regime had contributed to a reduction in Cold War tensions and to 'serious arms control negotiations'.[58] In contrast to the Nazi regime whose leaders were brought to trial after the war, the GDR had belonged to the United Nations since 1973, gained great international prestige and was never indicted before any judicial institution. 'While the Nazi regime was anti-communist, the GDR was anti-fascist. The importance of this difference cannot be overestimated'. The Nazi regime completely destroyed democratic institutions while, according to the Commission, 'state socialism' integrated the concept of 'socialist democracy' in some areas of work and local government, hindered though it was by democratic centralism. The ideological origins of the two regimes were fundamentally different. Fascist (the report did not use the term 'Nazi') ideology was rooted in mysticism and irrationalism 'and above all the anti-human racial doctrine', while Marxist–Leninist ideology was 'bound to the rationalism and humanism of the Enlightenment and was directed against nationalist and racial hatred'.[59]

The economic structures of the two regimes were distinct. Capitalism persisted in fascism while 'state socialism' organised a non-capitalist economy. While the Nazi regime abolished social and labour rights, the GDR brought about an 'improvement in the social position of working people'. It enhanced equality of opportunity in education, careers, culture, social security, the right to work, the elimination of unemployment, women's rights, health, and child care. In these matters, according to the Commission, the GDR could compare with advanced capitalist societies. Although the SED claimed to be a 'dictatorship of the proletariat', in fact the leadership of the SED, not the working class or the SED as a whole, governed. It would be more precise to refer to a 'Stalinist-influenced dictatorship of the SED leadership' which had authoritarian and dictatorial but also democratic components. In conflict with Marx's intention, 'socialism and democracy and real emancipation remained separate' in the GDR.[60] The East German regime had to be understood in the context of German history since World War I, including the experiences of the Weimar Republic, 'fascist barbarism', the international constellation of the postwar years and the role of the occupying powers. While comparisons of the two dictatorships would contribute to reflection and research, 'it would be completely mistaken' to try to compensate for the missed opportunities in the confrontation with the Nazi past in West Germany after 1945 with 'rigorousness in the examination of the history of the GDR'.[61]

The Commission, despite a right-of-centre majority, was also remarkably kind to East Germany in the area of its foreign policy. The GDR represented a 'radical break' with the international politics of 'imperialist Germany', that is, Nazi Germany. The 'anti-fascist and anti-imperialist character of its foreign policy' comprised part of the historical legitimacy of the GDR. The GDR contributed to presenting a new face of Germany to the peoples of Eastern Europe. In Europe, the GDR advocated peace and security. In a stunning piece of revisionist history, the Commission laid the blame for Germany's division on the West while the East sought a 'unified, demilitarized and neutral Germany'. According to the Commission, East Germany sought arms control in Europe, helped to overcome the crisis of medium range nuclear weapons and sought normal relations and 'security partnership' with the Federal Republic.[62] In foreign policy, it intoned that 'the GDR supported overcoming colonialism, an equal incorporation of the developing countries in international relations and a new economic world order. It also practised practical solidarity with the countries of the Third World. All of this brought the GDR sympathy and great respect which persists after it has ceased to exist'.[63] It described in neutral tones East German foreign aid in the realm of education, health and economic support which went, 'above all to the states and national liberation movements of the third world that were anti-imperialist and socialist'. The worst the Commission said about East Germany's policy towards the developing world was that it contributed to an 'instrumentalisation' of developing countries in the East–West conflict. In the 1970s, the GDR won 'worldwide recognition' for its support for détente. To be sure, it refused to liberalise internally despite détente. Yet in the area of foreign relations, it 'did not correspond to historical realities' to call the GDR an 'unjust state' (*Unrechtstaat*). To do so would contradict the 'views of the international community of states'. No state that had diplomatic relations with the GDR spoke of it as an 'unjust state'.[64] The Commission did not dwell on the fact that the GDR was the only member of the Soviet bloc that had no diplomatic relations with Israel. The presumably so very critical, West German-dominated, Enquete-Kommission presented a view of East German foreign relations that would give little cause for protest in the former GDR. It offered no examination of the intersection of anti-Semitism and anti-Zionism in East German foreign policy.[65] The Enquete-Kommission stressed that contributing to a 'reconciliation between and among the people of the GDR and of the Federal Republic' was part of its 'essential mission'.[66] Perhaps this drive for reconciliation among the Germans stood in the way of addressing difficult issues such as the East German record in the Middle East. As the American historian David Blight has pointed out so well in *Race and Reununion: The Civil War in American Memory*, the desire for reconciliation among former adversaries fostered apologia and myth more than an honest confrontation with difficult past.[67]

The shadow of the erroneous and politically motivated historical comparisons of the historians' dispute of the 1980s was clearly on the minds of the scholars invited to testify. Everyone, especially conservatives, was determined to avoid a repetition of comparisons that obscured differences. Horst Möller, Director of the Institut für Zeitgeschichte in Munich and a historian with impeccable conservative and anti-communist credentials asserted, 'a fundamental difference [between Nazi Germany and the DDR] certainly lay in the fact that there was no racism under Communism'.[68] Instead, Möller continued, millions were killed in the Soviet Union due to 'class murder' (*Klassenmord*), not racially motivated mass murder as in Nazi Germany. Despite this obvious difference, Möller pointed to commonalities: a loss of contact with political realities; an inability to learn; antagonism to the West and to liberal democracy in a way that continued a German 'special path' with different political coordinates. Yet 'the racism and anti-Semitism' of the Nazi regime was 'foreign to the GDR', whose ideology instead emerged from Socialism and the Enlightenment.[69] Yes, there were episodes of an anti-Semitic nature in the early 1950s, but they were less serious than analogous events in the Soviet Union, Poland and Czechoslovakia. The Nazi regime and the GDR, he continued, could not be equated in terms of the 'degree of criminal inhumanity. Such an equation contains a certain (*Verharmlosung*) minimization of Nazi crimes'.[70] While the Nazi regime fostered extreme nationalism, the GDR was 'far removed from' it.[71] Without equating East Germany to the Nazi regime, Meuschel in *Legitimation und Parteiherrschaft* had examined the GDR's integration of anti-western nationalism with Marxism–Leninist anti-imperialism. Yet her trenchant analysis did not find an echo in Möller's or other expert papers, or even in the Commission's final report.

The participants in the hearings were selected by the political parties to establish a balance between Right and Left. An interesting moment in the hearings took place when, to the surprise of many, Jürgen Habermas, one of Germany's most well-known left-of-centre intellectuals, expressed his complete agreement with Karl Dietrich Bracher, the dean of right-of-centre liberals in the German historical profession and the leading exponent of the heuristic value of the concept of totalitarianism. Bracher noted that he had been sharply criticised when, in 1976, he referred to the GDR as 'the second German dictatorship'. This was bad form in a period when Willy Brandt and Egon Bahr were describing this same government as West Germany's 'security partner'. Using a word such as 'dictatorship' not to mention 'totalitarianism' was regarded in that climate as a threat to détente and thus to 'peace policy'. In 1994, Bracher told the Commission that, although the GDR did not approach the level of criminality of the Nazi regime, he thought that its authoritarian state structures and 'totalitarian ideology' drew on authoritarian and illiberal attacks on freedom in recent German history.[72] Bracher also argued that the contrast of democracy and dictatorship in West and East affected the process of coming to terms with the Nazi past. While coming to terms with the past over time became a key question for the legitimacy of West German democracy, the forms of that endeavour in the GDR were established by a 'counter-dictatorship' (*Gegendiktatur*). It was only in the Federal Republic that a real debate about the Nazi past could, and did, take place while in the GDR, 'the burning question' of a second democracy after Weimar was suppressed in 'an authoritarian, partly totalitarian system'. The result was a 'long error laden development' instead of a frank assessment of the Nazi era. Bracher warned against 'anxiously careful, ideological and apologetic avoidance of any comparison between right wing and left-wing dictatorships'. The work of comparison and distinction was essential for both forms of dictatorship 'were closely bound up with one another'.[73]

West Germany, Bracher continued, differed from both East Germany and the Weimar Republic because its 'long and always contentious' and 'self-critical learning process' about a difficult past contributed to the 'strengthening, consolidation and stabilization of the second German democracy'.[74] The history of the Federal Republic had shown that despite many shortcomings its reckoning with the Nazi past had contributed to political learning. 'Without the relentless and unsparing, non-partisan confrontation with our contemporary history of both right-wing and left-wing dictatorship, it would not have been possible to stabilize and secure a second German democracy after the collapse of the first (the Weimar Republic)'.[75] Examination of the past, political learning and the stabilisation of democracy had all been closely connected in West Germany since 1945. At every point, public discussion of the difficult past had to overcome apologetics as well as arguments about efficiency (and the supposed need for expert holdovers from the old regime). Repeatedly the advocates of facing the truth about the past had to overcome the resistance of others who argued that a statute of limitations on actions in the past should be upheld in 'the interests of internal peace'. Yet, he continued, 'as we experienced after 1945, pursuing that policy at the judicial level would undermine the credibility of democracy as a state based on the rule of law both in the eyes of the victims as well as of the followers and supporters of the dictatorship'.[76] In other words, just as an eventual detailed, well researched and judicially thorough confrontation with the nature and the crimes of the past dictatorship was essential for the legitimacy and stability of West German democracy after 1945 and 1949, so it was essential for a unified Germany to do so regarding the East German communist dictatorship after 1989/90. The shortcomings of the 1950s should not serve as a pretext to avoid looking clearly at the facts of the communist dictatorship after 1989. Indeed, the German confrontation with the communist dictatorship could learn from the shortcomings of the effort to face the crimes of the Nazi past in the 1950s. In making these arguments, Bracher took issue with those such as the philosopher Herman Lübbe who had argued that 'a certain silence' had been a precondition for the emergence of West German democracy. Such an argument confused political expediency with the need for stability based on an honest confrontation with the past.

Jürgen Habermas followed Bracher. He said that, although politics had played a role in his selection, 'I fear that here I can't take any position other than that of Mr. Bracher' though he arrived at the same conclusions from a different starting point.[77] Those who juxtaposed the destabilising impact of facing the past with the supposedly stabilising results of forgetting and silence posed a false alternative. The West German experience had shown that just the opposite was the case. At a broader level, 'for the first time in the 1960s', the confrontation with the Nazi past had contributed to transforming trust in the system into 'constitutional loyalty' (*Verfassungsloyalität*) that was fundamental for a 'liberal political culture'. This did not happen primarily because West Germans turned to the past for affirmative role models. Rather, for individuals as well as for the collective awareness of peoples, learning came from reflection about 'negative experiences and disappointments that we want to avoid in the future'.[78] The sequence of the two dictatorships one after another could offer an 'instructive clarification of their totalitarian commonalities'. Yet the focus on 'the second past must not be allowed to weaken the memory of the first', and especially its defining feature of state-ordered mass murder. 'This horrible fact brings to us consciousness of the normative core of the democratic state based on the rule of law. I refer to the symmetrical relationship of recognition that secures every person the same respect'.[79]

Habermas recognised that the Left was inclined not to make comparisons which conservatives were more comfortable with. That said, there were commonalities between 'these totalitarian regimes'. The Left should 'apply the same standards to both', while 'the right should not underplay or obscure the differences between them'.[80] Moreover, he believed that in 1994, 'for the first time an anti-totalitarian consensus' that 'deserves the name' could be built in Germany because, in contrast to the 1950s, it would 'not be selective'. Doing so would be easier for the younger generations to do than for his own. While the 1950s had their share of hypocrisy and double standards, Habermas's comment passed over the consistent application of the term totalitarianism by Cold War liberals such as the previously mentioned Kurt Schumacher, the young Willy Brandt and Richard Lowenthal, all of whom attacked totalitarianism of the Left and the Right with equal vehemence. It was the communists in the 1950s and then the new Left variants of Marxism in the 1960s that attacked the application of the term totalitarianism to the communist states. Habermas argued that liberal and democratic values could emerge in the absence of a political climate freed from, 'a polarizing general suspicion against internal enemies' and riven between anti-communism and anti-fascism. This German discussion of totalitarian dictatorship, more than those of the 1950s, reflected the central role that the Holocaust had come to play in reflections on the Nazi past.

Habermas and Bracher argued that the West German confrontation with the Nazi past, and the Holocaust in particular, distinguished it from East Germany's post-Nazi discussions. In order for democracy in a unified Germany to be placed on a firm foundation, the distinctively West German tradition of coming to terms with the past needed to be extended to the East. While both Bracher and Habermas spoke much of political learning, neither spoke of learning from the traditions of East German anti-fascism. Unification meant that the results of 40 years of democratic debate in West Germany would trump the frozen and codified official anti-fascism of the GDR. There would not be any reconciliation between West and East in this matter. The memory of the Nazi past in West Germany would remain the core of such memory in unified Germany. The triumph of the results of memory in democracy over those of official anti-fascism seemed complete.

Yet despite the impassioned talk of no more double standards applied to dictatorships of the Right and the Left, the Commission did not take testimony about East Germany's support for the Arab states in the Six Day War of 1967; the opening of a consulate of the Palestinian Liberation Organisation in East Berlin in 1970; aid to Palestinian and Arab terrorists who were attacking Israel; or active participation in the passing of the 'Zionism is racism' resolution in the United Nations in 1975. It was ironic that, while the interest in remembering what Nazi Germany did to the Jews aroused huge scholarly interest, the only actions of a German government after the defeat of Nazism that caused death and injury to Jews or harm to the Jewish state received no attention at all from a Commission known for reviving the use of terms such as 'dictatorship' and 'totalitarianism' when applied to the GDR.

Aside from the work of Angelika Timm, a historian now living in Tel Aviv who was a former member of the East German foreign ministry, and some of my own work on the more easily accessible documents of East German foreign policy, there has been remarkably little interest by German scholars in this issue. This disinterest has continued despite the existence of whole research centers – in Erfurt, Potsdam and Berlin – with sizable staffs, bristling with criticism of East German communism. To be sure, East Germany's antagonism to Israel did not result in mass murder. It pales in importance compared with the Holocaust. Yet if the United States had not remained an ally of Israel, or if the Soviets had won the Cold War in Europe, then East Germany would have to take credit also for putting the survival of the Jewish state at risk as well. If East German policy had been successful, the Jewish state might have been destroyed and replaced by whatever the PLO of the 1970s and its Soviet bloc backers wanted to put in its place. So perhaps, despite assertions to the contrary, the desire for German–German reconciliation did thwart a frank look at the second German dictatorship in this regard.

Conclusion

The end of the Cold War and the collapse of East German and European communist governments introduced an era of intellectual flux and fluidity in Germany and Europe. The word "totalitarianism" achieved renewed intellectual and political respectability at least in some quarter and, for perhaps a brief time, there existed a willingness to apply this most devastating of political labels to the communist as well as the Nazi regime. Compared with the binaries and double standards of so much political debate during the Cold War, the debates of the past 15 years display a comparatively refreshing willingness to look at the truth about both German dictatorships without having to equate one with the other, or use the discussion of one to minimise the crimes and injustices of the other. Germany's preoccupations with post-totalitarian narratives since 1989 marked, one hopes, the passing of the strange idea that a close look at the genocidal policies of the Nazi regime should stand in the way of examination of the violations of human rights and democratic principles by the East German dictatorship.

If it is too much to hope that the era of dictatorships and double standards was being consigned to the past, the history examined in this essay suggests that the practitioners of such ideological contortions were being placed on the defensive, and had been deprived of the arrogance and clear conscience with which they had focused only on one or another of Germany's twentieth-century dictatorships.

Notes

1. This essay was originally delivered at a conference with the same title at the University of Wisconsin – Madison on 28–29 April 2006.
2. See Hannah Arendt, *The Origins of Totalitarianism* (New York: Harcourt, Brace, 1951); Karl Bracher, *Zeitgeschichtliche Kontroversen: Um Faschismus, Totalitarismus und Demokratie* (Munich: Piper, 1984). On the role of radical anti-Semitism in Nazi propaganda, ideology and policy, see Jeffrey Herf, *The Jewish Enemy: Nazi Propaganda During World War II and the Holocaust* (Cambridge, MA: Harvard University Press, 2006).
3. See Jeffrey Herf, *Divided Memory: The Nazi Past in the Two Germanys* (Cambridge, MA: Harvard University Press, 1997).
4. On the early years of the anti-totalitarian consensus, see Jeffrey Herf, *War By Other Means: Soviet Power, West German Resistance and the Battle of the Euromissiles* (New York: The Free Press, 1991); and Richard Lowenthal and Hans-Peter Schwarz (eds). *Die Zweite Republik* (Stuttgart: Seewald, 1975).
5. On the political culture of East German see Sigrid Meuschel, *Legitimation und Parteiherrschaft in der DDR* (Frankfurt am Main: Suhrkamp, 1992).
6. On German battlefield losses see Rüdiger Övermann, *Deutsche militärische Verluste im zweiten Weltkrieg* (Munich: R. Oldenbourg, 1999)
7. On the connections between facing the Nazi past and foreign policy considerations in the 1950s see Thomas Schwartz, *America's Germany: John J. McCloy and the Federal Republic of Germany* (Cambridge, MA: Harvard University Press, 1991),
8. See Jeffrey Herf, "Multiple Restorations vs. the Solid South: Continuities and Discontinuities in Germany after 1945 and the American South after 1865," and other essays in Norbert Finzsch and Jürgen Martschukat (eds). *Different Restorations: Reconstruction and "Wiederaufbau" in the United*

States and Germany: 1865–1945–1989 (Providence, RI: Berghahn Books, 1996), pp.48–86. Also see Wolfgang Schivelbusch, *The Culture of Defeat: On National Trauma, Mourning and Recovery* (New York: Metropolitan Books, 2001).

9. See Jeffrey Herf, *Divided Memory* (note 3), pp.201–67.
10. Cited in Herf, *Divided Memory* (note 3), p.253. Also see Kurt Schumacher, "29.6.1947: Grundsatzreferat Schumachers auf dem Nünberger Parteitag der SPD: 'Deutschland und Europa'," in Willy Albrecht, *Kurt Schumacher: Reden-Schriften-Korrespondenzen, 1945–1952* (Berlin: J.H.W. Dietz, 1985), p.508–509.
11. Nahum Goldmann, cited by Herf, *Divided Memory* (note 3), pp.318–19; also Nahum Goldmann, speech at Bergen-Belsen, 30 November 1952, Bundesarchiv Koblenz, NL Theodor Heuss B122 2082, p.1.
12. On these issues, see Robert Moeller, *War Stories: The Search for a Usable Past in the Federal Republic of Germany* (Berkeley, CA: University of California Press, 2001).
13. Theodor Heuss, cited by Herf, *Divided Memory* (note 3), pp.321–5; Theodor Heuss, "Dies Scham nimmt uns niemand ab!," *Bulletin des Presse-und Infomationsamtes der Bundesregierung*, 2 December 1942, pp.1655–6.
14. See Rebecca Wittmann, *Beyond Justice: The Auschwitz Trial* (Cambridge, MA: Harvard University Press, 2005).
15. Thomas Schwartz, *America's Germany: John J. McCloy and the Federal Republic of Germany* (Cambridge, MA: Harvard University Press, 1991).
16. On these issues see Norbert Frei, *Adenauer's Germany and the Nazi Past*, pp.69–100; and Jörg Friedrich, *Die kalte Amnestie: NS Täter in der Bundesrepublik* (Frankfurt am Main: Fischer Taschenbuch Verlag,1984), pp.272–81.
17. See Herf, *Divided Memory* (note 3), pp.291–2. Also see Hans-Jürgen Döscher, *Verschworene Gesellschaft. Das Auswärtige Amt unter Adenauer zwischen Neubeginn und kontinuität* (Berlin: Akadamie Verlag, 1995); and Ulrich Brochhagen, *Nach Nürnberg. Vergangenheitsbewältigung und Westintegration in der Ära Adenauer* (Hamburg: Junius, 1994).
18. During the occupation years, the American occupation authorities carried out extensive surveys that probed German political views. The findings were grim. An OMGUS (Office of Military Government United States) survey of March 1947 summarized the results of surveys of the previous two years as follows: "four in ten Germans are so strongly imbued with anti-Semitism that it is very doubtful that they would object to actions against Jews … Less than two in ten could probably be counted on to resist such behavior." OMGUS, Opinion Survey Section, Report no. 49 (3 March 1947), NARA rg. 260, 5/233-3/5, cited by Frank Stern, *Im Anfang war Auschwitz: Antisemitismus und Philosemitismus im deutschen Nachkrieg* (Göttingen: Bleicher Verlag, 1991), p.126.
19. On West German restitution see Constantin Goschler, *Schuld und Schulden: Die Politik der Wiedergutmachung für NS-Verfolgte seit 1945* (Göttingen: Wallstein Verlag, 2005), 543 pp.
20. On West German–Israeli relations, see Inge Deutschkron, *Israel und die Deutschen: das Schwierige Verhältnis* (Cologne: Verlag Wissenschaft und Politik, 1991); and Lily Gardner Feldman, *The Special Relationship between West Germany and Israel* (Boston, MA: Allen and Unwin, 1984).
21. These issues remain contentious. See Andrei Markovits, *Uncouth Nation: Why Europe Dislikes America* (Princeton, NJ: Princeton University Press, 2006); and essays by Jeffrey Herf, Andrei Markovits and Angelika Timm, in Jeffrey Herf (ed.), *Antisemitism and Anti-Zionism in Historical Perspective: Convergence and Divergence* (London: Routledge, 2006).
22. Theodor Adorno, "Was bedeutet: 'Aufarbeitung der Vergangenheit," in *Theodor Adorno: Gesammelte Schriften*, vol. 10:2 (Frankfurt am Main: Suhrkamp Verlag, 1977), pp.555–72.
23. See David Cesarani, *Becoming Eichmann: Rethinking the Life, Times and Crimes of a 'Desk Murderer'* (Cambridge, MA: Da Capo Press, 2006).
24. On this see Rebecca Wittmann, *Beyond Justice: The Frankfurt Auschwitz Trial*(Cambridge, MA: Harvard University Press, 2005); and Devon O. Pendas, *The Frankfurt Auschwitz Trial, 1963–1965: Genocide, History and the Limits of the Law* (New York: Cambridge University Press, 2005).
25. See Herf, *Divided Memory* (note 3), pp.337–42.
26. See Lucy Dawidowicz, *The Holocaust and the Historians* (Cambridge, MA: Harvard University Press, 1981); and Karl Bracher, *Zeitgeschichtliche Kontroversen* (note 2).
27. Elements of the history of the West German new left and "the Jewish question" exist but a fully adequate historical study remains to be written. See Dan Diner, *Beyond the Conceivable: Stuides on Germany, Nazism and the Holocaust* (Berkeley, CA: University of California Press, 2000); Martin Kloke, *Israel und die deutsche Linke: Geschichte eines schwiergen Verhältnisses* 2nd edn (Frankfurt: Haag and Herchen, 1994); Gerd Koenen, *Das Rote Jahrzehnt: Unsere kleine deutsche Kulturrevolution,*

1967–1977 (Munich: Fischer Taschenbuch Verlag, 2002); Wolfgang Kraushaar, *Die RAF und der linke Terrorismus* (Hamburg: Hamburger Edition, 2006); and his *Die Bombe im jüdischen Gemeindehaus* (Hamburg: Hamburger Edition, 2005).

28. For a comprehensive collection of the public contributions to the debate about constructing a memorial in Berlin to the murdered Jews of Europe, see Ute Heimrod, Günter Schlusche and Horst Seferens (eds), *Der Denkmalstreit – Das Denkmal? Die Debatte um das 'Denkmal für die ermordeten Juden Europas': Eine Dokumentation* (Berlin: Philo Verlag, 1999).

29. See Jeffrey Herf, *Divided Memory* (note 3), pp.13–200.

30. The phrase "leveraged into power" is Ian Kershaw's. See his *Hitler: 1889–1936 Hubris* (New York: Norton, 1999). The phrase is more historically accurate than the more familiar "Nazi seizure of power." Hitler did not seize power. Conservative politicians gave it to him in the naive hope that they could control him.

31. On the construction of heroic biographies in place of life's shades of grey, see the excellent study by Catherine Epstein, *The Last Revolutionaries: German Communists and their century* (Cambridge, MA: Harvard University Press, 2003).

32. On Merker and the Communists in Mexico City, see Jeffery Herf, *Divided Memory* (note 3), pp.40–68. At the same time that Merker, drawing on published sources, was making this argument, Franz Neuman, working in the Research and Analysis Branch of the United States Office of Strategic Services in Washington, was writing that the Nazis would not murder the Jews because they needed a scapegoat for diverting the frustrations caused by German capitalism. See Franz Neumann, *Behemoth: The Structure and Practice of National Socialism, 1933–1944* (New York: Oxford University Press, 1944). Also see Richard Breitman and Norman Goda, "OSS Knowledge of the Holocaust," in Richard Breitman, Norman J.W. Goda, Timothy Nafthali and Robert Wolfe, *U.S. Intelligence and the Nazis* (New York: Cambridge University Press, 2005), pp.11–44.

33. "Aufruf der kommunistischen Partei Deutschlands, 11.Juni 1945," in Walter Ulbricht, *Zur Geschichte der Neuesten Zeit: Die Niederlage Hitlerdeutschlands und die Schaffung der antifaschistische-demokratische Ordnung*, 2nd edn ([East] Berlin: Dietz Verlag, 1955), pp.370–79; see also discussion in Jeffrey Herf, *Divided Memory* (note 3), pp.27–31.

34. On "Lessons of the Trial Against the Slansky Conspiracy Center," see Jeffrey Herf, *Divided Memory* (note 3), pp.126–9.

35. See Jeffrey Herf, *Divided Memory* (note 3), pp.106–61; and his "Dokumentation: Antisemitismus in der SED: Geheime Dokumente zum Fall Paul Merker aus SED- und MFS-Archiven," *Vierteljahrshefte für Zeitgeschichte* (October 1994), pp.1–32.

36. Paul Merker. "An die Zentral Kontrollkommission des ZK. Der SED, Berlin: 'Stellungnahme zur Judenfrage' (1 June 1956), Paul Merker, NL 102 102/27, SAPMO-BA ZPA, p.16; cited in Herf, *Divided Memory*, pp.155–6.

37. This discussion draws on Herf, *Divided Memory* (note 3), pp.190–200.

38. Jeffrey Herf, *Divided Memory* (note 3), p.200.

39. Cited by Herf, *Divided Memory* (note 3), pp.364–5. Also see "Dokumentation: Gemeinsame Erklärung der Volkskammer," *Deutschland Archiv* 23, no. 5 (May 1990), pp.794–5; and "The East Germans Issue an Apology for Nazis' Crimes," *New York Times*, 13 April 1990, pp.A1, A7.

40. On debates among intellectuals concerning German unification, see Jan Werner-Müller, *Another Country: German Intellectuals, Unification and National Identity* (New Haven, CT: Yale University Press, 2000).

41. "Beschlußempfehlung und Bericht der Enquete-Kommission 'Aufarbeitung der Geschichte und der Folgen der SED Diktatur," Deutscher Bundestag, *Enquete-Kommission 'Aufarbeitung von Geschichte und Folgen der SED-Diktatur in Deutschland*, vol. 1 (Frankfurt am Main: Suhrkamp Verlag, 1995), pp.152–3.

42. "Bericht der Enquete-Kommission" (note 41), p.193.

43. On the intellectual demobilization of the distinction between democracy and dictatorship from the 1960s to the 1980s see Jeffrey Herf, *War by Other Means: Soviet Power, West German Resistance and the Battle of the Euromissiles* (New York: The Free Press, 1991).

44. "Aufgaben der Enquete-Kommission 'Aufarbeitung der Geschichte und der Folgen der SED-Diktatur," *Enquete-Kommission*, vol. 1 (note 41), p.153.

45. Deutscher Bundestag, *Enquete-Kommission 'Aufarbeitung von Geschichte und Folgen der SED-Diktatur in Deutschland*, 9 vols (Frankfurt/Main: Suhrkamp Verlag, 1995); and "Aufgaben der Enquete-Kommission" (note 41), pp.156–7.

46. Rainer Eppelmann, "Vorwort, Bericht der Enquete-Kommission," in *Enquete-Kommission*, vol. 1 (note 41), p.182.

47. "Zur Rolle des Antifaschismus," in *Bericht der Enquete-Kommission* (note 41), p.287.

48. "1.21.Zur Entwickling des Antifaschismus, "in *Bericht der Enquete-Kommission*," vol. 1 (note 41), p.278.
49. "Zur Funktion des Antifaschismus in der DDR," in *Bericht der Enquete-Kommission* (note 41), p.279.
50. *Bericht der Enquete-Kommission* (note 41), pp.279-280.
51. "Die Haltung der SED zu Juden und Jüdischen Gemeinden," *Bericht der Enquete-Kommission* (note 41), p.282.
52. *Bericht der Enquete-Kommission* (note 41), p.282.
53. Jeffrey Herf, "*Der Geheimprozess*," *Die Zeit*, *Dossier* 41 (14 October 1994), p.7.
54. Sigrid Meuschel, *Legitimation und Parteiherrschaft in der DDR* (Frankfurt am Main: Suhrkamp, 1992).
55. "Zum Diktaturvergleich von NS-Regime und SED-Staat," in *Enquete-Kommission*, vol. 1 (note 41), p.708.
56. *Enquete-Kommission*, vol. 1 (note 41), p.709.
57. *Enquete-Kommission*, vol. 1 (note 41), pp.709–710.
58. For examination based on recently opened archives of East Germany's support for the Soviet hard line in the 1980s see Michael Ploetz and Hans-Peter Müller, *Ferngelenkte Friedensbewegung? DDR und UdSSR im Kampf gegen die NATO Doppelbeschlusss* (Munster: Lit, 2004); and Michael Ploetz, *Wie die Sowjet Union den Kalten Krieg verlor: Von der Nachrüstung zum Mauerfall* (Berlin: Propylaen, 2000).
59. "*Zum Diktaturvergleich von NS-Regime und SED-Staat*," in *Enquete-Kommission*, vol. 1 (note 41), p.711.
60. *Enquete-Kommission*, vol. 1 (note 41), pp.712–13.
61. *Enquete-Kommission*, vol. 1 (note 41), p.713.
62. "Zur außenpolitischen Akzeptanz der DDR," *Enquete-Kommision*, vol. 1 (note 41), pp.715–16.
63. *Enquete-Kommission*, vol. 1 (note 41), pp.716–17.
64. *Enquete-Kommission*, vol. 1 (note 41), pp.717–18.
65. On the hostility of the Nazi regime towards Zionism, see Jeffrey Herf, "Convergence: The Classic Case: Nazi Germany, Anti-Semitism and Anti-Zionism during World War II," in Jeffrey Herf (ed.), *Antisemitism and Anti-Zionism in Historical Perspective* (note 21), pp.50–70. On East Germany's stance toward Israel, see Angelika Timm, *Hammer, Zirkel, Davidstern: Das gestörte Verhältnis der DDR zu Zionismus und Staat Israel* (Bonn: Bouvier, 1997); and "Ideology and Realpolitik: East German Attitudes towards Zionism and Israel," in Herf, *Antisemitism and Anti-Zionism in Historical Perspective* (note 21), pp.186–205.
66. "Schlußteil," *Enquete-Kommision*, vol. 1 (note 41), p.737.
67. David Blight, *Race and Reunion: The Civil War in American Memory* (Cambridge, MA: Harvard University Press, 2001).
68. Horst Möller, "Zur Auseinandersetzung mit den beiden Diktaturen in Deutschland in Vergangenheit und Gegenwart, 1. Teil," in *Formen und Ziele der Auseinandersetzung mit den beiden Diktaturen in Deutschland, Band IX, Materialien der Enquete-Kommission 'Aufarbeitung von Geshichte und Folgen der SED-Diktatur in Deutschland* (Frankfurt am Main: Suhrkamp Verlag, 1995), p.579.
69. *Formen und Ziele der Auseinandersetzung* (note 68), p.592.
70. *Formen und Ziele der Auseinandersetzung* (note 68), p.593.
71. *Formen und Ziele der Auseinandersetzung* (note 68), p.595.
72. Karl Dietrich Bracher, "Zur Auseinandersetzung mit den beiden Diktaturen in Deutschland in Vergangenheit und Gegenwart, 1. Teil," *Formen und Ziele der Auseinandersetzung* (note 68), p.680.
73. *Formen und Ziele der Auseinandersetzung* (note 68), pp.681–2.
74. *Formen und Ziele der Auseinandersetzung* (note 68), p.682.
75. *Formen und Ziele der Auseinandersetzung* (note 68), p.684.
76. *Formen und Ziele der Auseinandersetzung* (note 68), p.685.
77. Jürgen Habermas, "Zur Auseinandersetzung mit den beiden Diktaturen in Deutschland in Vergangenheit und Gegenwart, 1. Teil," *Formen und Ziele der Auseinandersetzung* (note 68), p.686.
78. *Formen und Ziele der Auseinandersetzung* (note 68), p.688.
79. *Formen und Ziele der Auseinandersetzung* (note 68), p.689.
80. *Formen und Ziele der Auseinandersetzung* (note 68), p.689.

The 'Examination of Conscience' of the Nation: The Lost Debate About the 'Collective Guilt' in Italy, 1943–5

LUCA LA ROVERE

Premise: Italian Scholars and the Memory of Fascism

The historiographical debate about the legacy of the fascist dictatorship in Italy has for a long time been hampered by the cultural dominance of the so-called 'anti-fascist paradigm'. As is well known, in the postwar years the exaltation of the resistance to Fascism – be it during the regime or after its collapse on 8 September 1943 – as a popular struggle which announced the 'second *Risorgimento*' of the Italian nation, eclipsed the compromises which occurred between diverse sectors of Italian society and the regime. Such a narrative was implemented by the new – or newly re-organised – political parties to establish a clear separation between a would-be sound civil society, which had stubbornly refused to fit the ideal-type of the 'new fascist men', and a caste of fanatical dominators, regarded as the only responsible agents for Italy's catastrophe.[1] In so doing, anti-fascism, initially intended as an ethical and political programme of democratic rebirth, was transformed into the myth of the foundation of the Republic. One of the most prominent personalities of the anti-fascist movement, Vittorio Foa, has recently declared: 'We strove to create an image of Italy during the fascist regime as a country uncompromised by the regime. That was surely a mythological feature, far from being real, which we succeeded in implementing as the salient narrative of post-war history'.[2] In the subsequent years, such a representation was uncritically adopted by the anti-fascist historiography, with the relevant consequence that the study of the complex relationship between Italian society and the fascist regime was completely neglected.[3]

The end of the so-called 'long postwar' in Italy has resulted in a phenomenon which has been defined as the *'ritorno del rimosso'* [return of the suppressed memory].[4] In Italy, as well as in other countries with the most extreme fascist heritage, the debate concerning the participation of society in the totalitarian experience has reopened in an attempt to overcome the interpretative schema from the past. The end of collective identities based on an ideological and conflicting *Weltanshauung* [worldview] has revealed the lack of a shared memory able to establish a national identity.[5] Furthermore, the cultural and political crisis of the national narratives about fascism has necessitated the redefinition of the nexus between identity and memory.

In the wake of Renzo De Felice's groundbreaking investigations into the relationship between society and fascism, Italian historiography has finally reached agreement in identifying the cultural deficit of studies into the transition to democracy within the limits and contradictions of an anti-fascist discourse about fascism.[6] By the middle of the 1980s, the historian Nicola Gallerano spoke clearly of an irreversible crisis of the 'anti-fascist paradigm' and of its capacity to feed a shared memory of the past, and, thus, to constitute an effective unifier of national identity.[7] Since that time, the theme has been repeatedly revived. More recently, Sergio Luzzatto has pointed out that the 'crisis of antifascism' – as the title of his book states – will not be overcome without carrying out a serious attempt to re-found the cultural basis of such a civic tradition and historiographical trend.[8]

The road toward the development of a new season of studies directed at deepening the knowledge of Italy's history under fascism and, above all, at augmenting an understanding of the transition to a post-fascist era, is proving difficult. In fact, from an unconditioned adhesion to the 'anti-fascist paradigm', Italian historiography seems to be oriented toward uncritically accepting a new stereotype, namely that of the opportunistic and easy suppression of the memory of the dictatorship, in order to avoid the moral and penal consequences connected to the anti-fascist de-fascistisation policy. It is clear that both positions trivialise the meaning of the fascist experience: the former maintained that Italians had not been fascist at all; while recognising the widespread consensus of Italian society to the fascist regime, the latter stresses that they were able to easily reconvert themselves to democracy. For example, Giovanni Miccoli has acknowledged that in postwar Italy fascism was the object of a heated public controversy, but the result was a clear 'trend to obliterate the problem of fascism from the Italian society's history'.[9] One prominent representative of anti-fascist historiography has underscored that Italy would have experienced a type of hurried exorcism of fascism by the 'invention of an anti-Fascist past'.[10]

Both interpretations support the implicit assumption that the fascist regime was not a totalitarian one and, consequently, that after its collapse Italians could re-start their usual way of life which had been only partially, or not at all, affected by the fascists' attempt to 'regenerate' the nation according to its values and myths. For some historians the rapid mass conversion of Italians to anti-fascism reveals the 'transformist' attitude of Italians as the main feature of their national character: as they had been previously fascist purely for motives of conformity or opportunism, in the new political phase they promptly adhered to anti-fascism for the same reasons. In both cases, the grip of fascist ideology on society and, consequently, the personal political commitment of Italians had been weak and ephemeral: according to this interpretation, the 'imperfect totalitarianism' would have been replaced by an 'imperfect democracy'.[11] Even those who stress the permanence of a 'fascist mentality' – generically identified with the eternally conservative and 'moderate' attitude of the majority of the Italians, which marked the entire course of the national history – fail to assess the real consequences of the totalitarian dictatorship.[12]

In my paper I will reconstruct the early postwar discussion about the legacies of the dictatorship. Even a cursory examination of the press published between 1943 and 1945 – that is to say, before the consolidation of the anti-fascist narrative – shows the emergence of the theme of Italians', 'collective guilt' and of the country's need for moral redemption. Focusing on the topic of the suppressed memory of fascism, scholars have generally neglected the question of guilt. Also, those who have investigated the postwar debate on fascism – such as Pier Giorgio Zunino – have not detected a specific question of guilt.[13] That is why I will call it the 'lost debate'.

As will be made clear, I am interested neither in the topic of the de-fascistization process, which has already been investigated by other scholars,[14] or in assessing Italian guilt from the juridical or moral standpoint. I will try, instead, to reconstruct the Italians' self-image of fascist and post-fascist experiences, and to assess the discursive strategies that emerged in postwar Italy in order to deal with an awkward past. I do not deny that the final result of the struggle between conflicting narratives was to draw a veil of oblivion over the past. I would simply suggest that for a better understanding of the awkward relationships between Italian society and its fascist past it is necessary to put aside a moralistic approach toward a common tendency among contemporaries to forget the past, and to try to evaluate it as the dramatic consequence of the totalitarian experience for millions of persons. In order to do so, it is essential to analyse the way in which the 'question of guilt' was dealt with by contemporaries.

Italians and Fascism: the 'Question of Guilt'

Already in the days following the breakdown of the regime, some intellectuals and politicians attempted to open up the question of the Italian peoples' collective guilt. As was to happen in Germany after 1945, that was a position supported by a restricted minority.[15] These men, from different cultural backgrounds and belonging to different political parties, were firmly convinced that a frank discussion about the recent past was the only effective antidote against the revival of the totalitarian temptation, and the necessary viaticum for the reconstruction of society after the moral and material devastation caused by fascist rule. They asserted that the responsibility for the imperialist war of fascism and for the, by then, almost inevitable military defeat, could not be discharged completely on the regime's ruling class, but was the effect of 20 years of Italian society's active support of fascism. Italians had renounced the values of freedom and progress brought about by the *Risorgimento,* and willingly submitted to a brutal and liberticidal dictatorship. Thus, only a loud pronunciation of '*mea culpa*' would have produced a deep understanding of the tragic consequences of the blind faith of the overwhelming majority of the Italians in the myths of the fascist ideology. Remembering past mistakes was considered the beginning of the tough path of expiation and redemption. In that sense, for the anti-fascists the collective 'examination of conscience' would have represented the tool for developing a new consciousness of democratic citizenship based on a renewed ethics of accountability and memory. At stake was the attempt to produce a psychological and ideological break with the former regime, in order to allow millions of individuals considered to be still affected by its ideology and propaganda to find a new identity and integrate themselves into the democratic system.

There was another factor contributing to such awareness: since the very onset there were clear warning signs of a general tendency to avoid an awkward discussion about both individual and collective guilt, and to invoke a general pardoning in the name of a 'new beginning'. In this sense, the advocates of collective guilt also reacted to such a tendency. The debate brought to light the existence of two different Italys, so to speak: people who had lived different experiences during the *'ventennio'* (the 20 years of fascist dictatorship) disagreed now on the way of conceiving the nation's relationship with its past and, thus, on the way of building the country's future. It has to be stressed that in Italy the question of guilt was not systematically formulated, as was later done by Karl Jaspers in Germany. Nevertheless, it was openly evoked in numerous articles which used the same language, the same categories and, above all, the same moral inspiration that one would have found in Jaspers's book two or three years later.[16]

Three separate phases can be identified in the development of the debate:

(1) The phase following the breakdown of the regime, characterised by the public remembrance of what had happened in an early attempt to construct a pedagogy of memory. The collective guilt in this phase was conceived mostly in political and moral terms.
(2) The phase after 8 September 1943 when, after the signing of an armistice with the Allies, the intellectual debate on the past was driven to face an unexpected political evolution: the rebirth of fascism under the auspices of a Nazi ally demonstrated that it had not yet been defeated, as too hastily it had been believed to be, and its ideology was still attractive for a large proportion of Italians. Guilt was mostly attributed by the anti-fascist parties to the neo-fascists, considered as deserving harsh punishment or to be judged by criminal courts.
(3) The phase opened by the liberation of Rome (4 July 1944): while the return of freedom allowed the greater extension of the debate, the need for the political reconstruction of public life under the banner of anti-fascism gradually eclipsed the question of 'collective guilt'.

Elsewhere I have investigated the changing position of the whole spectrum of the political parties and public opinion.[17] In this paper I cannot do anything but limit my survey to a few examples.

The topic of the 'examination of conscience' was a traditional one for Italian Catholics. And indeed it surfaced for the very first time in an article published by the monthly review of the young Catholic intellectuals belonging to the *Azione Cattolica* (Catholic Action), only one month after the fall of fascism.[18] In an August 1943 issue Sergio Paronetto, a young manager of the State Agency for Industrial Reconstruction and leader of the Graduated movement of the AC, stated firmly that the same regime that everyone was now ready to criticize had been able to seize power and to maintain it for more than two decades because of the consent of Italian society as a whole. According to him, not only those who had actively supported the regime were guilty, but also the millions of Italians who had omitted for fear or moral disengagement to denounce its tyrannical nature. The latter had to be regarded as objective accomplices of the dictatorship and of its misdeeds. Thus he established a direct link between the individual and collective responsibility:

> A necessary complicity links the collective sin to individual sins: if the discipline was transformed into blind conformism, the order into sceptical sluggishness, the hierarchy into servile obedience, the strength into violence and abuse, the faith into renouncing intelligence, the patience into quietism, the reasonableness into opportunism and cynicism, the ardour into hatred, all this has not happened without a direct participation and a personal responsibility of each of us.[19]

In the same period, other Catholic writers pinpointed the close link between the moral decadence among Italians who had followed fascism, and the rejection of the Church's teaching of Christian love and solidarity. Writing in the same review, an anonymous Catholic priest described the process of a progressive slipping of Catholics into a full acceptance of the dictatorship. They had exchanged the essential liberties of the human being for an illusory idea of law and order and the ephemeral advantages produced by the Concordat with the fascist regime. Catholic intellectuals had shown their incapability in orientating public opinion and failed at directing popular feelings against the tyranny. The Catholic press had passively followed the orders of fascist propaganda, driving the people toward acceptance of a passive conformism. Also, the clergy had carried out only a superficial and formal action of indoctrination that had proved incapable of reaching the souls of the Italians and of contrasting with the dangerous effects of fascist ideology. In the new political age it was necessary to face the 'question of the Catholics' responsibility': they had frankly to recognise that the faith in the imperial dreams, the 'conformism without ideals' in which the new generation had grown up, the passivity shown toward the dictator's decisions had produced a deep 'weakening of religious, moral and civil feelings' and almost completely destroyed the 'Catholic tradition of life'.[20] The Catholic historian Arturo Carlo Jemolo went further. If the Italians' capacity for discernment between good and evil had so dramatically weakened, he observed, that was in part the result of the renunciation of the Church of the exercise of its high moral authority under fascist rule.[21]

The theme of the 'examination of conscience' was not only a prerogative of Catholic opinion. In the same period, the new director of the *Corriere d'informazione*, the liberal anti-fascist Mario Borsa, urged the Italians to face the immediate past without reticence, and to plead guilty:

> The true, humiliating, unforgivable guilt was ours. For this reason I have stated and I repeat that if we want to make an effort to relieve our distress, we ought to confess, to yell loudly as Tolstoj's Nikita: 'We did it! We did it!'. We were those who gave him [to Mussolini] the push to power, placing at his feet all our liberties and guarantees, showing a sadist will to be humiliated from the human standpoint, to be annihilated from the civic one, being eager to *ruere in servitium*.

Italy as a whole had revealed an extreme 'lack of religiousness', of 'civic sense', of 'personal courage'. Even the sacrifice of 'noble minorities', which had paid for their ideal coherence with years of exile and imprisonment, was not enough to counterbalance the sins of the rest of the population.[22]

As another journalist wrote in the same newspaper, an examination of conscience was necessary to dismiss behaviour and mentalities which were affected, often unconsciously, by fascist ideology and values and to re-establish a custom of seriousness and dignity: 'We should feel the desire to expiate every sin, also the sins we have not committed, also the crimes and the horrific misdeeds that others have committed in our name. We should be able to offer as a sacrifice, without a single complaint, all our distress and our material lost'.[23]

According to their interpretations of fascism as respectively a spiritual and a moral crisis, both Catholics and liberals insisted particularly on the concept of moral guilt, a kind of sin to be assessed by everyone's personal conscience. In this meaning the function of the acknowledgement of the collective guilt was neither revenge nor retribution, but atonement, a state of mind and conscience, so to speak, vital if one were to be set free from the sins of the past. Others, even among liberals, furthered an extensive meaning of the concept of guilt, openly speaking of the Italians' political guilt: as citizens of the fascist state, who had abolished civic freedom, persecuted internal minorities and pursued an imperialistic war against free peoples, they were subdued to the discretional power of the victors, both in the international and internal arenas. As the liberal journalist Gabriele Pepe wrote in the official daily newspaper of the Italian Liberal Party, the political irresponsibility of the peoples would have assumed the meaning of returning to a 'medieval political custom'. Conversely, he asserted: 'even if that is painful, we ought to accept the juridical–economical concept of the nation's responsibility for the deeds of its rulers: if the country has not been able to halt them, it means it was not ripe for freedom'.[24]

The topic of the awkward relationship between guilt and responsibility was dealt with by the socialist leader Paolo Treves, who had just returned to Italy after years of exile abroad. He believed that on 25 July 1943 only the regime's façade was finally ruined, but fascist habits and mentalities were still alive: thus it was not enough to erase the regime's symbols from the public buildings to eliminate the influence of 20 years of fascist domination over the Italians' consciences. For that reason the problem of the responsibility of fascism could not be skipped over by simply praising a new political system based on freedom. At the same time it was fundamental to clearly discern between 'guilt' and 'responsibility'. Only those who had consciously co-operated to support the 'political mistake' and 'criminal deeds' had to be regarded properly as the bearers of the 'fascist guilt'. While those who had simply been unable to halt them could be charged with a generic 'moral and political responsibility'. In this respect, Italians had to accept the responsibility for fascism and to act coherently both in the domestic and in foreign affairs, avoiding the temptation to yell Italy's innocence. Moreover, Treves reacted to the moderate force's attempt to involve anti-fascism in a general verdict of guilty: the faults of those who had strenuously fought against fascism could not be compared to the faults of the convicted fascist, who had willingly supported the regime or to those individuals who had simply kept themselves away from politics out of fear, or as a subtle desire for self-defence. In his conclusion, he reasserted the need for memory and self-consciousness: 'It is not a good approach to start by denying the disease. For if we want be respected by other people, as we do have the right to be respected, we have the duty to accept our collective responsibility'.[25]

Almost all contemporary observers agreed on the point that eliminating the dangerous effects of totalitarian rule from the individual's personality meant starting a long and difficult action of re-educating the Italians as the first step toward joining the ranks of the other European democracies. The acknowledgement of collective guilt – the regime's mass support – went hand in hand with the claim of a deep de-fascistization of Italian society. This was one of the major concerns of the socialists. The editor of the socialist national newspaper, the writer Ignazio Silone, argued that the reconstruction of Italy was not a material matter, but mainly a moral and political matter: 'Indeed we Italians – he wrote in July 1945 – urgently need coal; but perhaps we have a need even more urgent than any other. We need to eradicate the totalitarian disease ... from the intimacy of our conscience'.[26]

The Communists, too, believed that the collective examination of the conscience should primarily have a political function: the eradication of the roots of fascism from Italian society and the promotion of a deep renewal of national political life. In effect, the Communist party's leader, Palmiro Togliatti, detaching himself from the Third International's official interpretation, had developed as early as the mid-1930s a sharp analysis of the totalitarian phenomenon and of its penetration among the masses.[27] As he wrote in 1943: 'It is undisputable that the Italian people have been poisoned by fascism's imperialist and thuggish ideology. [...] The poison has flowed among the peasants, workers, and especially the petty bourgeoisie and intellectuals. In other words, it has spread among the people'.[28] Consequently, for the Communist leader, it was a hard or, better said, almost impossible task to distinguish those who were responsible for fascist misdeeds, especially because there was no sign of a popular opposition to the ruling classes' policies.

If the official discourse of the Marxist parties stressed principally the responsibility of the fascist ruling class and of its accomplices (the ruling classes, big business, royal institution), they were also concerned about that overwhelming majority of normal people who had been exposed for 20 years to fascist ideology and propaganda. Clearly, merely ascertaining Italian mass consent to Mussolini's dictatorship was sufficient to uphold the thesis of collective guilt for its crimes. Those who had adhered to fascism out of conviction were expected to admit their own fault. As the young jurist Vezio Crisafulli wrote in the Communist daily newspaper L'Unità, the process of self-criticism was of basic importance for reactivating the capability of individuals accustomed to conforming passively to the fascist commandment 'believe, obey, fight', to instead choose consciously their new place in the country's political life. Therefore, they should carry out a 'silent examination of conscience' in order to recall the states of mind that had led them to join with fascism, and later on to convert to anti-fascism. It was extremely important to assess one's 'intimate reactions' in the face of the most important events of the regime's history, from the murder of the socialist deputy Giacomo Matteotti to the declaration of war against France and Great Britain, and, above all, the personal contribution to the regime's political life. Above all, these individuals were requested to define exactly the 'process of self-criticism' which had brought them from an adhesion in 'good faith' to fascism, to reach real anti-fascist conviction. Such a criticism of the past political experience was the necessary condition for purifying one's personality from the influence of fascist ideology, and for making sure that the choice for a new political party would have been 'solid and fruitful for the future'.[29] In this sense, the Communist version of the 'examination of conscience' was a tool conceived to rehabilitate defeated enemies (former fascists), and to readmit them to political life after a process of ideological 'reversal'. At the same time, it was also considered as a useful mean to purify the individual not only from the 'fascist mentality', but also from bourgeois culture, in order to completely identify himself with the ideals and programmes of the working class.

The cultural and political need to understand the actual conundrum of the Italians' totalitarian infatuation led Riccardo Bauer, a member of the Action party, to propose in the fall of 1945 the assembly of a committee, within the Constituent Assembly, then about to convene, that would have been charged with the task of carrying out a national enquiry on fascism. By furnishing Italians with the 'documented evidence of their past degeneration', it was to disclose to them the 'road to redemption'.[30] Yet, the attempt to institutionalise the claim for a collective 'examination of conscience' passed virtually unnoticed. This was a sign of the existence among Italians of a widespread desire to simply overcome the past.

The Myth of Popular Anti-fascism in the Making: from Guilty to Victims

The Italian government's measures, issued on 27 July 1944, for implementing sanctions against fascists coincided with the apex of the debate about guilt.[31] The call for a wide purge, especially from the left-wing anti-fascist parties, overheated the debate about collective responsibility: those affected had by now to face the actual menace of being held responsible for personal acts and behaviour which could be punished by Italian law. This made the articulation of a discourse on fascist experience inspired exclusively by pedagogic and civic concerns more difficult. Moderate sectors of Italian society, the petty bourgeoisie that had directly supported the regime and was mainly employed in the civil service about to be purged, were particularly vulnerable to the sanction, which, based on the victors' retroactive laws, they viewed as unjust.[32] This sector of public opinion was well represented by a new political movement – the *Qualunquista* movement, which aimed to represent the feeling and needs of the 'man on the street', founded by the play-writer Guglielmo Giannini – whose growth of consensus was related to a strong anti-anti-fascist attitude.[33]

Also the moderate press (Catholic and liberal) began to invoke forgiveness in the name of the need for a national pacification. What was considered the failure of the purge in punishing the high ranks of the fascist regime turned into a rejection of the attempt to hit the 'small fishes', the ordinary people who had joined the party to ensure their family – as it was soon commonly asserted – had their daily bread. Furthermore, the brutality of the crimes perpetrated by Nazis and their Italian neo-fascist allies in Northern Italy led to a general fading away of the quest for guilt directly related to the 20 year dictatorship of Mussolini, because such guilt was considered – as we have seen – to concern *only* political and moral matters.[34]

Already during the middle of 1944 the question of guilt was gradually minimised and marginalised, though it was not yet openly negated. To achieve such a result, a wide spectrum of narrative strategies was deployed. One of the most popular was the thesis of the Italians' 'good faith' in following fascism: they had believed fascism was 'law and order', the restoration of the national traditional values of 'God, fatherland, and family', and the basis of a strong government able finally to fulfil the already unachieved goals of the *Risorgimento* and to make the country stronger and more respected abroad. For example, commenting on the political party line concerning the de-fascistization process, *L'Unità* clearly stated that there was no intention to prosecute 'those who have not been criminals, but victims of fascism, those who were deceived by fascism or compelled to adhere to the party by the well known various forms of moral and material coercion'.[35] The use of the term 'criminals' in reference to fascists is symptomatic: identifying the fascist regime with a phenomenon of political criminality meant essentially to avoid explaining the vast consensus it had aroused among Italians, and to restrict the question of guilt only to the fascist ruling class and the business classes who, according to Marxist interpretations, were behind fascism and had implemented the regime's policies. At the same time, it implicitly suggested that Italians had been – and perhaps still were – afflicted by a form of political immaturity which had prevented them from understanding the true nature of fascism.

On the other side of the political spectrum, the anti-anti-fascist propagandist Guglielmo Giannini wrote that the 'ordinary man' could not be charged with a deep ideological commitment to fascism, but only for having 'trustingly' and superficially adhered to the party. Those to be blamed and punished were, therefore, only the 'professional political men', who had joined fascism with the cynical purpose of making the grade and becoming rich.[36]

The tendency to identify the bearer of the guilt with the ruling class and with the monarchy was also shared by socialists, actionists and republicans. Yet, the idea of the Italian peoples' political un-responsibility based on the assertion of sole guilt lying with the fascist ruling class led paradoxically to the identification of the ultimate guilt of the fascist misdeeds with the Duce's personal responsibility. Recalling Mussolini's absolutism, and the less formal power wielded by the *gerarchi*, the fascist leadership, Rino Parenti, one of the founders of the first *Fascio di combattimento*, the movement from which the Fascist party originated, and the former chief of the Fascist federation in Milan, could naively affirm while under trial: 'finally, is it our fault if one day the King gave the power to Mussolini?'[37] In this way, more than 20 years of totalitarian dictatorship, the catastrophe of the world war and the fratricidal civil war, were reduced to a personal affair between Mussolini and the King. Meanwhile the Italians were considered, implicitly, to be passive observers. The argument of the irresponsibility of the people produced by the concentration of power and the creation of a 'new plutocratic cast' during the dictatorship, led the leading newspaper of the Italian Republican Party to assert that Mussolini carried the 'essential responsibility not only for the destiny of the country, but also for that of the whole world'.[38]

Another position was based on the evangelical formula, 'may the one who is without sin throw the first stone'. To claim that 'everyone was doing it' was a clear attempt to generalise and, thus, relativise the question of guilt. Mussolini's regime had received widespread consent in Italy and abroad. Fascism's good relationship with the Church and international public opinion had contributed to make these convictions stronger and stronger and to convince the public of fascism's good nature: was it not true that pope Pius XI had been referred to Mussolini as the 'man sent by Providence'? It was inconceivable, thus, that after its defeat the same people who had glorified fascism could claim the right to judge the sins of the Italians. Moreover, they had opened their eyes and actively fought fascism from the 8 September 1943 until the end of the war. The spectacle of the dictator's corpse hung up for all to see in a public square in Milan in 1945 was a clear sign Italians had, at least finally, matured an anti-fascist conscience and found their own way to freedom and democracy. This interpretation was sturdily supported by the press during the Peace Conference in order to try to spare Italy the harsh consequences of the imperialistic fascist war. As the liberal writer Francesco Flora declared: 'our guilt finds a correspondence in the guilt and the mistakes of other countries that cooperated to create the atmosphere in which an abject phenomenon like fascism could have international resonance'.[39] Using the same arguments, Luigi Sturzo, an anti-fascist priest and founder of the Catholic *Partito Popolare* (the Catholic Popular Party), maintained that Allies should demonstrate their trust in Italian people to allow the newly reborn democracy to grow stronger:

> There is nothing worse for a people than to be humiliated by its 'friends' and 'liberator', to hear them justifying their broken promises by blaming faults that are not personal faults, although pressed down, like a crown of thorns, upon the brows of all people. This is all the worse when those faults, like that of having left Mussolini in power, are shared by the same Allies, who until 1940 supported Mussolini and paid no heed to anti-fascism.[40]

Strictly linked with this latter thesis was the idea that Italians had already expiated the sin of having trusted and willingly followed fascism into the tragedy of the war by enduring the distress, and the pain, of defeat and civil war. They had paid for their misjudgement with the blood of their children and the material devastation of their country. Thus, they did not deserve and could not accept further punishment. The conservative daily newspaper *Il Tempo*, edited in Rome, gave voice to this feeling, reminding: 'if we all committed sins, right now we all are crying'. In other words, if the suffering had purified the collective conscience, the only possible conclusion was that Italians were 'without any sins'.[41]

Benedetto Croce – the philosopher who strove to transform the Italians' sense of irresponsibility in a largely accepted interpretation of fascism – not only insisted on the international dimension of the fascist phenomenon,[42] but repeatedly supported the thesis of an anthropological incompatibility of Italians' 'feelings of moderation and humanness' with the brutal and clownish nature of the regime. Their secular heritage of humanism had preserved them from the moral decadence of public life under fascism. Compared with centuries of progress and civilisation, Croce asked rhetorically, what was the importance of a 'parenthesis of twenty years'?[43] Italians had accepted the dictatorship primarily out of necessity of self-defence and to keep earning a living. As Croce stressed, under fascist rule the Party card had became the '*tessera del pane*' (bread ration voucher).[44] Such statements had the paradoxical effect of denying the very existence of fascism as an historical phenomenon. If it had 'flourished abusively' on the sound body of the nation, the liberal journalist Panfilo Gentile implied that it 'has never existed in the deepest layers of the country's conscience'.[45]

Also the liberal-socialist intellectual Mario Vinciguerra, writing on the review which expressed the position of one of the most intransigent parties on the question of the purge, the *Partito d'Azione* (Action party), wrote that Italians could be charged only with a 'generic political responsibility' for their nationalistic infatuation, whose origin had to be individuated in the people's 'deep lack of political education'. Therefore, the priority of the new ruling class had to be the task of educating the Italians, and not of punishing them as a whole. He concluded by asking a rhetorical question which underlined the difficulty of judging the past attitude of an entire people: 'Even if all the people had adhered to fascism, who could call upon them to respond for their deeds without committing an iniquity?'[46]

Soon after public opinion in Italy began to reflect an attitude within which a clear acknowledgement of the complicity of Italian society with the regime – which was impossible to deny – vanished when faced with a rejection of the responsibility for the political, material and moral consequences of the tyranny. In this sense, the 'examination of conscience', initially conceived as a tool to realise a real renewal of political life and collective behaviour, became an easy 'shortcut' to avoid not only the political and penal sanctions of the purge, but also to avoid a moral judgment considered unjust and unacceptable.[47] As Croce put it, 'to examine the moral conscience and to acquit or punish' was a process which would have been accomplished 'by every man for himself, with only the help of inner examination, self-criticism and self-correction'.[48]

Moreover, the process of the 'trivialization' of fascism, underlying the political discourse on collective responsibility, had the effect of reinforcing the victimisation of former fascists. In fact, just as they could portray themselves as 'victims' of fascism's deception, in the new political climate they could become 'victims' of anti-fascism's thirst for revenge.[49] The refusal to face even a mere moral discrediting for any former affiliation to the fascist party led to the denouncement of anti-fascism's 'fascist' methods in the application of purgatorial legislation. The transformation of the guilty into victims was the first step toward the complete absolution of the Italians from fascist guilt.

But the rough attempts to conceal the question of guilt were only the symptom of a deeper inability on the art of Italians to believe they could have actually identified themselves with a regime that had led them to the moral and material destruction of the country. There were widespread signs in public opinion that the Italians had great difficulty in recognising and understanding their fascist past. For an independent, patriotic newspaper published in Rome in the winter of 1944, the idea of an ideologically based commitment of the people to the fallen regime was so incompatible with the human sense of dignity as to be simply unconceivable and, thus, unacceptable: 'If forty million human beings have let a gang of political adventurers dominate them for twenty years, if they have actually had to experience the military defeat to finally awaken themselves, can they truly be called men?'[50]

The sentence quoted underscores the dramatic divide between the individual's past fascist identity and the new anti-fascist or, at least, non-fascist consciousness. In the same way, the Socialist writer Leonida Repaci described the attitude of Italians during fascism with a metaphor: as spectators, they had observed themselves participating in the mass gatherings of the regime with astonishment and bewilderment, split between the desire to believe such a spectacle was nothing but a nightmare and the satisfaction of being there. Only as late as 25 July 1943 had the Italians demanded back their souls, souls previously lost to the 'devil'.[51] Evidence of this feeling of split conscience can also be detected in many private memories, by countless efforts to make clear to oneself the reasons which had led to the enthusiastic devotion to fascism, only later fully recognised as the essence of evil.

Psychology aside, one must strive to understand that a narrative about the past could not develop in other ways. It was part of a 'policy for the past', to quote a phrase used with reference to Germany,[52] that was implemented by political parties in the attempt to condemn fascist ideology, to exclude the former ruling class from high-ranking positions in politics and the civil service and, at the same time, to reintegrate the greater part of the former ordinary fascists back into the public life. This policy was based on the anti-fascist movement's necessity to deal with a matter of fact: on the one side the impossibility of carrying out a vast purge of Italian society without undermining the foundation of the new democratic state. On the other side this policy found support in strong collective expectations. As editor of *L'Unità*, Velio Spano wrote that, as anti-fascism was a 'minority phenomenon' and 'many millions of Italians had adhered to fascism', the claim to 'remake Italy with ten to twenty thousand people was an infantile sham'.[53]

That is the main reason why all Italian parties gradually substituted the topic of guilt with a self-absolutory narrative, based on the arguments we have discussed. As has been observed, the *amnesty* of 1946, following the demise of the Italian monarchy decided by a popular referendum and promoted by the justice minister Togliatti, brought about a phenomenon of collective *amnesia*.[54]

Conclusion

The early postwar discussion of the inheritance of the dictatorship demonstrates the emergence of the theme of *collective guilt* of the Italians and of the country's need for moral redemption. A close analysis of the press shows the contradictions and the excessive simplicity of a reassuring formula that stresses the immunity of Italians from fascist influence. In effect, any survey of public opinion represents a current chance to assess the impact of the regime's totalitarian project and its long-term effects on Italian society. This is, as one could imagine, a difficult question to deal with and, thus, a hotly debated feature among scholars. Yet, I believe that the contemporary observers' perception of the fascist regime and its impact on Italian society constitutes a very sensitive tool to assess its nature. Carried out in the years before the consolidation of the 'anti-fascist paradigm', the debate on fascism appeared to be completely free of the ideological overload of the subsequent Cold War political climate. It is remarkable that the observers' anti-fascist political affiliation made them trustworthy witnesses, for they were mainly interested, as anti-fascists, in underestimating the regime's effectiveness, which is precisely what was later to happen.

In the first place, the intellectuals' intervention in the debate, expressing their concern for the moral and political rebirth of the nation, disproved implicitly the image of the fascist regime as an 'imperfect totalitarianism'. They strove to make contemporaries recognise two basic facts: (1) that the fascist regime had not been merely a violent dictatorship imposed by force on an unwilling people, but had succeeded in producing a widespread consensus among Italians. In this sense, the question of guilt was recalled essentially as the sin of the collectivity to have believed and followed the fascist regime until its last days; (2) that the fascist organisational apparatus had not been a fictional device set out to conceal the regime's ideological vacuum and to compensate for its incapacity to grip society and indoctrinate the masses.

Conversely, they maintained that it had been able to reach and affect the lives of millions of citizens and that its ideology had penetrated as a dangerous poison into every sector of the Italian society. When they called for a harsh 'de-fascistiza-tion' of the country and the renewal of public life through the elimination of the negative influences of 20 years of fascist domination over Italians' consciences, they were concerned with the long-term effects of totalitarian pedagogy. As we have seen, even those sectors of public opinion which categorically refused to undergo the purge, or even to be criticized by others for their fascist past, were far from denying the vast involvement of Italian society in the totalitarian experiment. Catholics, also, were well aware that the bare fact of loyalty to the Church had proved useless in limiting the effects of the totalitarian attempt to make the 'new fascist Italians'. In this sense, the 'discovery' and the close analysis of the debate carried out by contemporaries about the collective guilt should compel historians to ask themselves whether the 'imperfect totalitarianism' theory still has any heuristic value.

In the second place, acknowledged as an aberration of the values of freedom and humanity, fascist experience was too painful to be absorbed into the collective memory. The first attempts to construct a realistic narrative of the past experience revealed the incapacity of individuals, and of the greater part of Italian society, to process the memory of the past. In this sense, the development of a strong drive towards forgetting was neither the face assumed by a traditional national attitude to conformism and opportunism – which is one of the strongest stereotypical characteristics attached to Italians[55] – nor simply the result of the political condition of postwar Italy: namely the necessity to convince the Allies that Italians were ready for democracy without undergoing a painful process of re-education.

The drive toward forgetting was, contrarily, one of the most visible consequences of the inability of the society to cope with its traumatic past, an effect of the cleavage produced in the continuity of collective and private history by the totalitarian experience. As has been pointed out, self-deception is the way to keep secret from ourselves the truth we cannot face and ensure a strategy of survival; the process through which self-deception itself is the only way to explain what might otherwise seem incomprehensible.[56] In this case, the deception was the effect of individuals' inbility to connect their present convictions with those of the recent past.

Nor is it possible to adopt a moralistic attitude toward this kind of behaviour. In fact, one must take into account that, after a traumatic experience the liar – a single person or a collective entity – begins to believe that the lie is not a lie, but true.[57] For the contemporary this phenomenon was evident. The young socialist intellectual Paolo Alatri remarked that, as an effect of the 'mass conversion' to anti-fascism, many of the former fascists sincerely believed themselves to have been good anti-fascists also in the past.[58] As has been noticed, this splitting of the individual's personality is what generally happens under totalitarian rule.[59] We should probably argue that it continues to operate even after the collapse of the totalitarian regime, as a long-term effect, due to the transition from a consolidated system of values and beliefs to a completely new one.

That is why the 'question of guilt' was mitigated and, finally, shelved via a continuous re-elaboration of the past that favoured the early development of interpretative stereotypes. The consolidation of an official memory in the years 1945–1948 produced a consequent marginalisation of those recollections which the official memory could not assimilate. The continuous process of re-elaboration of the immediate past resulted in a total negation of the question of guilt: Italians, who had previously acknowledged their responsibility in various forms, finally represented themselves as victims of fascism, and, thus, objectively anti-fascists.

Even the partial admissions of the consent of Italian society to fascism were progressively forgotten. This made it possible to recall the fascist period as a sort of silent but strong struggle fought by a society unified by its aversion to tyranny and its attempt to create the 'new man': it was the final affirmation of the 'anti-fascist paradigm'. As we said before, it was destined to be the dominant narrative of fascist experience during the years of the so-called 'First Republic'.

It is worth noting that the debate about the guilty and the victims in Italy developed completely with reference to former fascists, while the actual victims (the Jews, ethnic minorities, the colonial populace and the civilians of the countries occupied during World War II) remained completely hidden and voiceless.[60] It will take a long time before Italians will bring into question the consolidated image of the 'good Italian' and recognise the extent of the war crimes and of the persecution of the Italian Jews.[61] But this attitude toward the past was not a unique feature of postwar Italy. It was adopted in all the countries which had experienced the oppression of totalitarian rule.[62]

Contrarily to what many historians, in Italy and abroad, continue to believe, the fascist experience not only deeply affected Italian society, but continued to be a heavy legacy also in the postwar era.

Notes

1. See Filippo Focardi, *La guerra delle memoria. La Resistenza nel dibattito politico italiano dal 1945 ad oggi* (Rome-Bari: Laterza, 2005).
2. Vittorio Foa, "L'antiFascismo è un pilastro ma discutiamolo fino in fondo," an interview with G. De Marchis, *La Repubblica*, 19 December 2003.
3. Such an approach was first criticized in the mid-Seventies by the Communist leader and historian of the Italian Communist Party Giorgio Amendola. See Giorgio Amendola, *Intervista sull'antifascismo*, Piero Melograni (ed.) (Rome-Bari: Laterza, 1976), p.3.
4. Cf. Leonardo Paggi, *La violenza, le comunità, la memoria*, in Leonardo Paggi (ed.), *La memoria del nazismo nell'Europa di oggi* (Florence: La Nuova Italia, 1997), p.XII.
5. See Gian Enrico Rusconi, *Se cessiamo di essere una nazione* (Bologna: Il Mulino, 1993).
6. See Renzo De Felice, *Fascism: An Informal Introduction to its Theory and Practice*, an interview with Michael A. Ledeen (New Brunswick, NJ: Transaction Books, 1976).
7. Nicola Gallerano, "Critica e crisi del paradigma antiFascista," *Problemi del socialismo* 7 (1986), p.133.
8. Sergio Luzzatto, *La crisi dell'antiFascismo* (Turin: Einaudi, 2004). See also Alberto De Bernardi, "L'antiFascismo: una questione storica aperta," in Alberto De Bernardi and Paolo Ferrari (eds), *AntiFascismo e identità europea* (Rome: Carocci, 2004), pp.XI–XXXII.
9. Giovanni Miccoli, "Cattolici e comunisti nel secondo dopoguerra: memoria storica, ideologia e lotta politica," in Giovanni Miccoli, Guido Neppi Modona and Paolo Pombeni (eds), *La grande cesura. La memoria della guerra e della Resistenza nella vita europea del dopoguerra* (Bologna: Il Mulino, 2001), p.52.
10. Aurelio Lepre, *L'anticomunismo e l'antiFascismo in Italia* (Bologna: Il Mulino, 1997), p.99.
11. Even though from different perspectives, both Salvatore Lupo (*Partito e antipartito. Una storia della prima Repubblica, 1946–78* (Rome: Donzelli, 2004), p.83 ff. and Ernesto Galli della Loggia [*La morte della patria. La crisi dell'idea di nazione tra Resistenza, antiFascismo e Repubblica* (Rome-Bari: Laterza, 1996), pp.43–4] share this conviction.
12. For example, Mirco Dondi, "The Fascist Mentality after Fascism," in Richard J.B. Bosworth and Patrizia Dogliani (eds), *Italian Fascism. History, Memory and Representation* (New York: St Martin Press, 1999), pp.141–59.
13. See Pier Giorgio Zunino, *La Repubblica e il suo passato. Il Fascismo dopo il Fascismo, il comunismo, la democrazia: le origini dell'Italia contemporanea* (Bologna: Il Mulino, 2003).
14. See Lamberto Mercuri, *L'epurazione in Italia, 1943–1948* (Cuneo: L'Arciere, 1988); Roy Palmer Domenico, *Italian Fascists on Trial, 1943–1948* (Chapel Hill, NC: University of North Carolina Press, 1991); Hans Woller, *Die Abrechnung mit dem Faschismus in Italien 1943 bis 1948* (Munchen:

Oldenbourg, 1996); Romano Canosa, *Storia dell'epurazione in Italia. Le sanzioni contro il Fascismo, 1943–1948* (Milan: Baldini & Castoldi, 1999).

15. See Wolfgang Benz, "Postwar Society and National Socialism: Remembrance, Amnesia, Rejection," *Tel Aviver Jahrbuch für deuthsche Geschichte* (1990), pp.1–16; Michael Geyer, "La politica della memoria nella Germania contemporanea," in Paggi (note 4), pp.257–304; Jürgen Kocka, "Confrontarsi con difficili passati. Memorie collettive e politica in Germania dopo il 1945 e il 1990," *Mondo contemporaneo* 2 (2005), pp.103–18.

16. Karl Jaspers, *The Question of German Guilt* (1948), translated by E. B. Ashton (Westport, CN: Greenwood Press, 1978).

17. Luca La Rovere, "Gli intellettuali della 'seconda generazione' fascista e la transizione al postfascismo. Identità personale e memoria collettiva (1943–1948)," Ph.D dissertation, University of "Roma Tre," 2002–2003; L. La Rovere, "L'esame di coscienza della nazione: gli intellettuali, il problema dei giovani e la transizione al postFascismo," *Mondo contemporaneo* 3 (2006), pp.5–61.

18. See Renato Moro, *La formazione della classe dirigente cattolica* (Bologna: Il Mulino, 1979) and Richard J. Wolff, *Between Pope and Duce. Catholic Students in Fascist Italy* (New York: Lang, 1990).

19. Sergio Paronetto, "Morale professionale del cittadino," *Studium* 9 (July–August 1943), p.222.

20. L. V., "Le tappe di una crisi," *Studium* 10 (October 1943), pp.317–9.

21. Arturo Carlo Jemolo, "La tragedia inavvertita," *Il Ponte* 7 (October 1945), p.595.

22. Mario Borsa, "Sincerità," *Corriere d'informazione*, 22 May 1945. *Corriere d'informazione* was the new name chosen by the publisher for the former *Corriere della sera*, one of the oldest and most influential national newspapers, which compromised its reputation, becoming the official newspaper of the neo-Fascist Republic in Northern Italy.

23. Francesco Palazzi, "Esame di coscienza," *Corriere d'informazione*, 16 June 1945.

24. Gabriele Pepe, "Le due politiche," *Risorgimento liberale*, 22 June 1944.

25. Paolo Treves, "Colpa e responsabilità," *Avanti!*, 10 April 1945.

26. Ignazio Silone, "25 luglio," *Avanti!*, 25 July 1945.

27. See Giuseppe Vacca, "La lezione del Fascismo," in Palmiro Togliatti, *Sul Fascismo* (Rome-Bari: Laterza, 2004), p.LXXXVI ff. On the Communist interpretation of fascism during the 1930s cf. Pier Giorgio Zunino, *Interpretazione e memoria del Fascismo. Gli anni del regime* (Rome-Bari: Laterza, 1991), p.95 ff.

28. Letter to Vincenzo Bianco of 15 February 1943, quoted in Elena Aga Rossi and Victor Zaslavsky, *Togliatti e Stalin. Il Pci e la politica estera staliniana negli archivi di Mosca* (Bologna: Il Mulino, 1997), p.165.

29. Vezio Crisafulli, "Esame di coscienza," *L'Unità*, 28 June 1944.

30. Riccardo Bauer, "Esame di coscienza," *Realtà politica*, 1 September 1945.

31. Woller (note 14), p.134.

32. The civil servants menaced by the purge were around 300,000 units. As a result of the so-called 'Nenni's Act', from the name of the socialist leader charged with the task of the purge, issued in November 1945, the number decreased to 30,000 members of the upper grade of the public administration. In February 1946 only 4800 of them had been effectively purged. Woller (note 14) pp.521–3.

33. Cf. Sandro Setta, *L'Uomo qualunque, 1944–1948* (Rome-Bari: Laterza, 1975).

34. Mariuccia Salvati, "Tempo umano. A Roma dopo la dittatura, 1944–1945," *Passato e presente*, 64 (2005), p.43.

35. "Punire i responsabili della catastrofe della guerra," *L'Unità*, 13 July 1944.

36. Guglielmo Giannini, "Questi Fascismi," *L'Uomo qualunque*, 10 January 1945.

37. a. d., "Rino Parenti dice …," *Corriere d'informazione*, 3 August 1945.

38. Giovanni Antonelli, "Responsabilità e corresponsabilità," *La Voce repubblicana*, 3 October 1944.

39. Francesco Flora, *Ritratto di un ventennio* (Naples: Macchiaroli, 1944), p.57.

40. Luigi Sturzo, *Italy and the Coming World* (New York: Roy Publisher, 1945), pp.241–2.

41. "Italiani senza peccato," *Il Tempo*, 12 September 1945.

42. Benedetto Croce, "Il Fascismo come pericolo mondiale," in Benedetto Croce, *Scritti e discorsi politici, 1943–1947* (Bari: Laterza, 1963), vol. I, pp.7–16. The article first appeared in the *New York Times*, 28 November 1943.

43. Croce (note 42), pp.56–7.

44. Benedetto Croce, "Fiducia nell'Italia," *Risorgimento liberale*, 3 November 1945.

45. Panfilo Gentile, "Il Fascismo è morto," *Risorgimento liberale*, 16 January 1945.

46. Mario Vinciguerra, "Epurazione e depurazione," *La Nuova Europa* 1 (January 1945), p.4.

47. Cf., for example, Francesco Marano, "Verità," *Italia nuova*, 2 January 1945. *Italia nuova* was a monarchic newspaper, which harshly opposed the "de-Fascistization" process.

48. Benedetto Croce, "Intorno ai criteri dell'epurazione," (note 42), p.45.

49. The same phenomenon has been observed also in postwar Germany, where the distinction between 'criminals' and Nazis in 'good faith' produced 'reactions of self-pity and defiance rather than remorse and insight'. Benz (note 15), p.12. As Tony Judt put it: 'the war left a vicious legacy. In the circumstances of the Liberation, everyone sought to identify with the winners […]. This in turn entailed distinguishing and distancing oneself from those who had been the enemy'. Tony Judt, "The Past is Another Country: Myth and Memory in Post-war Europe," in Jan-Werner Müller (a cura di), *Memory and Power in Post-War Europe* (Cambridge: Cambridge University Press, 2002), pp.157–83.

50. Carpio, "Rialzarsi," *L'Italiano*, 26 Febbruary 1944.

51. Leonida Repaci, "Nascita di un giornale," *Epoca*, 5 Febbruary 1945.

52. Cf. Norbert Frei, *Adenauer's Germany and the Nazi Past. The Politics of Amnesty and Integration* (1997), translated by Joel Golb (New York: Columbia University Press, 2002), pp.XII ff. and 303 ff.

53. Velio Spano, "I nostri giovani," *L'Unità*, 1 August 1944. For the difficulties encountered by the deFascistization process in postwar Europe see Charles Maier, *Fare giustizia, fare storia: epurazioni politiche e narrative nazionali dopo il 1945 e il 1989*, in Paggi (note 4), pp.243–56.

54. Cf. Mariuccia Salvati, "Amnistia e amnesia nell'Italia del 1946," in Marcello Flores (ed.), *Storia, verità, giustizia. I crimini del XX secolo* (Milan: Bruno Mondadori, 2001), pp.141–61.

55. The topic of the Italians' 'national character' as a mythological construction has been investigated by historiography. See Giulio Bollati, *L'Italiano. Il carattere nazionale come storia e come invenzione* (1972) (Turin: Einaudi, 1983).

56. Cf. Sissela Bok, *Secrets: On the Ethics of Concealment and Revelation* (New York: Vintage Books, 1962), p.69.

57. 'In order to live with yourself, you allow yourself to be "taken in" by your own deceptive style'. Stanley Cohen, *States of Denial. Knowing about Atrocities and Suffering* (Cambridge: Blackwell, 2001) p.38.

58. Paolo Alatri, "Morte apparente del Fascismo," *La Nuova Europa* 24 (June 1945), p.10.

59. Hans Buchheim, *Totalitarian Rule. Its Nature and Characteristic*, translated by Ruth Hein (Middletown, CN: Wesleyan University Press, 1968), p.41.

60. See, for example, Fabio Levi, "Italian Society and Jews after the Second World War: Between Silence and Reparation," in Jonathan Dunnage (ed.), *After the War. Violence, Justice, Continuity and Renewal in Italian Society* (Market Harborough: Troubador, 1999), pp.21–31; Nicholas Doumanis, "The Italian Empire and *brava gente*: Oral History and the Dodacanase Islands," in Bosworth and Dogliani (note 12), pp.161–77.

61. On the myth of the 'good Italian' cf. David Bidussa, *Il mito del bravo italiano* (Milan: Il Saggiatore, 1994); Filippo Focardi, "'Bravo italiano' e 'cattivo Tedesco': riflessioni sulla genesi di due immagini incrociate," *Storia e memoria* 1 (1996), pp.62–6; F. Focardi, "La memoria della guerra e il mito del 'bravo italiano'. Origine e affermazione di un autoritratto collettivo," *Italia contemporanea* 220–221 (2000), pp.393–9; Claudio Fogu, "*Italiani brava gente*. The Legacy of Fascist Historic(al) Culture on Italian Politics of Memory," in Claudio Fogu, Wulf Kansteiner and Ned Lebow (eds.), *Politics of Memory in Postwar Europe* (Durham, NC: Duke University Press, 2006), pp.147–76; Angelo Del Boca, *Italiani, brava gente? Un mito duro a morire* (Vicenza: N. Pozza, 2006).

62. See for example Pierre Lagrou, "Victims of Genocide and National Memory: Belgium, France and the Netherlands, 1945–1965," *Past and Present* 154 (1997), 181–222.

Negotiating War Legacies and Postwar Democracy in Japan

FRANZISKA SERAPHIM

Japan's alleged failure to face its militarist past – to forget the past or even to falsify its most shameful moment – is a cliché of fairly recent vintage and often predicated on Germany's alleged success of acknowledging the crimes of Nazism. In light of widespread popular notions regarding national memory and amnesia, it seems only prudent to examine the contemporary contexts in which the inquiry into the politics of 'reckoning with the past' assumed such public prominence, as it clearly has today. It is a global phenomenon – and a phenomenon of globalisation – yet we continue to think of it in national terms. The crimes of totalitarian, militarist or fascist regimes affected people across national boundaries. Likewise, holding their perpetrators responsible was rarely an exclusively domestic process but also involved foreign interests. Careful contextualisation is crucial, but so are efforts to disaggregate the political mechanisms of 'working through the past' and to look at their various components.

This contribution begins with a critical look at the stereotypical (mis)conception of an amnesiatic if not outright irresponsible 'Japan' in contemporary popular and even in scholarly discourse. It is certainly true that the discourse about responsibility for the militarist past did not explicitly become a matter of 'official state policy' in Japan until the 1990s in contrast to West Germany, where this began at least two decades earlier. Instead, I contend that the main tendency of the Japanese state under the leadership of the Liberal Democratic Party (LDP) – the party in power for almost the entire postwar period – was to push substantive debates about the war and its postwar legacies onto the level of civic political activism and to influence the outcome indirectly. In turn, the 'social politics of the past' – namely the continuous yet shifting contest over the institutional, intellectual and social legacies of the war among organised social groups – became an integral part of Japan's postwar history. Different and 'conflicting' meanings of the past thus came to be woven into the fibre of postwar democracy, understood as guaranteeing various interests public space through political participation.

The key historical factors that influenced the place of the past in postwar politics in Japan included institutional continuities across 1945, the limits of legal justice, Japan's international position in the Cold War, and fierce interest group involvement in the treatment of war victims and in history education. During the years of foreign occupation by the United States (1945–52), reform efforts highlighted Japan's 'criminal past' with some lasting effects, both positive and negative. (Subsequently, America's wars in Asia, from Korea to Vietnam and more recently the Gulf Wars, provided urgent opportunities to call these effects into question.) From the 1950s through the 1970s, public contests over war legacies as integral parts of the postwar order focused on Japan's 'militarist past' within a 'national' framework, and remained largely a matter of issue-based domestic politics with few international repercussions. Since the late 1980s, however, Japan's 'colonial past' has become an important topic in the context of Asian regionalism and engages not only the Japanese public as a national public but the international community as well, particularly in neighbouring Asian countries. Social activism, which at times intersected with intellectual debates and was refracted in popular culture, embraced the complexity of Japan's militarist past within the institutional parameters of postwar Japan, and it changed with them over the six postwar decades.

The Japan that Cannot Say Sorry

On 12 August 1995, shortly before the fiftieth anniversary of Japan's defeat in World War II, *The Economist* in an article entitled "The Japan that Cannot Say Sorry" reported on the aftermath of a heated controversy in the Diet (Japan's parliament) over a proposed resolution to unequivocally state Japan's official apology for its aggressive war in the Asia-Pacific that had ended 50 years earlier. The 'Resolution to Renew the Determination for Peace on the Basis of Lessons Learned from History', as it was formally known, was the brainchild of then prime minister Murayama Tomiichi, the first Socialist in this office for 47 years, who presided over an unprecedented – and highly volatile – coalition government of the two main parties, the LDP and the long-term opposition party, the Japan Socialist Party (JSP). Murayama's quest to issue a formal apology to Asian nations on this fiftieth anniversary had in the preceding months been countered by a vigorous campaign staunchly opposed to the 'very idea of apology', launched by powerful nationalist interest groups such as the Japan Association of War-bereaved Families (Nihon izokukai) and eventually endorsed by 70 per cent of LDP Diet members, a quarter of all Diet members, and 5 million people. In the end, the Diet passed a statement that expressed only a 'sense of deep remorse', although Murayama himself offered a 'heartfelt apology' in his keynote speech on 15 August.

Taking no note of the larger political turmoil that produced the Diet resolution as well as the outrage against it, *The Economist* explained this outcome by way of Japanese culture. The abstract of the article read:

> Japan is still a nationalistic nation despite its great international economic ties, and is trying to hold its culture in place without influence from western nations. Japan does not want to lose its rich cultural heritage, and thus finds it difficult to apologize for its Asia invasion.[1]

Replace 'Japan' with the 'United States of America', and the above argument is no less valid; no American president has found it necessary to apologise for America's (failed) wars in Asia – from Korea to Vietnam and Iraq. And yet, in the original, the passage epitomises a perception of Japan that has taken firm root among the American – and increasingly the global – public: Japan, still nationalistic after all these years, has failed to join the civilised world, which embraces the need to officially atone for historical injustices.[2] In this classically orientalist view, Japan is not only 'lacking' but clearly 'lagging behind' the West, this time led by the 'model' apologiser Germany, for whom acts of denial or whitewashing of the past (of the kind that are common in Japan) are deemed 'unthinkable' or 'unimaginable'. The reason is almost always an amorphous, unspecified 'cultural heritage', imagined as unchanging, uncontested and separate from other cultures. Responsible reckoning with the past, in contrast, is narrowly understood – at least in the popular media – as a matter of political gestures on the state level for international consumption, that is, as governmental politics.

This cliché, while certainly not groundless, is disturbing because it resonates with stereotypes that were prominent 60 years ago when the war ended. In an August 1945 cartoon from the *Detroit News* and reprinted in the Sunday *New York Times*, the Japanese in defeat appeared to be 'primitive, childish, moronic, or emotionally disturbed' in the eyes of the American public.[3] While no one makes such a claim today, the manner in which Japan's supposed inability to apologise is reported has the reader similarly puzzling over Japan's lack of common sense. The American media coverage of Japan's 'memory problem' in the 1990s, animated by a seemingly steady stream of scandalous news – 'slippages of the tongue' by Japanese cabinet ministers effectively downplaying, if not outright denying, Japanese aggression in Asia, the appearance of a new and state-approved nationalist textbook adopted by less than 0.1 per cent of all schools, or the popularity of a flamboyant *manga* artist intent on justifying Japan's wartime conduct – indeed had the reader puzzle over 'the Japanese mind'.[4] In Germany, meanwhile, where 'reckoning with the past' (*Vergangenheitsbewältigung*) was understood as a uniquely German affair, Japan remained largely irrelevant as it had been even during the Axis Alliance in the 1940s. A notable exception is Gebhard Hielscher, Japan correspondent for *Die Süddeutsche Zeitung*, who specialises in teaching the Japanese how to come to terms with the past the right (i.e. the German) way.

There is no playfulness in the way that Asians, in particular Chinese and Koreans, remember their wartime hatred for the Japanese, and understandably so. Beginning in the 1980s with official complaints about Japanese textbooks and then prime minister Nakasone Yasuhiro's demonstrative 'state visit' to Yasukuni Shrine at the fortieth anniversary of the war's end, Chinese and South Korean governments have invoked Japan's 'militarism' with increasing alacrity. The broadly popular outburst of violent demonstrations in China in the spring of 2005 against the allegedly still militaristic Japanese, appeared to validate Iris Chang's dictum that Japan's 'denial' of its war crimes amounted to a 'second rape' of the Chinese people.[5]

In Japan, the cliché has served its own purposes. In the late 1980s, progressive intellectuals eager to revive an older debate about 'war responsibility' (*sensō sekininron*), invoked the comparison with West Germany to point to historical, cultural and societal factors for Japan's unresolved war legacies. Katō Shūichi argued that Japan lacked the political and moral 'backbone' to face its own responsibility. European or American ideas imported after the war never managed to change the old Japanese way of thinking but existed only as a skin-deep overlay, in his view.[6] Mochida Yukio and others found history and geo-politics at fault, which were beyond Japan's control.[7] Critics on the political right, meanwhile, inverted the cliché and insisted that Japan's first responsibility was to counter the postwar trend of contrition (in the face of foreign demands) and create pride in the nation's accomplishments, independent of other nations' memories of the war.[8] Nishio Kanji, a crusader against what he and others termed *Nihon dameron* (Japan-bashing) went on to co-found the Japanese Society for History Textbook Reform (Atarashii kyōkasho o tsukuru kai) in 1996 and edit a nationalist textbook that elicited international protests a few years ago. In this case, the cliché came full circle.

In contrast to the United States and People's Republic, where contemporary debates seemed to reconnect with wartime stereotypes, in Japan the focus lay on the long postwar period. On the political Right as on the Left, critics examined what had gone wrong (but also what had gone right) in the six decades that Japan kept the peace. The leftist critic Oda Makoto in fact considered pacifism the 'moral backbone' of postwar Japan, powerfully represented by the still unrevised Article 9 (the 'peace clause') of Japan's constitution.[9] Chalmers Johnson echoed this sentiment when he argued in a recent documentary that Article 9 represented Japan's official 'apology' for the war.[10] As constitutional revision becomes a realistic possibility, however, the debate about Japanese war memory in the broadest sense points foremost to the contextual changes that set it apart from 'the long postwar', which came to an end some time in the 1990s.[11] The confluence of geopolitical shifts after the end of the Cold War, the need for institutional reform, innovative legal procedures in dealing with historical injustices and changing patterns of civic activism produced a situation in which the politics of reckoning with the past assumed importance as a vital part of globalisation and regionalisation, in Asia as elsewhere. At the same time, questions of unresolved historical injustices served to localise these processes and endow them with political, legal, social and moral capital.

The current academic interest in these issues feeds on the potentially explosive conjuncture of global political shifts and specific local histories of injustice and their aftermath. Indeed, international contexts have always been crucial to domestic processes of reinvention after the collapse of a discredited regime, all the more so when the collapse came at the hands of unconditional defeat in a large-scale war. The history of Japan's empire and war in Asia is itself enormously complex, because it occurred against the background of Euro-American colonialism and coincided with a number of civil wars in different Asian countries before eventually linking up with Hitler's war in Europe. Unsurprisingly, the aftermath was no less complicated, when the dismantling of Japan's empire fed into various communist, nationalist and de-colonialist revolutions across Asia just as a new hegemonic structure – the Cold War – carved up the region once more. Japan's alleged 'forgetting' and 'falsifying' of its militarist past cannot be looked at in national or historical isolation. At a minimum, the United States as Japan's conqueror and later its principle ally in the world played a major role in this outcome, though certainly not the only one.

Victors, Perpetrators, Survivors and Japan's Criminal Past, 1945–52

Geopolitical shifts, new legal procedures, institutional reform and an explosion of civic political activism shaped the politics of the past not only after the Cold War but also in the years following Japan's unconditional surrender on 15 August 1945, albeit under vastly different circumstances. The dismantling of Japan's far-flung empire was a long and arduous process and, combined with the advent of the Cold War, disaggregated Asia politically and economically. Liberation from Japanese rule did not end occupation and war in China, Korea and many parts of Southeast Asia, but invited new occupying powers – the United States and the Soviet Union in Northeast Asia and the old European colonial powers in Southeast Asia – and fed the flames of ongoing or new civil wars. The pan-Asian project of collective resistance against the West, whether in the form of an early twentieth-century Chinese ideal (championed by Sun Yatsen) or its Japanese wartime incarnation of the Greater East Asia Co-Prosperity Sphere, had met a violent end.

Defeat in Japan was hardly less devastating than it was in Germany. The war had claimed close to 3 million Japanese dead (and more than 20 million across Asia) and left approximately 6.5 million Japanese (almost half of them civilians) stranded in Asia, Siberia and the Pacific Islands. Allied fire and atomic bombing of the Japanese home islands laid 66 cities to ashes, leaving 9 million people homeless.[12] When the American occupation forces under the leadership of General Douglas MacArthur, the Supreme Commander of the Allied Powers (SCAP), arrived in Japan in September, their first objective was not to alleviate the human catastrophe at their feet but to dismantle Japan's war machine and punish those responsible for it. 'Demilitarisation' was soon joined by 'democratisation', however, taught to the Japanese by Americans with a decidedly cultural, if not overtly Christian, mission of transforming that 'pagan, "Oriental" society' into a modern, American one. The special relationship between conquerors and conquered that ensued in these first years had a racial, 'erotic–exotic' quality that deeply coloured the Japanese people's view of the war. Indeed, John Dower characterised the occupation of Japan as 'the last immodest exercise in the colonial conceit known as "the white man's burden"'.[13]

The Early Postwar Debate about War Responsibility

The physical, psychological and political landscapes of defeat and foreign occupation engendered a diverse public discourse on war responsibility (*senso sekininron*) almost as soon as the war had ended. During a press conference about the management of the government on 28 August 1945, Prince Higashikuni Naruhiko, the first postwar prime minister, called on 'one hundred million to repent together' (*ichioku sōzange*), in effect declaring the people *in toto* responsible for the country's *defeat* and exempting no one but the emperor, in whose name the war had been fought.[14] This persistence of a wartime ideology had, in Yoshimi Yoshiaki's words, 'an undeniably distorting effect on the people's consciousness of war responsibility'.[15] Yet, taken on its own terms, 'one hundred million to repent together' also encompassed the historical reality that the majority of the people had cooperated in the war and would have to confront this individually, on their own terms. This, in turn, became central in the debate among intellectuals, who tried to come to terms with their own role under the wartime regime, although they rarely discussed the role of the people at large.

In sharp contrast to this attempt by the Japanese authorities to dilute responsibility among the populace, Allied occupation officials insisted on assigning individual responsibility to particular Japanese leaders for having started and supported the war. They arrested military officers, politicians and bureaucrats and put them on trial for war crimes, while they barred individuals and groups suspected of having supported the war from public office. The purge affected nearly 210,000 people, mainly business executives, journalists, right-wing leaders, schoolteachers, officials and former military personnel who had to resign from positions of public responsibility. In addition, SCAP's wide-ranging censorship policy rendered impermissible all public discussion of war propaganda and any kind of criticism of the occupation and its policies.[16] Yet, despite the Americans' very different notion of war responsibility, MacArthur agreed with Japanese government leaders to spare the emperor from legal indictment. In a remarkable transformation, the emperor was stripped of his status as sovereign of the nation (and as 'living deity'), and instead was made the symbolic cornerstone of Japan's new 'peace' constitution. This rendered the issue of his abdication a moot point.

Not so among the people, some of whom began to discuss specifically the emperor's role in the war, both as its foremost victim (as which he appeared on his travels around the country), but also as its foremost criminal. A mass meeting on the issue of war responsibility in Tokyo in December 1946, for example, displayed a banner that read, 'Pursue the war responsibility of the emperor, who deprived us of our livelihoods!' People from all walks of life looked back at the war years through the lens of defeat and foreign occupation in efforts to identify which aspects of Japanese society needed to be changed most urgently in order to reconstruct the social system as a whole. The term 'war responsibility' enjoyed great popularity in the mass media in the first postwar years, moving in and out of debates on the political issues of the day. War responsibility was a socio-political issue at a time when democratisation embodied everybody's hopes for a new and greatly changed society. It was a moral issue dictated by the war experience and postwar devastation, and it became an intellectual issue as academics, writers and critics debated the correct approach to this complex problem.[17]

The notion of individual responsibility clearly dominated the progressive discourse in opposition to the older idea of collective responsibility mostly held by conservatives. Liberal intellectuals accepted individualism as an essential part of democracy and thus made its absence a powerful part of their view of the wartime past. Nakano Yoshio, editor of the journal *Heiwa* (Peace), insisted that the Japanese people's morality during the war was a slave morality, and he, Nakano, was the first to take responsibility for having been a 'modern slave'.[18] Marxist writers, many of whom had been imprisoned during the war, scrutinised the wartime behaviour of writers and cultural figures and found an astonishing lack of individual consciousness and social responsibility among the wartime intellectual community. Odagiri Hideo, in June 1946, went as far as to publish a list of 25 names of war propagandists, a move that was highly controversial at the time. Others, for example the historian Hani Gorō, considered it more important that intellectuals examine their own actions and recognise their faults than to purge them from their public positions.

In passionately denouncing the war and emphasising democratic reform, the intellectual vanguard of the war responsibility debate set the past off against the present, thus validating the need for a radically different future. They called for nothing less than a complete break with the wartime past, which also offered the opportunity to make the left-liberal faction a legitimate power and important force in society. The lack of distance to the experience of war and defeat in a way dictated this intense concern with the restructuring of society. It should also be kept in mind, however, that little detailed information about the conduct of the war was available at the time. The early debate about war responsibility took place not only under Allied censorship but at a time when graphic descriptions of Japanese war crimes against Asians in particular had not been publicised to make people aware of the scope of Japan's responsibility. So soon after the end of the war, people clung to the hope for a better future rather than dwelling on the memory of the terrible past.

Legal Responsibility and the Allied War Crimes Trials

To define and raise public knowledge about Japanese war crimes, to allocate individual responsibility for them and to set a new precedent for international law conventions were the goals of the Allied war crimes trials in Japan (and similarly in Germany). Initially, there was much support for the legal pursuit of the leadership's responsibility for the war disaster among the Japanese population. Yokota Kisaburō, professor of international law at Tokyo University, wrote in 1946, 'The people are very interested in the current issue of war crimes ... but they don't clearly understand the notion of war crimes ... because it has changed dramatically with this war. ... Indeed, international law is being newly conceived ... and it amounts to nothing less than a revolution of international society itself'.[19] Yokota was referring to the expanded interpretation of 'crimes against humanity' to include unprecedented crimes, and especially to the new category 'crimes against peace' (provoking, planning and beginning a war). He welcomed these changes as central to the restructuring of international relations and Japan's place in them. Yokota considered the recognition of personal responsibility among the wartime leadership as the first step towards this goal, and called for a thorough investigation by Japanese courts themselves.

The war crimes trials that ensued, however, were solely an Allied affair. They included not only the high-profile International Military Tribunal of the Far East (IMTFE), known in Japan as the Tokyo War Crimes Trial (May 1946 to November 1948), but also 2244 regional Class B/C war crimes trials conducted by the Dutch, British, Australians, Chinese, Americans, French and Filipinos throughout Japan's former empire between 1946 and 1951. The Soviets held secret war crimes trials against Japanese they had captured in Manchuria, northern Korea and southern

Sakhalin, including 12 individuals associated with Unit 731, the now infamous bacteriological warfare research unit.[20] In Tokyo, 11 justices representing the Allied nations found 23 Class A war criminals guilty and sentenced seven to death by hanging, including Tōjō Hideki, Hirota Kōki (both former prime ministers) and Matsui Iwane (a former general in command of the troops during the Nanjing Massacre in 1938). Elsewhere, a total of 5700 individuals were indicted for Class B/C (conventional) war crimes, of which 920 were executed, including Taiwanese and Korean former subjects of the Japanese empire. Although these local trials dealt with such crimes as murder of civilians, the mistreatment of POWs and rape, few left an enduring mark on the public consciousness of these crimes. The unevenness with which they were conducted, especially the prosecutors' failure to recognise the peculiarities of the Japanese chain of command, coloured these trials as acts of vengeance in the minds of many Japanese.[21]

With the exception of the Chinese, those who sat in judgment of Japanese war criminals belonged to the old colonial powers (Britain, Holland, France, the United States and Australia) rather than to Asian nations that had suffered under Japanese colonialism. The brutal mistreatment of Allied POWs loomed large at these trials as systemic to Japanese military practices. In contrast, the organised sexual abuse of tens of thousands of Asian women who were forcedly recruited to provide 'comfort' to the Japanese troops at the front did not register as anything but individual misdeeds. Moreover, arguably one of Japan's most gruesome crimes – the development and use of biological and chemical weapons in China associated with Unit 731 – was deliberately covered up by American military personnel who found the data generated by Japanese scientists immediately useful for America's own biological weapons program. Far from making the crimes of using human guinea pigs for this research publicly known, the Americans helped the head of Unit 731, Ishii Shirō, and his staff to acquire new identities and start new lives in postwar Japan.[22] This was 'victors' justice' with both a racist and an unabashedly opportunistic edge.

The politicisation of legal justice rendered against Japan was nowhere more apparent than at the Class A war crimes trial in Tokyo. Here the objective was to prove Japan's singular liability for having conspired to wage an aggressive war, based clearly on *ex post facto* law and modelled after the Nuremberg trials as if wartime Japan had been analogous to Nazi Germany. Most jarring of all, as a handful of former military and civilian leaders were singled out to be personally embodying the evils of Japan's aggressive war, emperor Hirohito as former commander-in-chief, in whose name the war had been fought, remained aloof of the whole process, as if untainted by war crimes. Instead, the emperor was rein-vented as a pacifist under the new 'peace' constitution. The responsibility of the Japanese people, most of who had actively cooperated in the war effort, similarly played no role in the trial. It is little surprising, therefore, that nationalists in Japan would come to see the seven hanged Class A war criminals as having shouldered the responsibility both for the emperor and for the people, thus becoming 'martyrs' in the face of Allied 'justice'. (This logic lay behind the secret enshrine-ment of their souls at Yasukuni Shrine in 1978.)

The Tokyo War Crimes Trial was riddled by extraordinary contradictions as well as the hypocrisy of the Allies, who, as victors, ignored not only the larger historical context of imperialism and colonialism (past and present) but also war crimes of their own (e.g. the atomic bombings). By 1948, any positive expectations of the trial the Japanese public may have harboured had simply dissolved. 'I hope that never again and in no country on earth will there be another war crimes trial', wrote a 45-year-old physician in a letter to the editor of the daily newspaper *Yomiuri shinbun*. 'We need equality among the peoples of the world, freedom of trade, and open borders if we want to prevent another global war'.[23] But the commencing Cold War had changed the Allies' priorities. Soon after the seven convicted men had been hanged, the prosecutors released all Class A war crimes suspects who had not received the death sentence, citing insufficient evidence. As General Willoughby himself admitted privately to a friend, 'this trial was the worst hypocrisy in recorded history'.[24] The Japanese accepted the verdict quietly and stoically, but the whole notion of reckoning with the past through war crimes trials became discredited. Thereafter, only the Japan Communist Party called for independent Japanese trials, but none were ever conducted. The Japanese government officially accepted the Tokyo trial's verdict when it signed the San Francisco Peace Treaty in 1951, but the notoriety of the phrase 'Tokyo trial view of history' in the following decades suggests a widespread rejection of this imposition of the victor's version of history.

Institutional Reforms and Continuities

The desire to reinvent Japan as a peaceful and democratic society ran broad and deep among the people in the early postwar years. What 'peace and democracy' would look like, however, was at least initially contingent upon the occupation forces' reform agenda. John Dower described SCAP's 'demilitarisation and democratisation' policies as a potent mix of genuine liberal visions and self-interested, even arrogant, pragmatism. The American reform program succeeded in setting the institutional parameters of Japanese postwar democracy, most powerfully symbolised by the U.S.-imposed constitution, which went into effect in May 1947. Nonetheless, SCAP's policy shifts in response to changing world affairs demonstrated to Japanese both inside and outside of government the power-political nature of discrediting past institutions and replacing them with new and democratic ones. The deep ironies of the conqueror's mandate to establish peace at gunpoint and teach democracy through censorship were not lost on Japanese citizens. Indeed, the reform program provided the Japanese with inspiration and with structures but perhaps most importantly with opportunities to interpret the occupier's instructions as pragmatically as SCAP conducted its own policymaking.

In the fall of 1945, MacArthur set about dismantling what he considered to be the institutional pillars of wartime militarism and ultra-nationalism. SCAP targeted government ministries critically involved in war propaganda, closing various government ministries including offices of State Shinto, and cancelling the pension program for war-bereaved families. Education reform was likewise an important focus of demilitarisation as reflected in the substitution of textbooks and efforts to decentralise the educational structure. At the same time, the Bill of Rights issued in October 1945 established an impressive range of civil rights, liberated political prisoners (mainly communists), encouraged labour union activism and lay down the basis for a new system of social welfare. These individual liberties became the core of the new constitution; an ambitiously progressive document written and imposed by occupation officers after drafts by the Japanese government had proven to be unacceptable to SCAP.

The making of this constitution has attracted much scholarship, perhaps because it is the one democratic 'reform' of genuine American (or 'alien') origin that has remained unchanged until the present day. All other reforms, from polit-ical reorganisation at the central and local levels to reforms of the economy, labour, land allocation and education, were compromised to different degrees by SCAP's own policy inconsistencies, by the intervention of the Japanese government, and by postoccupation restructuring along conservative political lines. Here it is important to remember that MacArthur's General Headquarters (GHQ) formu-lated reform policies but implemented them through the Japanese government, which continued to operate legitimately. Institutional democratisation therefore involved the Japanese leadership – and even the public at large – more directly than was the case in Germany. The complicated process of drafting, translating and publicising the new constitution in fact revealed how fervently invested many Japanese people were in this issue. Ordinary citizens sent in personal drafts and debated their ideas for the constitution in public forums, while the cabinet under Prime Minister Shidehara fought hard to rescue any, even the smallest, part of the Meiji Constitution, which remained far from discredited in the elite's eyes.

In the end, MacArthur's draft prevailed with only minor linguistic alterations. It established popular sovereignty and guaranteed a broad range of civil liberties in line with American democratic ideals, but it retained the emperor as 'symbol' of the nation, now stripped of any political role. Most remarkably, the constitution contained a clause (Article 9) that explicitly renounced Japan's right to ever fight a war again or maintain an active military. While quickly considered a mistake by the Americans, who began to think of Japan as an indispensable ally in the Cold War, this clause was firmly embraced by a war-shattered populace and in time became the property of the Japanese people. Overall, a strong sense prevailed that the mistakes of the past could best be overcome by ensuring that they would not be repeated in the future, and the constitution with its Article 9 came to be seen as a powerful statement to that effect.

More precisely, underneath the glamour of newness, the American constitution managed at once to enshrine important continuities with the past, such as the imperial institution, and also to serve as a tool for citizens to combat the political ramification of other continuities, in elite personnel, bureaucratic institutions, as well as ideologies of nationalism. The occupation reforms did not, for example, eradicate the wartime organisational foundations of the postwar state.[25] The most powerful public institutions in postwar Japan, for example the Ministry of Finance and the Bank of Japan, were 'straightforward carryovers' from the war years.[26] Prewar political party lineages survived almost intact or were revived after SCAP lifted the military purge and released imprisoned war criminals by the early 1950s. One suspected Class A war criminal, Kishi Nobusuke, even became prime minister in 1957, and many more were able to rebuild their political careers. The mass media, too, reflect bold continuities with the past: all five of the main national newspapers not only survived but flourished during the war years. Many private organisations traced their organisational and ideological roots back to experiences in the 1920s and 1930s. The sense of 'starting over' in 1945, so compelling in the personal stories of individuals who lived through these times, was no more than a myth on the state level.

War Legacies as Special Interests

'Despite the ultimate emergence of a conservative postwar state', John Dower wrote in the introduction to his highly acclaimed book *Embracing Defeat*, 'the ideals of peace and democracy took root in Japan – not as a borrowed ideology or imposed vision, but as a lived experience and a seized opportunity'.[27] Whereas the state unapologetically capitalised on its prewar and wartime foundations and know-how during postwar reconstruction, civic organisations from across the political spectrum had to articulate their respective positions vis-à-vis the war and its legacies in order to legitimate their activism. Aided by MacArthur's Bill of Rights in the fall of 1945, the reconstructed Left gained political strength by founding labour unions, agricultural cooperatives and research groups, or reviving formerly suppressed organisations. Many professional organisations that had existed during and before the war changed their names and rhetoric to conform to new circumstances. Organisations identified as militarist by occupation forces were ordered to disband, but they, too, invoked the promise of participatory democracy and often re-established themselves in new guises. As a result, reckoning with the wartime past became intertwined with surviving defeat and foreign occupation and was used politically to lend legitimacy to interest-based struggles.

Shrine Shintoists and war-bereaved families were among those who organised nationally in the face of the occupation's demilitarisation policies. In response to MacArthur's Shinto Directive of December 1945, which ordered all State Shinto offices closed and declared public emperor worship illegal, leaders from various private Shinto organisations formed the Association of Shinto Shrines (Jinja honchō) in 1946, a national umbrella organisation of Shinto shrines, to negotiate a new status for Shinto under postwar democracy. Though critical of the wartime bureaucratic abuse of Shrine Shinto, the Association worked tirelessly to regain Shinto's huge losses both institutionally and in terms of its public image, and to revive the ties between Shrine Shinto, the Imperial House and the state through the use of Shinto rituals in public ceremonies. Families of the military dead, who had been honoured and privileged with sizable pensions during the war, found themselves in dire straights when MacArthur eliminated their government benefits. They organised nationally in 1947 to press for social welfare measures and formed the Japan Association of War-bereaved Families (Nihon izokukai) in 1952 to revive state recognition of the military war bereaved as the nation's foremost victims of war through proper pensions and official ceremonies for the war dead at Yasukuni Shrine. The Association of Shinto Shrines and the Association of War-bereaved Families evolved into powerful nationalist interest groups centred on resurrecting aspects of the wartime system that occupation policies had dismantled.

Nevertheless, the occupation's democratic reforms greatly favoured the political ambitions of the liberal Left, from progressive intellectuals to communist-inspired labour groups, who gained enormous public prestige and political momentum in the first postwar years, whether they had actively resisted the war or belatedly come to realise its unjustness. The defining moment for large national organising of groups critical of Japan's war effort came in the last years of the 1940s, when SCAP began to fear the possibility of a communist revolution and proceeded to retract some of the democratic rights MacArthur had granted the Japanese earlier, such as the right to collective bargaining. This was part of a broader policy change in the context of the Cold War that became known in Japan as the 'reverse course' and reflected not only American interests but also those of the conservative elites running the Japanese government. One of the most influential groups formed at this time, in 1947, was the Japan Teacher's Union. It opposed the continuation, indeed the strengthening, of bureaucratic structures, in particular the Ministry of Education, that had supported militarism during the war and threatened to undermine the opportunity to liberate teachers from the state and return them to the people – to transform teachers from passive agents of a militarist state into active agents of democratic change. The Teachers' Union established itself as a powerful voice that continuously raised public conscious-ness about state-sponsored information, interpretation and representation of the wartime past, not only in education generally but also in the public use of Japan's national flag and anthem, the revival of pre-war national holidays and Yasukuni Shrine as a site of national mourning for Japan's war dead. Not surprisingly, this activism made it the arch-enemy of right-wing organisations such as the Associa-tion of Shinto Shrines and the Japan Association of War-bereaved Families.

Many of the most prominent political interest groups formed within the context of the occupation and articulated their visions for postwar Japan on the basis of a selective reckoning with the legacies of the war. These organisations ranged from the far Right to the radical Left, although their respective political clout changed, in some cases considerably, across the decades. The end of the occupation in 1952 was the defining historical moment for these organisations, when their activities matured into interest politics that could be negotiated freely for the first time. Yet the manner in which these interest groups were able to command – or compete for – public space was immediately compromised by the domestic and interna-tional political landscape that emerged in the early 1950s. With Yoshida's official acceptance of the Tokyo War Crimes Trial verdict, which cast Japan as the sole aggressor in the war, the issue of crimes against other peoples was seemingly off the table. Public attention swung towards the legacies of the past that had been neglected under the occupation: the domestic experience of militarism and war, and its Japanese victims.

One-country Pacifism and Japan's Militarist Past, 1950s to 1970s

Despite Japan's defeat in 1945, no peace treaty was signed until 1951, and war continued in many parts of Asia. China's civil war finally came to an end with the Communist Revolution in October 1949. The following June, Korea's postwar division enflamed an ugly war involving the former allies China, the Soviet Union and the United States on Korean territory. Within this context, Japan's political options for international rehabilitation became narrowly circumscribed by its alliance with the United States in the deepening Cold War world. At the same time, a whole new range of discursive possibilities concerning Japanese reckoning with its wartime past opened up. The return of convicted war criminals to public life (and even national politics), the belated disclosure of the real horrors of the Hiroshima and Nagasaki atomic bombings, the stories of repatriates from Japan's former empire or bestselling collections of war testaments brought a flood of memories to public prominence and provided fertile ground for liberal demo-crats, pacifists, and nationalists of different vintages to formulate their own respective political agendas with great urgency.

Peace Treaties, Reparations and Compensation

In September 1951, Japan signed the San Francisco Peace Treaty with 48 countries, which ended the American occupation and restored Japan's national sovereignty in April 1952. Although regarded as non-punitive and non-restrictive, the peace treaty, like the resulting liberation from foreign occupation, turned out to be partial at best: excluded from the signatories were the entire communist bloc and most countries of Japan's former empire, in particular China and Korea. Okinawa and the Ogasawara Islands, moreover, remained American-occupied 20 years longer than the main islands, until 1972. Concurrently, Japan signed a separate alliance with the United States, the U.S.–Japan Security Treaty, which guaranteed the United States the right to station troops in Japan to protect Japan's internal and external security as part of the U.S. containment strategy in East Asia. The two treaties combined brought Japan firmly into the deepening Cold War confrontation, leaving no option for the political neutrality demanded by the left-liberal opposition on the basis of Japan's constitutional renouncement of war.

As feared by those who vehemently opposed the conservative and anti-communist trend at the time, the so-called San Francisco system established an international framework in which the official pursuit of Japanese culpability and atonement for the war was quarantined by the so-called bamboo curtain, a meta-phor for the Cold War division of Northeast Asia. American 'hard' Cold War policy, as it emerged even before the Korean War broke out, viewed Asia in bounds that ironically replicated Japan's wartime co-prosperity sphere, again with Japan at the centre, and again with a strongly anti-communist rationale. In 1948, George Kennan argued for 'the re-entry of Japanese influence and activity into Korea and Manchuria' as being 'in fact, the only realistic prospect for coun-tering and moderating Soviet influence in that area'.[28] When the Communist Revolution in China appeared imminent, however, U.S. planners actively promoted 'reopening some sort of empire to the south' – in Southeast Asia – in order to bolster Japan's economy and thus its importance in the 'great crescent' of containment, reaching from the Aleutians through Japan to the Philippines and Australia and extending further through Southeast Asia to India.[29] While the United States of course had no intention of recreating 'Japan's' co-prosperity sphere, the perceived strategic and economic necessity of such a sphere of influ-ence, now with 'America' at the centre, certainly resonated with Japan's wartime rationale of expansion as a matter of self-defence.

The reparations issue was closely bound up with the perceived need to build up Japan's economy in this broader Cold War context. Both the United States and the Chinese Nationalist government had drawn up their own reparations programmes well before the end of the war. In the course of negotiations between the two in the deteriorating Cold War environment of the late 1940s, however, the reparations program formulated by the U.S. State Department steadily shrank until its virtual renunciation in the San Francisco Peace Treaty against concerted Chinese and also Korean opposition. The nationalist Chinese regime on Taiwan, urged by the U.S. to conclude a separate bilateral peace treaty with Japan in lieu of signing the San Francisco Peace Treaty, waved its right to demand reparations in a 'magnanimous gesture'. As Okamoto Kōichi has argued, this represented the loss of a major opportunity to rebuild Japanese rela-tions with its neighbours and foremost victims of its colonial and war conduct on a fundamentally new basis of Japanese contrition and apology.[30] To be sure, the Japanese government had no independent foreign policy and thus no official say in this matter, but it nonetheless made clear that it regarded the reparations program as a way to build up East Asian trade and thus aid economic recovery rather than as compensation for the damages it had inferred on its neighbours during the war.[31]

Southeast Asia presented a different but equally instructive case. The Francisco Peace Treaty did specify in Article 14 Japan's obligation to pay reparations, but this was immediately qualified by the acknowledgment of Japan's inability to pay appropriate sums of money.[32] Prime Minister Yoshida Shigeru was thus able to reject Indonesia's and the Philippines' high demands ($18 billion and $8 billion. respectively) for reparations in 1951–2. Finally in 1954, members of the opposition Socialist Party intervened in a power-political move designed to oust Yoshida, and got reparations negotiations rolling again. In a series of bilateral treaties concluded throughout the 1950s, Japan committed itself to paying $250 million to Indonesia (1958) and $500 million to the Philippines (1956) over the following 20 years, and lesser amounts to Laos (1958), Cambodia (1959) and South Vietnam (1959). These payments later became tied to overseas economic aid (ODA) from Japan to Southeast Asia, which in time increased to substantial amounts, making Japan the world's largest ODA lender while simultaneously creating markets for Japan's export industry. The irony of Japan extracting economic gain from settling its outstanding war debts was not lost on Asian countries as they watched Japan's economy soar in the postwar decades. Nonetheless, Japan's ODA in Asia has also been seen as a long-term reconciliation endeavour that shows more sincere commitment to building peace and prosperity than formal apologies for wartime transgressions might.

People's Diplomacy

Reconciliation with China and Korea proceeded on other, more informal fronts until bilateral relations were normalised with South Korea in 1965 and with the People's Republic of China (PRC) in 1972. Both times, American interests were paramount in bringing these treaties about. The treaty with South Korea was highly desired by the United States in the context of its war effort in Vietnam but remained deeply controversial in both Japan and South Korea. Normalisation of relations between Japan and China followed on the heel of President Nixon's visit to Beijing and was greeted with euphoria in Japan. In fact, civic organisations in Japan had done much to keep cultural contacts and trade going with their counterparts across the East China Sea since the early 1950s. Of particular importance were the wide-ranging activities of the Japan–China Friendship Association (Nitchū yūkō kyōkai), which worked with academic, political, trade and peace groups in Japan to improve relations with the People's Republic of China via 'people's diplomacy' (*kokumin gaikō* in Japanese or *renmin waijiao* in Chinese), a term coined by the PRC's first premier Zhou Enlai.

The Japan–China Friendship Association, founded in October 1950, insisted on an official acknowledgement of Japanese war atrocities against China as the necessary basis for a rapprochement. To this end, it mobilised local groups to collect the remains of Chinese forced labourers in Japanese mines (most famously the Hanaoka Massacre of June 1945), return them to China and commemorate these victims in various ways. It succeeded in 1953–6 in helping to administer the repatriation of thousands of Japanese left in China after the war's end, including Japanese war criminals, who had been 're-educated' in China and voiced their criticism of Japanese aggression publicly. Throughout the postwar decades the Friendship Association worked to expand trade relations with China on an informal basis, spoke for the rights of Chinese residents in Japan, and especially since the 1980s, supported research into Japan's biological warfare and the 'comfort women' system.

People's diplomacy as championed by this and other left-of-centre organisations was at best ambiguous in theory and clearly compromised in practice. Never intended to be more than a temporary arrangement in Japanese–Chinese relations, it actually co-existed rather easily with official policy. Its success in managing Sino-Japanese relations in fact depended on the tacit consent of the government: the Friendship Association persistently lobbied the same state institutions it protested against, so as to be assured of its position in brokering relations with the PRC. To be sure, the Association deserved credit for creating and maintaining important channels of communication with the PRC until official relations were restored. Nevertheless, until then its activities also helped to perpetuate the political arrangement by which relations with China remained outside the political mainstream, while official policy focused predominantly on relations with the United States. Acknowledgment of and atonement for Japan's wartime aggression had its legitimate place in postwar public life, but as part of the special interest politics of certain interest groups on the opposition left, which were easily discredited as 'communist'.

With the end of the occupation, various organised victims of war were able to freely compete with one another for government compensation, as long as they had Japanese citizenship. Former imperial subjects from the colonies who had been Japanese nationals, however, abruptly lost Japanese citizenship when the San Francisco Peace Treaty took effect and became ineligible for government redress payments. As victims of wartime aggression, Chinese and Koreans in Japan became all but invisible, depending instead on the representation of those who worked to restore foreign relations. The real winners in the early 1950s turned out to be the families of the Japanese military dead represented by the Japan Association of War-Bereaved Families or Nihon izokukai. They campaigned aggressively (lobbying bureaucrats in the Health and Welfare Ministry and conservative politicians), first for social welfare privileges and then increasingly for the state's recognition of their losses as sacrifices to the nation. The first postwar piece of legislation concerning Japan's war victims accordingly was the War-injured and War-bereaved Families Support Act, which went into effect with the end of the occupation on 30 April 1952 and was revised four times in ways that significantly widened eligibility and payment amounts. The second piece of legislation, the Military Pension Law, introduced in August 1953, represented an explicit 'revival' of wartime pensions and thus bore the distinct flavour of wartime state ideology. This was a significant victory for nationalists critical of the reforms introduced under foreign occupation. Indeed, when the families of convicted war criminals became eligible for pensions in 1955, one could speak of the social rehabilitation of those who had been at the centre of militarist culture irrespective of their war conduct.

Anti-nuclear Allergies

Victims of the atomic bombings of Hiroshima and Nagasaki, known in Japan as *hibakusha*, were less successful in securing government compensation than the war-bereaved for a variety of reasons. First, under Allied censorship, *hibakusha* had limited access to medical treatment and could not organise support groups. No public discussion of the atomic bombings was allowed until 1949, and no photographs of the destruction were published until 1952. Second, A-bomb victims faced substantial social stigmatisation caused by ignorance and fear of the long-term effects of radiation. This was one important reason for what Monica Braw called the A-bomb victims' 'voluntary silence'.[33] Third, when Japan regained its national sovereignty, the question of government compensation of war victims was already dominated by the war-bereaved, war-injured, repatriates and other groups who demanded that the state recognise and compensate them for their losses in the line of patriotic duty. Atomic bomb victims, in contrast, were overwhelmingly civilians and powerful reminders of Japan's military defeat at the hands of the same power on which its future now relied. These factors undoubtedly discouraged the early peace movement to explicitly embrace the nuclear issue.

This changed in 1954 after the irradiation of a small Japanese tuna fishing boat, the Lucky Dragon Number Five, by nuclear fallout from a 15-megaton hydrogen bomb 'Bravo' experiment by the United States at the Bikini Atoll. A grassroots pacifist 'Ban-the-Bomb' movement sprang up in response to this tragedy and mushroomed into the first World Conference against Atomic and Hydrogen Bombs in August 1955. Under the leadership of Yasui Kaoru, a professor of international law at Tokyo Imperial University during the war, the anti-nuclear peace movement 'asserted nuclear victimhood to be a uniquely Japanese national experience' but clearly hoped that 'the voice of the Japanese people would sway the conscience of all the world's peoples'.[34] A year later, on the eleventh anniversary of the bombings, atomic bomb victims groups formed the Japan Confederation of A- and H-bomb Sufferers Organisations (Hidankyō) to demand 'state compensation based on the special nature of atomic bomb damage'.[35] The connection between the catastrophes of August 1945 and the March 1954 accident opened up a particular niche in public life in which *hibakusha* justified their demands for special government treatment in terms of a commitment to peace and a nuclear-free world, quite in contrast to the state recognition of wartime sacrifices that other war victims' groups claimed.

The Socialist-led opposition emerged at this time as the champion for the A-bomb victims to demand privileges comparable to those the ruling LDP had granted the war-bereaved in 1952. Although there was considerable bipartisan support for a *hibakusha* medical aid law (passed in 1957), the Socialist Party insisted on a more thorough political commitment to this war legacy: an end to U.S. military bases and a decisive anti-nuclear policy vis-à-vis the United States. Just as nationalist groups (including the war-bereaved) focused on the rehabilitation of aspects of the national past 'to console the spirits of the heroic war dead', so did the Socialist opposition embrace the *hibakusha* in the name of future world peace. The Lucky Dragon Incident seemingly extended nuclear victimhood to all Japanese, but more importantly, it divorced the Hiroshima and Nagasaki bombings from the conventional war that had preceded it. In Japanese public memory as well as in 1950s historiography, 'Hiroshima' inaugurated the postwar nuclear age. More so than ending World War II, it represented America's first strike in the Cold War (an interpretation that the U.S. historian Gar Alperovitz forcefully advanced ten years later).[36] It was the 'continuation' of America's military engagement in Asia that caught the Japanese public's attention in the mid-1950s, from the Korean War to nuclear testing in the Pacific.

Japanese victims' consciousness centred on the atomic bomb victims is routinely criticised in America and by some in Japan. Indeed, in museum and testimonial narratives, the bombs almost always fell out of the blue sky, like a natural disaster, with the focus on the lived experience of the horror that followed, while the questions of responsibility (the United States for dropping the bombs, Japan for having provoked them with its disastrous war) rarely surfaced. There are nonetheless contextual reasons for this development. They originate in the intersection of domestic and international politics in the 1950s: Japanese people began to work through the after-effects of the bombings at a time when the threat of nuclear war was once more a reality, and when Japan's future depended on its alliance with the world's number one nuclear power.

From the 1950s to the 1970s, war memory became closely tied to interest politics, whose legitimate public presence needed to be safeguarded as the most important lesson learned from wartime militarism as state coercion. In many ways, this was a left-dominated way of reckoning with the past, which came to an explosive peak in 1960 during the violent mass protests against the revision of the U.S.–Japan treaty, and several years later in protests against Japan's complicity in the Vietnam War. Although ostensibly about a foreign policy issue, what really mattered to the demonstrators, who represented 'the people', was to stand up to the 'state' which had taken neither voluntary responsibility for past mistakes nor pursued pacifist policies. 'Anti-nuclear allergies', as the popular opposition to nuclear weapons was later termed, and the firm embrace of Article 9 of the constitution (the peace clause), formed a pair of popular convictions designed to resist the gradual encroachment of the (conservative) state on the (democratic) public sphere.

Recent History in Scholarship and Education

The perceived split between the allegedly liberal people and the conservative government coloured various arenas of public life, but it became particularly entrenched in history education and scholarship. Occupation policies, but also Cold War politics, provided the backdrop against which both the independent historical profession and the official system of textbook production defined their objectives. The postwar history profession demonstrated its independence from SCAP's re-education programme early on, when it revived historical materialism as the interpretive lens through which to examine the war, and raised it to the level of an orthodoxy. This Marxist historiography, which paradoxically adopted the American terminology 'Pacific War', centred on the conflict with China (rather than with the U.S.) as the result of the contradictions generated by a worldwide system of imperialism. At stake was not the documentation of specific war crimes, or even the concrete realities of Japanese colonial rule, but the interpretation of the 15-year war within the context of the Second World War as well as the longer sweep of Japan's modern history. This was a history of imperialist oppression culminating in the authoritarian 'emperor-system ideology' (*tennōsei ideorogii*), which had victimised the Japanese and Asian peoples alike.[37]

Between 1956 and 1957, historians and other academics reopened their debate about war responsibility exclusively as a topic among progressive intellectuals. The driving force behind this effort was their realisation that a decade of postwar developments had failed to discard entirely the politics, thought and value system of the prewar and wartime periods. The term 'war responsibility' thus stood for both an investigation of wartime conduct and a critique of postwar trends. These intellectuals exhibited a stern opposition to the government for its attempt to reverse important democratic reforms; they demonstrated their anti-Americanism by attacking the American interpretation of the war and the conduct of the Tokyo War Crimes Trial, and they scrutinised their own role in society. Scholars like Maruyama Masao, Ienaga Saburō and Takeuchi Yoshimi pointed to Japan's path of development since the Meiji Restoration in 1868 to expose the roots of wartime behaviour and attitudes. Most of all, they aimed at discrediting the notion of the war as an aberration or 'historical stumble', as Yoshida Shigeru had phrased it earlier. In so doing, however, they in effect claimed that the war had been inevitable, given its pre-history. Indeed, the focus on the history of the war had a tendency to distract from the question of 'responsibility' for it.

From the late 1950s on, researchers affiliated with the government rather than the historical profession began to edit a multi-volume collection of military and diplomatic records of the war leading up to Pearl Harbor that had not previously been made available to historians.[38] Citing these new sources, scholars around the former military officer Hattori Takushirō and the conservative historian Tsunoda Jun launched a frontal attack against Marxist 'orthodoxy' by resurrecting the wartime term 'Greater East Asian War' (*daitō-a sensō*) to explain Japan's conflict with the United States (instead of Japan's imperial role in Asia). This revisionist approach made no difference between the militarist leadership and the people but postulated a nation united in its fateful entanglement in modern history. Hayashi Fusao provocatively titled his 1964 essays in the popular journal *Chūō kōron* "In Affirmation of the Greater East Asia War", and interpreted modern Japanese history since Commodore Perry as a 100-year war against the West.[39] Although bitterly denounced by established Marxist historians as an apologist attempt to whitewash the past, there was popular resonance – and even more governmental support – for a largely positive assessment of 'national' history at a time when Japan was clearly emerging as a rehabilitated member of the international community.

The challenge from the nationalist Right followed hot on the heels of changes in the education system, which brought textbook production more firmly under centralised state supervision through an approval procedure in the Ministry of Education. Here the issue revolved around the inclusion or exclusion of concrete historical details, for example war crimes, in the service of creating a positive national identity for citizens. The overt involvement of the state in the interpretation of the past mobilised a host of civic organisations in protest against bureaucratic control over public education, which had long been the Teachers' Union's objective. Ienaga Saburō, a high school teacher who had been involved in textbook writing since the early postwar years, spearheaded a prominent movement against official attempts to minimise or neglect information about Japan's war conduct by suing the Ministry of Education for textbook censorship in three different lawsuits.[40] His trials, which spanned three decades (1965–97), were never entirely successful or completely defeated, but they kept the issue of official control over textbooks in the political eye. More importantly, the textbook issue cast the dynamics of public memory firmly in the mould of liberal, responsible citizens struggling against an undemocratic and scandalously unapologetic government.

In the 1960s and 1970s, intensified public reckoning with the past was consistently conjured up by citizens organising across the political spectrum against what they perceived as state uses or abuses of war memory. The outburst of students', citizens' and environmental movements against politically constraining, socially discriminating and physically harmful consequences of government policies also fed upon new nationalist strategies led or sanctioned by the ruling LDP. The official revival in 1967 of the wartime national holiday *kigensetsu* (the birthday of the legendary first emperor Jimmu) on 11 February as *kenkoku kinen no hi* (National Foundation Day) was followed the next year by elaborate government-sponsored events marking the Meiji Restoration's centennial celebrations. This was postwar Japan's first large-scale public commemoration event celebrating a century of 'Japan in the world' by lightly skipping over the imperial and colonial quality of much of that history. Concurrently, nationalist organisations lobbied the LDP to support a bill that would bring Yasukuni Shrine back under state management and allow the resurrection of official ceremonies for Japan's 'departed heroes'. This did not come to pass. Central to the management of the past during these decades, however, was the dilution of Japan's militarist past in broad narratives of nation at the same time as concrete struggles against 'official' custodians of that past meandered their ways through every level of public life including the Diet, the courts, the academy and the mass media.

Internationalism and Japan's Colonial Past, 1980s to 2000s

The most significant shift in Japan's history of working through its wartime past occurred in the 1980s, when the interest-based, primarily domestic politics of negotiating meanings of the wartime past began to engage a global, rights-based approach to Japan's 'colonial past' and the question of restitution. The mushrooming, in the late 1980s and 1990s, of cross-national organisations representing the interests of long-neglected war victims, especially in Asia, compromised the once dominant position of special interest groups in the politics of memory by introducing an international dimension that could no longer be ignored in the post-Cold War era.

Emperor Hirohito's death in 1989, the end of the Cold War in the same year, and the collapse of the long hegemony of the conservative Liberal Democratic Party in 1993 marked a pivotal point, when issues of war and postwar responsibility for Japan's war conduct in Asia became prominently tied to the politics of redefining Japan's position in the world. This era of endings and putative new beginnings seemingly catapulted Japan's unresolved war responsibilities into the political limelight and made them an issue of broadly public debate rather than a tool exclusively of political protest. The massive production of Shōwa-retrospectives in the aftermath of the emperor's demise focused overwhelmingly on the war itself and connected with a suddenly prominent investigation of the emperor's war responsibility. The feminist movements in various Asian countries began to network and succeeded in bringing the long-neglected history of Asian women's sexual slavery at the hands of the wartime Japanese government not only to national but to global public attention. In the following decade, a host of still un-compensated and often ignored victims of war, including former Korean, Taiwanese, Chinese and Southeast Asian colonial subjects as well as atomic bomb victims, joined in a rapidly intensifying movement to press the Japanese government for official apologies and individual compensation payments.

Within this context, 'postwar management' (*sengo shori*) and 'postwar responsibility' (*sengo sekinin*) emerged as dual key terms in Japan's public life in the second half of the 1980s and preoccupied politics even beyond the fiftieth anniversary of defeat in World War II. International pressure, especially from China and South Korea, and rapidly increasing local and cross-national citizen networks pushed the issue forward until it became itself an important characteristic of the new 'post-postwar' era. Propelled by, but no longer confined to, a progressive intellectual discourse, the interpretation of the war's legacies and its practical ramifications in government politics drew on older conflicts over war memory but significantly expanded their parameters. Educational policies, war dead ceremonies, financial compensation and the like continued to define the contested territory of memory, but now this territory was recognised as a political issue in its own right that transcended national borders and included ordinary people as well as the highest wartime authority, the emperor.

At the same time, the inherent multiplicity of issues associated with compensation as a political, legal, social and ethical question elicited a variety of approaches and clashes of interests. Indeed, no sooner had former victims of Japanese aggression filed their lawsuits in Japanese courts than their individual claims were appropriated to long familiar problems of reckoning with the past, from school textbooks to museums and back to the Tokyo War Crimes Trial and Cold War politics. A case in point was Tokyo University professor Fujioka Nobukatsu's Liberal View of History Study Group (Jiyū shugi shikan kenky ūkai) and its notorious spin-off, the Society for the Making of New School Textbooks in History (Atarashii rekishi kyōkasho o tsukuru kai or simply Tsukuru-kai). Addressing themselves to students and teachers in Japan as well as abroad, these groups – new in the mid-1990s – not only resisted the onslaught of the global memory critique, but took issue with it and thereby strengthened the viability of conservative nationalism within contemporary discourses. They openly denied some of Japan's documented war atrocities and actively campaigned to eliminate references to the 'military comfort women' system in textbooks. More recently, the Tsukuru-kai succeeded in publishing – and getting the Ministry of Education to approve – its own nationalist textbook, albeit amid huge public outcries in Japan and abroad.[41]

A particularly dynamic link in cross-national civic activism grew out of feminist networks across Asia and led to the Women's International War Crimes Tribunal for the Trial of Japanese Military Sexual Slavery held in Tokyo in December 2000. This was a people's tribunal, organised by Asian women and human rights organisations, staffed by prosecution teams from nine countries across the Asia-Pacific region, presided over by four judges of international reputation and attended by over 1000 spectators and 200 media anchors every day for four days. On trial was Emperor Hirohito and the state of Japan 'for the crimes of rape and sexual slavery as crimes against humanity' during World War II. The testimony hearings of 64 survivors and two Japanese veterans formed the core of the proceedings, accompanied by the statements of academic historians, international law specialists and psychologists who contextualised the testimonies with respect to the Japanese wartime state, especially the role of the Emperor, the structure of the Japanese army and the psychological mechanisms of trauma. The final judgment found Emperor Hirohito guilty, and held the Japanese government responsible for adequately acknowledging and providing compensation to the victims of this atrocity.[42]

The tribunal – and the compensation debate of which it was a part – owed much of its significance to the recognition by all who participated in it that it took place 'belatedly' in biological time (its would-be recipients were near the end of their lives or had already died) and in world time (comparatively to other countries facing similar issues). Public hearings and other testimonies as well as oral histories assumed a now-or-never urgency sustained by a new realisation of the political consequences of half a century of silences and silencing. Of course Japan was not alone in this but was in fact in the good company of most of its Asian neighbours, who were also only now beginning to complicate and negotiate the politics of memory and restitution in their own countries and internationally. Moreover, the worldwide attention summoned by this intra-Asian memory debate suggested that war memory and responsibility were acute issues in other world regions as well. At the turn of the millennium, perhaps the most innovative attempts at conceptualising and addressing issues of historical responsibility and relating them to contemporary war crimes were taking place in Asia, organised by international teams of women and men.

Conclusion

In Japan, the politics of reckoning with the social and political legacies of the war remained intimately tied to public negotiations of postwar democracy for many decades. Justice for, and reconciliation with, clearly identified perpetrators, accomplices and victims of Japan's wartime imperial regime, in contrast, entered this larger discourse only selectively, at times of international involvement or as a matter of special interest politics. Japan's long history of memory as domestic political struggle figures as prominently in current debates about East Asian relations as regional geo-politics during the Cold War (and hence) conditioned patterns of negotiating war legacies. This is not so different in other Asian countries, most conspicuously South Korea and China, where questions of reconciliation were also kept at a safe distance until the late 1980s. The reasons are starkly political rather than vaguely cultural and must be sought in the confluence of a variety of factors including geo-political shifts, institutional reforms, the development of legal procedures in dealing with historical injustices, and changing patterns of local, national and global civic activism. 'Reckoning with the past' is a relational dynamic, an uneven process and by definition an unfinished undertaking, in Asia no more so than in Europe. For all its flaws, it bears enormous consequences for political and social relations today.

Notes

1. *The Economist* 336/7927 (12 August 1995), pp.31–4.
2. To be fair, *The Economist* ran a shorter article on 3 June 1995 explaining the party-political manoeuvring behind the challenge to the Diet Resolution and also suggests that the difference to Germany originates in part in the American occupation of Japan. "The Symbols of Japan Past," *The Economist* 335/7917 (3 June 1995), p.31.
3. John Dower, *War Without Mercy* (New York: Pantheon, 1986), p.190.
4. Kobayashi Yoshinori, *Shin gomanizumu sengen supesharu sensoron (Sensōron* and other *manga*) (Tokyo: Gentosha, 1998). An illuminating discussion of the 'history' theme in contemporary Japanese comic books is Tessa Morris-Suzuki, *The Past Within Us: Media, Memory, History* (London: Verso), 2005.
5. Iris Chang, *The Rape of Nanking: The Forgotten Holocaust of World War II* (New York: Basic Books, 1997). See particularly Part III "The Forgotten Holocaust: The Second Rape". A German analogue to this was Ralph Giordano, *Die zweite Schuld, oder: Von der Last Deutscher zu sein* [The Second Guilt: About the Burden of being German] (Hamburg: Rasch und Röhring Verlag, 1987).
6. Katō Shūichi, "Sensō sekinin no ukekata: Doitsu to nihon. Bukuletto ikiru," *Bukuletto ikiru* (Tokyo: Adobanteiji saabaa, 1993), pp.8–9.

7. Mochida Yukio, "Sensō sekinin to sengo sekinin." *Kamogawa bukuletto* (Kyoto: Kamogawa shuppan, 1994).
8. Nishio Kanji, *Kotonaru higeki: Nihon to Doitsu* (Tokyo: Bungei shunjūsha, 1994).
9. Oda Makoto, "Rikaishi yurusuna: sengo gojūnen, rekishi ni bunkiten ni tatte" *Wadatsumi no koe 99* (1994).
10. Chalmers Johnson in John Junkerman's documentary "The Japanese Peace Constitution," 2005.
11. Carol Gluck, "The 'Long Postwar': Japan and Germany in Common and in Contrast" in Ernestine Schlant and J.Thomas Rimer (eds), *Legacies and Ambiguities: Postwar Fiction and Culture in West Germany and Japan* (Washington, DC and Baltimore, MD: The Woodrow Wilson Center Press and The Johns Hopkins University Press, 1991), pp.63–78.
12. Dower, *Embracing Defeat* (New York: Norton, 1999), pp.45–53.
13. Dower (note 12), p.23.
14. Hosaka Masayasu. "Ichioku sōzange to iū katarushisu: Higashikuni naikaku," in *Haisen zengo no Nihonjin* (Tokyo: Asahi shinbunsha, 1985). Also, Dower (note 12), p.496.
15. Yoshimi Yoshiaki, "Senryōki Nihon no minshū ishiki: Sensō sekinin o megutte," *Shisō* (January 1992), p.74.
16. For a full list of censored topics, see Dower (note 12), p.411.
17. An excellent source for the diverse writings and interpretations on war responsibility is Okuma Nobuyuki, *Sensō sekininron* (Tokyo: Yuijinsha, 1948).
18. Nakano Yoshio, "Jikaku to kōdō nitsuite," *Jinbutsu hyōron* (October 1946). Cited in Nobuyuki (note 17), pp.138–42.
19. Yokota Kisaburō, "Sensō hanzai to kokusai hō no kakumei," *Chūō kōron* (January 1946), pp.31–40.
20. Dower (note 12), p.449.
21. An excellent analytical overview of the trials can be found in Dower (note 12), chap. 15.
22. Sheldon H. Harris, *Factories of Death: Japanese Biological Warfare, 1932–45, and the American Cover-Up* (London: Rutledge, 1994).
23. Kimura Gorō, letter to the editor, *Yomiuri shinbun* (13 December 1948).
24. Quoted in Dower (note 12), p.451.
25. This argument is most forcefully made in John Dower, "The Useful War," in *Japan in War and Peace* (New York: The New Press, 1993), pp.9–32.
26. Dower (note 25), p.11.
27. Dower (note 12), p.23.
28. Quoted in Dower, "Occupied Japan and the Cold War in Asia," in *Japan in War and Peace* (note 25), p.184.
29. Dower (note 28), pp.184–5.
30. Okamoto Kōichi, "Imaginary Settings: Sino-Japanese–U.S. Relations during the Occupation Years" (Ph.D. dissertation, Columbia University, 2000), p.183.
31. Kōichi (note 30), p.198.
32. Lawrence Olson, *Japan in Postwar Asia* (New York: Praeger, 1970), p.100.
33. Monica Braw, "Hiroshima and Nagasaki: The Voluntary Silence," in Laura Hein and Mark Selden (eds), *Living With the Bomb* (Armonk: M.E. Sharpe, 1997), pp.155–72.
34. James Orr, *The Victim as Hero: Ideologies of Peace and National Identity in Postwar Japan* (Hawaii University Press, 2001), p.52.
35. From Hidankyō's founding documents, quoted in Orr (note 34), p.143.
36. Sebastian Conrad, *Auf der Suche nach der verlorenen Nation: Geschichtsschreibung in Westdeutschland und Japan, 1945–1960* (Vandenhoeck & Ruprecht, 1999), pp.196–9.
37. See especially Rekishigaku Kenkyūkai (ed.), *The History of the Pacific War (Taiheiyō sensō)*, 5 vols (Tokyo: Tōyō Keizai shinposha, 1953–4).
38. Conrad (note 36), pp.199–202.
39. Hayashi Fusao, *Daitō-a sensō kōteiron* (Tokyo: Chūō kōron, 1964).
40. A good overview of these trials is Nozaki Ysohiko and Inokuchi Hiromitsu, "Japanese Education, Nationalism, and Ienaga Saburō's Textbook Lawsuits," in Laura Hein and Mark Selden, *Censoring History* (Armonk: M.E. Sharpe, 2000), pp.96–126.
41. Gavan McCormack, "The Japanese Movement to 'Correct' History" in Laura Hein and Mark Selden, *Censoring History* (note 40), pp.53–73.
42. For information on the trial and verdict, see http://www1.jca.apc.org/vaww-net-japan/english/womenstribunal2000/whatstribunal.html

Innocent Culprits – Silent Communities. On the Europeanisation of the Memory of the Shoah in Austria

EVA KOVACS

After the liberation in 1945, Austria found itself in a delicate situation: it had to produce an 'official' narrative acceptable to the whole society, of the *Judenverfolgung* ('the persecution of Jews' – at that time, the terms 'Holocaust' or 'Shoah' did not yet exist). Owing to the fact that the persecution of Jews totally destroyed the pillars of coexistence between them and non-Jewish Austrians, two kinds of national identity emerged: the identity of the persecuted Jews and that of the Austrians who made the persecution possible, either as culprits or accomplices or bystanders. In other words, the survivors of the Shoah had to give up their former national identity, which they had shared with the Austrian nation as a whole. They could not take their identity for granted in everyday cohabitation any longer but had to define it henceforth, in an indirect way, as a form of belonging to a national culture, a language community or a political system. Accordingly, the Austrians excluded the Jews from their nation, and after the liberation the survivors were only readmitted to the national community with certain reservations. This break in the Austrian identity led to a split in collective memory.[1]

The National State of Collective Memory: a Concise History of Remembering the *Judenverfolgung* in Austria

Since 1945, the memory of the *Judenverfolgung* has been divided into a Jewish and a non-Jewish one. For the Jews, remembering the Austrian past constructs a completely other landscape than for non-Jews. To put it simply, this bifurcation of Austrian memory was rooted in the controversial interpretation of the outcome of World War II. The Jews regarded the arrival of the Red Army as liberation while non-Jews considered it the beginning of a long and ignominious oppression.

Historians and sociologists like to contend that the Shoah provoked a massive social amnesia during the first two or three decades after World War II in Europe. By and large, they are right; however, in the first two years following the war, one witnesses totally different developments in the 'workshop' of the politics of memory. On 14 September 1946, an antifascist exhibition was opened in the Künstlerhaus in Vienna with the title 'Never Forget'. It was initiated by the Soviet occupants and organized by the Vienna City Hall and the three largest political parties. They decided to show 'the crimes of the Nazis to the public'. The exhibition, designed by the famous artist Victor Th. Shama, had 840,000 visitors.

As you can see in the posters (Figures 1 and 2), the victims were depicted in a very peculiar way: the official poster followed the old communist iconology of the labour movement. It did not show any real victims, but instead a strong, young worker with a hammer. At the same time, the poster exhibited of the politically persecuted used the figure of a former left-wing *KZ-Häftling* (concentration camp inmate) without referring to the millions of Jewish victims. Why did the Jews not appear in the posters, in the official discourse on World War II, or, as we will see soon, in the Austrian memory itself?

Figure 1. Exhibition poster (Shama).[2]

Figure 2.   Exhibition poster (Sussmann).[3]

The paradox of denazification (*Entnazifizierung*), that is, the ideological need for a new, non-Nazi political and economic elite that would restart governing the country after the war as well as the apparent lack of non-Nazi experts, is one of the well-known answers to this question.[4] One and a half million Austrians, 15 per cent of the adult population had been members of the NSDAP. Anti-Semitism, with its deep roots in Austrian society even after 1945, was also an important reason for disregarding the Jews when preaching anti-fascism. Contemporary newspapers displayed the murdered Jews as a bunch of anonymous strangers. The small group of Jewish survivors clearly disturbed the newly shaped social and political consensus.

According to a public opinion poll from 1946, 46 per cent of the Austrian population objected to the return of the Jews to Austria.[5] Not only Austrian society at large but also the political and intellectual elites prevented the survivors from coming back to their home country.[6] Moreover, if a person still returned to Austria, nevertheless, he or she had more difficult access to reparation than a former *Wehrmacht* soldier who had been forced to do *malenkaia rabota* in Russia.

At the beginning of 1947, with the first amnesty of the former NSDAP members, 90 per cent of the possible perpetrators avoided trial. This law gave back voting eligibility to former NSDAP members (6 February 1947). The general amnesty act for former Nazis was born 10 years later (14 March 1957). The new concept of integrating the former Nazis brought the Austrian political parties many new voters. The political discourse externalised the Nazi past of the Austrians (by projecting it onto the Germans) and constructed the new thesis of the Austrians as victim. According to this, the Austrians were the first and innocent victims of German National Socialism.[7] This claim could not be better symbolized than by the fact that, in 1947, Austria demanded reparation from Germany for the damages caused by the *Anschluss*.[8] The Nazi past was thereby converted into a heroic chapter of Austrian history.[9] The Jewish victims were subsumed under the category of the 'anti-fascist resistance fighter' and the *Antifa* movement institutionalised Austrian victimhood. This way of dealing with the Shoah showed a surprising consistency until the end of the 1970s.[10]

The long silence was broken by the American television series 'Holocaust'[11] in 1979. With this film, the new name for the *Judenverfolgung* began its worldwide career. Although the film was made partly in and about Austria, it was presented in the country relatively late, only after the premiers in the United States, Great Britain, Israel, Germany and France. The series led to a broad, painful discussion of the role the Austrian nation played in the Shoah. The descendants of the culprits woke up from their deep sleep and challenged the untouchability of the taboo of the indefensibility of Nazism, while the survivors criticized the Hollywood style of the film.

Seven years later, during the presidential elections, the biggest scandal ever of the Third Republic broke out with a little help from the American media. As is well known, it revolved around the *Wehrmacht* past of Kurt Waldheim.[12] The debate that ended with dubious results reproduced the old barriers between Austria and the world. It was not only the Austrian politicians but also the quasi-independent domestic media that tried to wash the mud of the Nazi past off Waldheim and to misinform the public by blurring historical reality, while the American newspapers published more and more hard facts about him. Nevertheless, in the final ballot, Waldheim got 53.9 per cent of the votes, the largest victory ever in Austria. In the same year, the right-wing populist Jörg Haider became the chairman of the Freedom Party of Austria (FPÖ).[13] In other words, Austria was unable to come to terms with the past in a self-reflexive way but repeated its social trauma by closing in on itself and sticking together, radicalising right-wing sympathizers and trying to suppress critical voices.

However, the jinni had already got out of the bottle. Under the aegis of the 50-year anniversary of the *Anschluss*, quite a few historical and sociological research projects were launched, and the media started to cover the Austrian history of Nazism as a hot issue. The new publications made it clear that a majority of the Austrian population welcomed the *Anschluss,* and soon after took part in bringing out (or at least tolerating) the Shoah.

This change in public discourse had an effect on political rhetoric, too. In 1991, for the first time since 1945, Federal Chancellor Franz Vranitzky admitted the responsibility of the Austrians for the *Judenverfolgung*.[14] In the second half of the 1990s, a large-scale restitution process began, reaching by now not only the survivors with Austrian citizenship but also the former forced labourers worldwide. Moreover, the research activities of the newly established *Historikerkommission* resulted in an unprecedented governmental program of commemoration. In 2003, the Mauthausen Memorial was inaugurated whose exhibition clearly shows the role of Austria in the persecution and execution of hundreds of thousands of Austrian and foreign citizens. Among the camps in Austria, only in Mauthausen, there were concentrated as many as 200,000 people from all over Europe, and half of them were killed. The exhibition, also accessible on the web, conveys three messages: (1) 'we were responsible for the Shoah'; (2) 'our responsibility goes beyond the border of our land'; and (3) 'we were responsible for killing not only the Jews but also the Roma and the Sinti, homosexuals and political prisoners' from all over Europe. The basic information on the Memorial was published in 30 languages.[15] Seemingly, Austria successfully joined the mainstream of the European culture of memory – seemingly.

But, what happened to the Austrian Jews? If we do an in-depth analysis of the web site of the Mauthausen Memorial or the other *lieux de mémoire* in Austria, we will recognize a – maybe unconscious – 'trick': the Austrian Jews as victims or survivors are missing or play a minor role in the daily practice of the politics of memory. One has the impression that the 'local Jews' have been overshadowed by the Europeanisation of the Shoah. In order to highlight this paradox, let me tell you an emblematic story about a small town in Austria where I made an anthropological case study on collective memory some years ago.

The Local Level: the Example of Rechnitz

When launching my research project on cross-border identity in Rechnitz (located in South-Burgenland, at the Hungarian border), my Austrian colleagues told me not to ask people about the scandal of the mass grave because, if I asked them, they would not tell me anything about their lives.

From the autumn of 1944 on, thousands of forced labourers were working in the vicinity of the town. They were commanded to build the so-called *Südostwall* (South-East Defence Line) that was supposed to stop the Soviet tanks. In spring 1945, a new group of forced labourers arrived on foot from Hungary (it was the so-called death-march/*Todesmarsch*).[16] On 24 March, following a party held by SS and SA officers, the leaders of the local administration and other notables (among others Count and Countess Batthyány – the latter was a Thyssen sister – who hosted the party in their castle), the drunken guests killed 180 forced labourers in an old horse stall called Kreuzstadl (Cross Barn). They also murdered another 11 people already on the road leading to the Kreuzstadl. In addition, 18 men were killed on the following day, after they had buried the victims of the massacre from the previous day.[17]

When the war ended, the doctor of a neighbouring village filed an accusation against an unknown perpetrator. While the legal procedure was unfolding, the evidence of the massacre somehow disappeared, and, under political pressure, the eyewitnesses did not testify against the accused. Furthermore, in 1946, two of the witnesses were secretly murdered in the wake of a pub fight in the town. Although the legal procedures lasted unusually long (the last trial ended in 1962), the perpetrators were not found. In the early 1990s, unknown culprits – perhaps young members of the Freedom Party – severely damaged the Jewish cemetery, the last relic of Jewish culture in Rechnitz. In 1993 and 1996, the Wiesenthal Center revived the case, and initiated an expedition to find the mass grave, without success. Subsequently, one of the leading Austrian newspapers, *der Standard*, stamped the people of Rechnitz *en bloc* as anti-Semites. The last unsuccessful search expedition took place in October 2005. An amateur historian from Salzburg is still searching for military aerial photographs from 1945 in Washington in order to locate the mass grave.[18]

Knowing this story, I went to Rechnitz and told my 80–90-year-old interviewees (what happened to be true), that I was researching the interwar period of Burgenland and would like to hear their life histories. After presenting his life, my first interlocutor, Mr H. showed me a couple of photographs. The black and white photos, which were probably produced by a talented – or even by a professional – photographer, portrayed Jewish genre-pictures of Rechnitz, e.g. excursions, swimming, walks, picnics, etc. On the backs of the pictures were names and dates with explanatory notes. As the interviewee said, the pictures showed members of the local community. When I asked him how he came to have these photos, he answered that he had got them from Mr K. before 1938, that is, just before the Jews 'left' town. The notes were produced by Mr H.'s son in the 1980s, who showed them to his friends from Canada. Mr H. explained to me further:

> The Jews of Burgenland were lucky because they could *emigrate*. They were transported to the Yugoslav border and then, English ships took them across the Adriatic Sea. The Braun family and other families, too, who had been hiding in Yugoslavia, returned to Rechnitz. *No, nobody had any difficulties.* But I say, all Jews were lucky, 'cause they could go away. Hitler came on the 12th of March, with the whole army, and the first – the first [Jews] left on the 8th of April, then on the 12th, 20th and 24th the whole [community]. One of them lives in America. Well, he's still alive. Our neighbours, you see, they also emigrated with their son to America. (An interview with H. H., original in German language, my emphasis)

My second interviewee showed me the same pictures. He told me, he had got them from Mr S. before the 'departure' of the Jews. I became more and more frightened by these comments, especially, when I saw the same pictures and listened to the same stories the third time in yet another house (see Figure 3). (Ironically, while preparing for this presentation, I found a similar photograph from Rechnitz on the website of the Washington Holocaust Museum. See Figure 4.)

In fact, the Jews of Rechnitz never appeared in the life histories of my interviewees. They began to mention the Jews only after finishing their own personal narratives. In terms of both their socio-linguistic and structural forms, the two narratives, the biographical and the thematic ones, were entirely different. While the life stories broke down in a natural and logical way at particular points of the narration, the stories of the Jews of Rechnitz were extremely coherent, almost

Figure 3.   Swimming in Rechnitz, before 1938 (private collection).

Figure 4.   The Kohn family poses with Lina Spitzer in front of her home in Rechnitz (United States Holocaust Memorial Museum).[19]

perfect. They must have represented a common local knowledge of this topic. This common narrative portrays a peaceful coexistence between Jews and non-Jews in Rechnitz and ignores the Shoah or if it does not, it stresses the survival of the Burgenland Jews (by the way, a gross exaggeration).

To understand the meaning of the pictures, we have to combine the micro- and macro-stories with historical, political and socio-psychological interpretations. First, we have to exclude the option that the town as a whole wanted to save the culprits, and therefore constructed an illustrated narrative of peaceful coexistence. However, there can be only a few current inhabitants who stayed in Rechnitz at the time of the massacre – please remember that most of the men were on the front, and anyway, most are not alive today.

It is also likely that nobody from the Jewish community gave his or her family photos to my interviewees freely. It is well known from historical research in Austria that virtually nobody helped the Jews when they had to flee. The Jewish community, which amounted to 20 per cent of the population in Rechnitz, one of the largest in Transdanubia, left Rechnitz for Croatia and Hungary in a single week.[20] The photos were probably found by the locals in an empty house afterwards, and even if my interlocutors told me the truth, somebody made copies and distributed them among their friends many decades later. But why did that happen?

Let us compare the pictures with the comments. My interlocutors were convinced that Rechnitz was a unique town at the border of Austria and Hungary. They told me the following with pride:

> Well, Rechnitz was always *unique in all of Europe*, always, always, three religions, the Protestant, the Catholic and the Jewish, and three nationalities, the German, the Croatian and the Hungarian lived together. And now, now this is also not a problem for us. At school I used to learn all three languages, I read not only Goethe but also Hungarian poets such as Petőfi. And at the Catholic school, there were not only Catholic children

enrolled, but also we, the Protestants and many Jewish children as well. There was no problem, nothing, never. I must say there was no difference between us. (An interview with J. S., original in German language, my emphasis)

The pictures serve to depict this unproblematic co-existence with happy Jews, and to reflect an atmosphere of trust in which they were handed over to my interviewees by their Jewish neighbours at the very last moment of their life in Rechnitz. But, looking at the pictures, one sees no non-Jews appear in them. The illustrated idyllic memory is probably only a cover story for the real one; I believe it helped them to ignore the story of the massacre. In 1938, the old men were 15–20 year olds; perhaps they observed the expulsion of the Jews from Rechnitz passively, and shortly after they started serving in the *Wehrmacht* or in the SS. On a deeper psychological level, this story covered up their guilty feelings about their role in World War II.

None of the Jews returned to Rechnitz after 1945. In local parlance they 'crossed the border', 'moved' or 'emigrated' in 1938, and nobody asks why they did not come back after the war. Similarly, they are not interested in whether or not their Jewish neighbours died in the Shoah, even if they were not deported to the concentration camps directly from Rechnitz but later from another Austrian or Hungarian town. Nobody talks about these issues openly. On the contrary, the town maintains a historical continuity, however fictive and absurd it may be, with the help of these cover stories. As long as the Jews lived here, we liked them; since they have not lived with us, we preserve their memory.

The Refuge of Memory?

The example of Rechnitz is not unique in Austria or Europe: local communities tend to have difficulties in remembering their own Jewish victims. Replacing the terms of expulsion and deportation with that of 'free emigration' is also well known in our continent among the forms of 'soft' denial of the Shoah.[21] Normally, however, this way of reckoning with the past does not produce a local 'master narrative' contributing to collective identity. In Rechnitz, the 'master narrative' has three elements: (1) the experience of peaceful co-existence before 1938; (2) the proximity of the state border (thus, the expulsion of the Jews also meant a 'simple' crossing of the border); and (3) last but not least, the massacre in 1945 in which, as is well-known from court procedures, the citizens of Rechnitz regarded the forced labourers as strangers, foreign Jews who came from Hungary. They did not consider the liquidation of these starving people and their agony as comparable to what they thought to be the fate of their own Jews.

While the local community has remained silent about the mass grave until now, in 1987, a small group of outsiders started commemorating the massacre, which led to the founding of the REFUGIUS association.[22] Nevertheless, this did not change the attitudes of the local people. As a matter of fact, the 'master narrative' overpowered the new initiative. What has happened to the memory of the Jews in Rechnitz during the last 15 years?

In 1991, a memorial stone was unveiled in the castle park (the Batthyány castle), dedicated not only to the almost 200 victims of the massacre *but also* to four of the town's resistance fighters. Moreover, everybody forgot about the original Jewish citizens of Rechnitz in the ceremony. Shortly after, in 1992, the founders of

Figure 5.   Kreuzstadl (aerial photograph).[23]

REFUGIUS declared in the constitution of the association that, in addition to remembering the Nazi period, they would also focus on the refugees of today. In 1994, the association donated to the Burgenland Federation of Jewish Communities the Kreuzstadl, the building where the massacre took place (Figure 5). Both institutions declared that this memorial was founded 'for all victims of the *Südostwall'.*

Parallel to this, in the mid-1990s, two pieces of art emerged out of the Rechnitz scandal: a film and a stage play. The film focused on the search for the corpses, while the play tried to reconstruct the day of the massacre.[24] Both collected historical materials and confronted the audience with the brutality of the Austrian perpetrators, many of them former inhabitants of Rechnitz. However, the artistic methods of coming to terms with the past did not result in a significant change in the attitudes of the locals.

While Rechnitz remained silent (and the eyewitnesses slowly began to die off), the programs of the REFUGIUS became international. Survivors from all over Europe, public figures and politicians from Hungary and local politicians from Burgenland come together every year in the Kreuzstadl and remember the victims of the *Todesmarsch*. As in the web site of the Mauthausen Memorial, not only the memory of the actual culprits but also that of the local victims fade away from this scene. However, Rechnitz is marketing the same kind of remembering on the 'retail of memory' as the Austrian or the German government when they sell the commodity of the non-existent European memory of the Shoah all over the world.

Conclusion

In the first part of the paper I discussed the ways in which the Austrian Jews as victims or survivors came to be missing or played a minor role in the daily practice of the politics of memory. One has the impression that the 'local Jews' have been overshadowed by the Europeanisation of the Shoah.

The second part presented the case of Rechnicz as a paradoxical example of 'creative forgetting' or 'forgetting by remembering'. The gap left in collective memory by the murdered Rechnitz Jews had been filled first by the tragedy of 'foreign' forced labourers coming from Hungary, until both were diluted in the European memory of the Shoah. Moreover, the Shoah has got 'anthropologised' in an association assisting the refugees of our time.[25] I also mentioned that the case of Rechnicz is not unique; it is rather part of the mainstream.[26] During the past decade, the memory of the Shoah has become a central issue of politics, culture and pedagogy of the European Union. The memorial landscape changed (cf. the monuments, documentation centres and museums dedicated to the memory of 'European' victims and addressed to the European public), and the tendency of Europeanization reached into deeper layers. After two years of preparation, an NGO named Task Force for International Cooperation on Holocaust Education, Remembrance, and Research[27] was established following an initiative from Sweden. Besides the EU member states, Argentina, Israel and the United States are represented in that NGO. As a first step, it suggested that 27 January, the date of the liberation of Auschwitz, become a memorial day. The member states accepted the suggestion in 2003. This does not mean only that throughout Europe the Shoah has to be commemorated on the same day, but also that remembering follows the same prefabricated scenario in more and more countries. Although the events of commemoration take place 'on the spot', they have less and less in common with the history of the given place.

The success of globalisation/Europeanisation originates in the lack of local memories. The Shoah destroyed the substance of European Jewishness, which depended on flourishing communities. The Jewish people and their communities disappeared from their physical and symbolic places. The survivors left their former homes because they did not want to be confronted with the crying emptiness of these places and the lack of solidarity of the neighbours. The forced migration of the survivors and the indignation of society at remembering resulted in the dislocation of the Shoah itself. In sum, it is no wonder that the memory of the Shoah became centralized and dislocated in Europe as a whole. Very concrete places – even in cities like Berlin, Prague, Lemberg and Cracow, which are full of 'Jewish spots' of tourist attraction – have become uniform in the past one and a half decades.[28] They turned into *non lieus*: few would remember those who had lived there.

Notes

1. See William Johnston, *The Austrian Mind* (Berkeley, CA: University of California Press, 1972); Emmerich Tálos, Ernst Hanisch, Wolfgang Neugebauer und Reinhard Sieder (eds), *NS-Herrschaft in Österreich* (Wien: Verlag für Gesellschaftskritik, 2000).
2. Victor Theodor Slama, Druck: Globus, Wien 1946, 37.4 × 27.4 in./95.0 × 69.5 cm, ÖNB-FLU, 16310699, available at www.onb.ac.at/sammlungen/plakate/siteseeing/wieder_frei/exhibition_1946/194603_text.htm (last accessed 15 May 2007).
3. [Heinrich] Sussmann, WStLB Poster collection, Signature P 11122, available at www.stadtbibliothek.wien.at/ausstellungen/1999/wa-237/naziverbrechen/P11122-de.htm (last accessed 15 May 2007).
4. See Robert Knight, *"Ich bin dafür, die Sache in die Länge zu ziehen." Die Wortprotokolle der österreichischen Bundesregierung von 1945 bis 1952 über die Entschädigung der Juden* (Frankfurt am Main: Athenäum 1988).
5. In: *Der neue Weg*, No. 29/30, 15. August 1946. Cit. Brigitte Bailer, "Der 'antifaschistische Geist' der Nachkriegszeit" (Paris 1999), available at www.doew.at/thema/antifageist/antifageist.html (last accessed 15 May 2007).

6. See Gerhard Benetka, "Entnazifizierung und verhinderte Rückkehr. Zur personellen Situation der akademischen Psychologie in Österreich nach 1945", *Österreichische Zeitschrift für Geschichtswissenschaften* 9/2 (1998), pp.188–217.

7. However, the concept of the 'first victims' was developed by The Moscow Declaration on Austria (30 October 1943): 'The Government of the United Kingdom, the Soviet Union and the United States of America are agreed that Austria, the *first free country to fall victim to Hitlerite aggression*, shall be liberated from German domination'. See Robert H. Keyserlingk, *Austria in World War II* (Kingston–Montreal: McGill–Queen's University Press, 1988), p.207.

8. See Walter Manoschek: "Verschmähte Erbschaft. Österreichs Umgang mit dem Nationalsozialismus 1945–1955", in Reinhard Sieder, Heinz Steinert and Emerich Tálos (eds), *Österreich 1945–1955. Gesellschaft, Politik, Kultur* (Wien: Verlag für Gesellschaftskritik, 1995), p.100.

9. See e.g. the Austrian Monuments of War from the 1950s. In Heidemarie Uhl, "Das 'erste Opfer'. Der österreichische Opfermythos und seine Transformation in der Zweiten Republik", *Österreichische Zeitschrift für Politikwissenschaft* 1 (2001), pp.19–34.

10. To the mechanisms of the taboo making see: Gerhard Baumgartner, "Erinnerte und vergangene Zeit", in Emil Brix, Ernst Bruckmüller and Hannes Stekl (eds), *Memoria Austriae – Menschen, Mythen, Zeiten* (Wien: Oldenbourg Verlag, 2004), pp.530–44.

11. *Holocaust – The Story of the Family Weiss* (R: Marvin Chomsky). NBC, New York.

12. See Gerhard Botz and Gerald Sprengnagel, *Kontroversen um Österreichs Zeitgeschichte. Verdrängte Vergangenheit, Österreich-Identität, Waldheim und die Historiker* (Frankfurt am Main: Campus, 1994).

13. The United States answered for these with adding of Waldheim's name to the watch list of the Ministry of Justice and, from 1987, Waldheim was not allowed to enter the United States.

14. However, the new thesis was not fully accepted by the Austrian society. See Ruth Wodak, *"Wir sind alle unschuldige Täter!": diskurshistorische Studien zum Nachkriegsantisemitismus* (Frankfurt am Main: Suhrkamp, 1990).

15. See www.mauthausen-memorial.at (last accessed 15 May 2007).

16. See Udo Fellner, "Bittere Heimatgeschichte. Das Schicksal der jüdischen Zwangsarbeiter in Krottendorf und Kalch", in Gerhard Baumgartner, Eva Müllner and Rainer Münz (eds), *Identität und Lebenswelt. Ethnische, religiöse und kulturelle Vielfalt in Österreich* (Eisenstadt: Prugg, 1989), pp.128–32.

17. See Eva Holpfer, *Der Umgang der burgenländischen Nachkriegsgesellschaft mit NS-Verbrechen bis 1955 – Am Beispiel der wegen der Massaker von Deutsch-Schützen und Rechnitz geführten Volksgerichtsprozesse* (Wien: Diplomarbeit, 1998); a shorter version was published in Italian language: "Il massacro di Rechnitz", *Storia e Documenti*, 6 (2001), pp.205–21. See also: www.nachkriegsjustiz.at/ns_verbrechen/juden/rechnitz_eh.php (last accessed 15 May 2007).

18. See http://derstandard.at/?url=/?id=2344618 (last accessed 15 May 2007).

19. USHMM, #33984, available at: www.ushmm.org/education/foreducators/guidelines/historical.php (last accessed 15 May 2007).

20. See Gert Tschögl, "Geschichte der Juden in Oberwart", in Baumgartner, Müllner and Münz (eds) (note 16), pp. 116–27.

21. A survivor of Burgenland formulated this difference in the following: 'Nobody emigrates, if it isn't necessary. I wouldn't ever leave Austria from my free will. I didn't escape from Burgenland to Vienna or to America in the Dollfuß-Schuschnigg area (1934) although I could. However, there were really bad times, too'. In Eva Deinhofer and Traude Horvath (eds), *Grenzfall. Burgenland 1921–1991* (Veliki Boristof, 1991), p.63.

22. See www.refugius.at ; www.memorial-museums.net/ (last accessed 15 May 2007).

23. See www.mkoe.at (last accessed 15 May 2007).

24. In the movie the basic truth forms the background of a 'Cat and Mouse' game between Shoah survivor Isador Sandorffy, who wants to find the location of the mass grave in order to give these Jews a proper burial, and the people of Rechnitz who give wrong clues and object to the search. See *"Totschweigen"/Wall of Silence*, Directed by Margarete Heinrich and Eduard Erne. A co-oproduction among Austria, Germany and Netherlands, 1994; *"März. Der 24. Ein fiktiver Versuch über einen real geschehenen Massenmord"/24th of March. A Fictional Attempt at a Real Happened Mass Murder"*, Directed by Peter Wagner (Oberwart, 1995). See Peter Wagner, *Tetralogie der Nacktheit/Tetralogy of the Nakedness* (Oberwart: edition lex liszt 12, 1995).

25. This kind of anthropologisation led to the mushrooming of institutes of genocide research all over the world. The notorious reaction to the paradox that the matter concerns very specific victims and very general perpetrators is strongly criticized by Dan Diner in response to an essay by Jaspers on the question of guilt. See Dan Diner, "On Guilt-Discourse and Other Narratives: Epistemological Observations Regarding the Holocaust", *History & Memory*, 9/1–2 (1997).

26. For example, an object (on a 4 × 1 m ground plate, two 2 m high yellow triangles) designed by an Austrian artist, was erected in Budapest and transported to Ebensee through 40 towns and villages following the direction of the former death march. The opening commemoration of the "Mobile – Memory – Project" was held 17 April 2004 in the new Holocaust Museum in Budapest. The project, supported by the Austrian government, still exists; the last commemoration took place in in St Peter in der Au, Göstling and Bratislava Petržalka in 2007. See http://www.erin-nern.at/bundeslaender/niederoesterreich/institutionen-projekte/projekt-mobiles-erinnern   (last accessed 15 May 2007).

27. See: www.holocausttaskforce.org (last accessed 15 May 2007).

28. For more details see Ruth Ellen Gruber, *Virtually Jewish: Reinventing Jewish Culture in Europe* (Berkeley, CA: University of California Press 2002).

Should France be Ashamed of its History? Coming to Terms with the Past in France and its Eastern Borderlands[1]

LAIRD BOSWELL

For over 50 years, France has wrestled with the question of how to come to terms with the Vichy régime and its legacy. Recognising that Vichy had been the greatest crisis of the French twentieth century and understanding the nature of that crisis took over a generation. Well into the late twentieth century Vichy was, to borrow the words of Henry Rousso, a past that could neither be digested (*un passé qui ne passe pas*) nor fully confronted.[2] Today, this era has come to a close. The gradual disappearance of a war cohort that had so much at stake in how the period was remembered and interpreted has dulled the passionate spark of the debate. The generation of politicians – from Charles De Gaulle to François Mitterrand – who lived through the Vichy era and later instrumentalised it for their own benefit, has also faded from the scene, and the Vichy question no longer finds itself at the heart of political discourse. The turning point surely came in 1995 when President Jacques Chirac recognised France's responsibility in the Holocaust. For the first time the head of the French state accepted the nation's culpability in the deportation of Jews; Chirac spoke of an 'irreparable' act, a 'collective fault' and acknowledged that 'the French people, the French state assisted the criminal madness of the occupier'. It was time, Chirac argued, to 'recognise the errors of the past and the faults committed by the state' and be in line with 'an increasing number of the French who are resolved to face up squarely to their past'.[3] Chirac thus turned his back on earlier arguments, made by both De Gaulle and Mitterrand, that France could not be held accountable because these acts had been undertaken by the Vichy Regime and not by the Republic. For Chirac, France was a perpetrator, though one that had *assisted* the Nazis in their murderous enterprise.

Chirac closed the door on an enduring interpretation of the Vichy regime – one that survived among politicians, judges and bureaucrats longer than among historians – that presented Vichy as a parenthesis that bore little relationship to the Republics that preceded and followed it. By the time Chirac rejected this argument in 1995, the evidence of the nation's wartime responsibility had been fully established. Indeed, when in 1993 Socialist President François Mitterrand had attempted to disassociate the Republic from the crimes of Vichy at a ceremony commemorating the mass arrests of Parisian Jews in 1942, he met with widespread scepticism. Chirac's 1995 speech thus gave a long overdue official stamp of approval to the Republic's responsibility for acts committed by the Vichy Regime. His recognition came at the end of a long, arduous and bitter process that saw French society slowly come to grips with the Vichy regime's legacy.

Just as the issue of victims and perpetrators began to recede after the last of the trials for crimes again humanity held in France in the 1990s, the issue resurfaced in a different geographical and temporal setting: the Algerian War and colonialism. Over the last decade, the Vichy regime has been displaced as the centrepiece of the debate concerning how the nation needs to confront its past. Part of this, no doubt, is attributable to the disappearance of the World War II generation and of the controversies that it brought to the public sphere. Historians have also played a vital role in this shift, helped in their task by a more liberal access to the Algerian War archives beginning in 1992. Scholarship on all aspects of the German occupation, which once dwarfed interest in other areas of contemporary history, is not as important as it once was. Instead, scholars have turned their attention to the Algerian War and the French colonial enterprise. The 'dark years' in French history increasingly refer to the Algerian War, not the Vichy regime.

Ironically, as the nation faced up to Vichy's legacy the colonial past has brought the problem of national responsibility back to fore and underlined France's persistent difficulty in addressing intractable moral and judicial issues. Growing research on the army's use of torture during the Algerian War, on the role of the French judicial system and on the violent nature of colonial rule has placed the issue of victims and perpetrators front and centre.[4] In the decades that followed Algeria's independence in 1962, participants of all kinds presented themselves as victims and often sought recognition of that status. The Algerian case has particular resonance in the present because victims and perpetrators, be they of Algerian or European origins, sometimes live side by side on French soil. The question of French responsibility in Algeria has crucial implications for a generation of French citizens of Algerian heritage, just as it is of critical import for France's relations with its former colonies.

Recognising responsibility, however, is a long, tortuous and difficult path that demands political vision and courage. The process has encountered setbacks and has been instrumentalised by the political world. When right-wing deputies in the French National Assembly passed a bill in February 2005 requiring that school curriculums 'recognise in particular the *positive role* of the French presence overseas, and notably in North Africa',[5] they signalled unambiguously that the pendulum had swung too far. Colonisation was something to take pride in; the culture of repentance was deeply damaging to French national self-understanding. Nicolas Sarkozy embraced this vision during his 2007 presidential campaign: he transformed the past into a key campaign issue, and went one step further than the Assembly by extending the process of rehabilitation to World War II. Sarkozy urged the nation to turn its back on the 'fashion' of repentance pushed by those, 'who want to resuscitate the hatreds of the past by demanding of sons that they expiate the alleged misdeeds of their fathers and their ancestors'. It was time to honour the nation's past. France should not be 'ashamed of its history' [*la France n'a pas à rougir de son histoire*] he proclaimed, 'she did not commit genocide, she did not invent the Final Solution. She invented the rights of man and is the country in the world that has fought the most for liberty'. Sarkozy thus moved away from Chirac's courageous recognition of France's responsibility in the Holocaust, and at the same time he asked citizens to honour the French colonial enterprise. 'Not all the colonists were exploiters', he argued; the truth, he continued, 'is that there were not many colonial powers in the world that worked so hard for civilisation and development and so little for exploitation'. France was neither a nation of perpetrators nor a nation of victims. It was a country united by a common destiny 'stronger than hatred and vengeance'.[6]

It took over one generation for France to address the Vichy past head on. At the war's end, like many other nations just freed from German occupation, the French undertook extensive purges. The first wave took place during the Liberation of France and resulted in the execution, without the validation of legally sanctioned trials, of 8000–9000 suspected collaborators, Vichy militia members and auxiliary police forces. French men, including resistance members, reasserted their masculinity by shearing the heads of approximately 20,000 women accused of various forms of collaboration with the Germans; some of these women were subject to further public degradation by having swastikas branded on their bodies or by being forced to parade in public with their 'German babies' on display.[7] Once the state reasserted its authority, the judicial apparatus kicked into gear and investigated over 300,000 individuals for crimes of collaboration; close to 125,000 people were later tried – 50,000 were imprisoned and 6763 condemned to capital punishment (though only 767 death sentences were carried out). In addition, the state launched extensive inquiries on the behaviour of civil servants, eventually punishing 22,000–28,000.[8] In the short term, the purges provided the satisfaction of identifying culprits who had collaborated with the Germans, while at the same time they helped the French forget the uncertainties and the ambiguities of their wartime behaviour. By targeting a restricted number of individuals for crimes of collaboration – the percentage of those investigated sentenced in Holland and Belgium was substantially higher[9] – France managed to disassociate itself from bearing responsibility for the events that transpired during the German occupation. Collaboration was the work of individuals, associations and corporations; the postwar French state could not be blamed for their acts. Over the long term, however, there was no closure: the purges left a distinctly bitter taste along with the nagging impression that justice had not been accomplished.

During the 1950s and 1960s, the nation was more concerned with forgetting the divisions of the war years and adhering to a Resistance myth, known as *résistancialisme*, which played a crucial role in restoring French national pride. The Resistance myth was the foundational building block of the two largest political parties of the Fifth Republic, the Gaullists and the Communists, and both derived much of their legitimacy and appeal from posing as 'inheritors' of the Resistance. The

Communists claimed, erroneously, to be the party of the '75,000 executed' and placed the commemoration of their 'martyrs' and heroes on centre stage.[10] De Gaulle's magnetism derived in no small part from his leadership of the Free French and his uncanny ability to incarnate the resistance and thus, in a substantial leap of logic, the nation. The Resistance myth held together as long as he was alive: it allowed him to minimise Vichy's significance while he simultaneously worked with former *Pétainistes* whose support was critical to his success.

By the mid 1970s, however, the tide turned and the Resistance slowly fell out of favour thanks to the ever-growing eruption of the Vichy years on the French political and cultural scene, the growing interest of film directors and writers, and the works of historians such as Robert Paxton, who argued that collaboration was not a policy that was imposed on the French, but was on the contrary proposed and sought out by the Vichy regime.[11] The extensive explorations of French collaboration with Germany, including France's role in the Final Solution, spurred acrimonious debate and forced the nation to confront its past. They also produced an understanding of that past from which German responsibility was to, an increasing degree, absent. The courts played a central role in this process. The growing judicialisation of the past in the 1980s and 1990s, highlighted by three trials for crimes against humanity (Klaus Barbie in 1987, Paul Touvier in 1994 and Maurice Papon in 1997) that garnered international attention, also raised difficult issues about the relationship between history and the judicial system. This new wave of trials, over 40 years after the end of the war, was spurred by the complaints of victims, their descendents, and their lawyers (notably Serge Klarsfeld) and not by an initiative on the part of the French state.[12] More recently, the pendulum has swung back to the centre: in *La France à l'Heure Allemande* [France under the Germans], Philippe Burrin argued that accommodation – more so than collaboration – characterised French people's relationship to the German occupiers. France under German rule was a grey zone that resisted easy characterisation and analysis.[13] Since the late 1970s, the study of the Resistance has also been rehabilitated and its definition, character and strength significantly re-evaluated.[14]

Clearly, France's Dark Years have become less contentious since the mid 1990s. The passage of time has given a new generation of historians the distance to interpret the regime in all its complexity, and the disappearance of the war generation has made their findings less contentious. The expanded access to critical archives has made it possible to plumb the regime's darkest corners in depth.[15] These historiographical shifts have had a decisive impact in determining France's relationship to its past. One of the most striking analyses of late – because it rehabilitates the actions of French civilians – is the Israeli historian Limore Yagil's dissection of the relationship between Christians and Jews under Vichy. Instead of returning to the much discussed question of French complicity in the arrest and deportation of 75,000 Jews, Yagil reverses the common question and asks why three-quarters of the Jews living in France survived the war – one of the highest survival rates after Denmark, Finland, Bulgaria and Italy. Her answer, developed in painstaking detail, is that as early as 1940 French citizens at all levels, Protestants and Catholics, intervened in ways large and small to assist and save Jews. Numerous civil servants disobeyed orders, and so did police forces, prefects and other members of the upper echelons of the state administration. Men and women of Christian Democratic inspiration, committed to civil disobedience and active in the resistance, played a critical role in saving French Jewry. Jews in France were thus not saved by the Jews in the Communist resistance or by Jewish escape networks, but by engaged individuals rarely connected to the dominant Gaullist and Communist resistance movements.[16] For Yagil, widespread grass-roots civil disobedience, much more than complicity with the Nazis and their local accomplices, characterised the wartime years in France.

The competing and ever-changing understandings of the Vichy Regime have destabilised traditional questions. Which past, after all, does one need to address and come to terms with? One of collaboration or accommodation? Of courageous civil disobedience or of ordinary accommodation? One of complicity in the arrest and deportation of tens of thousands of French Jews or one that highlights the extraordinary work of individuals who saved an even greater number of Jews? Clearly, it is not an either/or proposition; in fact, the work of historians has underlined that understanding the complexity of the past is more profitable than pinpointing an elusive responsibility. We have reached a point where historians – neither the rapidly disappearing war generation, nor a culture obsessed with the Vichy period – play the leading role in structuring and reframing the past.

There remains, however, one major blank spot in France's attempt to address its history during World War II. In the border region of Alsace–Lorraine, the period of the German occupation has barely been confronted – a state of affairs that has endured with the tacit approval of regional and national elites. The deep-seated amnesia in Alsace–Lorraine, coupled with the difficulty of confronting the Algerian and colonial experiences, and the frank and extensive discussions of the Vichy regime, suggests that in France coming to terms with the past has not been a linear process. In fact, the ability to address history is both intertwined and determined by powerful questions of geography and ethnicity.

The relationship between victims and perpetrators has been more difficult to untangle in Alsace than in the rest of the nation because of the province's distinct war experience. No region had been more torn by the war than Alsace and Lorraine, and in no province had the events of 1939–45 assumed such complexity and had the human toll been so important. The ordeal of the border provinces began in the early days of the Phoney War (September 1939) when civil and military authorities evacuated some 600,000 Alsatians and Lorrainers to central and south-western France, where many of them remained until May 1940. For the great majority, this constituted their first extended stay in the 'interior' of France – a sojourn that brought to light the profound chasm that separated them from local inhabitants. The south-westerners, who could not understand why these imagined paragons of French patriotism (a myth constructed while the Provinces were under German rule between 1871 and 1918) spoke a German dialect and brought with them separate educational and religious institutions, gave them a reserved and sometimes hostile welcome. It was not infrequent for the Alsatians and Lorrainers to be called contemptuously *boches*, or because they spoke German, *ya ya*. The bewildering experience of being 'foreigners' in their own country pushed many to return to Nazi-annexed Alsace–Lorraine in the late summer of 1940.

After its lightning victory, Germany promptly annexed both provinces *de facto* and ruled them with *Gauleiters* based in neighbouring regions. The Nazis banned the use of the French language and undertook widespread Germanisation. The Germans expelled some 100,000 Lorrainers and 45,000 Alsatians to the interior of France on the grounds of ethnicity (Jews, Gypsies, immigrants, *français de l'intérieur* [French from the interior]), ideology (communists, French nationalists) or service to the French nation (high-ranking civil servants). German civil and administrative law was introduced. Germanisation walked hand in hand with Nazification. The National Socialist Party and its ancillary organisations undertook the *Gleichschaltung* of society. But the Nazis found willing accomplices in both Alsace and Lorraine, and collaboration, in ways large and small, with the Nazi regime during the first years of the war may well have been more extensive than historians have recognised. In August 1942 the Germans began drafting Alsatians and Lorrainers into the *Wehrmacht* – a development that would leave deep scars in the postwar years. Over the course of the war, some 130,000 Alsatians and Lorrainers, who became known as the *malgré-nous* [against our will – or literally 'in spite of ourselves'] or as the *incorporés de force* [forcibly conscripted], were conscripted into the *Wehrmacht* and over 90% of them sent to fight on the Eastern Front. By the war's end, an estimated 30,000 had died in battle, 10,000 were missing in action never to return, 20,000 had been captured by the Soviets and languished in POW camps and some 32,000 had been wounded during the course of the conflict.[17] To this day, few in France know that 16% of the 250,000 French military casualties in the World War II died in German uniform and came from the border provinces. And how could they, given that secondary and university level textbooks pass over this difficult episode in total silence?

In the postwar years the problem was how to reconcile the experiences and memories of those who had been, willingly or not, on opposite sides: those who hid underground or fled to the interior of France to escape conscription; the *malgré-nous* who had fought in German uniform; the members of the small Alsatian resistance; those who had been evacuated to south-western France in the autumn of 1939 and had chosen not to return; those who had been expelled by the Germans; those interned in concentration camps and prisons; surviving Jews; and those who had collaborated with the Nazis in ways large and small, joined NSDAP organisations and volunteered for the Waffen SS. A significant cross section of the Alsatian and Lorrainer population stood on both sides at the same time, having compromised itself in ways large and small with the Nazi regime while sometimes resisting in spirit, in language (by singing the Marseillaise) and humour, and more rarely, in acts, the totalitarian regime.[18] The lack of in-depth investigation of these issues makes it difficult for historians to evaluate if collaboration with the Nazis was a surface phenomenon, designed to protect local inhabitants, or if it reflected some measure of acceptance for the Nazi regime.

In the short term, reconciliation or even accommodation proved elusive. The widespread *épuration* [purges] undertaken in the two provinces fuelled denunciations and pitted local inhabitants against each other. The percentage of the population that was purged was ten times higher in Alsace and Lorraine than in the rest of France, and the percentage of guilty verdicts in the appellate court of Colmar, the highest in the nation.[19] True, the courts condemned few Alsatians and Lorrainers to death, but authorities interned some 12,000 suspects and, in the darkest pages of the postwar purges, sent many to the Struthof (Natzweiler), the only Nazi concentration camp on French soil, and others to a former Nazi security and re-education camp located in nearby Schirmeck.[20] At the war's end, the infamous Struthof had been hastily reconverted into an internment camp where conditions remained tough and spartan. The internees were a heterogeneous group of Germans, French and foreigners: former SS, members of the *Légion française des volontaires*, accused collaborators of all stripes, Nazi party members and innocent civilians wrongfully accused by the Resistance. Some children were also interned with their families. In early 1945, authorities launched an investigation into extensive mistreatment by prison guards.[21] The internment of perpetrators and civilians, some of whom had been brought in on dubious charges, in the grim concentration camp that had been a symbol of Nazi persecution in France (though most who died there were foreigners) illustrated how indifferent French administrators and military officials remained to the persecution of Jews and others, and how little they understood about the Nazi regime.

The *épuration* rekindled the profound conflicts that fractured Alsatian and *Lorrain* society, and it evoked in disturbing fashion the large-scale purges conducted by the French in the wake of their victory in 1918.[22] The purges were also generated by continuing French desires to reconstruct an Alsatian and Lorrain identity devoid of all remnants of a German past, and divorced from the regionalist and autonomist leanings that had structured the region's interwar social and political life. The purges were aimed at identifying victims and punishing perpetrators, but they also sought to cleanse the region according to vaguely defined ethnic and national criteria. In Alsace and Moselle head shavings and attempted lynchings appear to have targeted 'pro-Nazi' women (and some men) who had been evacuated to Germany, and who slowly trickled back in the midst of the Reich's defeat. While few women appear to have been shorn as retribution for their sentimental links to Germans, the sexual content of head shavings was rarely far from the surface.[23] Punishing women for crimes of collaboration was more difficult here than in the rest of the nation given the generalised accommodation with the Nazi regime, the presence of Alsatians in the ranks of the NSDAP and the large numbers conscripted in the German army, not to mention the fact that the dividing lines between French and Germans were not always easy to untangle. The reassertion of French masculinity, however, was far more problematic in Alsace, because men had been deeply implicated (willingly or not) in the Nazi war machine.

The tension between the official discourse, embodied by De Gaulle, of a patriotic Alsace and Lorraine enthusiastically returning to the maternal fold, and an *épuration* whose purpose was both to re-establish full control over the province and to punish those too compromised by Nazism or too sympathetic to Germany, gradually eased during the late 1940s. It resurfaced with a vengeance at the occasion of a famous 1953 trial. In June 1944, the Waffen-SS *Das Reich* Division, on its way to the front lines in Normandy, had encircled the sleepy town of Oradour-sur-Glane in the rural Limousin and massacred 642 men, women and children. Oradour, much like Lidice in Czechoslovakia, quickly became the symbol of French suffering at the hands of the Nazis. Nine years later, 21 soldiers who had participated in the slaughter, including 13 Alsatians who had been forcibly incorporated in the German army and later transferred to the SS, were tried by a military court in Bordeaux.[24] To witness Alsatians side by side with Germans on the bench of the accused infuriated Alsatian public opinion, and all the more so given that Parliament had passed a law of 'collective responsibility' in 1948 enabling the prosecution of French citizens for war crimes.

The dramatic prosecution of the 13 Alsatian *malgré-nous* marked a turning point in Alsace, and made it exceedingly difficult for the province's inhabitants not to adhere to a common interpretation of the war that mixed denial and victimisation.[25] The *Procès de Bordeaux*, as it became known in Alsace, served to crystallise the discourse of victimisation – a discourse that has remained at the centre of Alsace's relationship to the war, not to mention its identity, to this day. Alsatians claimed that the *malgré-nous* could not be held responsible for their actions at Oradour because they had been forcibly incorporated in the German army. The *malgré-nous* were victims, not torturers. This was a powerful argument in a region where, given the scope of forced incorporation, virtually all towns and villages had suffered losses and most inhabitants counted a *malgré-nous* among their family or their friends. The narrative of victimhood underlined that Alsace had been *abandoned* in a cowardly fashion by France in 1940. Neither the *malgré-nous*, nor civil servants, nor the province as a whole could be held accountable for their acts during the war. Responsibility lay in French and German hands. The Alsatians had been victims of maleficent forces they could not control.

The Bordeaux military court swept these arguments aside when it found all 13 Alsatians who had been conscripted into the German army guilty of the crimes for which they had been charged. The verdict created a massive uproar in Alsace. The entire region, led by the association of *malgré-nous* veterans, rose up in protest: from small municipalities, to the region's elected officials, Protestant and Catholic churches, associations large and small, and all political parties save the Communists. Bells tolled in mourning, flags were set at half mast and Alsatians gathered in silence before monuments to the war dead. Faced with embarrassing, massive civil disobedience from a province that remained central to French national identity, one that had vital political and economic clout, the Chamber of Deputies promptly voted to amnesty those who had been 'forcibly incorporated in the German armies'.[26] In so doing, they implicitly recognised that Alsatians could not be guilty of war crimes against French citizens. As Sarah Farmer has argued, the nation's elected officials chose to sacrifice the poor, communist-leaning region where the massacre had taken place to the interests of the nation. France's pardon of the *malgré-nous*, and by extension of all Alsatians, however, would quickly be forgotten by the vast majority of Frenchmen, who considered it as an act of political expediency, and the Oradour massacre would continue to poison relations between Alsace and the interior of France for the next half-century. Following the 1953 Oradour Trial, the border region remained absent from historical and political debates that centred on France's responsibility during the war, and in the wake of the Oradour trial, the *malgré-nous* argued that it was time to turn the page, to forget the past (and notably the Bordeaux trial), and not continuously to revive it. To this day, the *malgré-nous* argue that the Bordeaux trial was an 'insult' to the border provinces.[27]

In Alsace, the association of *malgré-nous* veterans – known as the *Association des déserteurs, évadés et incorporés de force* (ADEIF) [Association of Deserters, Escapees and Forcibly Conscripted Soldiers] – reaped the benefits of the Oradour trial.[28] From the very beginning, the ADEIF had come to the defence of the accused and had argued that the *malgré-nous*, betrayed by France in 1940, were victims, not perpetrators. These were French patriots whose plight was just as distressing as the plight of civilian victims of Oradour, and it was time for the French nation to recognise this. The Oradour trial, in combination with the often vociferous defence of the Association of *malgré-nous* veterans, anchored in Alsatian public opinion the view that the tragedy of French soldiers in German uniform was identical to the tragedy of Alsace itself.[29] The malgré-nous were victims of a cause 'that was not theirs'.[30] This powerful, if simple, narrative which survived for decades left little room for other actors whose role in the war had been substantially different.

The ADEIF was founded shortly after the war's end to defend the honour of those who had fought in German uniform, proclaim their attachment to their French homeland (thus their motto 'Honneur et Patrie' [honour and fatherland])

and call for the return of Alsatian and *Lorrain* prisoners of war held in Soviet camps. Only 62 would return between 1948 and 1955. Throughout the 1950s and well into the 1960s, however, the *malgré-nous* pressed relentlessly for the release of thousands of unaccounted Alsatians and Lorrainers believed to be held against their will in the Soviet Union. The fate of some 11,000 missing Alsatians and Lorrainers made it difficult to turn the page on World War II and address the past head on. Up until the mid-1960s the *malgré-nous* veterans portrayed themselves as a profoundly patriotic organisation whose fidelity to France could not be questioned; local *malgré-nous* sections organised pilgrimages to monuments of the war dead, inaugurated flags and pennants, built their own memorials to commemorate their fallen comrades – and undertook these tasks with the blessing of local Catholic and Protestant churches. The *malgré-nous* veterans also worked tirelessly to obtain pension rights, veteran's benefits and reparations for their members – and they grew frustrated with a Parisian bureaucracy that dragged its feet on these contentious issues. By 1968, the tone had changed. The *malgré-nous*, angered by the lack of response, increasingly characterised themselves as having been 'sacrificed', and as 'Alsatian youth subjected to an unprecedented war crime'.[31] The 1970s saw the *incorporés de force* seek reparations for the 'war crime' to which they had been subjected.[32] By the 1980s and 1990s, their tone became even more strident: soldiers in German uniform, argued G. Nonnenmacher, the president of the *Malgré-nous* association, had been the object of a 'disguised genocide', 'a crime against humanity'.[33] The slippage in terminology was revealing. To equate the *malgré-nous* with the fate of the Jews at a time when France was addressing its complicity in the Final Solution, illustrated the deep memory rift between the border region and the rest of the nation, and also underlined how the discourse of victimisation was intertwined with anti-Semitism.

The growing militancy of the *malgré-nous* veterans was a response to the nation's complete ignorance of their plight. After half a century of lobbying to ensure that French soldiers in German uniform would be recognised as having fought for the nation, the *malgré-nous* veterans had been unable to make a dent in national consciousness. Secondary school and university textbooks studiously ignore them, and the border provinces shine by their absence in French histories of World War II. The Alsatians and Lorrainers could only be integrated in the national community by forgetting their recent past and especially their Germanic past. Even the emergence (in the 1990s) in the public arena of the *malgré-elles* [in spite of themselves, or more literally 'in spite of herselves'] – the 20,000–30,000 Alsatian women conscripted during the war in the *Reichsarbeitsdienst* [obligatory work service] or the *Kriegshilfsdienst* [war relief service] – whose role was repressed during the postwar years, has done little to bring the complex position of wartime Alsace into new relief.[34] While the *malgré-elles* have struggled (with little success) to obtain the same financial compensations as their male counterparts, they have adopted the same discourse of victimisation. This new group of victims, however, raises crucial questions about the gendered nature and memory of victimhood.

The culture of victimhood was further developed and relayed by the extensive *malgré-nous* memoir literature that has appeared ever since the early 1950s. Usually published by small, regional publishers, this literature relates the experience of Alsatians and Lorrainers in German uniform; it circulated widely in the region and occupies a place of choice in local bookstores. The vast majority of these memoirs – over 150 of them – are characterised by a similar structure that begins with forced drafting into the German army, the campaign on the Russian front, and more often than not, incarceration in Russian prisoner of war camps.[35] The tale is invariably similar: the *malgré-nous* portray themselves as the tragic victims of forces beyond their control, victims who under the harshest of conditions retained their allegiance to the French nation. One *malgré-nous* argued that incorporation into the Wehrmacht was equivalent to the deportation of all the province's young men to Germany, and thus equated French soldiers in German uniform with those deported because of their political activities.[36] More troubling is the fact that the memoirs are overwhelmingly silent when it comes to reprisals directed against Russian partisans and the behaviour of the Wehrmacht vis-à-vis civilian populations. Of the roundup and execution of Jews there is no mention. The *malgré-nous*, however, who were disseminated in a wide range of German army units on the Eastern Front, surely witnessed exactions of all kind. But their memoirs are an exercise in silence: they skirt the issue, preferring to underline their own resourcefulness and craftiness, the incompetence of their commanding officers and the cruelty of Russian soldiers. Often deeply anti-communist because of their tough sojourns in Soviet POW camps, the *malgré-nous* share with German soldiers marked prejudices toward the Russians, whom they routinely described as 'primitive' 'barbarian' and 'uncivilised'.

French soldiers who had fought in German uniform played a critical role in the diffusion and enforcement of a culture of victimhood in Alsace. Any challenge to this view was an affront to the *malgré-nous*, and was transformed into a denial of the province's suffering. This 'perverse victimisation', as the sociologist Freddy Raphaël has judiciously termed it, survives to this day and has placed off limits a critical examination of Alsatian collaboration during the war and of the province's moral responsibility; it has tended to consider *all* Alsatians as victims – something that does a profound injustice to those who chose exile or resistance, not to mention a range of other victims, civilians in particular, who paid a heavy toll during the war.[37] To this day, a critical discussion of the role Alsatian and Lorrain soldiers on the Eastern Front remains off limits, and an examination of the circumstances surrounding their forced incorporation into the German army remains a taboo topic. Were the sons and daughters of Nazi party members that reticent to go? The fate of Alsatian Jews is equally buried under silence. Evidence suggests some degree of public approval when the Nazis expelled Alsatian Jews to France in 1940 and confiscated their property; when Jews returned, in 1945, their welcome was, at times, lukewarm and recovery of their property difficult.[38] In some cases German soldiers had used Jewish gravestones to build anti-tank barriers during the winter of 1945 Battle for Alsace, and inhabitants later recycled these stones as building and paving material.[39]

The critical point, however, is that ever since the 1953 Oradour trial no Alsatians or Lorrainers have been prosecuted for crimes committed during World War II; no leading local politicians or public figures have seen their careers tarnished by revelations about their past; nor have any significant historical inquiries of the region's history provoked wide-ranging debate in civil society. In Alsace and Lorraine victims do not appear to have filed complaints in courts against perpetrators of all kind. The contrast with the rest of the nation, obsessed with Vichy in the 1980s and 1990s, could not be more striking. The pervasive image, relayed by regional histories, was that Alsace was quashed under the Nazi boot.[40] Alsatians, wrote one historian of the *malgré-nous*, echoing language President Sarkozy would use for France one decade later, 'should not be ashamed of this painful episode in their past'.[41] From 1953 until the present, silence has characterised the region's relationship to the Nazi occupation, and it is a silence that has met with the approval of the vast majority of the region's elites, social and political actors – and of the French government.

Political and bureaucratic elites subscribed to and reinforced this sanitised version of the province's history. Charles De Gaulle in particular embraced and nurtured the fiction of Alsace as a patriotic war victim because this helped cement the province's political support, minimised the profound fractures of the period of occupation, and underlined the timeless unity of the French nation. De Gaulle, of course, could count on his image as the Liberator of Alsace – a liberator who had stood up to Eisenhower and refused to evacuate the city of Strasbourg during the German army's December 1944 counteroffensive in the Ardennes. As early as December 1944, De Gaulle travelled to Alsace and he would do so repeatedly throughout the 1950s and 1960s in order to reinforce his image as a French nationalist; his attentiveness paid off handsomely at the polls as the region became the bastion of the Gaullist movement in France. In the 1960s the Gaullists controlled the overwhelming majority of the region's seats in the Chamber of Deputies and dominated legislative elections. Spurred by their desire to refuse the past, Alsatians and Lorrainers embraced Gaullism and patriotic politics because it allowed them to reintegrate the nation without addressing the ambiguities of their history. Victimisation made history palatable to Alsatians, Lorrainers and the French.

The Alsatians and Lorrainers were, of course, not alone in draping themselves in the mantle of victimisation. In the 1950s Germans (soldiers in particular) argued that they had been victims of Nazism and the war. By the 1980s, however, Germans were engaged in an intensive public debate about the Nazi past – one that addressed the question of responsibility head on and gave way to a more complex understanding of the nation's relationship to its history.[42] Austria surely provides the best comparison with the case of the French border provinces. Alsace has long shared with Austria – and this is cause for reflection and for concern – the distinction of having failed to come to terms with its role during World War II. The war was all about suffering and victimhood at the hands of the Germans, not about contrition and assuming responsibility. In both Alsace and Austria, war veterans (the *malgré-nous* and, in Austria, the *Kamaradenschaftsbund*) instrumentalised public sympathy to ensure that a critical discussion of the war years remained off limits. There are, however, significant differences between the two cases. In Austria, the extensive debate in the late 1980s surrounding Kurt Waldheim's wartime role in the Balkans polarised the political world, but it eventually led to an extensive debate about victims and perpetrators, and to a civic movement focused on confronting the Nazi past.[43] Nothing comparable has taken place in Alsace or Lorraine.

There is thus a striking contrast between a French nation that has attempted in fits and starts to confront its history, and that has done so with increasing resolve over the last 30 years, and a region within France, critical to the national sense of belonging, where an extensive debate about the past remains in its infancy. Strasbourg, home to the European Parliament and the Council of Europe, may well symbolise Franco-German reconciliation and France's Europeanisation, but it is also the capital of a region that lives in the denial of the past. The French nation bears considerable responsibility for this state of things. There was no interest on the part of the state to press Alsatians and Lorrainers to investigate the past in any depth, nor was there any interest on the part of civil society to ask questions about a region that occupied a mythic place in the French imaginary. Facing up to history in the border provinces might have revealed a disquieting acquiescence with Nazism at the grassroots, and a range of responses to the German occupation that was not replicated in other areas of the country. It would have questioned the moral responsibility of the nation – of the entire French nation – in the conduct of the war. Confronting the past head on – and this was the fear both in Alsace and in France – risked reviving questions about the border region's place within the French nation, a place that had been left in silence since 1918. The awkward truth is that National Socialism had done more to cement Alsace and Lorraine to the French nation than did 20 odd years of reintegration following the Great War, because it gave inhabitants of the border provinces little choice but to turn their backs both on autonomism and on a political culture deeply marked by the German annexation between 1871 and 1918. The Alsatian case illustrates how contentious border areas often remain immune to larger debates about victims and perpetrators taking place nationally. Local and national political elites, afraid that questioning the past will revive longstanding conflicts over national and regional belonging, end up condoning in these regions a silence that is no longer acceptable on a national level.

There are timid signs that in the twenty-first century silence is slowly giving way to an engagement with the complexities of the region's history. Representatives of Alsace, the city of Strasbourg, and the *malgré-nous* attended the commemorative ceremonies held on the occasion of the 60th anniversary of the Oradour-sur-Glane massacre in 2004. And in the summer of 2005 the region inaugurated a museum, the Mémorial de l'Alsace-Moselle, whose objective is to introduce the public to the region's complex past while fostering Franco-German reconciliation in the present.[44] The Mémorial addresses the experiences of all border province inhabitants during the war, from those who resisted and were deported, to those who joined the Nazi party and those incorporated in the German army. Commemorating all these protagonists together, however, makes it appear as if their experience and their suffering are comparable and can be understood on the same plane. Even more problematic, a substantial discussion of the fate of Alsatian Jews is absent from the Museum. The Mémorial is located in the prime Alsatian memorial site of the World War II. Built in Schirmeck near a Nazi 'security' camp where numerous Alsatians were interned, and within sight of the Struthof concentration camp, the Mémorial's location is all about commemoration and victimisation – not about contrition or responsibility. The Mémorial's ability to provide a clear account of the experience of French soldiers in German uniform, and of the Nazi experience in the border provinces, is compromised by its location. Still, the museum, whatever its faults, signals a fresh attempt to engage the past, and needs to be understood as part of the larger 'museum-ification' of France's experience in World War II that includes the Mémorial de Caen in Normandy and the Centre de la mémoire in Oradour-sur-Glane.

Given the time that had elapsed since the end of World War II, should the past best remain buried, and energies devoted to more pressing issues in the present? The problem, however, is that the culture of silence and denial that developed in the war's wake continues to have a disturbing impact in the present. Ever since 1984, Alsace and Lorraine have been among the foremost bastions of Jean Marie Le Pen's *Front National*. The Party's scores in national elections have regularly approached the 25% mark – and this in a region where support for the European Union runs higher than in the rest of the nation, and where unemployment rates have been consistently lower than the national average. What struck and puzzled observers, and what still holds true in the present, can be summarised as follows: the National Front scored well throughout the region, both in urban, de-industrialising areas beset by social crisis and in the parts of the picturesque Alsatian countryside where one finds few social problems and even fewer immigrants.[45] The striking resurgence of the extreme right also finds its expression in other, more disturbing, realms. Over the past 25 years, Jewish cemeteries throughout Alsace have been the target of repeated desecrations and a renewed wave of vandalism in 2004 brought this phenomenon to national attention. This subterranean anti-Semitism, closely linked to a negationist subculture, provides a window into the region's tension-ridden relationship with its Jewish heritage. Alsatian neo-Nazism has also been on the rise and the reaction of local political elites has been timid. One crucial factor that explains both the passivity toward Jewish grave desecrations and the strength of the *Front national* is the region's inability to come to terms with its unsavoury recent past. The National Front, the neo-Nazis, and the grave desecrators all benefit from this culture of denial much more than they work together for common goals. Until the discourse of victimisation has been demystified, and until Alsatians have a better understanding and take responsibility for their complex, contradictory history (a history not just imposed by the French and German states), the extreme right's propaganda will find fertile soil. In Alsace, as in Austria, confronting the past is the *sine qua non* to challenging the discourse of the extreme right. The issue today is no longer one of identifying or punishing perpetrators, but an honest appraisal of the past is vital to the creation of a vibrant political culture. Just as French society (and Republicanism) needed to come to terms with the legacy of Vichy, and today still needs to turn the page of Empire, so too does Alsace need to address its history. At a time when the region is being transformed by transnationalism on the Franco-German border, and by the presence of large numbers of French citizens of Turkish and North African heritage, there is no more important task.

Notes

1. "La France n'a pas à rougir de son histoire" [France should not be ashamed of its history], Nicolas Sarkozy, Speech given in Nice, 30 March 2007, www.sarkozy.fr (last accessed 30 October 2007).
2. Eric Conan and Henry Rousso, *Vichy. Un passé qui ne passe pas* (Paris: Fayard, 1994).
3. Speech given by President Jacques Chirac at the commemoration of the roundup of Jews at the Vel' d'Hiv on 16 and 17 July 1942; http://elysee.fr/elysee/elysee.fr/francais/interventions/discours_et_declarations/1995/juillet/allocution_de_m_jacques_chirac_president_de_la_republique_prononcee_lors_des_ceremonies_commemorant_la_grande_rafle_des_16_et_17_juillet_1942-paris.2503.html (last accessed 14 January 2008).
4. Raphaëlle Branche, *La torture et l'armée pendant la Guerre d'Algérie, 1954–1962* (Paris: Gallimard 2001); Sylvie Thénault, *Une drôle de justice: Les magistrats dans la guerre d'Algérie* (Paris: La Découverte, 2001). For historiographical overviews see also Thénault, *Histoire de la guerre d'indépendance algérienne* (Paris: Flammarion, 2005) and Raphaëlle Branche, *La guerre d'Algérie: Une histoire apaisée?* (Paris: Seuil, 2005).
5. Emphasis mine. See article 4 of Law no. 2005-158 of 23 February 2005 'portant reconnaissance de la Nation et contribution nationale en faveur des Français rapatriés', in *Journal Officiel de la République française* 46 (24 February 2005). Faced with growing opposition from teachers and from overseas

French Departments, and confronted with a growing political controversy, the government repealed article 4 on 15 February 2006.

6. Speeches of Nicolas Sarkozy at Caen, 9 March 2007, and Nice, 30 March 2007, available at www.sarkozy.fr. For excerpts and comments see *Libération*, 6 April 2007; *Le Monde*, 10 April 2007; and Marc Olivier Baruch, "Eloge de la repentance," *Le Monde*, 12 April 2007.

7. Fabrice Virgili, *La France 'virile': Des femmes tondues à la libération* (Paris: Payot, 2000), pp.77–8.

8. Henry Rousso, "L'épuration, une histoire inachevée," *Vingtième siècle: Revue d'histoire*, 33 (1992), pp.78–105; see also François Rouquet, "L'épuration: histoire d'un chiffre, mémoire du nombre," in Marc Olivier Baruch (ed.), *Une poignée de misérables: L'épuration de la société française après la Seconde Guerre Mondiale* (Paris: Fayard, 2003), pp.516–29.

9. See István Deák, Jan T. Gross and Tony Judt (eds), *The Politics of Retribution in Europe: World War II and its Aftermath* (Princeton, NJ: Princeton University Press, 2000), p.161.

10. In fact, 23,000 people (of all political leanings) were executed during the war. Stéphane Courtois and Marc Lazar, *Histoire du Parti communiste français* (Paris: Presses universitaires de France, 1995), pp.217–18.

11. Robert O. Paxton, *Vichy France: Old Guard and New Order, 1940–1944* (New York: Columbia University Press, 1982), p.51.

12. On all these issues see the illuminating analyses of Henry Rousso, "Une justice impossible: L'épuration et la politique antijuive de Vichy," and "Juger le passé? Justice et histoire en France," in *Vichy. L'événement, la mémoire, l'histoire* (Paris: Gallimard, 1992).

13. Philippe Burrin, *La France à l'heure allemande, 1940–44* (Paris: Seuil, 1995).

14. For an excellent historiographical overview, Laurent Douzou, *La Résistance française: une histoire périlleuse* (Paris: Seuil, 2005).

15. For recent examples, Jean-Marc Dreyfus, *Pillages sur ordonnances. Aryanisation et restitution des banques en France, 1940–1953* (Paris: Fayard, 2003); Raphaël Delpart, *Les convois de la honte: enquête sur la SNCF et la déportation, 1941–1945* (Neuilly-sur-Seine: Lafon, 2005).

16. Limore Yagil, *Chrétiens et Juifs sous Vichy (1940–1944): Sauvetage et désobéissance civile* (Paris: Editions du Cerf, 2005).

17. Gaël Moullec, "Alliés ou ennemis? Le GUPVI-NKVD, le Komintern et les '*Malgré-nous*', Le destin des prisonniers de guerre français en URSS (1942–1955)," *Cahiers du Monde russe* 42 (2001), pp.667–78. For a general survey of the *malgré-nous*, Eugène Riedweg, *Les 'Malgré-nous'. Histoire de l'incorporation de force des Alsatiens-Mosellans dans l'armée allemande* (Mulhouse: Editions du Rhin, 2005), see figures on casualties p.294; Pierre Rigoulot, *La tragédie des Malgré-nous* (Paris: Denoël, 1990).

18. The moving diary of Marie-Joseph Bopp chronicles the behaviour of the citizens of Colmar during the war. See *Ma ville à l'heure nazie. Colmar, 1940–1945* (Strasbourg: La Nuée Bleue, 2004).

19. Jean-Laurent Vonau, *L'épuration en Alsace. La face méconnue de la Libération, 1944–1953* (Strasbourg: Editions du Rhin, 2005), p.171; Baruch (ed.), *Une poignée de misérables*, (note 21), p.525.

20. On the Struthof, see Robert Steegmann, *Struthof. Le KL-Natzweiler et ses kommandos: une nébuleuse concentrationnaire des deux côtés du Rhin, 1941–1945* (Strasbourg: La Nuée Bleue, 2005).

21. Archives départementales du Bas-Rhin (Strasbourg), 544D49.

22. For the post-World War I purges, see Laird Boswell, "From Liberation to Purge Trials in the 'Mythic Provinces': Recasting French Identities in Alsace and Lorraine, 1918–1920," *French Historical Studies* 23 (2000), pp.129–162.

23. Virgili, *La France 'virile'*, pp.158–69.

24. Fourteen Alsatians were placed on trial, but one of them had volunteered for the SS. He was charged with treason, not war crimes.

25. The best book on Oradour is Sarah Farmer, *Martyred Village: Commemorating the 1944 Massacre at Oradour-sur-Glane* (Berkeley, CA: University of California Press, 1999).

26. Farmer, *Martyred Village*, p.162.

27. *Bulletin de liaison. Association des incorporés de force d'Alsace et de Moselle* 211 (2004).

28. In the mid-1950s, the ADEIF simplified its name to Association des évadés et incorporés de force.

29. *Bulletin de Liaison. Association des déserteurs, évadés et incorporés de force. Groupement du Haut-Rhin*, 1er Trimestre 1953.

30. *Bulletin de Liaison. Association des évadés et incorporés de force* 36 (1960).

31. *Bulletin de Liaison. Association des évadés et incorporés de force* 68 (1968).

32. *Bulletin de Liaison. Association des évadés et incorporés de force* 96 (1975).

33. *Bulletin de Liaison. Association des évadés et incorporés de force* 164 (1992).

34. Nina Barbier, *Malgré-elles. Les Alsaciennes et Mosellanes incorporées de force dans la machine de guerre nazie* (Strasbourg: La Nuée Bleue/Editions du Rhin, 2000).

35. See Alfred Wahl, "L'incorporé de force d'Alsace-Moselle. Analyse de récits de guerre," in *Mémoire de la seconde guerre mondiale. Actes du Colloque de Metz* (Metz: Centre de recherche Histoire et civilisation de l'Université de Metz, 1984). For one example from a large literature see Georges Starcky, *Malgré nous! Le drame des Alsatiens et des Lorrains* (Paris: Editions France-Empire, 1995).

36. Eve Cerf, "Récits de guerre alsaciens: Mémoires et oublis," *Revue des sciences sociales de la France de l'Est* 20 (1992–3), pp.36–50.

37. See Pierre Rigoulot, *L'Alsace-Lorraine pendant la guerre* (Paris: PUF, 1997), p.122, and Freddy Raphaël and Geneviève Herberich-Marx, *Mémoire plurielle de l'Alsace: Grandeurs et servitudes d'un pays des marges* (Strasbourg: Publications de la société savante d'Alsace et des régions de l'Est, 1991).

38. Freddy Raphaël (ed.), *Le Judaïsme alsacien: Histoire, patrimoine, tradition* (Strasbourg: La Nuée Bleue, 1999), p.16; For a list of the Jewish deportees see René Gutman, *Le Memorbuch. Mémorial de la déportation et de la résistance des juifs du bas-rhin* (Strasbourg: La Nuée Bleue, 2005) and Jacky Dreyfus and Daniel Fuks, *Le Mémorial des Juifs du Haut-Rhin Martyrs de la Shoah* (Colmar: Jérôme Do Bentzinger éditeur, 2006).

39. Freddy Raphaël and Geneviève Herberich-Marx, "Une singulière présence des Juifs en Alsace: La construction d'un oubli," in Raphaël and Herberich-Marx (eds), *Mémoire de pierre, mémoire de papier. La mise en scène du passé en Alsace* (Strasbourg: Presses universitaires de Strasbourg, 2002), pp.125–6.

40. For a recent use of this term, see Pierre Barral, "L'Alsace-Lorraine: trois départements sous la botte," in Jean-Pierre Azéma et François Bédarida (eds), *La France des années noires*, vol I (Paris: Seuil, 1993), pp.233–149.

41. "Les Alsaciens n'ont pas à rougir de cet épisode douloureux de leur passé," Riedweg, *Les 'Malgré-nous'*, p.294.

42. The problem of Germans victimhood is particularly complex. My point here is that Germans have addressed the past in ways that Alsatians have not. See Bill Niven (ed.), *Germans as Victims: Remembering the Past in Contemporary Germany* (Basingstoke and New York: Palgrave Macmillan, 2006).

43. On the 'victim culture' in Austria, see David Art, *The Politics of the Nazi Past in Germany and Austria* (Cambridge: Cambridge University Press, 2006), pp.101–44.

44. http://www.memorial-alsace-moselle.com

45. For interpretations of the National Front in Alsace see Bernard Schwengler, *Le vote Front national. L'Alsace: un cas particulier?* (Strasbourg: Editions Oberlin, 2003); Daniela Heimberger, *Der Front National im Elsass: Rechtsextremismus in Frankreich. Eine Regionale Wahlanalyse* (Wiesbaden: Westdeutscher Verlag, 2001).

From Invisibility to Power: Spanish Victims and the Manipulation of their Symbolic Capital

IGNACIO FERNÁNDEZ DE MATA

Repression and its Handmaiden: Invisibility

The foreigner who turns an interested eye toward contemporary Spanish politics might be surprised by the sight of the entire country, 70 years after the civil war that devastated it, dug up in the search for mass graves that contain the remains of those killed during General Francisco Franco's uprising in towns that were conquered by the insurgents and in the repression that followed. After decades of official but unspoken silence, the most hidden and alienated dead whose very blood generated opprobrium during the dictatorship, emerge in the Spanish public scene with a surprising and deafening clamour. Their disinterment, and the power of the skeletons inscribed with visible signs of material and symbolic violence, has generated an intense debate about the war, its victims, and their memory.

This process has been made possible by the process of historiographical revision carried out during the last 20 years by scholars on the progressive Left, as well as by amateur revisions lacking academic rigour. The conflicting setting of today's public memory is witnessing a similar conservative revisionism, which reiterates theses already shuffled by the dictatorship, although made more sophisticated by scientific enquiry and objectivity, and points to the need for 'reconciliation'. Many among the Right trusted that the physical disappearance of those who had lived through the most violent period of Francoism's repression would silence the latent controversies of the civil war. But the truths and the suffering of the victims had been transmitted from one generation to the next, given the lack of closure imposed on the families by the mass burials of their loved ones' remains, and the active silencing of their murders. The interim of the dictatorship and the transition had in fact been the calm before the storm.

The victims who, from their opened graves, are now indirectly contributing to the construction of a counter-hegemonic narrative of the past, are those who were killed in the rearguard of the zone under insurgent military command. They were not war casualties, but civilians who were captured, many picked up from their homes under the complicit cover of night, and assassinated without due process. Many had turned themselves in when they found out that their names were on 'a list' in the hands of the victorious insurgents.

This process of extermination, concentrated in the first six months of the war, took the lives of approximately 59–70% of the total of victims during the civil war, and the subsequent dictatorship. The number of those killed by the insurgents during this period of 'hot terror' was around 90,000 (plus 5000 more produced by Franco's post-war 'justice'). Those assassinated by the Republican faction amount to nearly 55,000 dead, not a negligible number by far.[1]

This systematic exercise was so clearly geared toward the complete extermination of the Republicans that there were so-called 'second and third rounds of cleansing' meant to eliminate those that had been missed in the first killings.[2] Politicians and those affiliated to parties in the Popular Front, members of leftist unions and members of the *Casa del Pueblo* [People's House], those who had publicly proclaimed Republicanism as their creed, suffered imprisonment and murder in areas which had already been pacified. This was what Mola's 'exemplary punishments' evidently came down to.[3] Punishment did not stop there, however – the relatives of those assassinated were also victimised, as they suffered the loss of loved ones, the ignominious behaviour of neighbours and the constant marginalisation in their communities. Added to this was economic hardship, as the main provider of the household was dead, and they were impeded from acceding to certain jobs, and in many cases properties were taken from them. Female relatives were specifically targeted, as their humiliation symbolically increased the punishments of their husbands, fathers, sons or brothers. They were denigrated publicly, beaten, arbitrarily incarcerated, made to render domestic services for the military commanders and so on.

This violence of extermination in which the political rival had to be physically eliminated did not come from processes born in the brief and recent Second Republic. Its roots went back to the last third of the nineteenth century at least, when the conflicts of identity owing to the weak and incomplete consolidation of the Spanish nation-state became increasingly untenable. Throughout the first third of the twentieth century, moreover, Spanish political culture had not grown accustomed to the democratic process, and recourse to armed force became politically normalised. The lack of commitment to Republican democracy vitiated the Second Republic on both the Left and the Right. Finally, there existed an extreme socio-economic inequality that led to a radically polarised political situation. But the developments that took place between 1936 and 1939 were unthinkable at the societal level; the fact that some people had voluntarily turned themselves in attests to this fact. Nothing like the type of violence unleashed then had ever taken place before, not during the divisive civil wars of the nineteenth century, nor during the dictatorship that was still fresh in everybody's memory, that of General Miguel Primo de Rivera's regime from 1923 to 1929.[4]

This extreme and organised violence generated irreparable damage to and fractures in the social fabric of the communities involved. That a sector of civil society virulently attacked and repressed their next-door neighbours was severely shocking, for despite tensions, relations of subordination, and conflicts, co-existence was premised on the minimum respect of the life and property of all community-members.

Silencing and Invisibility

More than 60 years would go by before Spanish society acknowledged that such killings and marginalisation had indeed taken place – that people had been killed for the mere fact of their political identity or activities, that the killers had had absolute impunity and had sometimes benefitted from their crimes. The imposed silence and invisibility that excluded the relatives of those assassinated from being an integral part of national society, keeping their memory and experience from being integrated into post-war national narratives, is still one of the many elements of Francoist repression that endures within our democracy.

This seeming societal indifference was fed by two factors: first, the state's denial that any politically motivated massacre had taken place (outside those perpetrated by the 'Reds'); and second, the tacit prohibition regarding any public discussion of the massacres, among other politically sensitive subjects. To Spanish society at large, the relatives of those massacred by the supporters of the victorious regime were invisible as a social sector that was part of the nation. To their neighbours in provincial towns and cities where killings were known to have happened, they were visible only as the embodiment of the vanquished past, their loss understood as directly related to the wrong-headed ideologies that their relatives had espoused.

Thus the relatives of the assassinated republicans suffered both a social invisibility, and an even more painful silencing that became, indeed, the continuation *on them* of the repression against their dead relatives. They were not allowed to mourn their dead or to bring flowers to the mass graves whose site was often known. They had to live side-by-side with the executioners of their loved ones, and not only could they *not* pursue justice against them, but they had to subordinate themselves socially and politically to them. They were the ones who carried on them the stigma of pariahs, they the ones expected to 'apologise' for being related to a *fusilado* [those executed without trials and buried in mass graves at the beginning of the Spanish Civil War], and not the actual killers.

The Logic of Violence and Construction of the Victims During the Dictatorship: Understanding Repression from Within

In part, Spanish society could believe that there had been no politically motivated massacres, and simultaneously believe that those who died were guilty of *something*, because the logic constructed by the Francoist regime to explain the undeniable fact of tens of thousands of murders in non-combat zones made this plausible. Because they denied that their adherents had committed these atrocities, they could not posit, for instance, that zealous townspeople had let things get out of hand in their just desire to help the insurgents cleanse Spain of the blemish of the 'Reds'. No: it was 'envy and petty hatreds' – *malos quereres* – that led some to take advantage of the disorder provided by war, following the unruliness of the Republican period, and kill people whose behaviour singled them out for killing. The regime thus tacitly acknowledged that the victims were indeed Reds, but denied that the perpetrators were acting on state-sponsored, state-sanctioned anti-Red feeling.[5]

In this environment of denial, official silence and ongoing state repression against political dissidence (which included the questioning of governmental statements-of-fact), the relatives of the deceased had to continue living their lives. Given the impact of the trauma, their incapacity to express their pain or reach closure, and the extra economic hardships that most suffered in addition to the emotional and social distress, one can argue that the world of the families of the repression's victims was 'ruptured'. In order to rebuild their lives on these broken foundations, families needed to construct a logic to the violence, to understand what had happened to them, why their loved ones had died, why their world had been turned upside down. Two aspects are important to understand how and why the relatives of the victims constructed the explanations that they did. First, families had to do this without the benefit of actual information, within a rigid system of censorship that made access to knowledge about what had actually happened virtually impossible for them, and their quest to find information dangerous. Second, the regime's discourses, imposed on them as the defeated side – and therefore, the wrong side – would evidently become the hegemonic context in which the relatives constructed their own narratives.

Not knowing that there were indeed orders given from senior officals to compile lists of 'Reds' and give them exemplary punishments, the first and second generation of the relatives of the victims believed that the local context was the only stage of the political violence. They witnessed, or heard from their parents, instances of local people demanding the execution of particular persons – even some who had been freed by the authorities – and just as importantly, they saw the economic and political benefits that accrued to some of the local instigators of violence. They remembered the quarrels that tore at the social fabric of their society, and they lived through a time when the absolute marginalisation of social pariahs was normalised to the extreme. Many relatives of assassinated Republicans accepted the thesis that the murders were the product of the envies, petty hatreds, greed and *revanchismo* [vindictiveness] that moved sectors of the townsfolk against the other, defeated, sectors.

As part of this 'logic of violence' constructed by the relatives, the assassinated were not random victims of senseless acts of violence. Their names were put on a list because of their political or social activism; or even because they were mistaken as political or social activists when they had nothing to do with politics. In reality they were murdered so that a particular person or family could accede to a job or secure an illegitimate source of wealth.

The responses and discourses of different relatives of both the second and first generation reflected different adaptations to the reality of death and silence. For some, it became important to underline that their deceased relatives had been totally and completely 'clean' of political blemishes – they were not 'Reds'. The stigma that such a label carried with it implied an almost immediate justification of their 'legal' or extra-legal execution. The murder of a 'Red' was not to be blamed on the one who pulled the trigger, but on the Red himself for placing himself outside the bounds of the political body of the nation, threatening the moral order of society and practically 'forcing' the hand of his killer to react by attacking him. Because of this, it was logical that in their effort to underline the dignity and personhood of their murdered loved one, some people preferred to 'misremember' the deceased person's political activism and construe them as devoid of political ideology. In the end, they were murdered because they had become involved in politics unknowingly. They had been misled, misinformed, they had made a fatal mistake. Only then could the relatives say, 'he did nothing: his death was entirely unjustified'. The insidiousness of this construction lies in its equation of political activism and wrongdoing: the relatives who so constructed the victims of the repression had indeed internalised the regime's construction of political activists as inherently evil, genetically flawed, essentially 'othered'.

Other relatives rejected the construction of 'Reds' as 'killable others' by emphasising that their murdered loved one had done nothing wrong – as opposed to, had done nothing, period – and that his or her political activism did not justify their assassination. They were murdered because this or that prominent townsperson was angry at the victim's temerity or pride. They were murdered because they had stirred things up at local level, they had tried to change the conditions of work, they had tried to improve the position of the underdogs; they had faced up to *caciques* and corrupt leaders.

In both these cases – which should be seen as schematic models which in reality are nuanced and sometimes mixed – the victim was an agent in his life and death – whether he or she was indeed politically active, or whether he or she was the object of envy or ill will. The killings were not random – local enmities and struggles framed their execution and logic. But in both cases, the victim was not a 'mere' victim – a bystander faced with the fact of his murder would say – if he was killed, he must have done *something*.

Dead Man Talking: Post-Authoritarian Constructions of Violence and Victims

Thirty-nine years passed between the most egregious massacres of the Second Republic's supporters and the death of the dictator. Five years more went by before democracy was tenuously restored. Within two years of the restoration of democracy, the Socialist party was in power in Spain. But the relatives of the victims, the families that had seen property taken from them, and had had humiliations heaped upon them for years, were still invisible, still silenced, not only during the transition to democracy, but during three consecutive Socialist administrations. Their demands to have the remains of their loved ones exhumed and given proper burial went unheeded, and the frustration of the first generation of relatives increased as they themselves reached old age and feared they would die and never be able to fulfil their duties to their dead fathers and brothers and uncles who lay in unmarked graves. The politicians responded by saying 'it is not the time', or 'we should not reopen the wounds of the past' to people whose present was still an open wound, and for whom the right time could no longer be delayed. Between 1978 and 1981, groups of relatives in fact undertook citizen-led exhumations, despite the lack of archaeological assistance that could have identified the remains of each victim, but the failed coup of 1981 revived old fears and cut even that option short.

It was not until the summer of 2000, after the exhumation of a grave in El Bierzo, in the northern province of León, that the claims of the relatives of the victims of the repression finally crystallised in the public sphere. Santiago Macías and Emilio Silva, the latter the grandson of one of those exhumed at El Bierzo, founded the Asociación para la Recuperación de la Memoria Histórica [Association for the Recovery of Historical Memory; ARMH, Spanish acronym], dedicated to the recovery of the remains of those murdered and concealed in unmarked mass graves during the Spanish Civil War. In a matter of weeks, ARMH expanded like wildfire across the whole country, as chapters were formed in various locales, encouraged by an illustrated report published in the Sunday edition of *El País*, Spain's most important newspaper. That article was followed by a barrage of thousands of letters and e-mails from people around the country asking for guidance in the task of recovering their relative's remains.[6]

Silva and Macías presented a claim before the Working Group on Enforced or Involuntary Disappearances of the United Nations, which in itself became a piece of news of high social and political impact. This generated increasing pressure on the Spanish government to respond – or react – to the demands of the relatives agglutinated in the ARMH, and in the various other organisations dedicated to the same objectives that multiplied throughout the country.

Most importantly, the defeated were suddenly made visible at the societal level, as if indeed 'a large amount of memory floated around; it had not evaporated, even though it had been swept under the rug of history, because prudence, the need to coexist, or fear, had compelled it to be put there'.[7] Different media finally picked up the stories of these people who had been killed, buried in unmarked graves, and then blamed for their own deaths, and the stories of their family members who had lived with the terrible suffering of mourning in silence, often feeling shame for the crime that was committed against them. Local and national radio stations, newspapers and popular texts started creating a counter-hegemonic narrative of the invisible and silenced past. Not only were the stories of the dead occupying these public spaces – those assassinated by Francoists – but the stories of their survivors' vexations, impoverishment, expropriations and exploitation were also made public for the first time. The concept of 'victim' was undergoing a fundamental transformation and broadening. But the acceptance by many of Francoism as a legitimate regime, the still present (though weakened) stigmatisation of the 'Reds' and the long neglect that their assassinations continued to receive under conservative and Socialist administrations alike, revealed that Spanish society had still not absorbed the magnitude of the injustice and the atrocities committed during the 'hot terror' and its aftermath.

In response, many among the movement for the recovery of historic memory have attempted to redefine the victims of Francoist repression from the discourse of the universal principles of *human rights*. Their insistence on the inviolability of the individual's humanity was meant to break the shell of social indifference that did not see the massive assassination of 'Reds' as an attack on the very foundations of Spanish society and human morality. The restoration of democracy made available information and knowledge that were impossible to accede before – especially the knowledge that the military insurgents of 1936 had developed plans of extermination,[8] and that the orchestration of 'lists' of marked individuals had followed orders developed at the top of the regime. This piece of information (new at a general social level, although scholars had been talking about it for some time) has derived from the construction of a counter-hegemonic explanation for the massacres. In this narrative, intra-community tensions and local dynamics did not play an important role in the execution of violence – the blame was on the insurgent government. There is a clear tendency among some studies and associations to insist upon this external origin of the repression, considering local tensions and struggles as irrelevant in the extermination process. If this were the case, the victims were fully, totally and merely victims: their personalities, their actions as members of highly divided communities and the hatred or greed of their neighbours had little to do with their death. Only their political activism, or the perception of the regime about their political activism, singled them out. In this new construction of victimhood, the deceased – their bones now exposed by the exhumation process, handled by the hands of forensic scientists, journalists, family members and members of NGOs and associations – are abstracted from their social–historical context and made malleable Victims. The real and increasingly violent tensions of the Second Republic, as well as the immitigable culpability of the local perpetrators who murdered neighbours and strangers in cold blood and with complete impunity, were left on the wayside of this logic.

The discourse about the victims is re-defined in this new context: by underlining the outside force – the orders of extermination – the innocence of the victim is 'consolidated' in his or her abstraction from a complicated milieu in which good and bad things were happening, in which messy problems and tensions could potentially lead a bystander to say, 'if he was killed, it must have been because of *something*'. The murdered men and women become total victims because their fate was in the hands of a removed entity that did not even know them, an entity that saw in them embodied ideologies and not persons when they were, first and foremost, human beings. But there is a series of problems with this narrative of the victims. First, the grounding of the victim's personhood, and the experience of the relatives who were also surviving victims, is denied the importance that it indeed had and that forms an important part in the relatives' memories about how they lived through the dictatorship. Second, the narrative lets in through the back door the notion that, if indeed the victims had in life been involved in messy political struggles, or had performed unpopular measures at local level, they had 'done something' and were therefore partly to blame for their own assassinations.

In any case, the struggle of the movement for the recovery of historic memory has indeed made it increasingly untenable for people to say out loud that, if a person was killed either by the Francoist regime or in the pacified zones during the war, they probably had *some* guilt. The victims of repression are increasingly understood as such – as victims, and therefore, as unjustifiably victimised.

Victims as Symbolic Capital: Redefinition of Victimhood in Light of 11 March

On 11 March 2004, a terrorist attack on Madrid's urban train system profoundly altered the political and cultural terrain in which the definition of 'victim' was attached to a 'logic of violence'. A notion of a 'victim of absolute innocence' emerged in this incident, as Spanish society poured into the streets to protest and mourn the death of men, women and children who had done nothing other than go on with their everyday, only to be met by an act of extreme violence that cut their lives short. The loss of these individuals was seen as a loss for the universe of Spanish society, and the culprit or culprits – in the immediate aftermath, they were still unknown – carried all the blame.

This representation of victims of armed violence was entirely new in Spain. The 11 March thus inaugurated the social acceptance of the claim to innocence demanded by other victims but never totally obtained. But nothing about the actions or personalities of those who died from the attacks on the trains of Madrid could explain these deaths to their relatives, who were therefore seen to suffer the ultimate injustice. Entirely removed from their assassins, nothing about their ethnicity, nationality, social class, religious affiliation or political ideology justified their death even to the attackers. Inserted in the global context marked by The War on Terror, these were the most innocent victims of twentieth-century Spain.

For days, Spanish newspapers printed small biographies of each of the victims in an exercise of humanisation and individualisation that contributed to validating the feeling of global loss felt by society for each of these lives. From this, let us say, purification of the concept of 'victim', the other victims of armed 'political' violence in Spain are being imbued with newfound humanity – the victims of Francoist repression and the victims of the Basque terrorist separatist organisation ETA – as evidenced in their treatment in the general press.

ETA and Francoism: Similar Exclusion and Similar Experiences of Victimhood

Somewhat paradoxically, given its early anti-Francoist politics, ETA and the Francoists operated in similar ways, and produced similar social processes of victimhood. Both the Francoists and ETA defined their victims *a priori* as outside the national body politic, and thus *othered*, proceeded to 'eliminate' them in order to protect and maintain the purity of those who remain inside, who, unlike 'those others', are social persons. Francoists applied the ultimate ostracism – assassination – to those labelled 'Reds' and as such, not true Spaniards, while ETA ostracises those who are declared as not deserving to belong to the Basque people.

The victims of ETA, like the victims of Francoism, tend to be paradoxically inscribed with a degree of guilt – a notion that, if they were not randomly chosen, they must have some responsibility or play some part in the political universe that made ETA take their lives. Many testimonies of relatives of those murdered by the terrorist organisation affirm that they were treated as if they were a plague, guilty of *something*. More than receiving the solidarity of their neighbours, they were treated with suspicion. In a similar vein, some relatives of Francoist victims claimed that other family members distanced themselves, as if they feared they would somehow become 'contaminated' by their condition of *desafectos al regimen* [dissidents]. Blame was not entirely in the hands of the killers.

Significant sectors of Spanish society likewise believed that political militancy or belonging to police or military corps explained – and partly justified – the death of most of these victims of ETA. The logic of their deaths was therefore similar to the logic and construction of victims and violence of Francoism. Moreover, ETA's victims were mediated before society by their political affiliation to the parties and organisations that 'patrimonialised' their deaths as 'one of theirs', and not a member of Spanish society as a whole.

The Victims of Armed Violence as Symbolic Capital

From the total innocence of the victims of 3–11 emerges a symbolic capital that not only redefines the concept of victim, and therefore affects the victims of Francoism and their relatives as well as ETA's victims. It charges the political terrain with meanings embodied by the 'victims' that go beyond themselves and, in fact, condense visions of the past and the future that also inform ideas about the Spanish nation.

When the attack of 11 March took place, the governing party – the conservative Popular Party (PP) – clung to the idea that ETA was the culprit. The PP government had evident political interests in this version – general elections were about to take place in three days, and the PP had taken onto itself the mantle of Spain's own domestic 'war on terror' and ETA was the main enemy. Such a shocking attack by ETA made the PP the evident choice on the ballot. But immediately after the attacks, Spanish society clamoured for a thorough and objective investigation into the incident, as links to Islamic terrorism became apparent. The PP's refusal to admit that indeed evidence pointed away from ETA was evidently tied to the fact that Spanish society had rejected the country's entry into the war on Iraq, and would now perceive the terrorist attack as indirectly caused by the PP's illegitimate entry into the war.

The Socialist Party [Partido Socialista Obrero Español, PSOE], on the other hand, had insisted from the beginning, along with other parties and organised elements of civil society, that the victims and the relatives of the victims had a right to know what was being investigated and what had actually taken place. They had also previously made electoral promises related to removing Spain immediately from the war, and related to the fully fledged support of the Movement for the Recovery of Historic Memory and the relatives of Francoism's victims. When, three days after 11 March, the PSOE found itself in control of the government, they had become the defenders of the victims of 11 March and the defenders of Francoism's victims. The symbolic capital that this accrued to them as managers of the pain and memory of these groups of innocent victims was so significant that the opposition party, the PP, attempted to gain some of this capital itself.

The 11 March victims increasingly embodied the refusal of the PP to take into account the largest peaceful demostration in contemporary Spanish history;[9] and then, their incapacity to admit the truth about a major incident because of vested electoral interests. They embodied, therefore, a commitment to the democratic process and a fundamental respect for the right to life beyond political or religious ideologies. Having led Spain to become part of the coalition of the War on Terror, the PP sought to capitalise on these Spanish victims of this same war, not only to deflect their own blame, but to impede the electoral and political benefits accruing to the PSOE as the governing party that successfully managed the issues suffered by the victims of 11 March. After the intervention of Pilar Manjón before the National Chamber of Deputies,[10] president of the Asociación 11-M Afectados de Terrorismo, the Regional Government of Madrid, controlled by the PP, created a parallel association of victims called the Asociación de Ayuda a las Víctimas del 11-M to counteract the support that they perceived accrued to the government in its successful management of the victims' situation. This association has declared through its president its dissidence from the original group based on the politicisation of that group, and its desire to remain independent from the government and to criticise what it perceives to be unnecessary measures such as the creation of a Commissioner of Victims that responds to all 'categories' of victims of armed violence in the country.

On the other hand before 11 March, the symbolic capital of the only officially recognised group of victims of armed violence – ETA's victims – had been politicised by all the parties concerned. But insofar as the PP had taken the mantle of Spanish national security and an exclusivist Spanish nationalism reminiscent of Francoism that left little room for 'separatist' ideologies, ETA's victims are particularly meaningful. The PP's capture of one of the most important organisations of victims, the Association of Victims of Terrorism, is evident in the fact that José María Aznar was named honorary president of the association, and in the various public statements that place AVT in conflict with other victims' associations, especially Pilar Manjón's.

Finally, another very recent process that affects the visibility of all victims and their use as capital was the so-called (failed) *permanent ceasefire*, declared by ETA (from 22 March 2006 to 30 December 2006). All political speeches regarding the process of peace began with a message of support and solidarity with ETA's victims, without the usual labelling of the victim's political affiliation or ideological affinity. This shift from the partisan patrimony that, until recently, characterised the treatment accorded the victims of ETA is arguably informed by the new terrain of innocent victimhood and global social loss initiated by the attacks of the 11 March. A process of peace negotiation with ETA became the road assumed by the PSOE-led government, which underlined the need for reconciliation with justice, or truth, or both – while the PP operated from a logic of 'defeat' as the only way to maintain society and the nation. A game of mirrors juxtaposes the symbolic meanings embedded in the victims of Francoism and ETA for the PP: for the former, reconciliation is prescribed and imposed without any redress, reparations or recognition; for the latter, 'negotiation' with terrorists implies a reconciliation that the victims should in no way accept, for it would demean the death of their loved ones. In this way, the PP was the only party to vote against a resolution passed in the Chamber of Deputies that named 2006 as the Year of Memory, in honour of the 75 years of the proclamation of the Republic and to commemorate the 70 years after the start of the Civil War. A spokesperson of the PP said that the year should be declared the 'Year of Concord', underlining the divisiveness that is rekindled by 'memory'.

Conclusions

Perhaps two normative points regarding scholars' responsibility in the transformation of Spanish historic memory and the construction of true social reconciliation are the best way to conclude this paper. First, in order to promote the respect that is indispensable for a truly integrative social and historical interpretation of the conflicts of the past, it is necessary to reflect on the experience and suffering of the Civil War and the repression associated with it. Confronting the conflicts that led to and that were unleashed by the repression from an ideological standpoint does not bring us closer to a solution on how to negotiate this traumatic past. To break the perpetual reproduction of an exclusivist history of the victors that became hegemonic memory that left no room for dissidence or difference, we must document and listen to people's testimonies and experiences[11]. It is necessary to connect emotional, personal and communal experiences with the wider national context to understand how central orders or programmes intermingled with local spheres to produce diverse and particular types of violence.[12]

Second, we must understand that those 'Reds' (and Francoists) assassinated far from the battle field during the Civil War were indeed innocent: their assassination without due process was entirely unjustified. Their loss was a loss for all of Spanish society, not only for 'the Republic', the party or the family they belonged to. Through their adherence to the principles of the Universal Declaration of Human Rights, the Movement for the Recovery of Historic Memory had already touched on this new significance of innocence, victimhood and violence. But they had not entirely succeeded, and scholarly resarch can provide stronger foundations for the construction of new meanings. Spanish society and Spanish political organisations must learn that the loss of civilian life in the hands of political criminals, both in the past and the present, has negatively affected all Spanish national society. This injustice should not be 'capitalised' for electoral or political purposes through the celebration of partisan 'lists of martyrs.' If we can do this, we will have taken an important step as a mature democratic society in the construction of a truly polyphonic and integrative society.

Translation: Yesenia Pumarada Cruz

Notes

1. Julián Casanova, "Una dictadura de cuarenta años," in Julián Casanova (coord.), *Morir, matar, sobrevivir: La violencia en la dictadura de Franco* (Barcelona: Crítica, 2002), pp.8 and 19 and 20. Julián Casanova, "Rebelión y revolución," in Santos Juliá (coord.), *Víctimas de la guerra civil* (Madrid: Temas de Hoy, 1999); Julián Casanova, "La historia que nos cuenta TVE," *El País*, 3 April 2005.
2. Stanley Payne, in *Los militares y la política en la España contemporánea* (Madrid: Sarpe, 1986), pp.438–9, describes some claims for the unjustified assassinations of these lower-class people.
3. Emilio Mola Vidal, *Obras completas* (Valladolid: Librería Santarem, 1940).
4. See the books of Stanley Payne, *Politics and the Military in Modern Spain* (Stanford, CA: Stanford University Press, 1967); *Spain's First Democracy. The Second Republic, 1931–1936* (Madison, WI: Wisconsin University Press, 1993); *The Spanish Civil War, the Soviet Union, and Communism* (New Haven, CT: Yale University Press, 2004); *The Collapse of the Spanish Republic, 1933–1936: Origins of the Civil War* (New Haven, CT: Yale University Press, 2006).
5. Ignacio Fernández de Mata, "The "Logics" of Violence and Franco's Mass Graves. An Ethnohistorical Approach", *International Journal of the Humanities*, 2/3 (2006), pp.2527–35.
6. Emilio Silva and Santiago Macías, *Las fosas de Franco. Los republicanos que el dictador dejó en las cunetas* (Madrid: Temas de Hoy, 2003). The ARMH is not the only association concern with *historic memory*. Other organizations include: Archivo Guerra Civil y Exilio, AGE; Asociación de Familiares y Amigos de Represaliados de la II República por el Franquismo; Asociación de Amigos de la Fosa de Oviedo; and Foro por la Memoria. However, the impact of the ARMH in the Spanish society has made it the main protagonist of the present process.
7. Iñaki Gabilondo, "Prólogo. Generosidad," in Carlos Elordi (ed.) *Los años difíciles* (Madrid: Suma de Letras, 2003).
8. Julián Casanova (coord.), Francisco Espinosa, Conxita Mir and Francisco Moreno Gómez, *Morir, matar, sobrevivir. La violencia en la dictadura de Franco* (Barcelona: Crítica, 2002). Francisco Espinosa, *La columna de la muerte: el avance del ejército franquista de Sevilla a Badajoz* (Barcelona: Crítica, 2003); Francisco Espinosa, *Contra el olvido: historia y memoria de la guerra civil* (Barcelona: Crítica, 2006).
9. 15 March 2003.
10. 15 December 2004.
11. Walter Benjamín, "Tesis de filosofía de la historia," in Walter Benjamin, *Ensayos escogidos* (Buenos Aires: Editorial Sur, 1967). See Thesis 9.
12. Philippe Bourgois, "The Continuum of Violence in War and Peace: Post-Cold War Lessons from El Salvador," *Ethnography*, 2/1 (2001), pp.5–34; Veena Das, Arthur Kleinman, Mamphele Ramphele and Pamela Reynolds (eds), *Violence and Subjectivity* (Berkeley, CA: University of California Press,

2000); Nancy Scheper-Hughes, "Coming to Our Senses. Anthropology and Genocide," in Alexander Laban Hinton (ed.), *Annihilating Difference: The Anthropology of Genocide* (Berkeley, CA: University of California Press, 2002), pp.348–81; Nancy Scheper-Hughes and Philippe Bourgois, "Introduction: Making Sense of Violence", in Nancy Scheper-Hughes and Philippe Bourgois (eds.) *Violence in War and Peace. An Anthology* (Malden: Blackwell, 2004).

The Legacy of the Authoritarian Past in Portugal's Democratisation, 1974–6

ANTÓNIO COSTA PINTO

Democratic transitions challenge both the social elite and society as a whole to face up to the legacy of dictatorial regimes; however, the literature on regime change has paid little attention to the question of how the type of transition may determine the extent of the elimination or retention of authoritarian legacies. In a pioneering effort to understand the links between authoritarian legacies and the 'quality' of consolidated democracy, Katherine Hite and Leonardo Morlino argue that the three key variables are: the durability of the previous authoritarian regime; the institutional innovation of that regime; and the mode of transition. In other words,

> the more durable and institutionally innovative the authoritarian regime, the greater the potential influence of authoritarian legacies. The more privileged the authoritarian incumbents in the mode of transition from authoritarian rule, the greater the potential influence of authoritarian legacies.[1]

Changes of regime oblige new authorities to come to terms with the legacy of the past, and democratic transitions have been fertile ground for attitudes that are more or less radical in relation to the elimination of authoritarian legacies, and, in particular, the political punishment of the elites and dissolution of the institutions with which they are associated.[2] Samuel Huntington argues that the emergence, or non-emergence, of 'transitional justice' is less a moral question, and more one relating to the 'distribution of power during and after the transition'.[3] In simple terms, 'only in those states where political authority radically collapsed and was replaced by an opposition did the possibility of prosecution present itself'.[4] In transitions by reform, in which the authoritarian elite is a powerful partner in the transitional process, the scope for the introduction of retributive measures is limited. Huntington was writing in 1990, when the transitions in central and eastern Europe were only just beginning and in many cases the calls for punishment and reparations continued, even in the negotiated transitions that had already resulted in consolidated democracies, in apparent counter-examples to his assumptions.[5]

However, when we take an overall view of the democratic transitions of the end of the twentieth century, if we differentiate between transitional and retroactive justice *tout court*, we see that Huntington was correct, since we are dealing with the former, and not the latter. That is to say: when 'proceedings begin shortly after the transition and come to end within, say, five years', we are referring to what Elster calls 'immediate transitional justice'.[6] We are dealing with a dimension of regime change: the processes of retribution as a dynamic element of democratic transition. Accountability is central to the very definition of democracy and new processes can be unleashed in any post-authoritarian democracy, even although the time dimension tends to attenuate the retributive pressures, particularly when there has already been a degree of retribution during the initial phase of democratisation. On the other hand, the factors that can unleash retroactive justice processes after the transitions may already have another much larger set of factors being, for example, one more weapon of party conflict, as was the case in some central European countries in which there are examples of the successful democratic and electoral re-conversion of former communist parties.[7]

During their initial phase, almost all democratisation processes create 'retributive emotions' that are independent of the type of transition.[8] In the case of right-wing authoritarian regimes, the criminalisation of a section of the elite, and the dissolution of the repressive institutions, constitutes part of the political programme of the clandestine opposition parties. Even in the Spanish case, which is a paradigmatic example of a 'consensual decision to ignore the past', these demands were present. In 'post-totalitarian' regimes (to use Linz's term[9]), the pressures for criminalisation were present from the very earliest moments of the transitions.[10] On the other hand, even when dealing with the majority of cases of elite-driven processes, where public opinion data exists, it tends to show that the elites were 'meeting a societal demand'.[11] Its successful implementation depends on the type of transition.

The type of dictatorial regime is vitally important for determining the extent of success of regime change, and for the legacies for a successful democratic consolidation.[12] However, even over the long term there is a positive correlation between the degree of repressive violence and the persistence of 'retributive emotions'; the conduct of the old regime does not explain the extent and degree of these emotions after its fall. Some authors suggest that those dictatorial regimes with the most 'limited pluralism', and which have a more discrete record of repression during their final years (for example, Portugal, Hungary, Poland), would face little pressure for retribution. However, the examples of Southern Europe, Latin

America and Central Europe do not confirm this hypothesis, because such pressures were present even in these cases.[13] We also argue that the nature of the transition is superimposed on the nature of the authoritarian regime, and the extent of its record of 'administrative massacres' in the appearance of a transitional justice.[14]

In this respect, the Portuguese transition is a particularly interesting case because of the authoritarian regime's longevity and the *ruptura* [rupture] nature of its regime change, with the collapse of the New State on 25 April 1974. Moreover, because Portugal was the first of the so-called 'third-wave' of democratic transitions, there were few models available to inspire it, and none to directly influence it. Portugal was, as Nancy Bermeo has claimed, an example of 'democracy after war',[15] in which the military played a determining role in the downfall of the dictatorship, opening a swift and important state crisis during the initial phase of the transition.

The comparative literature on transitions has always incorporated the Portuguese case. However, some of its characteristics, particularly the role of the military, the crisis of the state and the dynamics of the social movements, constitute elements that are difficult to integrate into the comparative analysis of democratisation.[16] As Linz and Stepan have noted: 'we all too often tend to see [Portugal] in the framework set by later transitions processes',[17] forgetting the greater degree of uncertainty and the 'extreme conflict path'[18] of a regime change that, according to some authors, 'was not a conscious transition to democracy'.[19] In fact, one of the limitations of some analyses of Portugal's transition is their assumption of finality, based on the subsequent consolidation. This assumption underestimates both the state crises and the 'revolutionary critical juncture' of the transition. The author of one of the best studies of political mobilisation and collective action in Portugal during the 1970s notes the methodological difficulties involved in 'assimilating *a priori* the State crisis with the transition to democracy', but it is precisely this that represents the challenge for any analysis of Portuguese democratisation.[20]

The nature of the Portuguese dictatorship tells us little about the nature of the country's transition to democracy. Salazarism was close to Linz's ideal-type of authoritarian regime:[21] it was a regime that survived the 'fascist era', and was not too dissimilar in nature from the final phase of neighbouring Spain's Franco regime, despite its single party being weaker, and its 'limited pluralism' greater.[22] In 1968, Salazar was replaced by Marcelo Caetano, who initiated a limited and timid regime 'liberalisation' that was swiftly halted by the worsening colonial war in Angola. The inability of Salazar's successor to resolve some of the dilemmas caused by the war provoked the outbreak of a *coup d'etat* in April 1974. This was a 'non-hierarchical' military coup, which had a political programme that promoted democratisation and decolonisation.

Unlike Spain's *ruptura pactada* [negotiated rupture], Portugal underwent a transition without negotiations or pacts between the dictatorial elite and opposition forces. However, there is no direct causal link between this marked discontinuity and the subsequent process of radicalisation: other transitions by rupture did not cause comparable crises of the state.[23] As we will show below, the simultaneous character of the democratisation and decolonisation processes was one factor in the crisis, while the latter was the main reason for the conflict that broke out in the immediate wake of the regime's collapse between some conservative generals and the Movimento das Forças Armadas (MFA, Armed Forces' Movement), which had planned and executed the coup. This conflict was at the root of the military's generalised intervention in political life following the dictatorship's overthrow. The rapid emergence of transgressive collective action can be explained by this crisis, although it was not these that provoked the State crisis.

The institutionalisation of the MFA transformed it into the dominant force behind the provisional governments. The 'interweaving of the MFA in the State's structures' and its emergence as an authority for regulating conflicts, which substituted, dispersed and paralysed the classic mechanisms of legitimate State repression, prevented 'the re-composition of the State apparatus'.[24] This was the main factor explaining why, in the Portuguese case, the movement for the dissolution of institutions and purges exceeded those of classic purges in transitions by rupture and, in many cases, came to be a component of the transgressing social movements.[25]

Below we will argue that the nature of the Portuguese transition, and the consequent state crises, created a 'window of opportunity' in which the 'reaction to the past' was much stronger in Portugal than in the other Southern European transitions.[26] The transition's powerful dynamic (state crises and social movements) served to constitute a legacy for the consolidation of democracy, in itself.[27] In other words, we will observe how the nature of Portugal's transition affected the legacy of authoritarianism, superseding and transmuting its impact on Portugal's democracy.

The Nature Of Portugal's Transition To Democracy

The Portuguese military coup of 25 April 1974 was the beginning of democratic transition in southern Europe.[28] Unshackled by international pro-democratising forces and occurring in the midst of the Cold War, the coup led to a severe crisis of the state that was aggravated by the simultaneous processes of transition to democracy and decolonisation of what was the last European colonial empire.

The singularity of the collapse of the dictatorship resides in the nature of military intervention by the captains, a rare if not unique case in the twentieth century.[29] The war on three fronts that was being waged by the regime in Angola, Mozambique and Guinea-Bissau from 1961 onwards made them protagonists in the country's political transformation.[30]

The prior existence of a semi-legal and clandestine opposition to Salazarism, although disconnected from the military officers that led the coup, was of crucial importance. It constituted a political option legitimated by the struggle against dictatorship. The replacement of Salazar by Marcello Caetano in 1968 for health reasons gave rise to a two-year liberalisation process, and although it was cut short, it allowed for the consolidation of a 'liberal wing' of dissidents opposed to the dictatorship. The creation of the Sociedade para o Desenvolvimento Económico e Social (SEDES – Society for Economic and Social Development) in 1970 further consolidated this dissident 'liberal wing'.[31] Thus, despite the surprising action of the military, there were alternative elites who had close connections with various sectors of civil society, and who were ready to play a leading political role in the democratisation process.

The 'revolutionary period' between 1974 and 1975 was the most complex phase of the transition if one considers the transition as the, 'fluid and uncertain period in which democratic structures are emerging', but in which it is still unclear what kind of regime is to be established.[32] During these two years powerful tensions emerged within Portuguese society, which began to subside in 1976, when a new constitution was approved and the first legislative and presidential elections were held. The mobilisation of diverse anti-dictatorial forces was crucial in the first days after the coup of 1974. It was especially important in the immediate dissolution of the most notorious institutions of the New State, as well as in the occupation of various unions, corporatist organisations and municipalities. Some of the military elite, the leaders of some interest groups and a part of the first provisional government sought the rapid establishment of a presidential democratic regime immediately following the convocation of elections.

The disagreements concerning the nature of decolonisation, which was the initial driving force behind the conflict between the captains who had led the coup and General Spínola and other conservative generals, led to the emergence of the MFA as a political force. This subsequently opened a space for social and political mobilisation that exacerbated the crisis of the state, and which can perhaps explain why the moderate elites were incapable of directing, 'from above', the rapid insitutionalisation of democracy. Many analyses of the transition rightly emphasise the powerful 'revitalisation of civil society' as a factor leading to the process of radicalisation. As Philippe Schmitter notes: 'Portugal experienced one of the most intense and widespread mobilisation experiences of any of the neo-democracies'.[33] It is important to note, however, that this mobilisation developed in parallel with and in the presence of this protective cover: indeed, it is difficult to imagine this mobilisation developing otherwise.

Initiatives of a symbolic rupture with the past began to evolve soon after April 1974, culminating in the rapid and multi-directional *saneamentos* [purges]. Following a quick decision to remove the more visible members of the dictatorial political elite and some conservative military officers, the purge movement began to affect the civil service and the private sector. It became increasingly radical, affecting the lower ranks of the regime bureaucracy, albeit unevenly. There were immediate calls for the agents of the political police and of other repressive bodies to be brought to justice.[34] Already in May 1974, the purge was the third demand of a group of 149 labour disputes, and it remained on the top of the list of demands made by workers and strikers throughout the following year.[35]

It was at this time that the parties that were to represent the Right and centre-Right, the Centro Democrático Social (CDS – Social Democratic Centre) and the Partido Popular Democrático (PPD – Popular Democratic Party), were formed.[36] The formation and legalisation of political parties to represent the electorate of the centre-Right and Right, the PPD and the CDS, pointed in this direction. A great effort was made to exclude from these parties any persons associated with the New State and find leaders with democratic credentials. Indeed, the CDS, which integrated sectors of Portuguese society that espoused conservative authoritarian values, was on the verge of being declared illegal up until the first elections for the Constituent Assembly on 25 April 1975.

The overthrow of General Spínola along with the MFA's shift to the Left and the implementation of agrarian reforms and nationalisation of large economic groups were symbols and motors of an ever worsening state crisis that was sustaining powerful social movements. The MFA's decision to respect the electoral calendar was a significant factor in the founding legitimisation of the democratic regime, and the realisation of these elections as scheduled greatly enhanced the position of the moderate political parties.

It is too simplistic to consider the 'hot summer' of 1975 simply as an attempt by the Partido Comunista Português (PCP – Portuguese Communist Party) to impose a new dictatorship with the support of the Soviet Union. Naturally, the democratic political elite made much of this argument in its founding discourse, but this does not provide a full explanation of events. The situation was more complex: conflict was fed by the development of strong grass roots political organisations such as the workers' commissions, the growing challenge posed by the extreme Left during the crisis, and its influence within the military. At the same time extreme left-wing journalists 'occupied' the Catholic radio station, Rádio Renascença and the newspaper *República* [Republic], which up until then had been the mouthpiece of the moderate Left, and houses, shops and factories were occupied throughout Lisbon.[37] The importance of internal divisions within the armed forces in driving these events forward means that they cannot be explained as part of a 'programmed conspiracy'.

Portuguese society began to polarise, with the emergence of an anti-revolutionary (and anti-communist) movement in the north of the country.[38] It was in this context of increasing mobilisation, on 25 November 1975, that moderate MFA officers organised a successful counter coup that toppled the radicals. The Partido Socialista (PS – Socialist Party) and the Partido Social Democrática (PSD – Social Democratic Party) backed the moderates, leading mobilisations in Lisbon and Oporto. In the provinces to the north of the River Tagus, the hierarchy of the Catholic Church and local notables supported parish-level mobilisations, with the local military authorities remaining neutral and/or with them being complicit in the activities. As elements of the extreme Right and Right, military officers and civilians alike began to mobilise, the anti-Left offensive became violent. Attacks were made on the offices of the PCP, the extreme Left and associated unions, and there emerged right-wing terrorist organisations, the Movimento Democrático para a Liberação de Portugal (MDLP – Democratic Movement for the Liberation of Portugal), and the Exército para a Liberação de Portugal (ELP – Portuguese Liberation Army).[39]

During 1974–5, Portugal experienced significant foreign intervention that influenced the formation of political parties, unions and interest organisations, as well as shaping the anti-Left strategy that evolved over the 'hot summer' of 1975. The Portuguese case was a divisive issue in international organisations, within the North Atlantic Treaty Organisation (NATO) and the European Economic Community (EEC), affecting relations between these two organisations and the Socialist Bloc countries led by the Soviet Union. All the evidence makes it clear that in 1974–5 Portugal was an issue of 'international relevance'.

Caught by surprise by the coup, the international community – and the United States in particular – concentrated on supporting democratic political forces of the centre-Left and centre-Right in the capital, as well as on intervening in the rapid process of de-colonisation, particularly in Angola.[40] The same post-war methods deployed to deal with Italy were used in the Portuguese case. The moderate political parties were financed by the U.S. administration, which together with the international organisations of the European 'political families' – these often mediating the U.S. role – also supported the training of party cadres.[41] However, the impact of foreign aid was limited: it was drowned out by the powerful political and social mobilisation led by the Left, an economy strongly marked by a large nationalised sector, as well as capital flight and the actual flight of members of the economic elite from the country. Although domestic political factors played a critical role in enabling both the triumph of moderate civilian forces and the final withdrawal of the military from the political arena, international support was more important than the early literature on the transition suggests.

The nature of the transition, and especially the state crisis that this unleashed, is essential for explaining some of its more radical characteristics, as well as some of the attitudes with respect to the country's authoritarian past during this period. Both flowed together into a double legacy for the consolidation of democracy.

Settling Accounts with the Dictatorship: Portuguese 'Transitional Justice'

Only a few months after the coup, Portuguese transitional justice displayed all the contradictory faces of an attempt to punish both the authoritarian elites and the agents of, and collaborators in, the dictatorship's repression. The second wave of score settling reached the economic and entrepreneurial elites. Most of the actual and symbolic punitive measures against the most visible and better known collaborators took place between 1974 and 1975, before the establishment of the new legitimated democratic institutions. This was a period marked by the crisis of the state, powerful social movements and military intervention that shaped social attitudes concerning the punishment of those associated with the old regime, and in which the judiciary played almost no role.

The non-hierarchical nature of the coup, with the almost immediate intervention of the democratic elite and popular mobilisation, accentuated both the real and the symbolic break with the past. The brief resistance offered by those forces most associated with the dictatorship's repression, such as the political police and the anti-communist militia (the Legião Portuguesa [LP – Portuguese Legion]), and the imprisonment of many of the former organisation's members were significant elements driving the political movement for their criminalisation.

The first measures implemented by General Spínola's Junta da Salvação Nacional (JSN – National Salvation Junta), which was in full accordance with the MFA Programme, provided for a minimal and swift purge of the armed forces. Members of the former regime who wished to join Marcello Caetano were immediately deported to Madeira, from where they mostly continued on to exile in Brazil. In this way, the new government avoided having to respond to popular demands that the former leaders face criminal trials in Portugal. Both the political police and the anti-communist LP, which had attempted to resist the April coup, were immediately disarmed, with some of their leaders being placed in custody. The single party and the official youth organisation were, along with many of the regime's institutions, closed down. The MFA proposed that 60 generals, most of whom had publicly declared their support for Marcello Caetano on the eve of his overthrow, should be placed on the reserve.

The main demand, which was nearly unanimous, was to ensure criminal trials of certain members of the political police. These demands were made as a consequence of the military coup's own dynamics and the surrounding of the political police's headquarters in Lisbon, which resulted in the surrender and arrest of many of the agents who had sought refuge in the building. Some attempts made were to ensure the survival of the political police in the colonies, given the collaboration between them and the armed forces. Nevertheless, the organisation was eventually abolished. Many former agents remained prisoners, whilst others fled the country within days of the coup.

It did not take long for the new authorities to create the Comissão de Extinção da PIDE-DGS, MP e LP (CEPML – Commission for the Abolition of the Political Police, Portuguese Legion and Portuguese Youth), which was led by military officers. This body began arresting people who had acted as informants for the previous regime's political police. The life of this commission was agitated: there were frequent denunciations of political manipulation by extreme left-wing groups and the PCP. The role of the commission was to prepare criminal proceedings of the trial of former police agents and to cooperate with other purge institutions, given its monopolistic access to the about 3 million files kept on individual citizens. In July 1975, Constitutional Law 8/75 provided for the trial by military tribunal of members of the political police, as well as those government officials directly responsible for repression on the basis of a 'revolutionary legitimacy' referred to in the preamble. The law also provided sentences of 2–12 years, and no statute of limitations was established for criminal proceedings.[42] At local level, the Movimento Democrático Português (MDP – Portuguese Democratic Movement), a front organisation with links to the PCP, took over local posts at the city council level and removed former regime leaders from their posts. Several of the authoritarian regime's union organisations were taken over by the workers, who removed the former leaders from their positions.

The first public statements by left-wing political parties were generally quite cautious regarding the issue of purges, with the PS and the PCP both issuing moderate statements. The first purges were spontaneous, with strikers calling for the removal of regime supporters within the business community. Some professors and bureaucrats in the universities of Lisbon and Coimbra, who had collaborated with the former regime, were almost immediately denied access to their faculties by student associations.

In response to these movements, the provisional government promulgated the first regulations on public administration purges. Two months after the fall of the old regime, the Inter-ministerial Comissão Inter-Ministerial de Saneamento e Reclassificação (CIMSR – Purge and Reclassification Commission) was created. It answered directly to the Council of Ministers and was charged with coordinating existing purge commissions or with creating new ones to cover all the ministries. Decree Law 277, dated 25 June 1974, charged it with the scrutiny of behaviour that 'contradicted the post-25 April 1974 established order'.[43] These commissions remained active until 1976, and the legislation governing them was revised several times in order to keep up with the radicalisation of the political situation. Decree Law 123 of 11 March 1975 already referred to the former regime as 'fascist', and threatened to purge the civil service for acts committed during the dictatorship.[44] That same month, when General Spínola fled the country, a widespread anti-capitalist sentiment emerged, resulting in a renewed wave of purges. In February 1975, official reports on the purge process stated that approximately 12,000 people had, legally or illegally, been either removed from their posts or suspended.[45] It is estimated that, between March and November 1975, the number of removals and suspensions must have increased significantly (see Table 1).

Various organisations were involved in the purge process. Aside from the measures adopted by the JSN and the MFA immediately after the coup, the PCP and the small but influential parties of the extreme Left were the main actors involved. Purge movements in the private sector, and even in the state bureaucracy, often escaped party political control. The establishment of *comissões de*

Table 1. Elites and forms of punishment

Elite	Punishment	Formal agent
Political, military, administrative	Administrative purges	Governmental and official commissions
Police (repressive) (PIDE-DGS)	Trial and administrative purges	Military tribunal and official commissions
Economic and entrepreneurial	Purges, workplace occupations, state intervention, nationalisation	Workers' commissions and government commissions

saneamento [purge commissions] within the public administration was approved by the first provisional governments, which included representatives of the PCP, PS and PSD. These commissions sought to establish a legal framework for many of the dismissals that were taking place as a result of the purges.

The *comissões de trabalhadores* [workers' commissions] often called for purges. These were established independently of the unions within businesses, and the PCP shared their control with the parties of the extreme Left. The commissions implemented the great majority of 'wild' purges, which the PCP often did not control.

Generally speaking, the purge process was not governed by a clear strategy and revealed no coherent pattern, varying greatly from sector to sector. The concept of 'collaborator' also shifted during the pre-constitutional period. In 1974, the first purges were limited by a strict definition of collaborator. By 1975 various types of authoritarian attitudes among the industrial and entrepreneurial elite were considered to be associated with the former regime.

The Armed Forces

For obvious reasons, the first institution to undergo a purge process was the military. Immediately after the coup, the MFA handed General Spínola the names of the 60 generals who had pledged their allegiance to the authoritarian regime, and who were subsequently placed on the reserve by the JSN. The purge of the armed forces was part of the MFA's political programme and, against the wishes of General Spínola, the process widened to affect a greater number of officers. The first list comprised persons who were deemed to have given political support to Marcello Caetano in a political ceremony in March 1974, and who had stood against the then clandestine MFA and generals Spínola and Costa Gomes.

In the months that followed the 1974 coup, special military commissions administered the purges demanded by the MFA. By October 1974, 103 naval officers had been removed from active service and placed in the reserves.[46] By the end of the year, 300 officers of all ranks, and from all three services, had been removed from active duty. Incompetence became the official criteria for removal, as it became impossible to sustain political criteria such as 'collaboration with the old regime', given that the whole defence establishment had collaborated with the New State during the colonial war.[47]

When General Spínola went into exile following the attempted coup of March 1975, the purge movement was reinforced, and the majority of the officers working with him were removed from their posts. The purges also affected the Guarda Nacional Republicana (GNR – National Republican Guard), Portugal's militarised police force. The Council of the Revolution, the MFA's supreme body, issued Decree Law 147C of 21 March 1975, which stated that any officers who did not 'obey the principles espoused by the MFA' would be placed in the reserve.[48]

With the consolidation of democracy, and as a result of the profusion of military movements during the transitional period, more officers were removed from the active list or subjected to processes that removed them from the armed forces and forced them into exile. Following the victory of the moderates within the MFA, those officers who had been associated with revolutionary left-wing movements, or with the Communist Party, were dismissed. Sympathisers of these parties within the armed forces were removed from their posts, while others went into exile in Angola and Mozambique, which were by that time governed by socialist regimes. After the dissolution of the Council of the Revolution, some MFA leaders were also forced to leave the armed forces, although many were reintegrated – only to be immediately relegated to the reserves as a consequence of the extremely drawn-out judicial processes that continued into the 1990s.

The military was the institution where the break with the past was clearest.[49] A new generation quickly rose to the top ranks of the armed forces as the old elite associated with the New State had been forced to retire. The institutionalisation of democracy in Portugal therefore entailed an important change in the lives of military officers, and it was here that the impact of the transition was most sharply felt.

Purging the Civil Service

The first legislation stated that civil servants could be purged for three reasons: non-democratic behaviour in the course of duty after the coup; inability to adapt to the new democratic regime; and incompetence. The minimum punishment was transferral to another post, whilst the maximum was dismissal.[50] Maximum penalties were applied according to priorities that were later defined by the government: members of the dictatorship's governmental elite; political police collaborators; leading members of either the MP, the LP or the single party; and heads of the dictatorship's censorship board.[51] The purge process was directed by the various commissions and presented to the CIMSR, which ratified the penalty to be applied, in each case implemented by the head of the relevant ministry. As a result of the protests from the trade unions and commission members about the indecision, the slow pace and bureaucratic nature of the purges, new legislation was introduced in March 1975. The new law provided for purges that were based on individual political behaviour prior to the fall of the authoritarian regime.

It is difficult to determine how the purges affected the state bureaucracy on a quantitative level. The process evolved differently from ministry to ministry, and depended on the amount of pressure exerted by the trade unions and the limits imposed by the legislation. By the end of 1974, eight months after the coup, about 4300 public servants had been subjected to a purge process.[52] According to the global analysis made by the commission coordinating the process, the action of the various ministerial commissions was very uneven, and depended upon the party to which the minister belonged and the degree of public opinion and trade union pressure.

One of the least affected was the Ministry of Justice, particularly magistrates and the political courts of the dictatorship (the 'plenary courts'). A large part of the moderate Left elite associated with the PS was made up of lawyers who had participated in the New State's political trials, either as the accused or as lawyers defending communist activists. At the same time, the Salazarist elite included a large number of law professors, and the regime had always obsessively attempted to legitimate its acts in juridical terms.[53] Both these elements would lead one to believe that pressure to prosecute the legal elite could be high, but this was not the case. Institutional factors, and the moderation of socialist leaders, were important factors counteracting the desire to purge the legal profession and the Ministry of Justice.

Additional obstacles, such as the autonomy of the judiciary and the fact that the first ministers did not promote purges, limited the removal of magistrates. In response to public criticism, the secretary of the Ministry of Justice's purge commission recognised that it was neither 'necessary nor viable at this point to undertake more thorough purges'.[54]

Out of a body of 500 magistrates, 42 judges were submitted to a purge process in 1974–5, most of them for participating in political courts or for holding government posts or for being members of the regime's censorship bodies.[55] Two years later, some of the better known judges who had been dismissed or forced to retire were reinstated by the Comissão de Análise de Recursos de Saneamentos e de Reclassificação (CARSR – Commission for the Assessment of Purge Appeals and Reclassifications). Despite protests from the moderate parliamentary Left, two judges who had gone through this process were subsequently appointed to the Supreme Court of Justice.[56]

The purges undertaken within the Ministry of Labour were more complex, far-reaching and radical. This new ministry replaced the regime's Ministry of Corporations and Welfare, which had overseen the regime's extensive corporatist apparatus. A large number of the 'wildcat' purges were 'legalised' by the inclusion in the purge law of those individuals who had maintained a formal relationship with the PIDE-DGS and those who had, in one way or another, collaborated with the political police. Additionally, nationalisation and state intervention in various private enterprises meant that the majority of forced removals took place in this sector, which was also the most marked by the anti-capitalism of the social movements.

Purges in the Ministry of Education, and throughout the education system as a whole, were also high: particularly in the universities. Famous university professors, schoolteachers and writers formed part of this sector's purge commission. The JSN removed all university deans and directors of faculties from their posts, and various high-ranking members of the ministry were transferred. In the secondary schools, the more radical actions by the student movement forced the military to intervene to protect the accused. However, given the very strong pressure exerted by the student movement, it was in the universities that both the legal and the 'wildcat' purges were most thorough. Some members of the commissions resigned in protest at the 'wildcat' purges which were often undertaken in the absence of any legal proceedings.

Students would, following votes in the student assemblies, simply deny professors access to the university, although only a small minority of those so 'condemned' were ever submitted to legal purge proceedings by the ministry's purge commission. The same applied to schoolteachers who were suspected of having collaborated with the political police. The most radical of the 'wildcat' purges took place in the University of Lisbon's law faculty, where an assembly dominated by a small Maoist party decided – against the will of PCP students – to remove some professors who were also members of the Council of State and leaders of conservative parties.

The repression of the pro-democratic student movement in the final years of the dictatorship, as well as the authoritarian behaviour of many professors, can explain some of the 'wildcat' purges. Legal proceedings against professors and other education workers were more solidly based on two criteria: holding high-level posts under the dictatorship; or collaborating with the political police's repression by denouncing students and opposition professors. As in the Ministry of Labour, the latter category was the most sought after, and purges also affected lower-ranking individuals who were accused of being police informants.

Some professors affected by the purges took up new professional activities, while others emigrated to Brazil. When the government introduced the *numerus clausus* [closed number] restricting access to the state university system, some of the professors who had been removed from their posts in 1974 became involved in the creation of private universities, although the large majority was later reintegrated into the state system.

Within the Foreign Ministry, the purge process was limited to a few members of the diplomatic corps who had held government posts under the dictatorship. When he was nominated to the position of foreign minister, the Socialist Party leader, Mário Soares, merely transferred some ambassadors. The purge commission, although fully established, only worked in those consulates in which collaboration with the political police had been more obvious, particularly in countries with large Portuguese immigrant communities such as Brazil and France, where consular officials had been involved in controlling and monitoring the activities of political exiles.

In total, purges within the state apparatus were uneven and limited. Where strong pressure was exerted by trade unions and worker commissions, as was the case in the Ministries of Labour and Education, forced removals were more frequent. Indeed, while reports indicate that most of those purged belonged to the higher levels of the administration, in these cases lower ranking civil servants were also affected, particularly for collaboration with the political police. However, long delays in purge proceedings reduced the overall scope of the process, and made it possible to reintegrate many of the purged individuals a few years later. Nonetheless, important changes did occur at the top levels of the state administration: while many were reintegrated between 1976 and 1980, the great majority never regained the strategic posts they had previously held.

Rupture at the Local Level

It is much harder to assess the break at the local level. On 24 April 1974 there were thousands of people running 304 municipalities and over 4000 parish councils. During the first months following the coup, the JSN and Ministry of the Interior designated provisional administrative commissions. The nominations were legalised assuming the authority of local members of the main democratic opposition parties. The MDP was the main purge agent at the local level. This party had succeeded the Comissão Democrática Eleitoral (CED – Democratic Electoral Commission), which in 1969 had obtained a significant majority in opposition to the Coligação Eleitoral de Unidade Democrática (CEUD – Electoral Coalition for Democratic Unity), the electoral front that was linked to the PS and the republicans. The MDP was dominated by the PCP, although it also had the support of independents and notables of the local democratic opposition.

During the 'hot summer' of 1975, anti-communist activity led to the collapse of several administrative commissions, which became increasingly isolated in the central and northern parts of the country. The parties of the centre-Right and the PS itself were poorly organised in 1974:[57] they lacked a proper party structure, and it was only later – during the pre-electoral period – that they began to call for positions at the local level.

Given the current lack of data, it is difficult to measure the levels of continuity and rupture within the local administration. Moreover, whilst constitutional legislation barred all leading local politicians who had been associated with the dictatorship from standing as candidates for the first elections, it must have had a limited impact.[58]

The Economic Elite

During the first two years of the transition, the economic elite had been hit hard by the process of nationalisation and state intervention, as well as by the flight of industrialists and entrepreneurs from the country. Despite attempts to reach an understanding between General Spínola and the leaders of the main economic groups, strike movements and strong pressure for state intervention led to the first wave of self-exiles. Some of the most important illegal purge processes were also initiated against members of the economic elite, visibly frightening them.

As has been noted above, demands for purges were among the most significant causes of industrial disputes during the weeks immediately following the coup. The 'symbols of rupture', signalled with the dismissal of most of the dictatorship's political elite as well as with the criminalisation of the political police, were important, even if purges of both public and private companies' administrations were rapidly transformed into a component of collective action that increasingly assumed radical traits. It is interesting to note that 73 per cent of the 102 industrial disputes associated with the purges assumed a radical form, often involving workplace occupation and worker self-management.[59]

It was only at the beginning of 1976, with the publication of Decree Law 52 of 21 January, that two purge commissions were given legal status and formal authority to deal with the banking and insurance sectors which had by then been nationalised. These commissions were subordinated to the commission governing purges in the public sector as a whole. Its main role at this point was to reintegrate those who had been subjected to 'wildcat' purges, without respect for the basic principles of due process.[60]

The exodus of important members of the economic elite became a regular occurrence in 1975, as did the nomination of new managers for the businesses taken over by the state. The 'wildcat' purges concentrated on large enterprises in the industrial area around Lisbon and in the banking and insurance sectors. In the business community, the dynamic overtook the desire to punish any individual's collaboration with either the political repression or with New State institutions, and it became an integral part of a wave of increasingly anti-capitalist social movements that railed against the business and land-owning elite. In the north of the country, where the unions and the workers commissions were relatively weak, there were fewer 'wildcat' purges.[61]

The nationalisation strategy aimed to dismantle the large economic groups and give the state control over the main sectors of Portugal's economy. Apart from direct nationalisation, the state indirectly controlled various businesses for a fixed period. The 1976 Constitution confirmed the nationalisation process, but reduced the level of intervention. One study allows us to conclude that 19 per cent of industrialists abandoned their posts (2 per cent were purged), and that the purges essentially affected the industrial area around Lisbon and Setúbal, hardly affecting the northern textile sector.[62] Brazil was the preferred destination for exiles, although many returned to Portugal between 1976 and 1980. When Mário Soares, as prime minister of the first constitutional government, visited Brazil in 1976, he called on members of the economic elite who had fled to return. Thus, the wave of nationalisations, purges and the forced resignations of the pre-constitutional period profoundly affected the entrepreneurial sector. Most of its members were reintegrated between 1976 and 1980, but nationalisation caused long-lasting changes to the Portuguese economic system: a key legacy of the transition to democracy.

The Print and Broadcast Media

The relationship between the state, the economic elite and the media underwent a profound transformation during the transition period.[63] Members of the administrative and management bodies of the print and broadcast media organisations were removed from their posts. Only a few directors of privately owned newspapers, which were already in the hands of the opposition under the old regime, were able to retain their positions. While the first purges were driven by the military, the main purge agents in this sector were journalists and typographers who were linked to the PCP and other extreme-Left organisations, and who were able to retain their dominant positions until 25 November 1975.

The censorship services were purged and dissolved. The official dictatorial press had a limited circulation that was essentially restricted to members of the state bureaucracy; the single party's newspaper, which was artificially sustained by an official subscription campaign, disappeared immediately following the occupation of its headquarters. The most important proceedings took place against non-official newspapers, where journalists and typographers linked to left-wing parties controlled the purges.

The media as a whole experienced profound change during the transition process: the political battle for control over the media had a great impact. The occupation of the Catholic Church radio station, Radio Renascença, by its own journalists, and the self-management system instituted thereafter, polarised public opinion. This radio station became an instrument of the extreme Left in 1975, until its powerful transmitters were destroyed on the instructions of the military, and the station returned to the Church.

The pro-democratic newspaper, *República*, met with a similar fate. Of all the daily publications, it was the only one to continue publishing throughout the New State period. *República* supported the PS, and became self-managed after its directors resigned in 1975, when it became a mouthpiece for the revolutionary Left until its old directors were restored in 1976. While the communists were not responsible for any of these events, the moderate Left associated with the PS made the 'República Case' one of their most successful 'anti-totalitarian' campaigns, in which they were successful in associating the 'Republica Case' with the threat of a PCP take-over of power.

After the nationalisation of the various economic groups that had controlled a substantial part of the print media, most of the press came under state control.

Later, at the height of the political radicalisation process, new newspapers emerged that were supported by the moderate Left and the parties of the Right, which re-employed some of the previously purged journalists. Many of these new newspapers relied, at least initially, on financial support from the western democracies.

Voluntarism and Memory

In 1974–5, several civic and state mobilisation initiatives were promoted to denounce the authoritarian legacy, and to 'democratise' certain sections of Portuguese society. Such was the nature of the *campanhas de dinamização cultural* (CDC – cultural action campaigns) developed by the MFA in collaboration with left-wing civilians and parts of the Serviço Cívico Estudantil (SCE – Student Civic Service). The government also created the Black Book Commission on Fascism, which was responsible to the presidency of the Council of Ministers, and which consisted of socialist and left-republican intellectuals and politicians. With access to all of the dictatorship's archives, this Commission published dozens of books containing primary documentation, which – among other issues – denounced the regime's repression, the treatment of political prisoners, censorship and the collaboration between economic groups and the political police. When it was dissolved in 1991 it was supposed to lead to the creation of a museum of resistance, a project that has yet to be realised. Other initiatives that were more emblematic of the 1974–5 period, but which were associated with the political parties as well as civil society and popular organisations, included the creation of the *Tribunal Popular Humberto Delgado* [Humberto Delgado Popular Court].

The CDCs were intended to 'democratise' the rural world. While established by the MFA, the campaigns were driven by left-wing intellectuals and communists who designed cultural initiatives denouncing the repression of the past, while promoting civic participation. Believing these campaigns to be little more than an attempt by the military to create its own propaganda department, the movements were immediately resisted by the northern conservative elites and criticised by the moderate political parties. Consequently, the campaigns were interrupted in the central and northern districts before finally being abolished in the aftermath of the events of 25 November 1975 and the dissolution of the PCP dominated Fifth Division.

The SCE was a product of two interrelated factors: the university system's inability to accept all candidates for higher education (which was itself a direct consequence of the rapidly expanding secondary school system), and an ideological climate that promoted contact between students and 'the people'. For one academic year prior to entering university, students were encouraged to work on literacy and other similar projects in the local communities. One of the projects that they were involved in was the collection of ethnographic material on popular memory. This material was intended to serve as the basis for a museum containing oral and material memories of the popular resistance to the New State by Portugal's 'peasants and the labourers'.[64]

Both the SCE and the CDCs met with resistance (albeit for different reasons) – particularly in the north of the country where conservative notables and priests were highly suspicious of left-wing initiatives, and where the urban middle-classes feared the consequences of students escaping the control of their families. The CDCs were closed down in 1975, with the ministry of education abolishing the SCE shortly thereafter.

The Humberto Delgado Popular Court was established to examine the regime's most notorious crime: the PIDE's assassination of the dissident general, Humberto Delgado, near the Spanish border town of Badajoz in 1965. Delgado had stood against Salazar's candidate in the 1958 presidential elections before fleeing into exile. The dictatorship consistently denied any involvement in the general's murder, while the family's first lawyer was Mário Soares, one of the regime's leading opponents. Established after the transition, the court sought to mobilise public opinion to demand the apprehension and conviction of the former PIDE agents who had committed this crime. In the end, those responsible for the assassination were tried and convicted *in absentia*.

The Constituent Assembly discussed a large range of proposals that were to lead to the criminalisation of both the authoritarian elite and the dictatorship's agents of repression. With the exception of the temporary measures that were introduced to ensure the prosecution of PIDE agents, the only legal legacy of the transition – in terms of punitive measures against the old regime – was the introduction of a clause in the 1976 Constitution prohibiting political parties that expressed a 'fascist ideology'. This clause was retained after subsequent constitutional revisions, and in the 1990s, despite criticisms about its continued utility, not only was it ratified by parliament, but it was even used against an extreme-Right group.

As we have seen above, the military, political, administrative and economic elite were all deeply affected (albeit to different extents) by the measures that were introduced during the first two years of the transition and which were designed to punish them for their collaboration with the previous regime (see Table 3).

As Table 2 shows, this process was a type of immediate transitional justice,[65] that took place very rapidly during the two transitional phases. The period of democratic consolidation marked the beginning of the rehabilitation process. Only the compensation of the 'anti-fascists' will be discussed below, as the legacy of the colonial war and the subsequent decolonisation was to drag on for the next 30 years.

The Dual Legacy and the Consolidation of Democracy

The moderate elite that dominated the consolidation period inherited a complex situation in 1976. The military intervention of 25 November 1975 marked the beginning of the process of democratic institutionalisation, albeit one that remained under the tutelage of the Council of the Revolution until 1982. In the economic sphere, the heavily nationalised sector and extensive state intervention- ism, combined with the introduction of austerity measures following the Portu- gal's first agreement with the International Monetary Fund (IMF), became symbols of recession and resulted in a drastic reduction in real salaries. In the

Table 2. Phases of transition and democratic consolidation and the purge processes

Fall of dictatorship	Crises	Democratic consolidation
April 1974 to March 1975	March 1975 to April 1976	April 1976 to October 1982
+ Legal purges – 'Wild' purges	+ Legal purges + 'Wild' purges	Reduction of penalties Reintegration

social arena, the return of hundreds of thousands of colonial refugees as a result of the decolonisation process brought problems. Some extreme right-wing terrorist activities briefly continued as a legacy of the 'hot summer' of 1975. They were soon to be joined by extreme left-wing terrorist activities.

The official discourse of the first two constitutional governments led by the socialist, Mário Soares, and the first democratically elected president, Ramalho Eanes, called for 'reconciliation' and 'pacification'. Under pressure from parties on the Right and centre-Right, the purges were soon brought to an end, and their role re-evaluated in light of the claim that they were an excess of the early transitional period. At the same time, a number of communists and left-wing civilians and military figures were removed from office: many members of extreme-Left parties and the PCP were dismissed from their positions within the civil service and state-owned companies. Members of the armed forces who had been associated with the former pro-communist Prime Minister, Vasco Gonçalves, and with the leader of the MFA's militant faction, Otelo Saraiva do Carvalho, were dismissed from service.

The extreme right-wing terrorism of the MDLP and ELP was carried out largely by serving and retired military officers. Their activities came to an end a few years later as they faded away following General Spínola's return from exile. While some of their members were jailed, the majority of cases dragged on for years, leading to vendettas that were a consequence of their extensive links with moderate elements during 1975's 'hot summer', and the promises made to them at that time that their crimes would not be 'forgotten'. The repression of the extreme-Left wing terrorist group, the Forças Populares–25 de Abril (FP-25 – Popular Forces of 25 April), with which Otelo Saraiva do Carvalho, the operational leader of the 1974 revolution and leader of the revolutionary Left, was involved, was a much more complex affair that dragged on right up until the turn of the century.

Despite this outburst of violence, a climate of political reconciliation dominated during the last years of the 1970s, determining the manner in which the government was to deal with the dictatorship's legacy. This was particularly true with respect of the trial of members of the former regime's political police. Following the so-called 'PIDE hunt', in which those who had not fled the country were tracked down, there followed a two year period during which PIDE-DGS agents awaited trial and punishment – either in protective custody or on conditional release. Their trials were conducted according to the new post-revolutionary political ethos, and as a result, those who had not taken advantage of their bail to flee the country received only light sentences from the military tribunals (normally they were sentenced to time already served), with those who had good military active service reports from the colonial war period receiving especially benevolent treatment. Although there was public demonstrations against and criticism of the sentences meted out, they did serve as notice that judicial legality and the rule of law had been re-established following the 'excesses' of the turbulent years, 1974–5. The two years that had passed since then had seen a significant diminution of 1974's revolutionary 'emotions', and the ruling political elite made it clear that they favoured continuing with institutional demobilisation.

Reintegration

Between 1976 and the early-1980s, steps were taken to reintegrate those who had been victims of the purges.[66] New legislation was passed and measures were quickly adopted to normalise the situation in the economic arena where 'wildcat' purges had been most severe. Soon after the introduction of these new laws, the Council of the Revolution ordered 'all officials of the armed forces who had been assigned to the purge commissions in private enterprises' to return to their barracks.[67] The government followed this up with a series of measures that were designed to allow the return of the exiles who had been forced out by the purges. Decree-law 471 of 14 June 1976 declared that the ideologically motivated purges realised by workers in the private and public sectors between 1974 and 1976, and 'which had not observed' the laws that were then in force, were legally null and void.[68]

Taking advantage of the new situation, the victims of the purges organised themselves into the Movimento Pró-reintegração dos Despedidos sem Justa Causa (MPDJC – Movement for the Reintegration of the Unfairly Dismissed), which could count on the new private newspapers to fight their corner.[69] The trade union movement protested against the reintegration of those who had been purged by holding strikes and even some sporadic sit-ins. But these actions, which mainly affected the recently nationalised state enterprises and the civil service, were largely unsuccessful.

The purge commissions in the ministries ceased to operate in 1976, and the Council of the Revolution, which took on the role of these commissions as well as the leadership of the CEPML, reinforced legal mechanisms to ensure that a process of rehabilitation took place. A moderate member of the Council of the Revolution, Captain Sousa e Castro, was given responsibility for the entire process. The CARSR was then created under the auspices of the Council of the Revolution, and continued in operation until the mid-1980s, rehabilitating the vast majority of appellants who came before it. This commission was composed of legally qualified military officials and civilians who had no links with the dictatorship. According to a report into its activities, the commission expressed the view that, 'it is necessary to repair the damage that was done' during the 1974–5 period when many of the purges were 'merely arbitrary'.[70] Most of those who had been dismissed during the purges had their punishment altered to compulsory retirement; the remainder often received a payment in lieu of lost earnings and restoration of their seniority for the purpose of calculating pension entitlements. In some cases in which trade union or student resistance to the reintegration was particularly vociferous, those who were to be reintegrated were simply transferred to other institutions or remained at home until emotions calmed down before returning to their posts. In some universities reintegration of those who had been purged did not begin until the early-1980s. One case, that of Veiga Simão, Caetano's Minister of Education, was decided by the Council of the Revolution itself; however, the great majority were left to Sousa e Castro and his CARSR.

Between 1976 and 1978 these commission reassessed around 3000 processes within the various government ministries and nationalised industries, most of which concerned officials of the previous regime's political police (see Table 3). In the case of PIDE-DGS agents, the CARSR followed the precedent established by the military tribunals: these tribunals had heard the cases against political police agents, and had decided that 'the fact that those being tried were former agents of the PIDE-DGS is irrelevant because it was not illegal in the past to be a member of the political police'. This principal restored their rights as public employees to them, but only if they had not 'taken part in illegal activities'.[71]

Table 3. Purge processes: measures applied by the purge commissions and CARSR action

		Purge commissions (1974–6)					
		Dismissed	Dismissed and compulsorily retired	Compulsorily retired	Suspended	Transferred	Unknown	Total
		289	2	107	13	56	1564	
CARSR (1976–8)	Dismissed	6	0	0	0	0	0	6
	Compulsorily retired	65	0	24	1	0	19	109
	Suspended	147	2	18	2	1	5	175
	Transferred	3	0	10	0	12	4	29
	Reintegrated	34	0	23	7	7	1282	1353
	Punishment annulled	33	0	31	3	33	30	130
	Archived	0	0	0	0	3	193	196
	Total receiving the same sentence as before	6	—	24	2	12	9	2031

Note: of the previous 1564 cases unknown, only nine remain unknown.

With the abolition of the Council of the Revolution, many of the outstanding appeals were transferred to the administrative courts, while the CEPML became little more than a document archive responsible to parliament. Parliamentary debates concerning the future of the archives were often heated and passionate, with some parties – particularly the CDS – calling for their destruction. Their incorporation into the national archive and consequent limited release to the public was a controversial victory for historians and left-wing parties.

The Politics of Memory in Democratic Portugal

An official exhibition of the twentieth-century history of Portugal, sponsored by the office of the presidency and the government, was inaugurated in November 1999 to coincide with the celebration of 25 years of Portuguese democracy. Directed towards both students and the public at large, thousands of Portuguese travelled through the dark passages of Salazarism, through the torture chambers of the political police, and along corridors that were lined with photographs of political prisoners, while opposition figures and the pro-democratic press were celebrated. There was a forebidding corridor dedicated to the colonial war, which culminated in a brightly lit area that celebrated the fall of the dictatorship. Significantly, the turbulent period of the first years of the transition were omitted, and the exhibition ended where democracy began, represented symbolically by thematic panels portraying the process of social and political change that had taken place during the 25 years since the fall of the Salazar regime.

Given the complex legacy of the first two years of the revolution, it would have been very difficult for an official exhibition to deal with this transitional period. According to the official discourse of Mário Soares's PS and that of the democratic parties of the centre-Right, Portugal's democracy was shaped by a 'double legacy': the authoritarianism of the Right under the New State, and the authoritarian threat of the extreme-Left of 1974–5.[72]

The impact of the return of right-wing exiles to Portugal, of press campaigns in favour of those who had been expropriated in 1974–5, and the search for some anti-communist 'military heroes' was hardly noticeable. By the end of the 1970s, the situation no longer favoured the political re-conversion of the dictatorship's 'barons', or of the populist military figures who hoped to make political capital out of their involvement in anti-communist activities during 1975. The process of de-colonisation, which was aggravated by their inability to mobilise the *retornados* [returnees], marked the end of an era for the radical Right in Portugal.

The relatively peaceful process of reintegrating the *retornados* was neither merely a consequence of the 'quiet habits' ascribed to the Portuguese, nor of state support: it was a product of the nature of the white community in Africa, with its relatively recent settlement in the colonies and the concomitant maintenance of family ties in Portugal.[73] Emigration to other countries, such as South Africa, also reduced the number of returning colonists and, consequently, the shock of social absorption.

The abolition of punitive legislation affecting the dictatorial elite, and the process of democratic consolidation, encouraged some of the old regime's leading figures to return to Portugal. The last president of the New State, Admiral

Américo Tomás (who maintained a 'political silence' until his death) and some former ministers eventually came back to Portugal. Marcello Caetano, though, refused and died in Brazil in 1980. None of those who came back sought to associate themselves with a possible rebirth of the radical Right, and few of them even joined democratic parties. Some exceptions prove the rule: Adriano Moreira, Caetano's Minister for the Colonies, developed a political career under the new democracy: he was elected to parliament and for a brief time and General Secretary of the CDS. Another former minister in Caetano's government, Veiga Simão, who was responsible for the modernisation of the school system on the eve of the regime's collapse, is another who reactivated his political career as a minister in António Guterres's socialist government.

On the eve of Portugal's accession to the European Community in 1985, the heritage of the double legacy was practically extinct. There was no party of the Right with parliamentary or electoral significance representing the old elite, or which could act as a repository of the authoritarian values inherited from Salazarism. Similarly, the legacy of state socialism and military guardianship had also disappeared following successive reforms of the constitution.

The new democratic institutions associated themselves with the legacy of political opposition to the dictatorship. The semi-presidential nature of the political system and the fact that, first General Ramalho Eanes, followed by two presidents who had been active in the anti-Salazar struggle (Mário Soares and Jorge Sampaio), have been symbolically important in reinforcing the anti-dictatorial image of the democratic regime. During the first 30 years of democracy, successive presidents have posthumously rehabilitated many of the dictatorship's victims, and decorated members of the anti-Salazar opposition with awards such as the Order of Freedom. The most emblematic of these decorations was granted to General Humberto Delgado, whose entire military honours were posthumously restored. Streets and other public places have been renamed after famous opposition figures – republicans, communists and Socialist alike – while Salazar's name has been removed from all public monuments, squares and also from the bridge over the River Tagus, which was almost immediately renamed the *Ponte 25 de Abril* [25 April Bridge].

Attempts to compensate activists who had struggled against the dictatorship were made from the 1970s onwards, although some of the proposals did not receive parliamentary approval.[74] Members of organisations opposed to the dictatorship had to wait until 1997, and the introduction of the PS government's legislation enabling them to seek compensation for the social security benefits and retirement pension entitlements for the years they were in hiding or exile.[75] In order to qualify, claimants must, through documents held in the PIDE archive, prove that they were persecuted, and that is not always easy.[76]

Another aspect of the attempt to symbolically delegitimise the authoritarian past was the alteration of national holidays. The date of the Republican revolution, 5 October 1910 (the republic had never been abolished by the dictatorship), assumed greater significance, while the 28 May holiday (which commemorated the 1926 military coup) was replaced with a new holiday on 25 April, celebrating the establishment of the new democratic regime.

There are, in Portugal, no museums documenting the dictatorship and its repression. All such proposals for such projects that were put forward during the first two years of the transition were abandoned on account of a lack of interest from civil society, the political parties (including the PS and the PCP), and a lack of enthusiasm on the part of the state. A 1991 suggestion to convert the Commission on the Black Books on the Fascist Regime into a museum of the resistance failed to garner the support of Cavaco Silva's centre-Right government. Some modest initiatives were undertaken by PS–PCP run city councils, including Lisbon, in the 1990s, the Museum of the Republic and Resistance being a case in point. It was only toward the end of the 1990s that private foundations were established with the explicit aim of consolidating the memory of resistance to Salazarism and the transition to democracy. This is true of the Mário Soares Foundation, which was established following the former president's retirement from office. With the passage of time, the 25 April Association – which is organised by former members of the MFA – has gradually developed an annual commemoration, and has kept alive the memory of those involved in the 1974 coup that overthrew the authoritarian regime.

As is the case with other democratic transitions, the fate of the defeated regime's archives was a topic of heated debate. Given the nature regime's fall, the military took possession of the PIDE-DGS archives, which consequently survived almost entirely intact. More importantly perhaps, Salazar's own personal archive survived. These documents, meticulously maintained by Salazar himself, had been kept in the Presidency of the Council of Ministers' offices following his death in 1970, contain an account of 40 years of Portuguese political life. Both the PIDE-DGS and the Salazar archive have been deposited in the national archive, where, like all other New State documents, they are open to public inspection.

Important public debate concerning the archives began in the 1990s, when they were first opened to the public. One 1996 controversy, provoked by a former socialist minister who had been a victim of the PIDE-DGS, concerned the duty to return letters, photographs and other material confiscated by the political police to their original owners or their heirs. Although some defended this course of action during the ensuing parliamentary, the negative reaction of the majority of historians ensured that these documents remained with the national archive.[77]

There are also occasional 'eruptions of memory' that arise from unresolved cases or from new revelations by members of the former regime. In 1998, the leader of the PIDE unit responsible for Humberto Delgado's assassination gave an interview to a Portuguese journalist in which he stated that he regularly travelled to Portugal, although he had been sentenced to eight years imprisonment *in absentia*. He was soon located in Spain, where he had been living under a false name; however, the Spanish court refused to allow the Portuguese authorities to extradite him, forcing the court that had originally sentenced him to admit that the statute of limitations applied, and that he was therefore free.

Conclusion

The Portuguese case is a good illustration of the absence of any correlation between the nature of the authoritarian regime, and the extent of retributive pressure during the transition process. It was the nature of the authoritarian regime's downfall and the character of the 'anti-authoritarian' coalition during the first provisional governments that provoked the symbolic break with the past. The new authorities felt that it was 'morally and politically desirable' to replace and to punish some members of the previous elite, and to dissolve the authoritarian institutions – particularly because the type of transition provided them with the political opportunity.[78]

Portugal's transition almost immediately began to eliminate some of the institutional legacies and the more important members of the elite that the dictatorship could have left to democracy. Not only were the regime's most important political institutions dissolved, but the 'authoritarian enclaves' that had survived many of the transitional processes of the 1970s and 1980s were either eliminated or subjected to complex processes that paralysed them. The dissolution of the more repressive organisations (such as the PIDE, and the Portuguese Legion) was a fact, and some of them were subjected to processes that involved purging and criminalising them.

The nature of the transition was certainly the main factor behind the rapid dissolution of authoritarian institutions, the criminalisation of the political police and administrative justice. However, the state crises also constituted an important 'window of opportunity' for the Portuguese type of transitional justice: simultaneously radical, diffuse and with little recourse to the judicial system. In the Portuguese case, particularly in public and private enterprises, the purges were transformed into a facet of the radicalisation of social movements. In fact, the state crisis and the dynamics of the social movements in 1975 exceeded the political punishment of the authoritarian elite, provoking the greatest 'fear' of the twentieth century amongst the country's social and economic elite.

The strong correlation between the dynamic of the purges, the state crises and the 'opportunity structure' that this afforded is temporally visible: with the 25 November 1975 coup that gave victory to the moderate military, supported by the parties of the Right and centre-Left, both legal and illegal purges came to an almost immediate end. This happened a few months before the new democratic institutions came into being. As Palacios Cerezales states, '25 November signalled the end of the state crisis and, with it, the final opportunity for many kinds of collective action', thus marking 'the passing of a critical and integrated juncture'.[79]

Elster notes that one of the factors in the diminution of the severity of punishments after the first phase of the transition was the natural 'abatement of the desire for retribution once it had been satisfied by he punishment of some wrongdoers'.[80] With the consolidation of Portugal's democracy, the parties of the Right made some attempts to criminalise the radical elites of 1975, but an 'informal agreement' to denounce both authoritarianism and the 'excesses' of 1975 marked the end of retroactive justice, and the reintegration of a large proportion of those who had been condemned.

Notes

1. Katherine Hite and Leonardo Morlino, "Problematizing the Links between Authoritarian Legacies and 'Good' Democracy", in Katherine Hite and Paola Cesarini (eds), *Authoritarian Legacies and Democracy in Latin America and Southern Europe* (Notre Dame: University of Notre Dame Press, 2004), p.25. For an extended version of some of the topics developed here see Antonio Costa Pinto, "Authoritarian Legacies, Transitional Justice and State Crisis in Portugal's Democratisation", *Democratization* 13/2 (2006), pp.173–204.
2. There is a very large bibliography dealing with 'transitional justice' processes, the most recent of which is by Jon Elster, *Closing the Books: Transitional Justice in Historical Perspective* (New York: Cambridge University Press, 2004), and *Retribution and Reparation in the Transition to Democracy*

(New York: Cambridge University Press, 2006). Of interest in relation to a comparative analysis of the Portuguese case are – as a general introduction to the phenomenon – the pioneering works by John H. Herz (ed.), *From Dictatorship to Democracy: Coping with the Legacies of Authoritarianism* (Westport, CT: Greenwood Press, 1982); James McAdams (ed.), *Transitional Justice and the Rule of Law in New Democracies* (Notre Dame: University of Notre Dame Press, 1997); and Alexandra Barahona de Brito, González-Enriquez Cruz and Paloma Aguilar (eds), *The Politics of Memory: Transitional Justice in Democratising Societies* (Oxford: Oxford University Press, 2001).

3. Samuel Huntington, *The Third Wave: Democratization in the Late Twentieth Century* (Norma, OK: University of Oklahoma Press, 1991) p. 215.

4. John Borneman, *Settling Accounts. Violence, Justice and Accountability in Post Socialist Europe* (Princeton, NJ: Princeton University Press, 1997), p.141.

5. Kieran Williams, Brigid Fowler and Aleks Szczerbiak, "Explaining Lustration in Central Europe: A 'Post-communist Politics' Approach", *Democratization* 12/1 (2005), pp.22–43.

6. Elster (note 2), p.75. To be more precise, we are dealing with 'the political decisions that were taken immediately following the transition and which were directed at individuals who were responsible for decisions made or implemented under the old regime'. See Jon Elster, "Coming to Terms with the Past: A Framework for the Study of Justice in the Transition to Democracy", *Archives Européennes de Sociologie* 39/1 (1998), p.14. Elster opposes this to what is called '"postponed transitional justice", when the first actions are undertaken (say) ten years or more after the transition' (note 2), p.76.

7. Helga A. Welshm, "Dealing with the Communist Past: Central and Eastern European Experiences after 1990", *Europe–Asia Studies* 48/3 (1996), pp.419–28. For more on the re-conversion of communist parties, see Anna M. Grzymala-Busse, *Redeeming the Communist Past: The Regeneration of Communist Parties in East Central Europe* (Cambridge: Cambridge University Press, 2002).

8. Elster (note 2), p.216.

9. Ibid., p. 62; Paloma Aguilar, "Justice, Politics and Memory in the Spanish Transition", in Brito, Cruz and Aguilar (note 2), pp.92–118.

10. Juan J. Linz and Alfred Stepan, *Problems of Democratic Transition and Consolidation: Southern Europe, South America and Post-Communist Europe* (Baltimore, MD: Johns Hopkins University Press, 1997), pp.38–54.

11. Williams, Fowler and Szczerbiak (note 5), p.33.

12. See especially Linz and Stepan (note 10), pp.38–65.

13. John P. Moran, "The Communist Torturers of Eastern Europe: Prosecute and Punish or Forgive and Forget?", *Communist and Post-Communist Studies* 27/1 (1994), pp.95–101.

14. Marc Osiel defines administrative massacre as 'large scale violation of basic humans rights to life and liberty by the central state in a systematic and organized fashion, often against its own citizens, generally in a climate of war – civil or international, real or imagined'. Marc Osiel, *Mass Atrocity, Collective Memory and the Law* (New Brunswick, NJ: Transaction, 2000), p.9.

15. Nancy Bermeo, "War and Democratization: Lessons from the Portuguese Experience", *Democratization* 13/3 (2007), pp.338–406.

16. Guillermo O'Donnell, Philippe C. Schmitter and Lawrence Whitehead (eds), *Transitions from Authoritarian Rule* (Baltimore, MD: The Johns Hopkins University Press, 1986); Linz and Stepan (note 10); Geoffrey Pridham, *The Dynamics of Democratization: A Comparative Approach* (London: Continuum, 2000).

17. Linz and Stepan (note 10), p.117.

18. Gretchen Casper, "The Benefits of Difficult Transitions", *Democratization* 7/3 (2000), pp.46–62.

19. Hite and Morlino (note 1), p.47.

20. Diego Palacios Cerezales, *O Poder Caiu na Rua: Crise de Estado e Acções Colectivas na Revolução Portuguesa, 1974–75* (Lisbon: Imprensa de Ciências Sociais, 2003).

21. Juan J. Linz, *Totalitarian and Authoritarian Regimes* (Boulder, CO: Lynne Rienner, 2000).

22. Antonio Costa Pinto, *Salazar's Dictatorship and European Fascism* (New York: SSM–Columbia University Press, 1996).

23. Robert M. Fishman, "Rethinking State and Regime: Southern Europe's Transition to Democracy", *World Politics* 42/3 (1990), pp.422–40.

24. Palacios Cerezales (note 20), pp.35–55.

25. For an excellent introduction to the comparative study of the role of social movements in the Portuguese and Spanish transitions see Rafael Durán Muñoz, *Acciones Colectivas y Transiciones a la Democrácia: España y Portugal, 1974–77* (Madrid: Centro de Estúdios Avanzados em Ciências Sociales, 1997).

26. Paloma Aguilar (note 9); Nicos C. Alivizatos and P. Nikiforos Diamandouros, "Politics and the Judiciary in the Greek Transition to Democracy", in James McAdams (ed.), *Transitional Justice and the Rule of Law in New Democracies* (Notre Dame: University of Notre Dame Press, 1997), pp.27–60.

27. Robert M. Fishman, "Legacies of Democratizing Reform and Revolution: Portugal and Spain Compared", paper presented at the annual meeting of the *American Political Science Association*, Chicago (2004).

28. Richard Gunther, P. Nikiforos Diamandouros and Hans-Jürgen Puhle (eds), *The Politics of Democratic Consolidation: Southern Europe in Comparative Perspective* (Baltimore, MD: Johns Hopkins University Press, 1995).

29. Philippe C. Schmitter, "The Democratization of Portugal in its Comparative Perspective", in Fernando Rosas (ed.), *Portugal e a Transição para a Democracia* (Lisbon: Colibri, 1999).

30. Norrie MacQueen, *The Decolonization of Portuguese Africa: Metropolitan Revolution and the Dissolution of Empire* (London: Longman, 1997); António Costa Pinto, *O Fim do Império Português* (Lisbon: Horizonte, 2001).

31. Tiago Fernandes, *Nem Ditadura nem Revolução: A Ala Liberal no Marcelismo (1968–74)* (Lisbon: Dom Quixote, 2005).

32. Leonardo Morlino, *Democracy between Consolidation and Crisis: Parties, Groups and Citizens in Southern Europe* (Oxford: Oxford University Press, 1998), p.19.

33. Schmitter (note 29), p.360.

34. António Costa Pinto, "Dealing with the Legacy of Authoritarianism: Political Purges in Portugal's Transition to Democracy", in Stein U. Larsen (ed.), *Modern Europe after Fascism, 1943–1980s* (New York: SSM–Columbia University Press, 1998), pp. 1679–717.

35. Fátima Patriarca, "A Revolução e a Questão Social: Que Justiça Social?", in Rosas (note 29), p.141.

36. Thomas C. Bruneu (ed.), *Political Parties and Democracy in Portugal: Organizations, Elections and Public Opinion* (Boulder, CO: Westview Press, 1997); Fernando Farelo Lopes and André Freire, *Partidos Políticos e Sistemas Eleitorais: Uma Introdução* (Lisbon: Celta, 2002).

37. John L. Hammond, *Building Popular Power: Workers' and Neighborhood Movements in the Portuguese Revolution* (New York: Monthly Review Press, 1988); Charles Downs, *Revolution at the Grassroots: Community Organizations in the Portuguese Revolution* (Albany, NY: The State University of New York Press, 1989).

38. Palacios Cerezales (note 20).

39. From June 1975 to April 1976 there were between 100 and 120 attacks on mainly Communist Party and communist controlled trade union offices. See António Costa Pinto, "The Radical Right in Contemporary Portugal", in Luciano Cheles, Ronnie Ferguson and Michalina Vaughan (eds), *The Far Right in Western and Eastern Europe* (London: Longman, 1995), pp.108–28.

40. Kenneth Maxwell, *The Making of Portuguese Democracy* (Cambridge: Cambridge University Press, 1995).

41. Walter C. Opello, "Portugal: A Case Study of International Determinants of Regime Transition", in Geoffrey Pridham, *Encouraging Democracy: The International Context of Regime Transition in Southern Europe* (Leicester: Leicester University Press, 1991), pp.84–102, Nuno Severiano Teixeira, "Between Africa and Europe: Portuguese Foreign Policy", in António Costa Pinto (ed.), *Contemporary Portugal* (New York: SSM-Columbia University Press, 2004); Rui Mateus, *Memórias de um PS desconconhecido* (Lisbon: Dom Quixote, 1997). The political police in the colonies remained active for the few weeks following the coup as the military hoped that it could be integrated into a military intelligence police. However, not even the colonial political police could escape the abolition of their service. On the criminalization of the Poltical Police see the excellent research of Filipa Raimundo, "The Double Face of Heroes: Motivations and Constraints in Dealing with the Past. The Case of PIDE/DGS", MA Dissertation, Institute of Social Science, University of Lisbon, 2007.

42. Artur Costa, "O Julgamento da PIDE-DGS e o Direito (Transitório) à Memória", in Iva Delgado, Manuel Loff, António Cluny, Carlos Pacheco and Ricardo Monteiro (eds), *De Pinochet a Timor Lorosae: Impunidade e Direito à Memória* (Lisbon: Cosmos, 2000), pp.39–53.

43. *Diário do Governo* 1/146 (1974), p.744.

44. *Diário do Governo* 1/59 (1975), p.375.

45. *O Século* 27 February 1975.

46. *O Século* 1 October 1974. Dinis de Almeida, who was at that time an important figure on the extreme Left of the MFA, divided the purges into four distinct periods. General Spínola and the MFA led the first series of purges. The second, which was based on the principal of 'incompe-

tence', was much slower and more complex. The third took place during the spring and summer of 1975, and involved the removal of right-wing officers. The fourth and final series of purges took place after 25 November 1975, when left-wing officers were removed. See Dinis de Almeida, *Ascenção, Apogeu e Queda do MFA* (Lisbon: Edições Sociais, 1978), pp.39–43.

47. António Costa Pinto, "Settling Accounts with the Past in a Troubled Transition to Democracy: The Portuguese Case", in Brito, Cruz and Aguilar (note 2), pp.65–91.
48. *Diário do Governo* 1/62 (1975), p.430–4.
49. Kenneth Maxwell, 'The Emergence of Portuguese Democracy', in Herz (note 2), pp.231–50.
50. There were four degrees of punishment: transfer to other duties at either the same or a lower grade; suspension for up to three years; compulsory retirement; and dismissal.
51. *Diário Popular* 5 September 1974.
52. *O Século* (note 46).
53. António Costa Pinto, "Salazar's Ministerial Elite", *Portuguese Journal of Social Science* 3/2 (2004), pp.103–13.
54. *A Capital* 19 April 1975.
55. There were very few purges in bodies that were responsible to the Ministry of Justice: 22 Judicial Police officers, 16 registrars and notaries, and four prison directors were removed from their positions. *A Capital* 19 April 1975.
56. See the speech delivered by the Socialist Party deputy, Raul Rego in *A Luta* 9 February 1977.
57. On the Socialist Party, see Vitalino Canas (ed.), *O Partido Socialista e a Democracia* (Oeiras: Celta, 2005).
58. *Constituição da República Portuguesa* (1986), pp.92–3.
59. Durán Muñoz (note 25), p.128.
60. *Diário do Governo* 1/17 (1976), pp.112–13.
61. Durán Muñoz (note 25), pp. 205–68.
62. Harry Makler, "The Consequences of the Survival and Revival of the Industrial Bourgeoisie", in Lawrence Graham and Douglas L. Wheeler (eds.), *In Search of Modern Portugal: The Revolution and its Consequences* (Madison, WI: University of Wisconsin Press, 1983), pp.251–83.
63. Kenneth Maxwell, *The Press and the Rebirth of Iberian Democracy* (Westport, CT: Greenwood Press, 1983).
64. Jorge Freitas Branco and Luísa Tiago de Oliveira, *Ao Encontro do Povo: 1-A Missão* (Oeiras: Celta, 1993), Luísa Tiago de Oliveira, *Estudantes e Povo na Revolução: O Serviço Cívico Estudantil* (Oeiras: Celta, 2004).
65. Elster (note 2), p.75.
66. This section owes much to Maria Inácia Rezola, who provided me with material concerning the Council of the Revolution and the purges. For more on this, see Maria Inácia Rezola, *Os Militares na Revoluçao de Abril* (Lisbon: Campo da Comunicaçao, 2006).
67. Council of the Revolution, Minutes of a meeting, 11 December 1975, Annexes T and P, Arquivo Nacional Torre do Tombo (ANTT). Sousa e Castro had already been nominated to take control of the purges, but he only took office after the events of 25 November 1975. See Council of the Revolution, Minutes of a meeting, 31 October 1975, ANTT.
68. *Diário do Governo* 1/138 (1976), p.1332.
69. From the *Jornal Novo* to the Socialist Party's own newspaper, *A Luta*.
70. Relatório de Actividades, CARSP 1976–1977–1978, p.1, ANTT/Conselho da Revolução.
71. Ibid.
72. To my knowledge, the only work dealing with the historical memory of 25 April and the transition within the most important political parties – the PS and the PSD – is Vasco Campilho, *Le Poing et la Fleche: Étude Comparative des Memoires Historiques de la Revolution des Oeillets au sein du Parti Socialiste et du Parti Social Democrate – Mémoire de DEA* (Paris: Institut D'Études Politiques de Paris, 2002).
73. Rui Pena Pires (ed.), *Os Retornados: Um Estudo Sociográfico* (Lisbon: IED, 1984).
74. *Diário de Notícias* 16 June 1976.
75. Law 20/97, 19 June 1997.
76. According to this law, the claimant must prove that their claim is related to time 'spent, either within the country or abroad, during which they were victims of political persecution that impeded their ability to engage in normal professional activities and prevented their social insertion into the community because of their membership of a political group, or their participation in political activities destined to promote democracy' at any time between 28 May 1926 and 25 April 1974.

77. If the person identified in the case is still alive, or has been dead for less than 50 years, their file may only be consulted with the permission from the individual concerned, or from their descendents. The majority of documents, expunged of names, are open for consultation.
78. Huntington (note 3), p.231.
79. Palacios Cerezales (note 20), p.176.
80. Elster (note 2), p.228.

Whom to Mourn and Whom to Forget? (Re)constructing Collective Memory in Contemporary Russia

ANATOLY M. KHAZANOV

The ways post-totalitarian and post-authoritarian countries deal with their disturbing pasts tells much about their contemporary political order as well as about the national identities they are seeking in the present. The issue is not whether horrors and crimes are remembered and commemorated, but whether society at large – outside the circle of survivors – makes the task of memory a public commitment.[1] Dealing with the past remains a painful problem in virtually all former communist countries. However, in Russia it acquires many specific characteristics.

Historians are still debating the total number of the victims of the Soviet regime, especially of those who were executed or imprisoned in the Gulag.[2] In any case, they number many millions. Additional millions of people were convicted on criminal charges but for political reasons that would not normally be considered criminal at all; they were victims of forced resettlements during the collectivisation process and of ethnic deportations and cleansings,[3] were incarcerated in labour armies or special settlements; were confined to the postwar filtration camps;[4] or died during artificially induced famines.

Perhaps their exact number will never become known because, as Keep[5] aptly remarked, the official Soviet sources are 'as reliable as the average mafioso's tax return'. But the victims were not only those who were executed or incarcerated in the Gulag. Even if they were not arrested, relatives of the repressed were victims as well because, in addition to emotional and economic suffering, they were discriminated against with regard to education, social opportunities, place of residence and in a variety of other ways. In addition, millions of people were subject to various discriminatory policies and practices, because they belonged to the 'wrong' social classes and strata, or ethnic groups.

Still, the crimes committed during communist rule play an insignificant role in the attitudes toward the Soviet past of the majority of Russians. The problem is not ignorance, but rather indifference, or an intentional desire to ignore the dark sides of the Soviet past. Nowadays, those who want to know the true history of the Soviet Union can do this. In the late 1980s and early 1990s, and even later, many eyewitness testimonies and memoirs of the survivors of the Gulag, document collections, archival materials, reference works, scholarly publications, literary works and articles in newspapers, documentary films and TV broadcasts have provided sufficient information on the political and state-sponsored crimes committed under communism. Some sites of mass murders, the very existence of which had been a state secret in the Soviet Union, were exhumed and made known to the public. Some NGO organisations, like the Memorial Society and the Sakharov Center, have emerged and devote their activities to commemoration of the victims and to revealing the true history of the Soviet regime.[6] This information was even included in some high school history textbooks published in the late 1980s and in the first half of the 1990s.[7]

However, the short-term interest in the repression, in the late 1980s, was mainly connected with the political struggle and desire to delegitimise the communist regime. This problem was solved in 1991. That was necessary but not enough. The repression as a national tragedy and crime has never been internalised and has not penetrated deeply into the mass consciousness. It has not become an indispensable part of the collective memory because attitudes toward the Soviet past are a matter of values much more than of knowledge. The disclosure of ugly truths is mainly rejected, or ignored, or contributes to a sense of victimisation, which, at present, is shared by many, perhaps even by the majority, of Russians.[8]

It is important what kind of collective memories are constructed. The extent to which they are self-critical is even more important. Today, the Soviet crimes occupy an insignificant place in the collective memory in Russia, if they exist at all. In any case, they remain diverse, fragmented, compartmentalised and localised. Communist crimes occupy a much more conspicuous place in the collective memories of ethnic minorities in the Russian Federation than in those of ethnic Russians. Among the latter they are remembered much more in such former centers of the Gulag, as Magadan, Norilsk or Vorkuta, than in Moscow or Saint-Petersburg. There are several reasons for this sad state of affairs.

First, one should take into account social changes and the growing temporal and historical distance from the Soviet past, especially from its Stalin period. After all, almost 70 years have passed since one of the major atrocities of Russian history, the Great Terror. This makes the repression much less emotionally charged. Of the two levels of memory, the factual and the experiential, the latter has already been eroded.

During Khrushchev's *Thaw*, Anna Akhmatova made a famous but incorrect prediction about two Russias that would have to face each other: the Russia that was imprisoned and the Russia that put it there. Nothing like that, however, happened in practice. Accounts between the two Russias were never settled. Imprisoning Russia looked at imprisoned Russia without great shame and embarrassment. Between 1953 and 1956, when survivors returned from the camps, they had to survive again, this time in a society at large that was not accidentally called the 'Big Zone' (in comparison with the 'Small Zone' of the camps). They had to merge into a still captive society. In the eyes of many Soviet functionaries and bureaucrats, not to mention KGB officers, the survivors bore a certain stigma. They were advised to keep their mouths shut and not to talk too much about their suffering and especially about those who had caused it. The secret letter of the Central Committee of the Communist Party of 19 December 1956 to all local Party organisations characterised some of those who had been pardoned or rehabilitated as people with, 'malicious attitudes toward the Soviet power'. In Leningrad some of those people were evicted from the city.[9]

Very little, and in many cases nothing at all, had been done with regard to the material compensation of the survivors and assistance in returning them to professional life. Rehabilitated survivors and the families of those rehabilitated individuals who had been executed or perished in the Gulag received two months' wages from their old jobs; in addition, they were sometimes assisted with housing. That was all. The survivors could also count their years in labour camps toward pensions, but this was hindered by bureaucratic procedures that not infrequently intentionally created obstacles in obtaining proper documentation.

Under the circumstances, many survivors were too traumatised, or frightened and intimidated, to convey their experience and suffering. Others were eager to demonstrate their trustworthiness and their unshakable loyalty to the Party and the Soviet regime in order to be reintegrated into society, and especially to be reinstated as Party members. If these people published their reminiscences, they were loathsomely false.[10]

Still, it is wrong to assume that all survivors kept silent. To the best of my knowledge those who were lucky enough to return from the Gulag did not experience 'survivor's guilt'. From the 1950s, some were eager to talk and actually did so, at least in private, behind closed doors: to family members or friends, sometimes to anybody who was interested in their stories. But there were not many who were really eager to listen to them.

Some families rejected the released from the outset. Others discovered that they could not find a common language with them anymore. The family of Varlam Shalamov, a writer of tragic fate, whose 'Kolyma Stories' greatly surpass Solzhenitsyn's work as a testimony to the Gulag and human behaviour there, collapsed because upon his return from the Gulag he rejected his ex-wife's demand 'to forget', while his daughter, always demonstrating her loyalty to the regime, did not want to maintain any ties to him. To her, and to many like her, her father had died long ago; this is what she always wrote in her personal particulars.[11] A writer, Yuri Dombrovsky, who returned to Moscow in 1995, after 25 years in camps and exile, wrote at that time:

> Even our children didn't feel
> sorry for us
> Even our wives did not want us.[12]

The information blockade was an indispensable part of Soviet ideological indoctrination. To construct a collective memory, individual memories need to be in contiguity with each other through public discourse and in a space provided by mass communications, public commemorations and historical narratives.[13] Few exceptions notwithstanding,[14] the stories of the survivors remained private. Most of the victims of the Gulag and other repressions, as well as the members of their families, were unable or unwilling to leave any record of their suffering, either oral or textual. The survivors remained isolated from each other and from the rest of society. Considering their political, social, ethnic and other diversity, it would be difficult for it to be otherwise even if the system were more open and liberal. But the Soviet system did not permit even an embryonic self-organisation. Solidarity and mutual support were possible at best on a very small-group level. Readjustment was mainly a solo act. Under the circumstances, the narratives of survivors did not contribute to the collective memory as much as was needed. The state prevented them from becoming a part of a remembrance.

In the late 1950s to the early 1980s, the regime remained repressive, but was much more sophisticated in this regard. Despite the creeping rehabilitation of Stalin, which became especially noticeable in the Brezhnev period, direct repression became much less arbitrary and far from always resulting in imprisonment.[15] The KGB preferred to resort to so-called 'preventive measures', like mass surveillance, harassment, threats, blackmail, psychiatric incarcerations, forced emigration and so on. The prevailing opinion in society, at that time, held that one had to do something really 'anti-Soviet' in order to be put in jail. Loyal or docile people could sleep well and not tremble at the knock at the door anymore. Thus, for ordinary Soviet citizens the very notion of victims and perpetrators underwent a significant change. In their opinion, innocent victims belonged mainly to the past.

Besides, in the late Soviet period, family background became much less important in impeding individual careers than it had been 20 or 30 years earlier. People were not penalised anymore for having the 'wrong' relatives if the latter were rehabilitated. But even having unrehabilitated relatives was not always an obstacle for their success. Personal loyalty to the Party and good connections mattered more than persecuted grandfathers, and even fathers. Gorbachev's paternal grandfather served nine years in a labour camp, and Yeltsin's father spent three years there, but this did not affect their successful careers. And since past abuses became less relevant to current realities, many descendants of the repressed were ready to consign them to oblivion, to let bygones remain bygones. Thus, the sharing of suffering became even more problematic.

Second, debates on the interrelations between historical memory and collective memory often ignore political power, which may exert a strong, sometimes even decisive influence over both of them. Remembrance and forgetfulness are always selective. They are connected not only with individual and collective life experiences; they are also an outcome of political choice and allegiances. One may say, tell me what you want to remember, commemorate and forget, and I will tell you who you are. This can be said not only about individuals, but also about nations and states, especially when memories are uncomfortable and should be followed by a need to repent and to atone. Members of all sorts of groups may make special efforts to promulgate their accounts of the past, but the modern state stands apart in the level of resources and authority it can master when creating a usable past and restricting competing efforts.[16]

In the Soviet Union up until Stalin's death those famous communists who had vanished during the Great Terror, or later, were mentioned only occasionally and only as traitors, spies and villains. Some of those who were rehabilitated during Khrushchev's thaw were incorporated as heroes and victims into the official pantheon. In both cases, this was very far from the truth. These people were executed for crimes they had never committed, but most of them had committed many other crimes that were never mentioned in the narratives and were not even considered crimes.

Besides, Khrushchev's rehabilitation was very selective. There was no national-level legislation or clear guidelines in this regard, and even those communists who had been convicted in the 1930s show trials were not rehabilitated at all. The official narrative of that time accentuated the persecution of veteran and other communists, but it did not condemn political persecution as illegal in principle. To Khrushchev the victims worthy of remembering were the loyal Party members (i.e. Stalinists), in the first place, and the non-Party loyalists, in the second place. By separating the Party from Stalin, Khrushchev presented the former as the main victim of his purges. The suffering of people from all other walks of life was largely ignored.

Stalin and but a few of his accomplices were made culprits, but the Party in general remained a sacred cow. Between 1954 and 1961 only about 50 individuals were executed or imprisoned, and about 350 people were expelled from the Party for 'violations of socialist legality'.[17] However, the main reason for their punishment was not their crimes but their association with Beria. Many KGB officers who were no better than those punished retained their freedom and even their positions.[18] The introduction of a statute of limitations in the late 1950s prevented the very possibility of prosecutions for crimes committed during the Great Terror. Thus, the policy of impunity remained dominant in the country. Still, for a short time, Stalin's dictatorship and his repressions not only became the topic of muted official criticism but of public debate as well, although the latter was limited to the narrow circle of the liberal-minded (in the terms of the 1950s) intelligentsia. But this debate was soon suppressed.[19]

During the *perestroika* period more leading communists were rehabilitated, and a few, like Bukharin, for a short time even became martyrs, sometimes with the assistance and blessing of western sympathisers.[20] The new myths once again ignored the fact that hurriedly canonised 'martyrs' had been perpetrators themselves until they fell victim to the system that they had created and supported. Actually, in 1986–1987, Gorbachev followed Khrushchev's pattern. For him, the main victims were the Party, the military and to a lesser extent the creative intelligentsia.[21]

Even this line met with a strong resistance by the KGB and some Politburo members, such as Andrei Gromyko.[22] However, under growing public pressure decrees issued in 1988 and in 1989 accelerated the rehabilitation of ordinary citizens persecuted from the early 1930s through the mid-1950s. By 2000, the President's Commission on rehabilitation of the victims of political repression created in September 1987 had rehabilitated more than 4 million people; of them some 800,000 victims were still alive at that time. Sometimes, rehabilitation was not devoid of politics. Thus, the Supreme Court rejected a plea to pardon Lavrenty Beria, although he had been executed not for his numerous real crimes but for allegedly being a British spy. At the same time, some of his bloody henchmen, like Pavel Sudoplatov, have been rehabilitated. Still, the comprehensive law rehabilitating the victims of political repressions from 7 November 1917 to the end of Soviet rule was adopted by the Russian parliament, the State Duma, only in October 1992.

However, the future of the Soviet past remained uncertain even during the heyday of Russian liberalism. In the late 1980s and in the 1990s, Russians were confronted with a range of competing accounts of this past, but attempts to produce new narratives based on a radical break with the previous official account of Soviet history to a large extent were unsuccessful. Individual and sometimes quite contradictory, mainly unpublished and often even unwritten recollections could not play a significant role in the construction of a collective memory which would be parallel to and independent of the official historical memory and master narrative. During *perestroika* and later, a collective memory could not just be resuscitated; it had to be constructed anew. Unfortunately, this never happened.

Actually, the Yeltsin government's attitude toward the Soviet past was quite ambiguous. The political elite that came to power in Russia, in the aftermath of the August 1991 coup, was mainly a direct continuation of the communist one. There was no real turnover of the administration, let alone of the bureaucratic apparatus, except that the many middle-ranking members of the *nomenklatura* advanced to its higher ranks.[23] The same can be said about the judiciary and power machinery. No wonder those people were not inclined to give a legal assessment of the Soviet period and especially of its individual culprits. There was neither an intensive nor a consistent engagement with the tragic and shameful aspects of the Soviet past. The state was repentant, or rather pretended to be repentant only for a short while.

In contemporary Russia, much more is known about the victims than about the executioners and persecutors. The Memorial Society continues to do its best to compile a list of all those persecuted, although there are still many lacunae in this regard. However, except for Stalin, Beria and some of their main henchmen, the names of other persecutors, not to mention rank-and-file executioners, remain unknown. To a large extent, the evil remains insufficiently personified.

The repentance was insincere, since the crucial questions of individual accountability and retroactive justice have never been raised, and the perpetrators, torturers and executioners mainly remained unidentified. Even proposals of non-penal sanctions and the public exposure of the offenders were rejected. Article 18 of the 'Law for the Rehabilitation of Victims of Political Repression' adopted by the Russian parliament in 1991, provided for criminal responsibility for those, 'who have been found guilty of committing crimes in connection with the administration of [Soviet] justice'.[24] However, this article remained only on paper. There was no criminal prosecution of the perpetrators whatsoever. In 1992, the State Duma mandated a release of the names of those who had borne direct responsibility for the Soviet crimes, but this decision was also sabotaged by the KGB and other state agencies and has never been implemented. In fact, the judicial prosecution and even public exposure of the perpetrators never became a popular demand; there was no strong public pressure in this regard. Unlike many other countries, there was no 'truth commission' in Russia either.

There is some convincing evidence that in East Central Europe, lustration in spite of some problematic aspects, has contributed to a consolidation of democracy.[25] In Russia, in the early 1990s, lustration was rejected outright not only by the government and the parliament but even by many those who called themselves 'democrats'. The publication of the names of secret informers was never on the agenda. It is not surprising that the most adamant opponents of lustration were the Party functionaries, KGB officers and secret informers. In this regard, a popular Russian writer Vladimir Voinovich[26] caustically remarked that the staunchest opponents of capital punishment are murderers awaiting execution.

The secret services were never put under any public control. On the contrary, in some ways they extended their influence over society. Many retired KGB officers penetrated businesses, parties, TV, mass media and even NGOs but retained ties with their former employer.[27] Already in 1996, the deputy head of the presidential administration, previously a high-ranking FSB (Federal Security Service, the successor to the KGB) officer, Evgeny Savostianov, publicly boasted that many KGB secret agents and informers had become prominent members of the political and economic elites.[28]

Those, who claimed that Russia needed its own Nuremberg were very small in number.[29] Most of them were forlorn dissidents of the Soviet era, whom even the 'new democrats' – in the recent past, the conformists, at best – preferred to ignore as much as possible or to label irremediable idealists, since the very existence of the former was a pang of conscience to them. No wonder that in the absence of strong public pressure the trial of the Communist Party had become a farce even before it began. Instead, in 1996, Yeltsin renamed, 7 November, Revolution Day, the Day of Accord and Reconciliation, which indeed brought neither accord nor reconciliation. In 2005, the Russian parliament decreed celebration of the Day of the October Revolution as a commemorative date.

Perhaps, the most bizarre attempt at false repentance was the reburial of the bones of Nicolas II and other members of his family, in 1998. At that time, Yeltsin claimed that this event symbolised that 'the current generation of Russian people is trying to atone for the sins of its ancestors'.[30] This claim was false because only the distant perpetrators were called the sinners, while many recent and willing accomplices attended the ceremony without any feeling of guilt for their own deeds.

Some other actions were unintentionally beguiling. The Central Bank first printed the 500,000-ruble note depicting the ancient Solovetsky monastery on an island in the northern White Sea, without crosses and cupolas, just as it was during Soviet times, when it served as one of the first and most notorious prisons. Instead of celebrating religion persecuted by the Soviets, Russia's most important financial institution inadvertently commemorated the Gulag.

Third, the collapse of the Soviet Union and the hardships of Russia's transition from communism backlashed in a widespread nostalgia for the 'glorious past', which can never be on the side of honest historical reckoning. The feeling of humiliation connected with Russia's defeat in the Cold War, the loss of its superpower status and the disintegration of the Soviet empire is widespread in the country. Many Russians also became nostalgic about the times when, in a way, life was easier and simpler because the state prescribed for them what to do and what to think but, in turn, provided them with employment, a social security net and the pride of living in a superpower.

Under the circumstances, it is too painful and difficult for the majority of Russians to admit that for more than 70 years they lived in a criminal state, in which forced labour camps, prisons, the Iron Curtain, domestic passports which restricted the right to voluntary chosen residency and shortages of basic foodstuffs and goods were an everyday reality, while the ruling communist elite followed the principle, which had first been formulated by Count Benckendorff, chief of the dreaded 'Third Section' (a kind of the KGB of that time) under tsar Nicolas I: 'Laws are written for subordinates, not for the authorities'.[31]

Fourth, there is no repentance without the feeling of guilt and responsibility. However, the vast majority of Russians categorically refuse to admit that they were voluntary or involuntary accomplices of the Soviet regime. The notion of collective guilt and collective responsibility is absolutely alien to them. Hence, their perpetual whining about the destiny of the unfortunate Motherland and their unwillingness to help it in practical terms. When Alfred Koch, a liberal Russian politician, stated that the Russian people themselves were to blame for their misfortunes, his words were almost unanimously perceived in the country as Russophobic and an unthinkable insult.[32] This is hardly surprising in a country where individuals were always subjects of the state, but never its citizens. Even in the late 1980s, when negative attitudes toward the Soviet regime were at their peak, only a very small group of radicals united in the uninfluential Democratic Union (its rallies were never attended by more than two or three dozen people) dared to promote the slogan: 'Shame on us all'.

One of several illusions of nineteenth-century Russian literature was a belief that suffering makes people better. This idea is still held by Alexandr Solzhenitsyn, but it was completely discredited by Varlam Shalamov and other inmates of the Gulag, who insisted that the camp experience always made people not better but worse. 'The Camp experience is completely negative, down to every single minute. A man becomes only worse. It cannot be otherwise'.[33] I was personally acquainted or friendly with about two dozen people who at one time or another were incarcerated in the Gulag. All of them confirmed Shalamov's opinion.

But the same can be said about the Soviet experience in general. The moral degradation and dehumanisation of an extremely atomised Soviet society, in which any form of social cohesion was deliberately weakened, was enormous and had long-standing consequences. Decades of terror and fear, the sacralisation of violence, brainwashing, spy mania, suspicion, denunciation, insecurity and deprivation, an atmosphere of intolerance, legal nihilism, social infantilism, depreciation of individuality, devaluation of human life and destruction of humanistic and/or religious values have left the majority of Russians with warped ethical principles and a broken moral backbone. Mistrust of and disdain for law and justice, residual disrespect for the truth and basic human rights, illiberal thought and attitudes are still evident today.

The Gulag not only left deep scars on the mentality of the people, who were its prisoners, and on their immediate families; it had a significant and negative effect on the psychology, behaviour, way of life, values and dehumanising attitudes of the general population as well. Directly or indirectly, the Gulag and other repressive agencies and institutions involved millions of people in their systems, serving as interrogators, prosecutors, judges, guards, officers, wardens, sentries, supervisors, managers and white-collar employees, engineers, technicians, physicians, political workers, and so forth. Their children were raised in an atmosphere of lies, violence and denunciations.[34] Those who shot and put other people in jail survived in greater numbers than those who were shot and imprisoned.

In the 1930s and 1940s, it was not uncommon for wives to denounce their husbands and for husbands to denounce their wives, for children to publicly repudiate their parents, and for relatives to disown their arrested kin. Millions of people were prone to mass psychosis and hysteria. At mass public meetings, they voted for capital punishment for the 'enemies of the people' and much later, for the suppression of the Hungarian revolution, for the invasions of Czechoslovakia and Afghanistan, and for any of the other disreputable and criminal deeds of the Soviet rulers.

Not only during the Great Terror but much later, until the very end of the Soviet Union, and apparently even now, a great number of people were secret collaborators and informers of the KGB, not disdained for denunciating their friends, colleagues and other people. In Stalin's period, voluntary informers and paid secret collaborators were ubiquitous: in factories and collective farms, in universities and research institutions, even in bread lines.[35] However, even after the death of the dictator, the situation did not change qualitatively. One may only speculate about the number of informers. In this regard, the Soviets hardly matched East Germany, but their number were very great.[36]

Voluntary denunciations made to settle scores and personal grudges with a disliked person, for career considerations, for an opportunity to travel abroad, or just because of a perverted sense of vigilance, were a common practice. In the Stalin period, they often resulted in arrests and even executions. Later, their consequences were usually less tragic, but there was never a shortage of those who were eager to become willing accomplices. Very few individual exceptions notwithstanding, these people have never been exposed in the post-Soviet period. The secret services still adamantly hold that snitches were good and loyal Soviet citizens, who never did anything wrong. Actually, collaboration with the KGB is not considered shameful in Russia today. It is not a secret in the country that the Orthodox Patriarch, Alexei II, in Soviet times was a KGB informer with the code name Drozdov. Nowadays, he preaches about the superior Russian morality and spirituality, and almost nobody finds this shameful. During the inauguration ceremonies he also blesses the Russian president, who in the not so distant past was a lieutenant-colonel of the same organisation. This situation is hardly proper for sincere repentance and atonement.

The Germans kept silent because they were burdened with guilt; the Japanese keep silent, because, if one followed Buruma,[37] they were burdened with shame; the French and Austrians belatedly confronted their troubled past in installments. Russians feel neither guilt nor shame. The Russian language even lacks a word remotely resembling the German *Vergangenheitsbewältiging*. The very idea of individual, and even less so of collective, responsibility remains too vague in Russian culture.[38]

In fact, there is nothing new in this attitude. Already in the late Soviet period, a growing number of people practiced a strategy of self-alienation and escape from Soviet society and its official values. Negative characteristics of the Soviet regime were privately acknowledged, discussed and criticised, but, as a rule, without any detriment to personal self-esteem. The guilty were the socio-political system and the communist rulers, never oneself.[39] Those who came of age at the time of disintegration of the Soviet Union are old enough to have concrete memories of 'the period of stagnation', yet young enough to discard questions of civic responsibility.[40] The very thought that they might carry the burden of responsibility for the deeds of their fathers and grandfathers is absolutely alien to them.

In no other country's history were the boundaries between perpetrators, accomplices and victims as blurred as in Soviet Russia. The guilt of Germans was more obvious, because the Germans mainly murdered the 'other'. One might say that, in Russia, in addition to the 'other', one's 'own' murdered other 'owns', and then other 'owns' murdered the murderers. But even this would be an oversimplification. Yesterday's perpetrators and executioners might later become victims. Most accomplices were simultaneously victims as well, and some victims, if they had managed to survive, later might become accomplices, or even perpetrators.

Thus, a problem of collective responsibility, even if it were admitted, poses many difficult questions.

The gnawing question in Russia, the question that can hardly be answered in an unambiguous way at all, is how to discriminate between the accomplices and the victims. The devilish device of totalitarian regimes was to turn the vast majority of people into worse than mere conformists. They made them active or passive accomplices to their crimes, sometimes involuntarily but nevertheless accomplices. As Vaclav Havel put it, in the Communist countries, everyone was in some measure co-responsible. Very few people escaped this trap, and of this few many had been accomplices too, at one time of their life or another.

No wonder that, nowadays, the majority of Russians consider themselves, and rather gladly, not accomplices but innocent victims. They were always the victims; the perpetrators were the others, although there is no consensus on who exactly these perpetrators were. The culprits were Stalin and his henchmen, communists, fascists, imperialists, Jews and other non-Russians. A certain homogenisation of victimhood through the construction of an 'us–they' opposition is taking place. 'Us' has become an undifferentiated category, and 'they' an abstract evil. Victimisation creates a sense of unity among the nation, but the price of this unity is quite heavy. Unwillingness to admit a society's own responsibility almost inevitably leads to its solidarity with the undemocratic power.

In post-totalitarian countries, generalising symbols and representation are important because, to some extent, they may impede forgetting and transfer subjective experiences into the collective memory. By demolishing monuments to the perpetrators and constructing memorials to the victims, a state and society reject their continuity with the criminal past. One of the most vivid images of the fall of the Soviet state came when a giant crane rumbled to the entrance of the KGB headquarters and hauled away the statue of 'Iron Felix', that is Felix Dzerzhinsky, the founder of the Soviet secret police and the brutal zealot and henchman. However, this event was not confirmed by other similar symbolic actions.

In Russia, the tragic events of Soviet history do not have an adequate symbolic representation. Moscow and Saint-Petersburg correspondingly have a Sakharov Avenue and a Sakharov Square; in the latter even a monument to Sakharov has been constructed, despite the protests of his widow. But his legacy is ignored. Very few memorials inspire people to think of and to feel the past as it really was. Many more, including those constructed in the post-Soviet period, which is marked by a fervour of statuomania,[41] suggest a glamourised version of that past. Monuments to the victims of repression pose more artistic, conceptual and political problems than monuments to heroes. Even their main purpose is arguable: are they supposed to mourn, to commemorate, to accuse, or to educate; or to combine all these functions? However, in Russia, the main reason for this commemorative neglect of the victims of repression is not a lack of tradition or conceptual problems, but a lack of will.

Very few places and spaces in the country inspire people to think of, to reflect on, and to feel the painful past as it actually was. Monuments to the victims of Soviet repression are very rare and consist mainly of inconspicuous commemorative stones, plaques, marks, and in but a few cases, statues. By 2002, they numbered only 420 altogether, and many of them were constructed not in Russia but in the other ex-Soviet republics.[42] Without the public initiative of NGOs there would be no monuments to the victims in Russia at all. Still, those that were constructed are quite ambiguous and may not even be perceived as a 'never again' statement.

Their predominantly abstract character eschews confrontation. They are deliberately de-politicised. They lack conventional symbols of suffering, repression and protest, such as chains, bars, bound hands or clenched fists. At best, they convey grief and sorrow, but they do not explain their causes, and they do not protest and accuse.[43] Most of them contain the inscriptions: 'To the victims of political repression'. Who was responsible for the repression is unclear. In the Czech Republic or Hungary analogous monuments contain an unambiguous answer: 'the communists'. In Russia, the perpetrators remain unidentified, and the evil anonymous. The very idea of political accountability is mainly ignored. (A rare exception is the stone on the Troitskaia Square in Saint-Petersburg dedicated to the victims of communist terror, and built mainly on donations of the former prisoners of the Gulag and the NGOs involved in their commemoration.)

Perhaps, the most revealing in this regard is the long history of the still not constructed national monument to the victims of the repression. The first time its construction was proposed by Khrushchev was at the 22nd Communist Party Congress in 1961. Remarkably by the victims he implied only 'comrades who became victims of arbitrariness'.[44] Gorbachev revived this proposal at the 19th Party Conference, in 1988, suggesting a monument to 'illegality and repressions' – a very vague definition indeed. Yeltsin promised the same, but again to no avail.

Today only a granite stone in Moscow marks the place where the planned national monument is to stand. This marker in Lubianka Square (in Soviet times, Dzerzhinsky Square), was brought by the Memorial society from the Solovetsky Islands in 1990, the site of the first forced labour camp, created under Lenin. Lubianka Square is itself noteworthy. It is located on the same square as the KGB headquarters, which doomed millions of people to suffering, torture and death. The monument to the victims was supposed to be built on the square of non-repentant perpetrators. Ironically, the notorious building on Lubyanka Square is now occupied by its arrogant heir, the FSB. However, the suggestion to move the stone to the place of the demolished monument to Dzerzhinsky and, thus, to attach to it additional symbolic meaning, was rejected by the Russian parliament. Likewise, demands to turn the KGB headquarters into a national museum of repression made by some members of the Memorial in the late 1980s are long forgotten.

Moreover, several attempts have already been made to restore on Lubyanka Square a monument to Dzerzhinsky. Remarkably, one of them was made in 2002 by Moscow mayor, Yuri Luzhkov, who personally supervised its toppling in 1991. So far, for political reasons, the Kremlin regards this action as inopportune, though by no means impossible.[45] Actually, several monuments to Dzerzhinsky have already been built in other places. Those who are promoting his positive image argue that he cared for homeless children, but fail to mention that he cared for them after he had murdered their parents. If these attempts succeed, the monument to the victims on the same square with the monument to the hangman would be another and even greater insult to their memory.

Perhaps it is for the best that a memorial to the victims of repression does not yet stand in the Russian capital. It may be that the modest granite stone is a more suitable symbol than a pompous, cold and false monument – one could not expect anything better in Russia's current political and artistic climate. The exceptions, like the modest yet interesting and moving memorial by the sculptor Mikhail Shemiakin in Saint-Petersburg, are very few in number. The monstrous Easter Island-type sculpture by the famous sculptor Ernst Neizvestny called the 'Mask of Grief', which gazed down at the Magadan harbour in the Far East, where thousands of barges carrying prisoners arrived at their final journey, illustrates better what might be expected were the national monument built. Considering Putin's repeatedly expressed desire to terminate all debates about victims and repentance, in all probability it would convey the patently false message: 'They are dead. But we have invested a lot of money in their commemoration. And now we do not own them anything'. But these were not the concerns of the Russian authorities when they decided to quietly put on hold the promise to build the national monument.

On every 30 October throughout the late 1980s and into the early 1990s, thousands of people, old and young, the persecuted, their relatives, liberal politicians and just those who condemned Soviet crimes, gathered at the Solovetsky Stone to commemorate the victims. Since 1974, political prisoners and dissidents in the Soviet Union have commemorated this day as the Day of Political Prisoners, and on 18 October 1991 the Supreme Soviet of the Russian Federation ruled that that 30 October be the Memorial Day for Victims of Political Repression. Nowadays, the number of those who come to the Solovetsky Stone on the day of remembrance has shrunk to several hundred at best, mostly the elderly. Some newspapers are not ashamed to mention their small number with a poorly disguised gloating delight.

The general public demonstrates complete indifference to the Solovetsky Stone and to those for whom it remains the main symbol of victimhood. In 1999, when I placed flowers on the Stone – I used to do this during all my visits to Moscow – my friend who accompanied me advised me to break the flowers' stems; otherwise they would be immediately stolen. In 2003, I witnessed how a few men used the Stone as a place on which they put several bottles of beer and snacks as they enjoyed a drink in the fresh air. They were certainly not ashamed of their behaviour because when I took my camera to take their pictures they affably waved their hands at me. Many people who happened to be nearby did not pay any attention to them and did not consider their behaviour repugnant.

It can be worse. In Vladivostok, a monument to a great poet, Osip Mandelshtam, who perished in the Gulag, has been defiled many times in the last few years, and eventually was removed to a secret location. It is not surprising either that in Saint-Petersburg a monument to the victims was defiled many times with graffiti like 'Judas', 'Too few were executed' or 'Long live great Stalin'.

Likewise, the burial grounds of the victims, even in the few cases when they are discovered and preserved, are not included into the mnemonic landscape of the country. Very little is done to preserve the Gulag camps as sites of national tragedy and horror. The only exception is Perm-36 camp for political prisoners, built in 1972. Neither monuments nor sites have become focal points of any significant state-initiated or public ceremonies.

Recently, a growing number of crosses and chapels reflect the Orthodox Church's desire to appropriate the suffering with the government's apparent consent and encouragement. It has become a common but dubious practice to erect crosses on the sites of the labour camps, the mass graves of victims and other commemorative places. The Orthodox connotations shut out a very significant number of victims: Protestants, Catholics, Jews, Muslims, Buddhists, non-believers, atheists and others. It is equally important that the Church commemorates suffering without any mention of its cause. It does not make a distinction between the victims and the executioners who later were executed too. It claims that through blood sacrifice they all became martyrs eligible for redemption. Far from everybody in Russia agrees with this claim. Thus, not only memory but commemoration too becomes diverse.

In all, memory contained in the monuments to the victims does not adequately reflect the real past. They become almost invisible – in the landscape, in meaning, and in the Russian imagination, because most of them do not evoke a strong emotional response. Memorialised history does not convey pain and condemnation. It looks toothless. But this is already almost an academic consideration. With Putin's ascendancy to power and the partial rehabilitation of the Soviet past, the construction of new monuments was actually blocked.

As regretful as this may be from a moral point of view, some examples from the postwar European experience prove that it is possible to transit to liberal democracy by playing down, or even forgetting the disturbing past.[46] But it is hardly possible to make the successful transition by glorifying it. If the past continues to drag Russia and its people backward, maybe it would not be such a bad idea to write certain things off for the time being. However, Putin is fond of repeating that there is no future without the past, and that Russians should not simply write off the past. The problem is, which past should be remembered?

Under Putin's authoritarian rule another revision of Soviet history is taking place, evoking very little protest because it reflects and simultaneously exploits the prevailing mood in Russia. The Grand Imperial style is in fashion again. Nostalgia for the musified and cinematicised version of an idealised Soviet past is actively propagated by the state-controlled TV and mass media as non-political, but, in fact, they are pursuing clear political goals. Instead of facilitating and encouraging the formation of a critical perception of the Soviet past, the Russian authorities conceal and abrogate its disturbing aspects.

Putin and the current Russian ruling elite, more than 25 per cent of whom were recruited from the military and secret services,[47] do not belong to the generation of repentance; they are the children of defeat. Putin frankly states that the greatest catastrophe of the twentieth century was not the two World Wars, not the Holocaust and Gulag, but the disintegration of the Soviet Union. At the same time, Putin and his advisors understand well the widespread disenchantment with democratic ideals in Russia. His authoritarian policies and nationalistic and pro-Soviet rhetoric meet with widespread public approval. After all, claims the Russian president, in Soviet times 'people did not live and work in vain'. His position can be summarised as follows: one should not humiliate the Russian people by constantly accentuating their shameful past. It is more expedient to present this past as not so shameful, or, even better, as not shameful at all. The repression, at best, is equated with space exploration and the Soviet ballet and is shifted to the distant periphery of the official narrative.[48] This position reflects the general mood; hence, the growth of pro-Stalinist sentiments in Russia.[49]

Perpetrators and their political successors always want a true history to be silenced and suppressed, at least played down and whitewashed. A near-total reclassifying of the state archives as secret, some of which were declassified for a short time, is only one, though revealing, part of the on-going process. In 2005, Putin warned, 'We are not going to compare and throw together crimes committed by Nazism and Stalinism'. The message was clear: there would be no Nuremberg in Russia; forget about it. An unapologetic former KGB officer, he personally contributes to attempts at restoring the false myth of the *chekists* as morally pure, self-sacrificing and noble knights with 'cool heads, warm hearts and clean hands', who did not have any other goal but honestly serving the Soviet state. Already in 2001, he assured his former colleagues that they should not be ashamed but proud of their history.[50] One of Putin's first acts as President was to restore the bust of Andropov in the FSB headquarters, together with his memorial plaque on its building.

The burden of history turned out to be unbearable for contemporary Russia. Memory there is divorced from knowledge. One is now witnessing the substitution of amnesia for justice and historical memory, and impunity for coming to terms with the past. The state again tightens its control over education and imposes uniformity in the teaching of history. Repressive Soviet history has again become repressed.

Russia lacks anything tantamount to the Polish State Institute for National Memory (*Instytut Pamieci Narodowej*). Dedicated volunteers and a few professional historians continue to publish new materials on the victims and repressions, especially in Russian regions. But even these materials are published in editions of very small circulations (a few hundred copies on the average) and are mainly aimed at scholars and interested individuals. The few NGOs, like the Memorial Society or the Sakharov Center, the custodians of the counter-memory, have managed to survive so far only because of international financial support. All these activities are very important indeed because in the current situation they become a kind of protest not only against the past, but also against the present. But they are insufficient.

Regretfully, there is very little protest against the re-revision of Soviet history because it reflects the prevailing mood in Russia. Not only the political elite but the public at large do not want to make Soviet crimes a focal point in collective rememberance. Putin's popularity has proven that nowadays descending from the KGB is not a stigma. On the contrary, the secret services are quite popular in a country longing for order and stability.

An excessive fear of being accused in the witch-hunt, and a desire to reach an accommodation with the communist *nomenklatura* so conspicuously demonstrated by the Russian liberals in the aftermath of the August 1991 putsch has backfired. In the countries trying to build a democratic order on the ruins of totalitarianism or authoritarianism it is not always necessary or expedient to put witches in prisons. However, they should be put in their place. Otherwise, the witches themselves begin hunting again, as is happening in Russia today.

Totalitarian regimes are always ideologically revolutionary. They imply mass mobilisation and mass participation. They are based on the explicit rejection of traditional moral standards which would make other people hesitate or feel guilty, and on the greater implication of the whole society in the repressive process.[51] In the Soviet Union, many millions of people not only followed orders, but faithfully served the communist regime. Under these circumstances, the distinction between a criminal leadership and an innocent nation is very dubious indeed. This is one of the reasons why, after totalitarian regimes are defeated or collapse, those who lived under them have a rather ambiguous attitude towards their totalitarian past and are reluctant to critically assess their own behaviour. The degree to which the majority admit that they were accomplices sets the limits of public remorse. Most of the people who lived under totalitarianism are incapable of sincere and complete repentance. Actually, there is nothing unusual in this regard. In the 1940s and in the 1950s, the majority of Germans perceived the Nazi regime as a handful of zealots, who deluded good and innocent German people.[52]

It takes one, or even two generations of waiting for repentance and for reckoning with the disturbing past and its uncomfortable moral issues. But the life and attitudes of these new, clean generations should be shaped by a liberal democratic order, civil society and economic prosperity. Only these generations with a radically different worldview and values sometimes, but far from always, are daring and honest enough to take their fathers and grandfathers to account.

All this is a far cry from current Russian realities. In Russia, 'the time is out of joint' again. Lived history, history taught at home, and learned history are bifurcated, just as they were in the late Soviet period. There is no national consensus with regard to the Soviet past today, and Russians still cannot draw a line between their past and present. Russian society has missed the opportunity of critical evaluation of the past. Instead, it has quickly become tired of suffering and of those who suffered.

It is not accidental that the master narrative of Putin's regime repeats and propagates a mythologised and sacralised version of World War II constructed in the Brezhnev period. Victory in World War II (the Great Patriotic War in the official lexicon) served as the legitimation of communist rule much better than the Bolshevik turnover in 1917.

In the early 1990s some attempts were made to re-examine many of the long-standing myths about the war, but their resurgence in the media began shortly after Putin came to power. Nowadays, the war occupies 6–8 per cent of all air time on the main, state-controlled Russian TV channels.[53] In this case, the constructed past influences the present quite successfully, and in a time of vanishing canons on the national heritage battlefield, this one still holds ground. As the Russian writer, Victor Astafiev remarked, 'the war made up, blocked out the war really fought'.

In the opinion of the vast majority of Russians, the war was the most important event in their twentieth-century history; there is little else left to take pride in. But at the same time, to a significant number of Russians, the war and the final victory still justify the repressive Soviet regime. Victory wrote off all disastrous blunders and the incompetence of the Soviet leadership, avoidable losses and unnecessary suffering of the ruled, and the unrepentant crimes of the rulers. It created a sense of national unity and extrapolated it into other periods of Soviet history.[54]

The higher the status that the glamour version of the war acquires, the more the memory of Stalin's repression is receding into the depths of the Russian collective memory, while the Great Stalin is idealised again by a growing number of Russians. According to the surveys of the Levada-Center, over the past 12 years, the perceived significance of the repression for Russian history has fallen from 29 to 1 per cent, while positive views of Stalin increased from 19 to 53 per cent between 1998 and 2003.[55]

This change in attitudes is actively encouraged and propagated by Putin's leadership. Suffice it to mention that on 21 December 2004, the date of Stalin's birthday, one of the leaders of the ruling United Russia party and the current speaker of the State Duma, Boris Gruzlov, after laying flowers on his tomb at Red Square, called for a reappraisal of the dictator's historical role. He claimed that some 'exaggerated' deeds should not be made to overshadow the 'remarkable' personality of a 'leader of our country who did a lot for Victory in the Great Patriotic War'.[56] Putin unveiled a plaque honouring the dictator's military leadership, and approved the minting of hundreds of silver coins bearing his portrait.[57]

Nowadays, young Russians reject traumatic historical knowledge and prefer closure. Public interest in Soviet crimes and sympathy toward their victims is rapidly diminishing. Downplayed in official narratives they are fading still further not only from collective memory but also from private memories. After all, why should one make a special effort to identify oneself with grandparents whom one has never seen in one's life, about whom one knows very little, and whose fate is already a distant history?

It seems that Russia may serve as an example for George Santayana's famous dictum that those who cannot remember the past are condemned to repeat it. History is intentionally sanitised to be made more suitable. It has again become a backward-looking projection of contemporary political attitudes and realities. Mass consciousness is becoming prone to the false idea that history can be corrected and improved without any need for repentance, and that everything can be destroyed and rebuilt anew.

No wonder that Russia has become a country of pseudos: pseudo-democracy, pseudo-capitalism, pseudo-historicity, pseudo-remembrance, pseudo-repentance. Only political power is real in the country, just as it always was. This situation will hardly change until a more general problem is solved: how to overcome the past without denying it? Whether, when and how this is done in Russia remains to be seen.

Notes

1. Charles S. Maier, "Overcoming the Past? Narrative and Negotiation, Remembering, and Reparation: Issues at the Interface of History and the Law", in John Torpey (ed.), *Politics and the Past. On Repairing Historical Injustices* (New York: Rowman & Littlefield, 2003), p.296.
2. See, for example, Steven Rosefielde, "An Assessment of the Sources and Uses of Gulag Forced Labor 1929–56", *Soviet Studies* 33 (1981), pp.51–87; Rosefielde, "Incriminating Evidence: Excess Deaths and Forced Labor under Stalin – A Final Reply to Critics", *Soviet Studies* 39/2 (1987), pp.292–313; Robert Conquest, *The Great Terror: A Reassessment* (Oxford: Oxford University Press, 1990); Edwin Bacon, *The Gulag at War: Stalin's Forced Labor System in the Light of the Archives* (New York: New York University Press, 1994); A.N. Dugin, *Neizvestnyi GULAG: Dokumenty i fakty* (Moscow, 1999); A.I. Kokurin and N.V. Petrov (eds), *GULAG: Glavnoe upravlenie lagerei. 1918–1960* (Moscow: Materik, 2000); Michael Ellman, "Soviet Repression Statistics: Some Comments", *Europe–Asia Studies* 54/7 (2002), pp.1151–1172; Alexander N. Yakovlev, *A Century of Violence in Soviet Russia* (New Haven, CT: Yale University Press, 2002), pp.233–234; Anne Applebaum, *Gulag. A History* (New York: Doubleday, 2003), p.578ff.; Barry McLoughlin and Kevin McDermott (eds), *Stalin's Terror. High Politics and Mass Represssion in the Soviet Union* (Basingstoke: Palgrave Macmillan, 2003); and many others.
3. The latter numbered over 6 million – see P. Polian, and N. Pobol, *Stalinskie deportatsii 1928–1953 godov. Dokumenty* (Moscow: Materik, 2005), pp.12–13.
4. Some 6 million people – see G. M. Ivanova, *Labor Camp Socialism. The Gulag in the Soviet Totalitarian System* (Armonk, NY: M. E. Sharpe, 2000), p.43.
5. John Keep, "Wheatcroft and Stalin's Victims: Comments", *Europe–Asia Studies*, 51/6 (1999), p.1091.
6. Nanci Adler, *Victims of the Soviet Terror. The Story of the Memorial Movement* (Westport, CT: Praeger, 1993), p.100ff.; David Remnik, *Lenin's Tomb. The Last Days of the Soviet Empire* (New York: Random House, 1993); Kathleen E. Smith, *Remembering Stalin's Past. Popular Memory and End of the USSR* (Ithaca, NY: Cornell University Press, 1996), p.78ff.
7. Arkady B. Tsfasman, "Stalin in Soviet and Russian History Textbooks from the 1930s to the 1990s", in Jerzy W. Borejsza and Klaus Ziemer (eds), *Totalitarian and Authoritarian Regimes in Europe. Legacies and Lessons from the Twentieth Century* (New York: Berghahn Books, 2006), p.561ff.
8. Lev Gudkov, *Negativnaia identichnost* (Moscow: Novoe Literaturnoe Obozrenie, 2004), p.83ff.
9. P. G. Pikhoia, *Sovetskii Soiuz: Istoriia vlasti* (Moscow: Izdatel'stvo PAGS, 1998), pp.167–8.
10. See, for example, Boris Diakov, *Povest' o perezhitom* (Moscow: Sovetskaia Rossiia, 1966).
11. I. Sirotinskaia, "Dolgie-dolgie gody besed", in V.V. Esipov (ed.), *Shalamovskii sbornik*, vyp.1. (Vologda: Izdatel'stvo Instituta povysheniia kvalifikatsii i perepodgotovki pedagogicheskikh kadrov, 1994), pp.134–5.

12. Anne Applebaum, "After the Gulag", *The New York Review of Books*, October 24 (2002), p.40.
13. Marina Loskutova, "O pamiati, zritel'nykh obrazakh, ustnoi istorii, i ne tol'ko o nikh", *Ab Imperio*, 1 (2004), pp.76–7.
14. For their analysis, see Leona Toker, *Return from the Archipelago. Narratives of Gulag Survivors* (Bloomington, IN: Indiana University Press, 2000).
15. V. A. Kozlov and S. V. Mironenko (eds), *Kramola. Inakomyslie v SSSR pri Khrushcheve i Brezhneve. 1952–1982* (Moscow: Materik, 2005), p.28ff.
16. James V. Wertsch, *Voices of Collective Remembering* (Cambridge: Cambridge University Press, 2002), p.68.
17. Smith (note 8), pp.166–7.
18. Pikhoia (note 9), 1998, pp.129–30.
19. Albert Van Goudoever, *The Limits of Destalinization in the Soviet Union: Political Rehabilitations in the Soviet Union since Stalin* (New York: St Martin's Press, 1986).
20. Stephen F. Cohen, *Bukharin and the Bolshevik Revolution* (Oxford: Oxford University Press, 1980).
21. Smith (note 8), p.42ff.
22. Pikhoia (note 9), pp.493–4.
23. Anatoly M. Khazanov, "What Went Wrong? Post-communist Transformations in Comparative Perspective", in Yitzhak Brudny, Jonathan Frankel and Stefani Hoffman (eds), *Restructuring Post-Communist Russia* (Cambridge: Cambridge University Press, 2004), pp.31–2.
24. For its analysis see Irina Flige, "Posle zakona o reabilitatsii: transformatsiia obshchestvennogo soznaniia", in Irina Flige (ed.), *Mir posle Gulaga: reabilitatsiia i kul'tura pamiati* (Saint-Petersburg: Nord-West, 2004), pp.55–61.
25. Natalia Letki, "Lustration and Democratisation in East-Central Europe", *Europe–Asia Studies*, 54/4 (2002), pp.529–52.
26. Vladimir Voinovich, *Anti-sovetskii Sovetskii Soiuz* (Moscow: Materik, 2002), p.407.
27. Alexei Miller, "The Communist Past in Post-communist Russia", in Jerzy W. Borejsza and Klaus Ziemer (eds), *Totalitarian and Authoritarian Regimes in Europe. Legacies and Lessons from the Twentieth Century* (New York: Berghahn Books, 2006), p.519.
28. *Izvestiia*, 17 October 1996.
29. Andrew Meier, *Black Earth. A Journey through Russia after the Fall* (New York: W.W. Norton & Company, 2003), pp.43–4.
30. *Moskovskaia Pravda*, 17 July 1998.
31. Richard Pipes, *Russia Under the Old Regime* (New York: Charles Scriber's Sons, 1974), p.290.
32. *New Times*, August 2005; see http://www.newtimeru/eng/detail.asp?art_id=1434
33. Varlam Shalamov, *Kolymskie rasskazy* (Moscow: Nashe Nasledie, 1992), p.194.
34. Ivanova (note 4), pp.XXII, 125, 184, 190.
35. Elena Zubkova, *Poslevoennoe sovetskoe obshchestvo: politika i povsednevnost'. 1945–1953* (Moscow: ROSSPEN, 2000), p.10.
36. I. A. Minutko, *Yuri Andropov. Real'nost' i mif* (Moscow: AST-Press Kniga, 2004), p.153; cf. Kozlov and Mironenko (note 15), p.53.
37. Ian Buruma, *The Wages of Guilt. Memories of War in Germany and Japan* (New York: Farrar Straus Giroux, 1994).
38. Catherine Merridale, *Night of Stone. Death and Memory in Twentieth Century Russia* (New York: Viking, 2000), p.337.
39. Igor S. Kon, "Identity Crisis and Postcommunist Psychology", *Symbolic Interaction*, 16/4 (1993), p.399.
40. Maya Nadkarni and Olga Shevchenko, "The Politics of Nostalgia: A Case for Comparative Analysis of Post-Socialist Practices", *Ab Imperio*, 2 (2004), p.510.
41. Anatoly M. Khazanov, "Post-Communist Moscow: Re-Building the 'Third Rome' in the Country of Missed Opportunities?", *City and Society. Annual Review* (1998), p.300ff.
42. http://lenta.ru/russia/2002/10/30/meeting/
43. Alexandr Etkind, "Vremia sravnivat' kamni. Postperestroechnaia kul'tura politicheskoi skorbi v sovremennoi Rossii", *Ab Imperio* 2 (2004), pp.68–70.
44. XXII S'ezd Kommunisticheskoi Partii Sovetskogo Soiuza, 17–31 Oktiabria 1961 goda. 1962. *Stenograficheskii Otchet*, vol. 2. (Moscow: Gospolitizdat), p.587.
45. *Izvestiia*, 20 September 2002.
46. Timothy Garton Ash, "Trials, Purges and History Lessons: Treating a Difficult Past in Post-communist Europe", in Jan-Werner Müller (ed.), *Memory and Power in Post-War Europe. Studies in the Presence of the Past* (Cambridge: Cambridge University Press, 2002), p.266ff.; cf. Tina Rosenberg, *The Haunted Land. Facing Europe's Ghosts After Communism* (New York: Vintage Books, 1995).

47. Olga Kryshtanovskaia, *Anatomiia rossiiskoi elity* (Moscow: Zakharov, 2004), p.264.
48. Yu Afanasiev, *Opasnaia Rossiia. Traditsii samovlast'ia segodnia* (Moscow: Rossiiskii gosuderstvennyi gumanitarnyi universitet, 2001), pp.155–7.
49. M. Ferretti, "Le stalinisme entre histoire et mémoire: la malaise de la mémoire russe", *Matériaux pour l'histoire de notre temps* 68 (2002), pp.65–81.
50. *Novoe Vremia*, 6 January 2002.
51. Juan J. Linz, *Totalitarian and Authoritarian Regimes* (London: Lynn Rienner, 2000), pp.105, 107.
52. Robert G. Moeller, "War Stories: The Search for a Usable Past in the Federal Republic of Germany", in David E. Lorey and William H. Beezley (eds.), *Collective Violence and Popular Memory: The Politics of Rememberance in the Twentieth Century* (New York: W.W. Norton, 2002), pp. 191–228.
53. http://www.eurozine.com/article/2005-05-03-gudkov-en.html.
54. Amir Weiner, *Making Sense of War. The Second World War and the Fate of the Bolshevik Revolution* (Princeton, NJ: Princeton University Press, 2001); Lev Gudkov, "Die Fesseln des Sieges Rußlands Identität aus der Erinnerung an den Krieg", *Osteuropa* 55/4–6 (2005), pp.56–73.
55. Boris Dubin, "Stalin i drugie. Figury vysshei vlasti v obshchestvennom mnenii sovremennoi Rossii", *Monitoring obshchestvennogo mneniia* 1/63 (2003), pp.13–25; 2/64 (2003), pp.26–40; cf. Aleksei Levinson, "Liudi molodye za istoriiu bez travm", *Neprikosnovennyi Zapas*, 4/36 (2004).
56. Lev Gudkov, "The Fetters of Victory", http://www.eurozine.com/article/2005-05-03-gudkov-en.html.
57. *The Moscow Times*, 4 May 2005.

Accomplices Without Perpetrators: What Do Economists Have to Do with Transitional Justice in Hungary?

JÁNOS MÁTYÁS KOVÁCS

Take a prime minister and an Oscar winning director, prominent 'moral entrepreneurs' in Hungary today. During late communism, the former served as finance minister and deputy prime minister, while the latter made persuasive movies on the troubled relationship between the artist and political power in a dictatorship. The former was a member of the Central Committee whereas the latter did not join the Communist party, and worked as deputy head of a film company during the 1980s. In the eyes of the dissidents, both had a few stains on their reputation, apart from those directly stemming from their formal positions. For instance, the former shut down the research institute of the Ministry of Finance in 1987, and fired his former friends and colleagues who were regarded by the party hardliners as radical reformers flirting with the anti-communist opposition. The latter took part in banning the presentation of his friend's sarcastic movie for similar reasons back in 1975. He called it an ideologically 'misunderstandable' film of 'harmful influence', which 'can be turned against the official cultural policy'.[1]

Such decisions belonged to the *modus operandi* of the political and cultural elite under János Kádár even two years before the collapse of communism. Nevertheless, they seemed inexplicably rough at the time. In respecting the Kádárist trinity of 'promoting, tolerating, prohibiting',[2] the censors preferred the second option to the third one. Why did our heroes become so overzealous? Was it a matter of personal jealousy? Were their harsh decisions part of a larger game within the top leadership? Why did the policy of small disloyalties turn into that of bigger betrayals?

I am not sure I know the answer today, although in the meantime a potential common *leitmotiv* of the two dismal stories has been revealed. Péter Medgyessy and István Szabó, to stop enigmatic narration, confessed (in 2002 and 2006 respectively) to having served the communist police at a certain stage of their careers. They kept their secrets until the truth about their double lives was unveiled in the media, and neither of them felt the need for repentance or to extend at least a blanket apology to the 'target persons', to use the language of the intelligence service.

Assuming, perhaps naively, that working in an authoritarian system as a stool-pigeon (a 'brick' as we say in Hungary)[3] is not the most decent occupation, this paper begins with the unease one feels in witnessing the peculiar pride of police agents. In retrospect, many of them refuse to regard themselves as perpetrators or, at least, accomplices, and prefer the role of the victim or even that of the hero. In defending their own case, they apply, among others, two basic arguments. They claim that (1) under communism in Hungary, opportunism was an almost unavoidable precondition for serving the common good, and (2) being an accomplice belonged to the idea of business as usual. While both arguments are necessary constituents of the discourse of self-excuse after communism throughout Eastern Europe, I will also emphasise their Hungarian specifics. First, the essentials of what I like to call 'fast forgiving' will be discussed. Then, turning to my own profession, I will show how profoundly economists, a *métier* usually disregarded in studying transitional justice, contributed to a moral relativisation of collaboration with the Kádár regime. Finally, after introducing the term 'academic remembering', it will be asked whether that contribution has now reached its end.

Respect for the Secret Agents

Coming to terms with the past in Hungary after communism can be characterised in a nutshell by three negatives. Unlike in the Czech Republic and Germany, *no* leading representative of the communist regime and agent of the communist secret police was excluded by law from public life, not even for brief periods of time; unlike in Germany, virtually *no* member of the ruling elite and agent of the secret police was convicted of crimes committed prior to 1989; and unlike in Germany (and currently in Poland, Romania and Slovakia), the secret files as a whole were *not* made accessible to the public. To put it simply, no *lustrace* was initiated, and no *Gauck*-type agency was set up to name the culprits.[4]

If János Kádár had not died in 1989 he would have been allowed to become an MP, the mayor of Budapest or even the President of the Republic, as happened in so many states of Eastern Europe. Screening was limited to certain professional groups and positions (for instance the clergy were exempt), only the files of domestic intelligence were examined, and the inspection was based exclusively on those materials which had been filtered through by the same service (that has not been radically purged until today). Even if it became clear that someone who belonged to one of the given professions/positions was filing reports or reading them, the sole sanction was that the fact (not the details) of his/her secret activities was made public. The police files were, however, accessible to all post-communist governments, and a notorious game of *kompromat* has been played in the political market.[5] The leading communist dignitaries were not put on trial, and even those few officers who were convicted of mass murder for slaughtering peaceful demonstrators after 1956 escaped imprisonment in one way or another.

It took almost one and a half decades to grant historians access to the files of the secret agents – more exactly, to certain files of certain agents. It is, however, still unclear whether the results of historical research may be published at all, or if the principle of protecting privacy will override that of freedom of information and publications, which have been rather rare anyway, will become illegal. As the man in the street says in my country (apologies for the vulgar metaphor), 'the shit emerges from the sewage drain extremely slowly'. This slowness provides the police informers with an undeservedly comfortable position. With time passing, the public became saturated with the political manipulation of the secret files; some of the agents turned into quasi-heroes, while those politicians and academics who still fight for clairvoyance are growing more and more suspicious in the public eye.[6]

In that moral chaos, Medgyessy and Szabó had no difficulty whatsoever in finding excellent excuses. The prime minister said that he, then a leading official in the Ministry of Finance, had warned his superiors at the counter-intelligence agency about the enemies of Hungary opening up to the West in the late 1970s and early 1980s, when the government was making secret preparations for joining the International Monetary Fund. He gave a brief, almost dry, explanation, and portrayed his clandestine activity as a predominantly analytic and exclusively international mission,[7] a patriotic deed risking an awful retaliation from the KGB:

> 'I am extremely proud of that period. … We wanted to join the IMF twice. In the early 1970s, it was the Soviet Union that prevented us to join. We tried again in the early 1980s. … We negotiated with the IMF and the World Bank under such a strict secrecy that even the relevant Hungarian authorities did not know about the negotiations. … So we embarked upon a road that led to NATO, and also EU membership became accessible.[8]

To put it bluntly, all his critics should be aware of the fact that, whenever they consume the goodies of life in present-day Hungary, they enjoy a small piece of Mr Medgyessy's noble soul itself.

The film director's story was much more plebeian in the beginning, but similarly solemn in the end. As a student, he was arrested right after the 1956 revolution, frightened to death, and blackmailed into spying on his colleagues. According to Szabó, he did not cheat his class-mates at the High School of Theatre and Film in Budapest but rather his principals at the police who had to struggle with his excessively detailed reports – about nothing. Allegedly, the primary goal that justified collaboration was to save a friend's life, who had taken part in the uprising, by confusing the detectives with long stories on the love affairs and financial problems of other friends and colleagues (and – for reasons of good conspiracy – of himself).[9]

Both the prime minister and the film director emphasised that their relationship with the secret service had lasted only for some years in the distant past, and been terminated thereafter for good. The former talked about free choice and courage, the latter about coercion and cowardice. Both stressed that their conscience was clean. Medgyessy did not mention if he had any scruples about his deeds at all while Szabó said he had revealed all his *angst* and moral dilemmas through his movies.[10] On one side of the picture they painted for the public one sees a descendant of the Transylvanian gentry, playing James Bond in the international financial markets, who, when exposed, behaves like a proud *hussar* officer. On the other, one faces, as in the case of an anti-Semitic pamphlet, the figure of a Holocaust survivor who was smart enough to fool the authorities after 1956, but who reacts to the disclosure today with quickly changing self-exculpations and a hysterical attack on certain enemies willing to kill him any moment. Both of them are self-confident left-liberals with a revealed identity of the 'elegant Westerner', who are happy to applaud to each other's successes.[11]

It was no wonder that the prime minister's party (the Hungarian Socialist Party, a successor of the communist party) continued to trust him after the scandal had broken out. This happened in the wake of the 2002 elections that he had won, due to a large extent to his image of a reserved technocrat famous for his economic expertise both before and after 1989. The Socialists have never been able to resolutely break with their own past, why would they have started soul-searching exactly at a moment in which Medgyessy's popularity was sky-rocketing despite (or because of) the disclosure. However, no one could foresee whether or not the coalition partner, the Alliance of Free Democrats (Liberals), a party deeply rooted in anti-communist opposition, would follow suit. After hesitating for a day, the liberal leaders who had been the main target of police surveillance under the old regime, also expressed confidence in Medgyessy, although their 'no' vote would have brought him down immediately. The price of their consent was a ritual promise: as so many times before, the Socialists pledged to finally open the files of the communist state security services.[12] Of course, the leading party in the national-conservative opposition (Fidesz, Young Democrats – Hungarian Civic Alliance), whose 'house newspaper' had exposed the D 209 affair (this was agent Medgyessy's code name), did its best to instrumentalise the story. However, its call for the prime minister's demotion proved incredible after many years of high-level cooperation with the extreme right led by István Csurka, another former police agent, and even more incredible later, following the cooptation in the opposition's satellite organisations of two former Politbureau members (Imre Pozsgay and Mátyás Szürös), once Medgyessy's superiors.

The backbone of the arguments still circulating today is this: counter-intelligence is a necessary element of security of any state; Medgyessy was a useful spy; that was a fair deal, he accomplished his task successfully (Hungary joined the IMF and the World Bank in 1982), thus, he deserved to be rewarded with money and promotion in the ministerial hierarchy. The opposition called him an opportunist but did not dispute the thesis of usefulness. This thesis was not challenged by most of the liberal critics either. True, they remarked that counter-intelligence under communism was not separated from other secret police activities, including the persecution of the dissidents, by a 'Great Wall of China'. These critics also reproached Medgyessy for unfair behaviour in the election campaign. A would-be prime minister, they said, has to inform the voters about his past as a whole, especially if it includes such a delicate episode exposing him to possible blackmail.

As regards István Szabó, it took his fans only a few days in January 2006 to organise a petition in his defence: 'For 45 years, István Szabó has made excellent and important films for us. Not only for Hungarians. He spread our fame all over the world. He wrote his name in the universal history of our culture. We love, respect and appreciate him.' The petition was signed by 240 people, many of them eminent representatives of the cultural and political elite.[13] The top leaders of the Socialists and the Liberals (not to mention those of the National-Conservatives) were in a hurry to shake Szabó's hand on camera. The media was full of passionate messages such as 'stop the witch hunt', 'don't deprive us of our youth/favourite films/moral idols', 'he has already confessed through his movies', etc. Those who disliked that 'sympathy rally'[14] did not condemn the director for his lack of courage in resisting blackmail in 1957. Instead, they called for compassion for other victims of the communist terror, including those who did resist and had to suffer, and those who just tried to survive but may have been endangered by Szabó's reports.[15] Also, they asked why he did not stop denouncing his colleagues in the 1970s, why he did not give himself up in 1989, and why he is still playing the role of the Knight of the Holy Grail. However, even the critics were ready to accept a clear distinction between the artistic value and the ethical posture of the author.[16]

In this way, the Hungarian public was asked to endorse the record of two, morally perhaps not quite impeccable, public figures, proud of their useful roles and right deeds who provided their country with high-quality political and cultural goods.[17] Allegedly, they contributed to a large extent to the demise of the communist system even if originally they had just wanted to improve it. Furthermore, no matter whether you call it modernisation, humanisation, westernisation or liberalisation, Medgyessy and Szabó proved to be outstanding representatives of these processes, and their collaboration dwarfed by their achievements in making the life of the people under (and after) communism easier.

Right deeds and useful roles – those who were brought up in the communist linguistic universe remember the correct versions of these idioms. They sound like these: *'objectively* right' and *'socially* useful' *in the final analysis*. These words are still music to my ears. The music demonstrates the continuity of an apologetic argument exactly at a time in which Hungarians are being increasingly confronted with the evidence of the hardness of the Kádár regime; a regime we have always thought to be rather soft, permissive even messy and sloppy, which prefers corruption to terror and mass mobilisation, as well as manipulation to indoctrination. Today, thanks to a small window of opportunity opened by the Medgyessy scandal, and the subsequent amendment of the law regulating access to the files of the communist secret services, we had better rethink, I believe, the convenient model of 'soft dictatorship', 'reform communism', 'the Kádárist compromise' and so on. If top officials in the government, Communist party leaders, scholars and artists of international fame, a large part of the high clergy, Kádár's 'court journalists' informed the secret police, many of them perhaps until the last breath of communism, then what we called 'the System' must have been much more authoritarian than assumed even by hard-core dissidents who were harassed by the police day by day before 1989.[18]

Why are István Szabó and Péter Medgyessy so proud today? Is this just an easy way of avoiding a guilty conscience, or a pragmatic technique of damage control? I am afraid that the underlying reason for their *hubris* is even more prosaic. They both firmly believe that it was worthwhile serving the secret police because in this way (and only in this way), they could bring their 'grand projects' into existence. Moreover, these projects, they think, did not suffer from the pact they made with the devil (although it is doubtful whether Medgyessy has ever imagined the intelligence service as hell).

As I am no historian of cinema, just a normal film-goer, let me condense my opinion on Szabó's *oeuvre* in two long sentences. If his movies had provided a brilliant portrayal of the guilty conscience of the collaborating artist or the demonic nature of the dictator, I would perhaps venture to repeat what one of his admirers wrote to a newspaper following his confession: 'to our luck, he chose to become a spy'.[19] To our bad luck, however, he permeated the theme of collaboration with the

sentimental self-praise of the talented but unmighty, a boring, self-justifying celebration of cowardice, and a perverse respect for the mighty; packaged his
messages in historical allegories (of Nazism rather than Stalinism) to avoid friction
with his communist protectors; and abandoned dealing with the Kádár era in
depth for the same reason. To avoid misunderstanding, I do not postulate here an
iron law dictating that moral imperfection leads to quality loss, but I do not deny
that in the case of István Szabó I suppose that is exactly what happened.[20]

And for Medgyessy – was the quality of his reformism affected by his
undercover activities? Did his role as a 'secret servant' reduce, for instance, the
significance of the introduction, under his guidance as finance minister, of the
first western-style tax system as well as the establishment of commercial banks
and the adoption of the first privatisation laws in a still-communist country
during 1987–8? Let me postpone the answer to this question for a while, and ask
another – somewhat rhetorical – question. Was not Medgyessy's position in the
government and the party at least as condemnable as that of the meanest 'brick'?
In his case, informing the secret service, I believe, was just the 'icing on the cake'
since reading the reports of the agents (and governing together with those who
read them and managed the machinery of oppression) could not be morally
superior to writing these reports.

Fast Forgiving

Let us leave the case of István Szabó behind, and focus on the economic reformer,
Péter Medgyessy. He is the real hero of my paper, or perhaps more exactly, all
possible Medgyessys in my country are, given their unbeatable contribution to
the *Zeitgeist* prevailing in Hungary today, which provides an easy refuge for
former collaborators of nearly any sort. As a matter of fact, I needed the spectacular cases of the two prominent secret agents to introduce the paradox included in
the title: as the archives slowly open up we see a growing number of crimes,
offences, wrongdoings and misdeeds, while in the narratives of the culprits one
finds almost exclusively victims, innocent bystanders and quasi-innocent accomplices while the crimes together with the perpetrators tend to vanish in the thick
of amorphous categories such as the nomenklatura, the party-state, the Soviets
and the like.[21]

Interestingly enough, the facelessness of the perpetrators does not result in
overloading the accomplices who, in the lack of identifiable political criminals,
would have to bear all responsibility for wrongdoing under communism on their
shoulders. Quite to the contrary, the accomplices are increasingly assuming the
role of the victim: allegedly, most of them were 'forced' to take certain – as they
say, 'perhaps indecent' – steps in the distant past, but have ever since been
'betrayed' and left to their own devices by the 'real' perpetrators who are still at
large. The perpetrators fade into accomplices who, in turn, aspire to the status of
bystanders or, not infrequently, to that of the victims. Mercy is meted out with a
reflex motion. More precisely, in the lack of sin there is no need for mercy or
remission. If there are no perpetrators, and the majority of society consists of
quasi-innocent accomplices, then the accomplices may always count on the
compassion of their fellow-accomplices. At the same time, attacking communism
head on yesterday may arouse distrust today. Was not the typical dissident actually an *agent provocateur*? – goes the nasty question. I do not think that in this
respect Hungary is a unique case in Eastern Europe.

This paper is *not* about the sociology or psychology of collaboration. Moreover, it does not want to condemn or forgive.[22] With a considerable dose of masochism (and with an interest in the Hungarian specifics of reckoning with the past), I turn to my own profession, the history of economic thought, to check the degree to which economists contributed to a dominant moral discourse that dilutes the concept of perpetrators and accomplices, and continue to celebrate their 'right' deeds in the framework of 'useful' collaboration.

Why, indeed, pick the poor economists? The vast and rapidly growing literature on transitional justice delivers dozens of explanations for ignoring, forgetting or forgiving crime without pinpointing that particular professional group. In the Hungarian fast-food restaurant of reckoning with the past, you find on the menu many dishes of moral relativism from the twentieth century and earlier. The menu includes excuses both for big and small wrongdoings, without making any principled distinction between the numerous forms of collaboration. The excuses oscillate between self-pity, legal scruples and cynicism, on the one hand, and an understandable claim of differentiation between big and petty crime, on the other: 'I was just a small screw in the machinery', 'others would have been even more harmful', 'I not only harmed but also helped people', 'I did it for my family', 'I didn't do it for money', 'I did it on others' orders', 'I was blackmailed/forced/tricked into doing it', 'my collaboration was formal', 'no one would have been better off if I had not collaborated', 'everybody served the System in a way or another', 'what I did was not against the law at that time', 'it has come under the statute of limitations by now', 'who has the moral right to be my judge?', 'the outcome will necessarily be some kind of *Siegerjustiz*', 'how can one prove any offence after so many years?', 'the culprits are old, why torture them?', and so on.[23] At the first glance, you do not find profound economic considerations in the background of these excuses.

There are also some other – specifically present-day Eastern European or Hungarian – dishes served in this restaurant to satisfy one's appetite for moral relativism. An indispensable ingredient of them is the blurring of historical boundaries; that is, postulating continuity between communism and capitalism as well as dictatorship and democracy to overshadow the 1989 revolution. Fast forgiveness is assisted by arguments such as these: 'if leading members of the nomenklatura were allowed to turn into prime ministers and business tycoons overnight, why should I, the small police agent be the scapegoat'; or conversely 'without my contribution made as a leading communist reformer we would still live under the old regime'; 'the first democratic parliaments in Eastern Europe were full of former apparatchiks and agents'; 'in 1989, justice-making would have been too early, today, however, it is too late'; 'the new regime also needs secret services'; 'does a multinational company not spy on its employees?'; 'is making justice a more important task than, for instance, combating unemployment or poverty?'; 'show me a Western leader who has not embraced a certain KGB officer called Putin yet'; 'is there a country in the former Eastern Bloc, in which decommunization, lustration, you name it, was implemented consequently *and* fairly?'; 'how come that Egon Krenz sits in prison while Mikhail Gorbachev is sipping champagne at a reception in Berlin?' Finally, let me quote a genuinely Hungarian syllogism:

> part of the anti-communist liberals (the Free Democrats) felt that it was kosher to enter the government of the ex-communists just five years after

the revolution; the other part (the Young Democrats) thought that it was kosher to make alliance with the extreme right at the same time, so nobody remained on the political scene to exercise moral authority any longer.

At any rate, goes the argument, clairvoyance in moral matters was already disturbed in 1989 by the 'roundtable agreement' between the communists and the opposition as a whole, that is, in a sense, between the representatives of the perpetrators and the victims. 'Revolution, that's what you should have made, dear friends' – this sarcastic remark was dropped by the late leader of the National-Conservatives, prime minister József Antall, in the early 1990s to explain that national reconciliation and negotiated change do not fit well with purging your negotiation partners sitting at the same roundtable.[24] To be sure, he referred not only to the ex-communists but also to both large camps in the anti-communist opposition, the National-Conservatives and the Liberals, suggesting that a great number of 'bricks' were built into their parties, too.

Antall himself was a revolutionary in 1956, then a history teacher and a museum director, a person also famous for another *bon mot*. When Kádár took power in November 1956, Antall said to his friends: 'I submerge and save myself until they leave'.[25] He resurfaced as late as 1989, and was confronted with the fact that one of his best friends had been spying on him. Following the victory of his party at the first democratic elections, he received from the last communist prime minister, Miklós Németh, a list of police informers active in the new political elite. With this sly move, a nationwide 'now you see it, now you don't' game began, in which various lists of names have been presented as trumps for a brief moment only to be withdrawn again. In this game, the very existence, quality and credibility of the secret files, that is, the principal pieces of evidence, were made questionable.[26]

If justice is impossible because, to put it simply, there is no unambiguous delict, identifiable culprit, fair procedure or morally clean judge, then it may seem to be the only reasonable and just solution to liquidate the potential proofs immediately, and forgive and forget (or forget and forgive) as soon as possible. 'Throw all secret files into the Danube!', demand more and more intellectuals and politicians in my country.[27] The only problem with this solution is that one cannot do the same with the victims ranging from those killed or forced to kill themselves, tortured, imprisoned, deported or driven mad, through those who were fired upon, spied on, harassed or blackmailed, whose property was confiscated, to those who 'only' did not have access to everyday civic liberties including the freedom of movement, association, speech and economic choice. What *can* be done, unfortunately, is to apply a large variety of techniques of relativising victimhood, ranging from the underestimation of the number of victims and the degree of their suffering, all the way to allegations concerning their political biases and business interests in the 'Gulag industry'. Why is forgiving fast? Because it demands forgetting before we could learn what is to be forgotten, thereby escaping from the pain of forgiving.

Does it make any sense, the reader may ask again, to associate the economists with all kinds of moral relativism and political machination on Earth? Actually, in the current history of Hungary one can easily detect the economists' traces at major junctures of political change. Let me proceed backward in time. The prevailing government coalition of the Socialists and the Liberals has been in power since 2002, but the formative years of their cohabitation in the Parliament elapsed between 1994 and 1998. In 1994, the surprising/embarrassing alliance between the ex-communists and the former liberal dissidents was forged in the spirit of opposition to the authoritarian ambitions of the national-conservative government.[28] But it also pursued pragmatic objectives formulated by economists and business-people – leaders, experts and clients of the two parties.[29] These objectives included the relaunching of stabilisation, marketisation and privatisation processes that were half-heartedly managed by the National-Conservatives between 1990 and 1994. The Liberals could not have been able to explain the reconciliation with the ex-communists to themselves and their own electorate without recourse to an alarmist rhetoric using 'the economy is on the verge of collapse'-style arguments.[30] At any rate, they entered a coalition led by the socialist prime minister, Gyula Horn, who never concealed the fact that, more than 30 years before cutting through the Iron Curtain, he had been a member of Kádár's militia, which mercilessly restored 'communist lawfulness' after the 1956 revolution.

One does not have to be a fan of conspiracy theories to discover, during the days of the 'negotiated revolution' in 1989, a similar sort of economists-inspired political alliance aiming to crown the trend of proto-liberalisation under late communism. That trend had been set in the second half of the 1980s in a joint effort by moderate reformers in the communist elite, and radical reform economists in both the academia and the anti-communist opposition. In 1989, many of the moderates joined the Socialist party led by Rezső Nyers, the father of the New Economic Mechanism in 1968, who was put on ice by Kádár for one and a half decades, while most of the radicals became founding members or fellow-travellers of the Free Democrats.[31] Incidentally, Péter Medgyessy was a recurrent top actor in all phases of the alliance until he was forced to step down in 2004 (to be sure, not because he had been a police agent). In the first two Socialist-liberal governments he worked closely together with quite a few experts whom he had fired in 1987. Thereby, the former frontlines were crossed, and the Socialists, who had suffered from an ongoing crisis of legitimation after 1989, had a chance to reclaim a large part of the radical reformist tradition.[32]

As a rule, conspiracy theories are dull and mean but occasionally they carry a grain of truth. Whatever goals the leading economists of Hungary originally wanted to attain, they did contribute to both the consolidation and the demise of communism as well as to the revival of social democracy and liberalism after 1989, not to speak of an alliance between the latter. By 'leading economists' one understood in Hungary a large group of experts representing an overwhelming majority of the profession. With the exception of a few textbook-Marxists, that group embraced nearly all influential scholars and a good part of high-level government and party officials in economic administration as well as enterprise managers, journalists and lawyers, as early as the end of the 1960s. Evidently, during the more than three decades of real socialism after 1956, the 'reform economists' included a great variety of experts: neo-Marxists, would-be Hayekians and sheer pragmatists, representatives of workers' self-management, entrepreneurial socialism and the social market economy, those who sought moderation and those who risked conflict with the communists, those who just gave advice to the party and/or the government and those who also took part in the implementation of the reform blueprints. Nevertheless, while this large array of academics and technocrats was wavering between the extremes of pro- and non-communism (perhaps also anti-communism), their cooperative attitude became often permeated with collaboration *sensu stricto*[33].

Back to the Golden Age

I have arrived at the gist of my argument. In the following pages, I would like to take a short-cut between fast forgiveness and the political economy of reform communism.

Those who mourn transitional justice in Hungary tend to think that its coffin was closed for good by the handshakes between the former dissidents and the ex-communists first in 1989 then in 1994. That may be true, but the relativising of communist crimes began much, much earlier, with the emergence of the idea of improvability of the System; an idea that began to blossom in Hungary during the 1960s, following the interlude of 'consolidation' under János Kádár.[34]

If one seeks *the* moment of 'original sin', after which one could hardly make a clear distinction between perpetrators, accomplices, bystanders and victims in Hungary under communism, one will actually find a whole series of shorter and longer moments during the 33 years separating the two revolutions. The story is too familiar to retell.[35] What interests me here is the general anomy at its end, best symbolised by the transformation of the image of János Kádár from the Soviet hangman into that of the Father of the Nation, who protects the Hungarians against the Soviets, in little more than a decade, comfortably beating the record held by Emperor Francis Joseph a century before.

As usual, anomy originated in a *trahison des clercs*, the capitulation of the bulk of the writers and other intellectuals (including church leaders) less than two years after the Soviet invasion.[36] They were followed by quite a few imprisoned revolutionaries released in the early 1960s and the émigrés, the majority of whom opted for a kind of co-existence with the counter-revolutionary establishment sooner or later. Their roles ranged from passive resistance to open collaboration that culminated sometimes in accepting high positions in public life. Altogether with more carrot and less stick than in most other countries of real socialism, Kádár managed to corrupt the citizens, including the cultural elite, into a regime they regarded first as perhaps acceptable, later as normal or even desirable.

The regime's founding doctrine, 'who is not against us is with us', justified the policy of reconciliation between communist rule and the people. Crude forms of terror, mobilisation and indoctrination were partly replaced by a pattern of social integration based primarily on the principle of 'live and let live', private consumption and popular culture, opening up to the West, welfare chauvinism toward the East, regulated embourgeoisement, depoliticising of public life, self-censorship and the like. 'Goulash communism', the 'happiest barrack in the camp' and other metaphors served to cement Kádár's populist model with discursive means reflecting the power holders' fraternisation with the citizens.

The emerging national(ist) pride reduced the sympathy felt by Hungarians for the Prague Spring and later for *Solidarnosc* to a minimum. Their protagonists were mocked (for instance Alexander Dubcek was derided as the proverbial 'dull Slovak'), and their antagonists were not hated. Internal solidarity between the social strata was hampered by a comprehensive ban on collective action, which was combined with incentives for individual coping strategies (primarily in the shadow economy), creating the petty bourgeois archetype of *Homo Kadaricus*. This archetype was reinforced by the image of the talented, entrepreneurial-minded, informal, tricky Hungarian who can profit even from communism, and by traditional elements of symbolic geography (Hungary as an integral part of Central Europe).[37]

Complying with the premise in the promise made by the regime – 'we do not provoke you if you do not rebel' – was tantamount to observing a set of taboos that ranged from the truth about the 1956 revolution, through the Soviet occupation, to one-party rule and state ownership. The taboos delineated the frames of an implicit 'social contract', in which one could find a relatively convenient place for him or herself but rarely an immaculate one. Under the aegis of that contract even a sort of passive resistance could mean collaboration. Moreover, the citizen was urged to be silent not only about the political crimes committed by the regime, but also about the privileges and the dubious business dealings of the nomenklatura. In exchange she was reassured that the party leaders would close one eye (this was the notorious winking by Kádár), if they recognised that the 'toiling masses' steal, cheat or lie to make ends meet. Thus, one did not have to join the party, denounce a neighbour, or remain quiet when others were punished for political reasons, to consider oneself a collaborator. It was enough to take home a tool from the factory, ask the party secretary for a favour or bribe a shop assistant to become a link in the chain of compromises sustaining the System, even if the shady behaviour of the citizen was dictated by reasonable self-defence. With time passing, one ceased to have a bad conscience: muddling along under 'authoritarianism with a human face' seemed to be the one and only solution.

Ostensibly, such a complex machinery of social coordination could not have been invented, operated and justified exclusively by writers, journalists, artists and philosophers, in other words, not infrequently by converted prophets of the 1956 revolution, or by opportunist church leaders. To turn a bloody retaliation into business as usual, Kádár needed not only opinion leaders with rhetorical skills and, if possible, a non-communist past on his side but also a rather innovative apparatus of the party-state and – more and more badly – social engineers with grand designs. Loyal to the pragmatic half of Marxist teachings, the latter were requested to deliver 'economic mechanisms' (to use a contemporary term) in support of his ambitious programme of reconciliation/corruption. To put it simply, Kádár needed more carrot, and did not have to wait long during the mid-1960s for an offer by the professional carrot producers, the economists, who had been experimenting with the technology of what they called 'socialist commodity production' since 1953.

That offer contained a series of reform programmes that tamed the command economy, and justified part of the 'stealing, cheating and lying' as regular bargaining strategies in the socialist market and the shadow economy. After over a quarter of a century of reform-making in Hungary, the designs of market socialism became occasionally more radical and sophisticated but their basic doctrine supporting the foundation philosophy of the Kádár regime did not change. Notwithstanding the fact that the economic programmes were assisted by sociologists, political scientists, legal experts and even historians, it was the reform economists who played a crucial role in construing the myth of sustainable and acceptable communism (a typical myth of a golden age), which had pre-programmed forgiving much before the crimes of communism became punishable in 1989.

While a small minority of the reformers cooperated with the nomenklatura under the assumption (which proved to be correct in the end) that the medicine they prescribed would become a poison in the long run, the majority believed in, or put up with, helping the system to survive by mixing a dose of 'the market' into central planning that had proven unable to keep the Kádárist promises. They were delivering the myth of long-term sustainability. Preaching acceptability meant that, in the lack of a first-best solution, one cannot but opt for a second-best one which, compared with the actual alternatives in the Soviet empire, still seemed to be the most efficient and humane.[38] In preparing for the New Economic Mechanism during the 1960s, Democratic Socialism, a concept mixing the ideas of the 1956 Revolution and the Prague Spring, was considered the first-best model by the reform economists. They needed about three decades (and a series of big disappointments) for the drift toward the ideal of democratic capitalism to take place. Until then, they accepted the most harmful thesis the philosopher, György Lukács ever formulated: 'the worst socialism is better than the best capitalism'.[39]

In the late 1970s, when economists realised that 'bad socialism' did not want to improve itself, they began to turn to *Realpolitik*: if one cannot expect communism to disappear soon or ever, let us make it the least unacceptable. This decision confused the moral frontlines anew. If prior to 1989, you asked a reform economist why she was cooperating with the Kádár regime either as a scholar working, for instance, in a research institute of the Academy of Sciences or as an official say, in the Central Planning Agency, she came up with one or two of the following answers: 'because I believe in socialism'; 'because it is superior to any kind of system in the world'; 'because on this side of the Yalta divide there can't be a better one'; 'because it satisfies the needs of the citizens at least to a certain degree'; 'because this is what I know'; 'because this is I am paid for'; 'because it can only be destroyed from within'. It goes without saying that the naive-constructive responses date back to the 1960s whereas, normally, the cynical-destructive ones (representing the local version of the 'better red than dead' principle) were characteristic of the 1980s.[40]

Desk Criminals?

Why pick the economists, one may ask again. What about other intellectuals, first of all, the 'Aczél boys' (named after the chief ideologue of Kádár, György Aczél), that is, writers, journalists and artists, among them the film director, István Szabó? Did they not justify cooperation with similar arguments, the only difference being that, when they were talking about the virtues of the Kádár regime, they put a greater emphasis on the relative political and cultural freedoms it granted than on its economic performance, that is on the circus rather than on bread? In defence of the economists let me answer this: while most of the Aczél boys regarded the market with disdain, especially in the field of social services and cultural goods, a typical reform economist did not subscribe to a severe limitation of political and cultural liberties by some kind of reformist dictatorship.

I hope I do not inflate the importance of my own profession by claiming that the carrot delivered by the economists was much bigger and fresher than the one produced by other Kádárist intellectuals. In the eyes of its producers and many of its consumers, it represented a comprehensive programme of systemic change within the economy, a programme that concerns the welfare of all citizens and postulates an authentic, modern but non-utopian model, which is scientifically proven and similar to certain well-established models in the West (without copying them), and results in a pioneering set of economic institutions that can be emulated in both the East and the West. The reformers were convinced that the *socialist* market (i.e. a liberalisation within the state sector under one-party rule) would resemble the *social* market of the capitalist welfare states. Although privatisation would be simulated, the party would withdraw from managing the economy, the citizens would be entrepreneurs without becoming capitalists and the country would open up to the West without leaving the Comecon. Furthermore, the new economic paradigm also had important political ramifications such as a leaner and more decentralised state or a less dirigist party, as well as an increase in economic and civic liberties with regard to consumer choice, cultural pluralism and access to the West. The reform economists offered the regime not only an allegedly viable system but also an allegedly progressive one, bursting ahead in large waves. This vision was condensed in the K.u.K. (Kádár und Kreisky) image of a *Sozialstaat* situated on the left, tolerated by the Soviets, celebrated by German foreign policy and blessed by the Pope.

Did this prove to be a utopia in the long run? Yes, definitely (partly, in the short run as well), but it dominated the principal moral choices of a whole nation until the middle of the 1980s, and also, to a certain extent, afterward. To use a telling phrase coined by a most original thinker among Hungarian economists, Ferenc Jánossy, in the 1970s, the result of the reforms was a *quasi*-market with *quasi*-entrepreneurs producing *quasi*-development.[41] Today, one is tempted to expand the thesis: such a quasi-development could only be represented by some kind of a quasi-ethic.

Despite international recognition in both politics and science, not to speak of the popular wing of Sovietology, reform economists lent their names to a controversial construct of liberalisation within, and by, the party state, which was compromised further in practice. Most of the experts became prisoners of these compromises, and had to witness not only the unfolding but also the repeated amputation of their reform programmes.[42] Thus, they themselves experienced being an accomplice and a sort of a victim at the same time. When someone's loyalty to the political core of the reform paradigm diminished, and as a newborn radical reformer turned to real capitalism instead of a simulated one, he could not in good faith demand radical forms of transitional justice following many years of close cooperation, bordering on collaboration, with the potential defendants.[43] Otherwise, he would have been trapped by accepting the task of naming the 'real' perpetrators and accomplices, and distinguishing them from the bystanders and the victims. Almost everyone was aware of the utmost difficulty of the task, suspecting the picture of society to be dominated by various shades of grey with some white and black spots on the margin. In other words, one could identify quite a few culprits, especially in the old guard of Kádár, the Ministry of Interior and the agit-prop machinery, but even among these apparatchiks one would find some who might be proud of a semi-reformist phase in their career. Probably, the identification of the victims could not have been too difficult either, though if one disregards the crimes of physical violence (which were relatively rare after the early 1960s), many of the victims also fall under the category of accomplices, provided they lived long enough under Kádár. To be sure, it was precisely this category that would have caused the biggest headache to the ethical taxonomist in a society whose basic organising principles were enfranchisement through corruption, rule-bending and a confusion of the 'us and them' dichotomy characterising a textbook dictatorship.

The above was not meant as a reproach to the reform economists: I am far from using the German term *Schreibtischtäter* (desk criminals) to describe their way of cooperation with the communist regime. In pointing to their contribution to social anomy, I do not want to suggest that it would have been better for Hungarians if, in an extreme case, all economists had resorted to passive resistance collectively, leaving the Hungarians behind in the morass of a highly inefficient command economy. In any event, a 'worse the better' strategy might have resulted in enormous hardships, and unleashed uncontrollable processes of social decay and political destabilisation. Moral intransigence vs serving the community – who could have the right today to decide about the benign forms of collaboration even if we have always known that several reformers attained vast privileges through that service? However, opting for its less benign forms, including reporting to the secret police, was avoidable, by which I mean more and more avoidable as years went by.[44] Nevertheless, the blurring of the boundaries between resistance, cooperation and collaboration in the open air made it very difficult to condemn collaboration in the secret world of state security (with the exception of the agent-zealots, of course).

A Consensual Maxim

In all probability, Péter Medgyessy could also have found smart excuses if he had really wanted to avoid joining the intelligence service. As disturbing as it may be, a parliamentary commission appointed upon his exposure named a dozen leading politicians active after 1989 who had informed the secret police before 1989. Among them, we find a deputy finance minister of the last communist government who became finance minister and president of the National Bank later, a director of the research institute of the Planning Agency who became minister for economic affairs, and his deputy in the ministry who had published a critical reform scenario in the 1980s, a top official of the National Bank who at the turn of the millennium was appointed to serve as a minister for EU affairs, a state secretary for privatisation in 1988–9 who became minister for foreign affairs ten years later – all belonging to those moderate reformers who joined the national-conservative camp after the revolution. Most of them were members of the communist party before 1989, like a few of their colleagues in the various post-communist governments, who had also belonged to the intelligence service (or its supervisory bodies) but remained in a party drifting toward social-democracy.[45]

One did not have to be a statistician to presume that the public saw just the tip of the iceberg;[46] the water probably covers many hundred other alleged or real agents – a sad prospect that could have accelerated the reckoning with the past in the profession. More sadly, its members still fail to ask questions about the moral aspects of their academic and political activities in the past. Regardless of the fact that normally their cooperation with the regime did not imply decisions about life and death, the memory of reform economists shows typically postwar patterns of repression: silence, trivialisation and externalisation. Almost 20 years have elapsed, but the memoirs written by, the life history interviews made with and the historical essays published on them still avoid touching upon the intrinsic moral ambiguity of the reformist position.[47]

Is the myth of the golden age still too powerful? Indeed, for a while, the silence could be explained by the initial advantages of Hungary in the Eastern European competition for the title of the best performer in post-communist transformation – a success story widely attributed to the economic reforms made under Kádár. Following the Medgyessy affair, however, I expected at least a modicum of introspection in the profession, in particular, when the process of disclosure went beyond the government and party leaders and reached the academic community. Undoubtedly, it was an easy solution to externalise responsibility by saying '*they,* the police agents among us were the perpetrators', and by failing to ask 'weren't we ourselves at least accomplices?' One could also suppress moral tension by questioning the credibility of the secret files, belittling the significance of the agents' reports and their scholarly performance, or simply remaining silent.[48]

As an historian of economic thought, I am *ex officio* interested in what can be called 'academic remembering'. As strange as it may be, we academics also remember but, as a rule, our views are subsumed in memory studies either under personal rememberence or under the sources of collective memory and the politics of history. Yet, studying the ways in which academics recall their own past or that of the research community may give the historian a unique chance to gain insight in ethical dilemmas that usually remain hidden, sometimes even from the academics themselves. In this closing section of the paper, I will focus on the case of the most prominent economic theorist in Hungary, János Kornai, exploring how he narrates his own victimhood and/or accompliceship. The reason for highlighting his story is twofold: (1) it shows the utmost complexity of moral choices an economist had to face even under a relatively permissive communist regime; (2) as an opinion maker, Kornai may determine not only the major patterns of economic interpretation of the Kádár era but also those of its ethical assessment.

In 2005, a professor of finance and banking, Tamás Bácskai who, as a renowned scholar and a leading official of the National Bank, took part in all possible reform projects after the late 1960s, admitted (upon exposure) that he had also worked for the police. He said that, shocked by the anti-Semitic atrocities he had witnessed in the days of the 1956 revolution, he spied on his colleagues at the Karl Marx University of Economics, Budapest, as well as on family members and friends (almost exclusively Jews, by the way), including his father and sister as well as the relatives of his sister, wife and former wife during the late 1950s and early 1960s.[49] Bácskai's confession did not shake the profession. Most members of the research community were just mildly embarrassed (above all because he denounced his close relatives), no one connected his morals with his scientific work, and also there was no scholar who, incited by the case, would have felt the need for introspection. Similarly, one could not find any historian asking whether Bácskai's stubbornly moderate reformism was not, *among other things*, also due to his commitment to the secret service. No one shouted *heureka*, I understand at last why he always called for self-restraint and precaution when we were writing our proposals for bank reform, currency convertibility, inflation management and the like in the 1970s and 1980s.[50] And no one said: 'Nonsense! You did not have to serve as a "brick" to exercise self-censorship'.

A spectacular example of continued silence combined with serious talk is provided by the memoirs[51] written by the role model of the majority of Hungarian economists, János Kornai, professor emeritus at Harvard who, prior to 1989, was always keen on avoiding any involvement in daily reform-making and mongering. At the same time, he was also famous if not notorious for denying any involvement with the anti-communist opposition before 1989. He refused to contribute to the work of the reform commissions appointed by the authorities but he did not remain silent if, for example, a minister asked for his opinion in a private conversation. Although he had deep reservations with regard to the rationale of reform economics, he avoided challenging its representatives in most of his publications.[52]

As a peculiar twist of fate in a small country, Kornai happened to be a close acquaintance of Tamás Bácskai (a friend of Bácskai's sister), and thereby an eminent target person for the agent. Apparently, he still despises the 'nasty role' Bácskai and all other 'bricks' (some of them were also Kornai's friends) who surveilled and denounced him played, but supposes that they may have been forced to betray him. He admits that shortly after 1956 he also betrayed his best friend, Péter Kende (not in a report to the police but in a scientific paper), and talks about small favours received from communist leaders.[53] Of course, these kinds of 'soft cooperation' cannot be compared to spying at all. I mention them only because Kornai brings them up, thereby raising the reader's expectations for clarifying the larger moral choices academic economists had to face under communism.

Kornai avoids cheap triumphalism in the case of Bácskai, but also refrains from deep-seated self-criticism concerning the ethical attributes of his own works. At the same time, he shows more understanding toward the reform economists than ever before: 'Sometimes I was also caught by reservations about the compromises the reform economists made with the power holders but I could eventually suppress these feelings and did not voice them publicly. I admitted that their activities were of more use than the harm their concessions could make'.[54] He thinks of the costs of his own compromises the same way. For instance, in appraising his *magnum opus*, the *Economics of Shortage*, published in 1980, Kornai does not conceal the fact that the book ventured to provide a comprehensive theory of the communist economy without analysing not quite negligible issues such as state ownership, the shadow economy, party control, militarisation and Soviet domination but adds: 'I am convinced that there is more than one life strategy that is morally acceptable'.[55] In his opinion, his own self-censored works and *samizdat* literature complement each other, and the *Shortage* contributed to the erosion of the Soviet empire like Solzhenytsin's, Orwell's and Koestler's works did. He is still proud of his book that was regarded by many as the *Das Kapital* of communism, and sure that it could not have been written and published if he had joined the dissidents. In his view, he exploited all possibilities of self-expression and reached the ultimate limits set by the censors.

János Kornai seems relaxed. He is firmly convinced that he was a victim (and a bystander at most) rather than an accomplice.[56] He does not raise counter-factual questions. Thus, the reader is tapping into the dark, asking herself in Kornai's style whether communism would not have eroded more rapidly if those – perhaps not quite negligible – issues had been studied by him. Or, to tackle a lesser problem, the scholar's responsibility for the evolution of economic sciences, Kornai disregards, somewhat surprisingly, the question of whether the economic theory of communism could not have surged if he had published (even if underground) his views on those issues at the end of the 1970s and the beginning of the 1980s.[57] The only thing the reader may know is that, despite all the efforts made by economists including János Kornai, communism had evaporated before it was profoundly analysed.[58]

Presumably, in Kornai's case, self-censorship led to a considerable loss of scientific quality by excluding essential variables from his explanatory model of the communist economy for quite a long time before 1989. Moreover, one cannot really measure how many original ideas were aborted *ab ovo* by a spontaneous contraction of the author's fantasy owing to self-imposed intellectual constraints. Nevertheless, that loss does not authorise anyone to disapprove his moral choice vehemently. I would especially dissuade those who would want to condemn him retroactively, enjoying the luxury of free speech in a democratic society.[59] Feeling sorry for the loss is, of course, a different issue.

And Medgyessy – did *his* undercover activities impair the quality of his reform-ism? I still owe the reader an answer to this question, and I am afraid I will continue to owe it for quite some time. Maybe, as is the case with Tamás Bácskai, Medgyessy's moderate reformism (as compared with the radicalism of some academic researchers) was simply due to his government responsibilities. Maybe he also reached the limits of his own terrain. At any rate, in the absence of any thorough knowledge of the secret files, the historian is unable to decide to what extent the police constrained its agents recruited from among the economists in devising and implementing reforms. Were those constraints harder than the rules of ordinary self-censorship? Or was a 'brick' sometimes permitted to act and/or think more freely than his colleagues? Thus far, no radical reform economist has been unveiled as a secret agent.

As for coming to terms with the past, the only consensual maxim the Hungar-ian economists have been able to discharge during the past 15 years sounds as banal as this: turning in your own friends and relatives to the police may betray bad manners. In each and every election campaign in Hungary during the last 17 years, the two major camps, the National-Conservatives and the Socialists, competed for the voters by means of Kádárist slogans. The Socialists are still debating whether they should really say good-bye to the Kádár era for good, or rather they might preserve some of its 'positive legacies' in the future. The liberal media carries bitterly nostalgic programmes featuring the popular saying from the 1980s: 'we are fine as long as Kádár is alive'. This culture of memory was chal-lenged by Imre Kertész, who a few years ago confessed that his Nobel Prize winning novel, *Fatelessness*, portraying his own tribulations in Nazi concentration camps with amazing sobriety, had actually been inspired by the depressing greyness and anomy of communism under János Kádár.[60] In a country in which 'Uncle János' has won every popularity contest of politicians during the past decades, I am afraid that Kertész' idea will not meet a warm reception in the foreseeable future.

Notes

1. See András Gervai, "Egy ügynök azonosítása" [Identifying an Agent], *Élet és Irodalom*, 27 January 2006. Today, the incriminated film director Gyula Gazdag is professor at the Department of Film of UCLA. The financial experts who were dismissed by the minister founded the first private insti-tute for economic research in Hungary before 1989. [See Ágnes Pogány, "A Pénzügykutatási Intézet története" [History of the Institute for Financial Research], in Hédi Volosin (ed.) *Lámpások az alagútban. Emlékek a Pénzügykutatóról* [Lamps in the Tunnel. Memories of the Institute for Finan-cial Research] (Budapest: Pénzügykutató Intézet, 1998), pp. 9–75.

2. This was the infamous "3T" principle of censorship (in Hungarian: *tiltás, turés, támogatás*).

3. The word "brick" (*tégla*) refers to the fact that the agent was built in by the police in the group under surveillance. I will use this term in the following though its synonyms show a great variety ranging from "spy" (*spicli* that comes from the German *Spitzel*) through "whisperer" (*besúgó*) all the way to BM-es (BM was the acronym of the Ministry of Interior). The word *titkosszolga* (secret servant) is a post-1989 neologism in Hungarian language.

4. For works on transitional justice in Eastern Europe (and beyond), see Hilary Appel, "Anti-Communist Justice and Founding the Post-Communist Order: Lustration and Restitution in Central Europe," *East European Politics and Societies* 19/3 (2005), pp. 379–405; Timothy Garton Ash, *The File. A Personal History* (New York: Vintage Books, 1998); Noel Ann Calhoun, *Dilemmas of Justice in Eastern Europe's Democratic Transitions* (New York: Palgrave Macmillan, 2004); Roman David, "Transitional Injustice? Criteria for Conformity of Lustration to the Right to Political Expression," *Europe-Asia Studies* 56/6 (2004), pp. 789–812; Istvan Deak, Jan T. Gross and Tony Judt, *The Politics of Retribution in Europe: World War Two and its Aftermath* (Princeton, NJ: Princeton

University Press, 2000); Jon Elster, *Closing the Books: Transitional Justice in Historical Perspective* (New York: Cambridge University Press, 2004); Jon Elster (ed.), *Retribution and Reparation in the Transition to Democracy* (New York: Cambridge University Press, 2006); Stephen Holmes, "The End of Decommunization," *East European Constitutional Review* 3 (1994), pp. 3–4; Tony Judt, *Postwar: A History of Europe Since 1945* (New York: Penguin Press, 2005); Csilla Kiss, "We Are Not Like Us. Transitional Justice: The (Re)construction of Post-communist Memory," *IWM Working Papers* (Vienna: IWM, 2006); Neil J. Kritz (ed.), *Transitional Justice: How Emerging Democracies Reckon with Former Regimes* (Washington, DC: US Institute of Peace Press, 1995); Natalia Letki, "Lustration and Democratisation in East-Central Europe," *Europe–Asia Studies*, 54/4 (2002), pp. 529–552; Charles Maier, "Doing History, Doing Justice: The Narrative of the Historian and of the Truth Commission," in Robert I. Rotberg and Dennis Thompson (eds), *Truth versus Justice: The Morality of Truth Commissions* (Princeton, NJ: Princeton University Press, 2000), pp. 261–279; Adam Michnik and Vaclav Havel, "Justice or Revenge?" *Journal of Democracy* 4/1 (1993), pp. 20–27; John Miller, "Settling Accounts with a Secret Police: The German Law on the Stasi Records," *Europe–Asia Studies* 50/2 (1998), pp. 305–331; Claus Offe, "Disqualification, Retribution, Restitution. Dilemmas of Justice in Post-Communist Transitions," *The Journal of Political Philosophy* 1/1 (1993), pp. 17–44; Tina Rosenberg, *The Haunted Land: Facing Europe's Ghosts After Communism* (New York: Vintage Books, 1996); Jacques Rupnik, "The Politics of Coming to Terms with the Communist Past. The Czech Case in Central European Perspective," *Transit Online* 22 (2002); Aleks Szczerbiak, "Dealing with the Communist Past or the Politics of the Present? Lustration in Post-Communist Poland," *Europe–Asia Studies* 54/4 (2002), pp. 553–572; Ruti G. Teitel, *Transitional Justice* (New York: Oxford University Press, 2000); Helga A. Welsh, "Dealing with the Communist Past. Central and East European Experiences after 1990," *Europe–Asia Studies* 48/3 (1996), pp. 413–428; Kieran Williams, Aleks Szczerbiak and Brigid Fowler, "Explaining Lustration in Post-Communist Eastern Europe," *Democratization* 12/1 (2005), pp. 22–43.

5. For more on the "my commie/agent is good, yours is bad" game, see János Kenedi, *Kis állambiztonsági olvasókönyv* [A Concise Reader of State Security] (Budapest: Magvető, 1996); *K. belügyi iratfelmérő jelentése a Kastélyból* [A Report by Police Documentalist K. from the Castle] (Budapest: Magvető, 2000); Krisztián Ungvári, "Der Umgang mit der kommunistischen Vergangenheit in der heutigen ungarischen Erinnerungskultur," in Bernd Faulenbach, Franz-Joseph Jelich (Hg), *"Transformationen" der Erinnerungskulturen in Europa nach 1989* (Essen: Klartext Verlag, 2006), pp. 201–221; László Varga, *Világ besúgói, egyesüljetek* [Whisperers of the World Unite] (Budapest: Polgart Könyvkiadó, 2007).

6. From time to time, the Liberals repeat their original suggestion (the so-called Demszky–Hack bill) to open the secret files, and a handful of historians publish on various kinds of prominent informers (church leaders, journalists, scholars, artists, etc.) in the framework of their research projects. Although the Liberals do not connect the claim of the so-called "informational restitution" with any kind of legal punishment, except for the pain caused to the brick by the revealing of the secrets, their bill repeatedly runs into resistance by the Socialists and the National-Conservatives. Below I will only refer to some of the most recent publications of liberal-minded scholars and politicians: Gábor Demszky, "Amnesztiát az iratoknak" [Amnesty for the Documents], in *A szabadság visszahódítása* [Reconquering Freedom] (Budapest: Új Mandátum Kiadó, 2001); Péter Hack, "Az ügynökvilág vége vagy újabb győzelme?" [The End of the Agents' World or Its Victory?] *Élet és Irodalom*, 13 February 2005; Gábor Halmai, "A köz érdeke és az ügynökminiszterek titka" [The Public Interest and the Secret of the Ministers of State Security], *Élet és Irodalom*, 13 January 2003; Miklós Haraszti, "Zsarolási haladvány" [Progression of Blackmail], *Élet és Irodalom*, 30 June 2000; János Kenedi, "'Stasi-operett' Magyarországon" ['Stasi Operetta' in Hungary], in *K. belügyi* (note 5); "Ügynök, ügynök über alles …" [Agent, Agent Above All], in *K. belügyi* (note 5); "A megismerés mint büntetési tétel" [Knowledge as Punishment], *Élet és Irodalom*, 24 March 2006; János Kis, "Az iratnyilvánosság és az alkotmány" [The Publicity of Documents and the Constitution], *Élet és Irodalom*, 25 March 2005; "Mit kezdjünk a volt ügynökökkel?" [What is to be Done with the Former Agents?], *Népszabadság*, 19, 21 August 1993; "Illusztráció az ügynökügyhöz" [Illustration to the Case of the Agents], *Élet és Irodalom*, 24 February 2006; Tamás Szőnyei, *Nyilván tartottak. Titkos szolgák a magyar rock körül* [The Registered. Secret Servants around the Hungarian Rock] (Budapest: Magyar Narancs, 2005); Péter Tölgyessy, "Az akták megítélése elválaszthatatlan a szocializmushoz való viszonyunktól" [The Evaluation of the Files is Inseparable from Our Attitude to Socialism], *Fundamentum* 7/1 (2003), pp. 33–36; Krisztián Ungvári, "Der Umgang" (note 5); "Mozgástér és kényszerpályák" [Room to Manoeuver and Forced Routes], *Élet és Irodalom*, 3 February 2006; "A beszervezés és az útibeszámoló" [The Enrollment and the Travel Report], *Élet és Irodalom*, 19 May 2006; László Varga, *Világ besúgói* (note 5);

"Gergő ... és az ő árnyéka, avagy amikor a jog a politika ügynökévé válik" [Gergő and his Shadow, or When the Law Becomes an Agent of Politics], *Beszélő*, 7/9–10 (2002), pp. 30–59. For an alternative approach among the Liberals, see Tamás Bauer, "Ügynöklicit" [Bidding for Agents], *Élet és Irodalom*, 26 February 2005; "Alkotmányos jogfosztás" [A Constitutional Deprivation of Rights], *Élet és Irodalom*, 18 March 2005; "Illusztráció az ügynökvitához" [Illustration to the Debate on Agents], *Élet és Irodalom*, 10 February 2006. A special genre of disclosure was invented by the writer Péter Esterházy, who published the reports filed by his own father to the police with detailed comments [Péter Esterházy, *Javított kiadás* (Revised Edition) (Budapest: Magvető, 2002)]. See also the bibliography of articles dealing with transitional justice in the weekly *Élet és Irodalom* between 1998 and 2006 (*Élet és Irodalom*, 3 February 2006).

7. See the transcript of the parliamentary investigation of Medgyessy's intelligence activities (session: 1 August 2002), http://www.nincstobbtitok.hu/index.php?article=00000103 (last accessed 13 January 2008). It is hard to believe that he did not have to report on his colleagues in the ministry. The suspicion was reinforced by a document leaked out from the police archives, according to which Medgyessy led a party investigation on the potential counter-revolutionaries in the main financial institutions back in 1976. See *Magyar Nemzet* 19 June 2002.

8. See *Magyar Hírlap*, 25 May 2001. While spying, he first became head of section in the ministry, then deputy minister. See also *Dokumentumok Medgyessy BM-dossziéjából* (Documents from Medgyessy's Files in the Ministry of Interior) I, II, III, IV, http://gondola.hu/cikkek/cikkek/11947 (last accessed 13 January 2008).

9. Allegedly, Szabó swore to his friend and another colleague not to reveal this secret any time in the future, and consulted them before filing his reports. According to another version of the story, he actually wanted to save himself. At any rate, he calls his friend in one of the reports a "counter-revolutionary," a most dangerous denunciation after 1956 (see "Pokolra kellett mennem" [I had to Visit Hell], *Népszabadság*, 29 January 2006; http://www.mtv.hu/magazin/cikk.php?id=102923, (last accessed 13 January 2008).

10. Szabó is less lucky than Medgyessy: his reports are available in the archives whereas most of the prime minister's files are still classified or lost.

11. In 2004–05, István Szabó was among the potential candidates of the left-liberal coalition in the presidential elections. He shot a whole series of films in the West before 1989, and is still the only Hungarian film director to win an Academy Award (1981). Péter Medgyessy worked as a successful businessman in the periods in which he was out of government, survived a few smaller corruption scandals, and received the *Légion d'Honneur* in 2000. When he was prime minister, the Parliament passed the so-called "film law" (a principal lobbyist was István Szabó), a law that granted large public funds to the film industry. The stories of the two gentlemen are not over: Medgyessy published his memoirs [the title is *Polgár a pályán* [A Citoyen on the Field] (Budapest: Kossuth Kiadó, 2006)], and Szabó promised that he would shoot a film focusing on his own tribulations in 1956 and later. Medgyessy said in an interview the following: "I refuse the claim that I must not like István Szabó because he filed reports to the police." *Népszabadság*, 21 February 2006.

12. Ironically, Szabó's past as an agent might have remained a secret forever if the Medgyessy scandal had not resulted in opening part of the files for the researchers. The prime minister's case triggered off a passionate debate in liberal circles, and even eminent former dissidents argued for the separation of ethical and political reasoning, and contended that Medgyessy must not be forced to step down on moral grounds. See János Kis, "Az erkölcsi minimum" [The Moral Minimum], *Élet és Irodalom*, 20 December 2002; Péter Nádas, "Az értelem kockázata" [The Risk of Reason], *Élet és Irodalom*, 3 January 2003; Endre Bojtár, "Kis-minimum" [The Kis Minimum], *Élet és Irodalom*, 3 January 2003; Miklós Haraszti, "A politikai minimum" [The Political Minimum], *Élet és Irodalom*, 10 February 2003.

13. The signatures show a strange mix, they include the names of famous '56-ers who sat in Kádár's prison and of police agents, as well as those of Kádár's court intellectuals and of leading former dissidents. (See *Népszabadság*, 30 January 2006.)

14. For a sarcastic counter-petition (expressing my own sentiments as well), see http://www.petitiononline.com/pityu/petition.html (last accessed 13 January 2008).

15. János Kis, a leader of the anti-communist opposition before and chairman of the Liberals after 1989, wrote the following: "It would not be appropriate to think of Szabó the same way as of Medgyessy who collaborated with the regime in order to promote his own career twenty years later. Péter Medgyessy was no victim. István Szabó was. But he was not the same kind of victim as those who did not join the police and therefore had to suffer or those who were the targets of his reports." See "A szembesítés gyötrelmei" [The Pains of Confrontation] *Népszabadság*, 4 February 2006.

16. A rare exception is provided by Iván Horváth's article who expressed serious doubts about the aesthetic value of Szabó's movies. See Iván Horváth, "A múltat végképp" [The Past is to be Deleted for Good], *Élet és Irodalom*, 10 March 2006.

17. In the public discussion, the names of Martin Heidegger, Bohumil Hrabal, Herbert von Karajan, Imre Lakatos, Carl Schmitt, and, in particular, Wilhelm Furtwängler were mentioned the most often as analogies. The destiny of Furtwängler fascinated István Szabó so much that some years ago he produced a picture ("Taking Sides") on the postwar screening of the German conductor. Szabó requested the script writer to include a new character in the original plot, a Soviet art historian who utters the following sentences: "In a dictatorship the arts belong to the party. ... One does need good connections. One does have to make concessions" (see Gervai, "Egy ügynök", note 1).

18. In the past couple of years, the biggest excitement among people at large was caused by the unveiling of cardinal/archbishop László Paskai (and five other archbishops and bishops), the most popular journalist of Hungary, György Szepesi, the soccer player and Olympic champion Dezső Novák and the rock singers Gyula Vikidál and Lajos Som. The liberal intelligentsia was most shaken by the cases of the writer Sándor Tar, the journalists Péter Molnár Gál and Tibor Fényi and the film director Gábor Bódy, who were all very close to the anti-communist opposition in the 1980s. See also note 45. On Molnár Gál's case, see György Spiró, "A Luzsnyánszky dossziéról" [On the Luzsnyánszky File], *Élet és Irodalom*, 10 January 2005.

19. See *168 óra* 23 February 2006.

20. In consuming the cultural goods produced by the collaborators, it is rather difficult for me to separate the author from his work. Of course, the fact that a soccer player spied on his team-mates does not invalidate in hindsight the memory of his superb goals. The same applies to a love song performed by a pop idol, to children rhymes written by a celebrated poet or to a theory proven by a natural scientist. Sometimes it is hard to suppress a bitter taste in one's mouth even in those cases. One feels betrayed, starts suspecting and the pleasure of reception fades. Bitterness may, however, turn into real fury if the pop idol used to sing protest songs, the poet used to write poems with heavy political messages and the theory was put forward by a moral philosopher. In these cases one cannot help raising the question of validity, credibility or, in one word, quality, especially if one has observed the authors from a close vicinity. Maybe, the future generations will look back on them without any indignation just like we do not really care about Villon's, Goncharov's or Rimbaud's wrongdoings today.

21. Ironically, since 1989, only three persons have been convicted in Hungary upon charges related to secret service activities under communism. József Végvári, major of the Ministry of Interior, who betrayed to the dissidents in December 1989 (!) that the surveillance of the "enemies of the system" as well as the liquidation of the secret files were not interrupted (this led to the so-called Duna-gate affair), was tried and reprimanded by the prosecutor for revealing state secrets. Two of his superiors got the same mild punishment for the liquidation of the secret materials (see László Varga, "Gergő", note 6).

22. How on earth could I pass judgements? I grew up in a nomenklatura family and was lucky enough to be sheltered from provocation by the state security services. I have no right to either condemn or forgive anyone. A few ironical remarks are, however, due to show that self-constraint on my part is not tantamount to affection toward the bricks, especially the proud ones.

23. Moral relativism has also been prompted by the recurrent quarrels between the '56-ers, the reluctance of the Socialists to break with the Kádárist tradition, and by the hypocritical anti-communist fervour of the right-wing parties, which culminated in establishing the House of Terror in Budapest. [See Éva Kovács, "Das zynische und das ironische. Zum Gedächtnis des Kommunismus in Ungarn," *Transit* 30 (2006), pp. 88–105.]

24. Debreczeni József, *A miniszterelnök. Antall József és a rendszerváltozás* [The Prime Minister. József Antall and the Systemic Change] (Budapest: Osiris, 1998), p.270. This is the context of the citation: "You cannot establish democracy and, at the same time, apply dictatorship in the sake of democracy. ... Revolution, that's what you should have made, dear friends. Do not require from those who managed the peaceful transition what one could demand from revolutionary leaders. Before the free parliamentary elections, one did not believe that there would be elections in this country. When we spoke of the secession of the Soviet troops, one did not believe that they would really leave. When we implemented all this, those who come up with very radical demands today, were silent. ... Do not expect from me to kick out a head of department in Sátoraljaújhely! ... We cannot do that because ours is a controlled, parliamentary government."

25. See Ferenc Fehér, "Az 'iskolamester'" [The Schoolmaster], *Beszélő*, 31 August 1991.

26. This game was also played by József Antall, who handed over envelopes to certain members of his party and coalition government (including those whom he wanted to discipline), and alluded to

the fact that some of the envelopes may contain unpleasant information on involvement with the communist secret services. [See Éva Kovács, "'Hütchenspiel' – Der ungarische Diskurs über die Restitution der Gerechtigkeit," in Krisztina Mänicke-Gyöngyösi (Hg.), *Öffentliche Konfliktdiskurse um Restitution von Gerechtigkeit, politische Verantwortung und nationale Identität* (Frankfurt am Main: Peter Lang Verlag, 1996), pp. 119–134.]

27. See G. M. Tamás, "Kenedi Jánosnak" [To János Kenedi], *Élet és Irodalom*, 26 November 1999; Tóth Klára, "Fájni fog" [It Will Ache], *Élet és Irodalom*, 22 April 2005. Both Péter Nádas and Péter Esterházy took an ambivalent but highly sophisticated approach in making moral judgements on collaboration: they did not reject justice-making as such but, in contrast to their attitude to the communist rulers, showed a fair amount of compassion toward the agents, and also admitted (just like Václav Havel did) their own responsibility for sustaining the *ancien régime*. To quote Nádas's words: "The dark and unchanging rule of the secret police is maintained not by petty informers who can be bought for a song, not by easily conned careerists or other nonentities, but by me." The same conclusion was drawn by Esterházy: "If … we said that the country (I, you, he/she, we, you, they) exchanged blood spilled in '56 for some money, then it also means that we, for instance, commissioned certain people, our fellow-citizens, to turn other fellow-citizens of ours (e.g., my father) into bricks, 'floor cloths'. This does not provide an excuse to either of the two parties, it is just so. I cannot extract myself from this in a clean state, this is not an issue of 'the others,' this is not a separate game between the rotten commies and the rotten bricks but it was played by all of us while we were not all (rotten) commies and bricks." See Péter Nádas, "Our Poor, Poor Sascha Anderson," *Common Knowledge* 8/3 (Fall 2002), pp. 526–547 [*Heimkehr* (Hamburg, 1999)]; Péter Esterházy, *Javított kiadás* (note 6), pp.122–3.

28. Actually, there were two conservative cabinets in Hungary between 1990 and 1994. Following Antall's death in 1993, Péter Boross, a company director under Kádár, became prime minister.

29. From among the former leading reformers László Békesi, Lajos Bokros, Péter Medgyessy, Péter Mihályi, György Surányi and Attila Károly Soós joined the highest echelons of the first Socialist-Liberal administration while Tamás Bauer and Márton Tardos, influential politicians of the Liberals, supported them.

30. Another important argument originated in the danger of a nationalist/populist/authoritarian distortion of the new democratic regime. Public intellectuals associated with the two parties founded the Democratic Charta in 1991 to face that danger.

31. At the roundtable talks, they often mediated between the hard-liners of the Communists and the opposition groups.

32. From among the former researchers, György Surányi, for instance, was president of the National Bank when Medgyessy became finance minister in the Horn government, and István Csillag was minister for economic affairs in Medgyessy's government. For a heroic story of reformism presented from the perspective of the Communists, see Iván T. Berend, *A történelem, ahogy megéltem* [History as I Lived It] (Budapest: Kulturtrade Kiadó, 1997). Today, the Socialists are coming close to subscribing to the tradition of the '56 revolution as well. The co-optation of a famous revolutionary and former Liberal, Imre Mécs, in the parliamentary faction of the Socialists in 2006 reflects the ambition of the progressive wing of the party to replace János Kádár with the leader of the revolution, Imre Nagy.

33. See my "A reformalku sűrűjében" [In the Thick of Reform Bargaining], *Valóság* 27/3 (1984), pp. 30–55; "Reform Bargaining in Hungary," *Comparative Economic Studies*, 28/3 (1986), pp. 25–42; "Reform Economics: The Classification Gap," *Daedalus* 119/1 (Winter 1990, pp. 215–248); "From Reformation to Transformation: Limits to Liberalism in Hungarian Economic Thought," *East European Politics and Societies* 5/1 (Winter 1991), pp. 41–72; "Compassionate Doubts about Reform Economics (Science, Ideology, Politics)," in J.M. Kovács and M. Tardos (eds), *Reform and Transformation. Eastern European Economics on the Threshold of Change* (London: Routledge, 1992), pp. 299–334; "Planning the Transformation? Notes about the Legacy of the Reform Economists," in J.M. Kovács (ed.), *Transition to Capitalism? The Communist Legacy in Eastern Europe* (New Brunswick, NJ and London: Transactions, 1994), pp. 21–46.

34. Of course, one can start telling the story of collaboration in the period following the defeat of the 1848 revolution, during and after the Council Republic in 1919 or, closer to our times, in the course of the 1930s when part of the left reconciled itself with the proto-fascist regime of Admiral Horthy. Probably, 1956 could have been the last moment before 1989 to make a fresh start in moral terms, if … if the revolution had not been defeated, had gone beyond the program of democratic socialism cum national liberation, and solved, in its honeymoon phase, the typical moral dilemmas of the time. These dilemmas were rooted in wartime collaboration, communist terror, the opportunism of the fellow-travellers, the victimhood of Communists under their own regime, the democratic

metamorphosis of Stalinists, etc. Too many "ifs," I know but the ethical choices became even more twisted after 1956.

35. Here let me just refer to some of the most recent works on the Kádár era: György Földes, *Az eladósodás politikatörténete* [The Political History of Indebtedness] 1957–86 (Budapest: Maecenas, 1995); Péter György, *Néma hagyomány* [Silent Tradition] (Budapest: Magvető, 2000); *Kádár köpönyege* [Kádár's Gown] (Budapest: Magvető, 2005); Tibor Huszár, *Kádár János politikai életrajza* [A Political Biography of János Kádár] (Budapest: Corvina, 2006); *Kádár – a hatalom évei* [Kádár. The Years of Power] 1956–89 (Budapest: Szabad Tér Kiadó, 2001–03); Melinda Kalmár, *Ennivaló és hozomány. A kora-kádárizmus ideológiája* [Food and Dowry. The Ideology of Early Kádárism] (Budapest: Magvető: 1998); János M. Rainer, *Nagy Imre. Politikai életrajz* [Imre Nagy. A Political Biography] (Budapest: 1956-os Intézet, 1996–99); János M. Rainer and György Péteri (eds), *Muddling Through in the Long 1960s. Ideas and Everyday Life in High Politics and the Lower Classes of Communist Hungary*, Trondheim Studies on East European Cultures and Societies, No. 16 (Trodheim: 2005); Sándor Révész, *Antall József távolról* [József Antall from Afar] (Budapest: Sik Kiadó, 1995); *Aczél és korunk* [Aczél and Our Era] (Budapest: Sik Kiadó, 1997); Éva Standeisky, *Gúzsba kötve. A kulturális elit és a hatalom* [Tied Up. The Cultural Elite and Political Power] (Budapest: 1956-os Intézet, 2005), Tibor Valuch, *Hétköznapi élet Kádár János korában* [Everyday Life in the Era of János Kádár] (Budapest: Corvina, 2006); *Magyarország társadalomtörténete a XX. század második felében* [The Social History of Hungary in the Second Half of the Twentieth Century] (Budapest: Osiris, 2001). As for the behavior of the intellectuals, censhorship, etc., it is still worth while reading Miklós Haraszti's book *The Velvet Prison* (New York: Basic Books, 1987). On the legacy of collaboration, see Gábor Gyáni, "A kollaboráció szégyene és dicsősége" [The Shame and Glory of Collaboration], *Élet és Irodalom*, 10 February 2006.

36. See Éva Standeisky, *Gúzsba kötve* (note 35); *Az írók és a hatalom* [The Writers and Political Power] 1956–63, (Budapest: 1956-os Intézet, 1996).

37. The old American anecdote about the smart Hungarian who enters the revolving door behind you but leaves it in front of you, began to spread in Hungary only in the 1980s. For the ongoing political instrumentalization of the myth of Central Europe, see my "Westerweiterung? Zur Metamorphose des Traums von Mitteleuropa," *Transit* 21 (2001), pp. 3–19.

38. Until the emergence of market socialism in China, the only serious alternative to the "Pannonian model" of reform economics was the "Illyrian model" of workers' self-management. For a most insightful appraisal of the Yugoslav economic policy in Hungary during the 1980s, see Attila K. Soós, *Terv Kampány, Pénz* [Plan, Campaign, Money] (Budapest: KJK, 1986). Cf. my "Narcissism of Small Differences. Looking Back on 'Reform Economics' in Hungary," in Christoph Boyer (Hg.), *Zur Physiognomie sozialistischer Wirtschaftsreformen* (Frankfurt am Main: Vittorio Klostermann, 2007).

39. See *Népszabadság*, 24 December 1967.

40. See my "Compassionate Doubts" (note 33); "Reform Economics" (note 33).

41. See Ferenc Jánossy, "Gazdaságunk mai ellentmondásainak eredete" [The Origins of Current Contradictions in Our Economy], *Közgazdasági Szemle* 16/7–8 (1969), pp. 806–829 (and in English, *Eastern European Economics*, 8/4 (1970)).

42. See Márton Tardos, "Reform: itt és most?" [Reform: hic et nunc?] *Mozgó Világ*, 9/2 (1983), pp. 8–23; "Ma jobban tudom, hogy senki se tudja" [Today I Know Better That Nobody Knows It], in Márton Tardos, *A liberális reformer* [The Liberal Reformer] (Budapest: Pénzügykutató, 1999). Tardos belonged to those few reform economists who could flawlessly harmonize dissidence and co-authoring papers with the Communist dissenter Rezső Nyers. See Rezső Nyers and Márton Tardos, "Milyen gazdaságfejlesztési stratégiát válasszunk?" [What Strategy for Economic Development Is To Be Chosen?] *Gazdaság* 13/1 (1979), pp. 5–25; "Vállalatok a gazdasági reform előtt és után" [Firms Before and After the Economic Reform], *Valóság* 24/3 (1981), pp. 9–19. For the ambiguity of my attitude to the legendary reform Communist, see "Nyers," *Élet és Irodalom*, 4 April 2003.

43. See note 6, in particular, the writings of Tamás Bauer.

44. Medgyessy seems to disregard this. I quote him: "There were two options. One of them was 'the worse the better' option, that is, to play for a quick collapse of the system. It would have been a great naiveté for someone to think like this in 1978. If one knows history and the international situation at the time, he/she cannot presume it to be a good option. ... Well, one can say with a clear conscience that in such a situation the only possible choice was to grant a normal life in the country; to do the work one had been taught, to work in the national economy and use the knowledge one obtained at the University of Economics about financial, professional, economic issues. I chose that way. I think I did it correctly. By the way, about ten million Hungarians chose the same

option." (See the transcript of the parliamentary investigation: http://www.nincstobbtitok.hu/index.php?article=00000103, last accessed 13 January 2008)

45. Among others, the names of the following economists were mentioned by the *ad hoc* commission led by Imre Mécs: László Bogár, Imre Boros, Szabolcs Fazakas, Zsigmond Járai, Béla Kádár, János Martonyi, Ferenc Rabár and Gábor Szalay (see http://www.nincstobbtitok.hu/index.php?page=0101, last accessed 13 January 2008). Many of them blocked the publication of their files by claiming that they were not public figures and referring to their rights for privacy. Part of them remained silent or said that they had only filed "travel reports" upon returning from their official visits to the West, or talked to certain officers but had not joined the secret police.

46. There were two delicate cases of collaboration (or the lack of it) with or without involvement with the secret police (the Hungarian or the Soviet one), which aroused much suspicion in the profession for many decades: (1) the mysterious suicide of György Péter in 1969, president of the Central Statistical Office after 1956, and the pioneer of reform thinking in Eastern Europe prior to 1956; (2) the "never-ending" presidency of Béla Csikós-Nagy in the Central Price Office, a prominent economist who flirted with Nazism before the war and was rehabilitated by the Communists thereafter. See Árvay János and Hegedüs B. András (eds), *Egy reformközgazdász emlékére. Péter György 1903–1969* [Remembering a Reform Economist] (Budapest: Cserépfalvi-T-Twins, 1994).

47. Besides the above-mentioned books by Berend and Medgyessy, see also the historical study written by László Csaba and László Szamuely on *Rendszerváltozás a közgazdaságtanban – közgazdaságtan a rendszerváltozásban* [Systemic Change in Economics – Economics in the System Change] (Budapest: Közgazdasági Szemle Alapítvány, 1998). József Böröcz's, László Lengyel's and György Péteri's writings are exceptions to the rule. See József Böröcz, "Reaction as Progress: Economists as Intellectuals," in András Bozóki (ed.) *Intellectuals and Politics in Central Europe* (Budapest: CEU Press, 1999, pp. 245–262); Lengyel László, "Adalékok a 'Fordulat és reform' történetéhez" [On the History of 'Turnaround and Reform']. *Medvetánc* 7/2 (1987), pp. 131–165; *Kétszög Hankiss Elemérrel* [A Diangle with Elemér Hankiss] (Budapest: Helikon Press, 2002); György Péteri, "Controlling the Field of Academic Economics: Hungary, 1953–1976," *Minerva* 34/4 (1996), pp. 367–380; "New Course Economics: The Field of Economic Research in Hungary after Stalin, 1953–1956," *Contemporary European History* November 6/3 (1997), pp. 295–327; "Purge and Patronage: Kádár's Counterrevolution and the Field of Economic Research in Hungary, 1957–58," *Contemporary European History* February 1/1 (2002), pp. 125–152.

48. A telling example: after the list provided by the Mécs Commission (see note 45) had been published, not a single colleague of the incriminated persons commented on their alleged wrongdoings, or, in general, on the moral dilemmas of economists under the Kádár regime, publicly. The rare comments concerned the controversial procedures of the commission, and the undoubtedly shaky proofs offered an excuse for silence. (See, e.g., Tamás Bauer, "Taps a kormánypártok padsoraiban" [Applause from the Benches of the Government Parties], *Élet és Irodalom*, 11 January 2003.)

49. Ironically, his code name was István Szabó.

50. In many cases the contacts with the secret service were not completely discontinued. Bácskai, for example, became an official in the Soviet satellite organization, the World Council of Peace in Vienna during the 1960s. As another agent from István Szabó's class in the film school wrote in a self-unveiling essay, the principals from the secret police reappeared in the life of the agents from time to time, keeping them in a state of permanent uncertainty and angst. (See Zsolt Kézdi-Kovács, "Jelentek" [I am reporting], *Élet és Irodalom*, 3 February 2006.)

51. János Kornai, *A gondolat erejével* [By Force of Thought] (Budapest: Osiris, 2005). (The quotations below are my translation.)

52. On this balance act, see, e.g., his "The Hungarian Reform Process. Visions, Hopes and Reality," *Journal of Economic Literature* 24/4 (1986), pp. 1687–1737.

53. Cf. *A gondolat* (note 51), pp.140–41, 225. (Kende, who left Hungary in the wake of the 1956 revolution, became a renown political scientist in Paris.)

54. *A gondolat* (note 51), p.290.

55. *A gondolat* (note 51)., p.264.

56. See note 27 on accompliceship as interpreted by two prominent writers in Hungary.

57. In social sciences it is doubtful whether delaying research will make its results more mature. Kornai's example demonstrates that, although those fields which he had excluded from his research program when writing the *Shortage* were included in his book on *The Socialist System* (Princeton, NJ: Princeton University Press, 1992), the postponement led to a decline in both

authenticity of analysis and depth of empirical inquiry. By the time Kornai broke with self-censorship and completed his book, the "insect" called planned economy died, moreover his interest turned to a new species, the emerging market economy.

58. See my "Business as (Un)usual. Notes on the Westernization of Economic Sciences in Eastern Europe," in Max Kaase and Vera Sparschuh (eds), *Three Social Science Disciplines in Central and Eastern Europe* (Bonn/Berlin and Budapest: IZ-Colbud, 2002), pp. 26–33.

59. Working rather close to János Kornai in the same research institute in Budapest for almost two decades, many of the younger colleagues including myself were convinced that he might have been less cautious without jeopardizing his life strategy. Today, with the benefit of hindsight, I am afraid that we were only right as far as the second half of the 1980s was concerned.

60. See Imre Kertész, "A Sorstalanságot a Kádár-rendszerről írtam" [I Wrote *Fatelessness* about the Kádár Regime], *Élet és Irodalom*, 30 May 2003; "A túlélés koreográfiái" [Choreographies of Survival], *Magyar Hírlap* 13 September 2003.

Crime and Punishment in Communist Czechoslovakia: The Case of General Heliodor Píka and his Prosecutor Karel Vaš[1]

MILAN HAUNER

The trials of Heliodor Píka and of Karel Vaš

On 15 June 2001, the Czech Press Agency (ČTK) briefly noted that Karel Vaš, a former military prosecutor, had been sentenced to seven years in jail. The senate of the Prague City Court found the 85-year-old man guilty of having forged evidence against General Heliodor Píka, accusing him of collaboration with the British secret service. This announcement seemed to indicate an extraordinary and singular moment in the post-communist jurisdiction of the Czech Republic (the former Czechoslovakia). For the first time a prominent perpetrator of communist repression had been successfully tried and sentenced. Other culprits, however, like the notorious torturers and interrogators of the 1950s, could not be prosecuted because either they had died, or their crimes had lapsed in the meantime because of the 50-year barrier, or, since they had already been punished (mildly) in the late 1950s, their lawyers could now successfully claim the old Roman Law principle – as happened, as we shall see, in the Vaš case – that one should not be prosecuted twice for the same crime.[2]

The victim, General Heliodor Píka (1897–1949), the head of the Czechoslovak Military Mission in Moscow during World War II and deputy chief of the General Staff after the war, had been selected as the prime target in the purges, initiated inside the Czechoslovak officer corps in the immediate aftermath of the communist takeover in February 1948. Karel Vaš, by contrast, epitomised the group of perpetrators of judicial crimes, regardless – and here his case becomes slightly complicated – of the fact that he himself had become victim in the 1950s under the same deadly mechanism of justice he helped to lubricate.

The seven year sentence against Karel Vaš, mild in itself, was considered as a *de facto* life sentence in view of the defendant's advanced age. In fact the presiding judge justified the relatively low sentence given to Vaš by referring to the advanced age of the defendant as a mitigating circumstance. His sentence, too, has been regarded as symbolic atonement for past crimes committed during the communist rule. It has been well received in the Czech Republic, though voices were heard sympathising with the aged defendant suffering from Parkinson's disease. However, most commentaries understood that the outrageous miscarriage of justice in the name of ideology of hatred, whether National Socialist or communist, had to be punished, even if it happened more than half a century ago, and the frail former prosecutor appeared to be, if not the first, then certainly the most important symbolic representative of the repressive communist system established since 1948.

Hearing the verdict, Vaš declared himself innocent. He and his counsel, Dr Čestmír Kubát, immediately dismissed the sentence as politically motivated and protested against the portion of the verdict that denied legal validity for the period of communist rule. Through his lawyer Vaš also rejected the charge that the evidence against General Píka was intentionally fabricated, maintaining that it reached him unblemished through legal channels. Both repeatedly said that they would appeal. The Czech Deputy Premier Pavel Rychetský, himself a lawyer by training, told the press that the sentence sets a moral and political precedent in that the same legal standards as applied to Nazi prosecutors and judges could be applied to communist crimes. Although almost 60 years have passed since General Píka's execution and another 40 years since the first attempts to rehabilitate him, the former resilient prosecutor of 'the enemies of the Soviet Union' looked as if he would not give in whatever the political circumstances. Admittedly, he was a hard nut to crack, but the Píka–Vaš interlocked case is one of the most intriguing in the entire postwar period of the Czechoslovak Republic. The Píka case still ranks first among military trials during the communist era, just as if Milada Horáková[3] became the symbol for the casualties among politicians, and Rudolf Slánský et al.[4] turned out to be the chief martyr for the communists and a sordid example of how communists had settled accounts among themselves.

Predictably, it was not the last word we have heard from Karel Vaš. Given the emotional involvement of the public, each judicial confrontation with the former military prosecutor Karel Vaš was perceived as a retrial of General Píka, whose rehabilitation trial of 1968 needed a symbolic end through imprisoning Vaš. In that respect the Vaš trials could be compared with the recent trials of octogenarian Nazi judges and prison guards, or Vichy administrators who had been accused of maintaining the façade of legality during World War II while collaborating closely with the German security services. In the case of Karel Vaš, however, he did not go to prison where he might have been allowed to die, which could have been interpreted as the crowning act of General Píka's incomplete rehabilitation.

Nevertheless, it was not Vaš's continuous illness and his very advanced age that prevented him from entering the prison to start his seven years' sentence. With the help of his energetic legal counsel, Dr Kubát, he exploited every paragraph of the law by inserting half-truths and full lies, never ceasing to appeal against the sentence, claiming that he himself was the object of a major miscarriage of justice – not General Píka.[5] Vaš and his lawyer went far beyond the legal norms re-established after the so-called Velvet Revolution of November 1989. They questioned General Píka's rehabilitation verdict from December 1968, making several outrageous hints that Píka's sentence of high treason for espionage in 1949 had been with all certainty justified since Píka himself, by signing the final protocol, *de facto* admitted that he had passed information to the British. In December 2001, Vaš and Kubát even had the impudence to call a press conference to present their brochure and to demonstrate Vaš's innocence. Moreover, no one could deprive Vaš as a World War II veteran of his pension with the 'liberation supplement', which has recently been increased. Naïve voices in the media, lacking the dialectical understanding of historical development that only Marxism could provide, were wondering whether Vaš received his supplementary 'liberation benefits' as a reward for the judicial murder of General Píka. As part of the campaign of catching the eyes and ears of the public Vaš has been seen participating quietly at numerous veteran parties and commemorations as if he was one of those selected for rewards rather than for condemnation. Survivors among the veterans have accused Vaš of being directly responsible for at least 12 death indictments, including that one of General Píka, and later in his capacity as military judge for more than 120 long-term sentences.[6]

Thus, the constant noise Vaš and his lawyer Kubát were making following the June 2001 sentence paid off. One year after passing the sentence on Vaš, on 15 January 2002, the Prague Supreme Court ruled that in 2001 the City Court had applied the wrong legal clauses in sentencing Vaš. It should have applied a certain military penal law of 1855, surviving from the Imperial Austrian era, but still valid in Czechoslovakia in the late 1940s. According to this penal law, Vaš's prosecution became barred under the statute of limitation introduced in 1994.[7] Before the assembled Czech media his lawyer triumphantly declared 'absolute victory'.

The former prosecutor Vaš obviously knows the value of studying law and its interpretation. Moreover, his lawyer has masterfully exploited *ad nauseam* the combination of old age and the incredible twists of his client's legal metamorphosis, frequently changing from the position of a perpetrator of crime into that of a victim. Can the free Czech society find means to resume legal proceedings against such notorious cases like Karel Vaš, which threaten otherwise to make the whole process of 'reckoning with the past' a travesty of justice?

Ne bis idem crimen iudicetur: General Píka and his Iron Prosecutor[8]

Who was General Heliodor Píka (1897–1949), whose judicial murder in 1949 fulfilled a similar function in launching the purges inside the Czechoslovak officer corps as the arrest and subsequent execution of Marshal Tukhachevsky in 1937 had done for the Red Army? General Píka was a professional officer loyal to former President Edvard Beneš and his London-based government in exile, who served, between 1941 and 1945, as the chief of the Czechoslovak Military Mission in Moscow. His was a most difficult job, since the able officer had to maintain a modicum of efficiency within the Soviet system of wartime exigency, under constant criticism of communist agents, while remaining loyal to the distant authority of President Beneš. How difficult this must have been can be illustrated by the example of the wireless communication between Moscow and the outside world, since the Soviets did not allow the Czechoslovak Military Mission to send out wireless messages; they had to be first decoded and delivered by hand to them. When Píka's request for an independent wireless continued to be ignored, he turned to British colleagues in

Moscow who did not want to know the cipher and dispatched his coded messages promptly without questioning. When this was reported to the Soviets, their reaction was predictable. Surrounded by NKVD agents, Píka had to be constantly on his tiptoes. They would try to take away soldiers from the Czechoslovak unit without asking his permission to train them as special agents for sabotage and terrorist activities, and then parachute them behind the lines. Owing to inadequate training and lack of contact with underground organisations, practically all these agents perished.[9] Píka's professional criticism of Soviet practices in recruiting agents for what practically amounted to suicide missions, his close personal contacts with British officers in Moscow and the respect his objective reporting from the German–Soviet battlefront earned him within the British Government,[10] his opposition to political agitation by Czech communists within the Czechoslovak army unit, his continuous loyalty to President Beneš's Government, his resistance to Soviet harassment and frequent attempts at blackmail to force him to collaborate with the communists against Beneš and his military superiors in London, all made him into a marked man after the communist 1948 February Coup.

When the war ended and Píka returned to Prague, he was promoted by President Beneš to deputy chief of General Staff. However, in May 1948, shortly after the communist takeover in Prague, he was arrested without a warrant by the communists on charges of espionage for British military intelligence. He was interrogated for the rest of 1948, during which time Reicin and Vaš collected evidence from the military archives and from witnesses until they had enough material to fabricate the indictment.[11] Píka was accused of working for British intelligence and for undermining the fighting qualities of the Czechoslovak armed forces in the Soviet Union during the war as well as after the war in his new position as the deputy chief of general staff. Indicted as a traitor and subsequently sentenced to death on charges of high treason in January 1949, Píka was executed six months later after all requests for clemency had been rejected by the highest executive organ in communist Czechoslovakia, the so-called 'fiver' [*Pětka*].[12] During the Prague Spring Píka's case was reopened and on 13 December 1968 the general was finally rehabilitated and acquitted of all charges contained in the 20-year-old death sentence.[13]

The institution that carried out the arrest and was in charge of the interrogation was the Army Security Intelligence Office, known under the Czech abbreviation 'OBZ'. It was run by communist officers who could be trusted by the NKVD. At the head of OBZ were Bedřich Reicin (1911–52) and his deputy Karel Vaš (1916–), who had both harboured a grudge against Píka since their first encounter in Russia during the war. Reicin arrived in the USSR under obscure circumstances some time in 1940 from the Protectorate, where he was registered at the Gestapo as a communist and a Jew.[14] Nevertheless, he was permitted to join a transport of Czechoslovak Jews, which travelled across the USSR to China. In Moscow he stepped out from the train and was arrested by the NKVD who refused to believe that Reicin was a member of the Czechoslovak Communist Party. Since he spoke German and his name sounded German, the Soviets concluded that Reicin must be a German spy and had him promptly dispatched to a labour camp. If anything, this life experience made him more cynical and subservient to the pressure of the NKVD. A similar fate had befallen Karel Vaš, when he tried to illegally cross into the USSR. Born in 1916 in Užhorod as son of a Jewish lawyer from the easternmost region of interwar Czechoslovakia, Subcarpathia Ruthenia (Ukraine), he became radicalized at a precocious age. Although Vaš claimed to be member of the Czechoslovak Communist Party since his student days, the Soviet authorities could not trust him and dispatched him to a Gulag camp like Reicin.

After the July 1941 agreement between Beneš and the Soviet Government, Czechoslovak citizens subjected to conscription who had been detained at the time inside the Soviet Union were released in order to join the Czechoslovak Army unit to be formed behind. First came former Czechoslovak soldiers who had been captured and interned by the Red Army following the collapse of Poland in September 1939.[15] Later former Czechoslovak citizens scattered in labour camps and captured Slovak soldiers who had fought along with the German troops were added. While Píka was in faraway Kuibyshev or Moscow, propaganda and intelligence matters at the newly formed Czechoslovak Battalion (Later Brigade and Army Corps) had been from the beginning in the hands of the communists like Reicin and Vaš, supervised by the NKVD.

When the war ended Píka was on the one hand promoted but on the other he became the target of a secret manhunt by the Reicin–Vaš team. His telephone conversations were tapped and he was shadowed by OBZ agents whether he was at home or travelling abroad. In early May 1948, shortly after the communist coup, General Píka was arrested, literally in a military hospital where he was undergoing surgery. Inhe beginning, Reicin himself conducted the interrogation. When he could not make any breakthrough, he angrily asked Vaš to take over and compel the general to admit his guilt that he was working for British intelligence. After a pause of four months Vaš thus started as chief investigator, and finished, in a serious breach – and as a lawyer he must have been aware of that – of legal practice, as the assistant prosecutor at the Píka trial.[16]

So complete was communist control of the military and judiciary apparatus soon after the February cup, and so weak the authority of the ailing President Beneš, that not even a warrant was required for the arrest of one of the most senior army officers. The Soviet-trained henchmen of the OBZ simply moved around and arrested whoever caught the attention of their chiefs,[17] and these were Reicin and Vaš at the time, both enjoying swift promotion from the ranks of lieutenants to colonels. Securing the military archives of the Beneš Government from London when the boxes arrived in Prague, Reicin began to sift carefully General Píka's correspondence with Gen eralIngr, Beneš's Minister of Defence. In parallel with the preparations for the Píka trial, Reicin assembled many disjointed sentences from the Píka–Ingr correspondence, which he started to serialise immediately after the announcement of Píka's sentence on 28 January 1949 in the army weekly *Obrana Lidu*. Under the pseudonym of Josef Bartovský it was to be published later as a propaganda brochure entitled: *The Path to the Bottom of Betrayal*. The brochure opened the assault against the pro-Beneš officers with a broadside against General Píka: 'although the [CP] Secretary General Rudolf Slánský warned of reactionary machinations against the Soviet Union already in the spring of 1946, it was only … when the former General Píka faced the tribunal that the hideous crimes of this clique were unmasked … which were carried out under the veil of military and resistance activities'.[18]

Vaš himself has described for obvious reason his strained relationship with Reicin in his reminiscences rather differently. Carefully avoiding the admission that he was Reicin's first deputy and over-emphasising the conflict-side of their relationship, he explains[19]:

> At the beginning of 1947 I was removed from counter-intelligence for conceptual disagreements with Bedřich Reicin, the chief of the 5th depart-

ment in the Army General Staff (intelligence). Among others I criticized his negative attitude toward officers who served in the west. After one-year service in the army judicial corps, I was entrusted in June 1948 with the investigation, of the case, among others, of General Heliodor Píka because there was justified suspicion that he had committed high treason. In the course of interrogating him I strictly followed the letter of the law. Neither physical nor psychological pressure was used against the general from myself; I would absolutely rule out that some one else should have tried it. I did not knowingly insert into his file any documents that might have been considered forgeries. I gathered impartially documents speaking for and against the general. In the draft summary of my charges against General Píka, which I had prepared following the advice of the deputy state prosecutor, I proposed a heavy jail sentence. I was at the time a mere assistant to the state prosecutor without the privilege of carrying out acts of prosecution. I did not wish the general's death. However, the selection of evidence ... including the final verdict were solely decisions taken appropriately by the court. It was not me who sentenced Gen.Píka to death in January 1949 but the State Court, in contradistinction with the proposal drafted by the deputy state prosecutor during the main hearing.[20]

Vaš then sums up in a telegraphic style what happened to him and Gen. Píka thereafter, mixing up his own rehabilitation with that of his main victim in 1968:

Eventually Gen.Píka was executed. He was then rehabilitated in 1968 under very problematic circumstances as a victim of the Communist regime. The judicial resumption of his case was however politically manipulated. It was preceded by the illegal negotiations of Píka's defense lawyers with the General's son with the President of the Republic in the presence of the prosecutor general and the president of the court. I happened to be arrested in 1951. Just like today I was accused of having tried unlawfully to impose capital punishment on Gen. Píka ... They were trying to force me to admit deeds, which I have never committed; besides I was to testify under false pretenses in the contemplated Slánský trial. I then spent a year and half in solitary confinement. There was no beating but I suffered hunger. When they thought I was done I began hunger strike. They capitulated but in July 1953 they managed to sentence me in a political trial. I received a life sentence. But that could take place only after the execution of Reicin in December 1952 ... After six years of imprisonment I was released ... and achieved full rehabilitation.[21]

The documents do not reveal whether the OBZ had acted upon the direct advice of Soviet 'counselors' in the Píka case. However, it is known that during his interrogations of General Píka, Vaš used to meet almost daily the resident NKVD agent in Prague, Mikhail Makarevich Khazanov, whose official function was 'legal counselor' at the Soviet Embassy in Prague. Khazanov requested and received every copy of the Píka interrogation protocol prepared by Vaš. He seemed to have unofficially advised Vaš how to conduct interrogation, according to Vaš's own testimony, since 'Moscow was eminently interested in Píka's indictment so that he should be prevented from fleeing to the West carrying with him all the Soviet military secrets he knew'.[22]

The close Khazanov–Vaš relationship continued throughout the period when Vaš was officially in charge of interrogating Píka – i.e. from 9 June to 17 November 1948 – in spite of the fact that at this time there was no official agreement between the OBZ and NKVD regarding the prosecution of Czechoslovak army officers considered pro-western, and that Vaš was in serious breach of the existing Czechoslovak Army regulations. Indeed, one is justified in asking who was in fact acting here as a foreign agent? Although Gottwald had made a request to Stalin in writing already in September 1949, it was not until the summer of 1950 that Soviet counselors (e.g. Makarov, Likhachev and others)[23] were brought in to assist with interrogations, such as the notorious Slánský group, in which the communists turned against their own ilk under the pretext of cleansing the party of 'Zionists, imperialist agents and other enemies of the Soviet Union'.[24] Reicin, as a suspicious 'cosmopolitan' communist, because of his Jewish origin, would figure as one of the prominent defendants in the Slánský trials. He was to be 'unmasked' as an ex-Gestapo and Anglo-American super agent in succession, who was at the time controlled by Píka. In order to protect himself and Slánský from also being 'unmasked', Reicin and Vaš had to prosecute Píka. Their 'Zionist' plot however, was uncovered two years later. Like Slánský, Reicin received the death sentence and was executed in December 1952. Now came the moment when Karel Vaš as Reicin's close collaborator must have felt the whiff of death as the merciless wheel of communist Nemesis threatened to entangle him as well.

Charged with espionage and high treason, Vaš was arrested in August 1951 and spent over one year in solitary confinement. At his trial in July 1953, hoping that it would be a mitigating circumstance, Vaš boasted of his decisive contribution in the Píka case and mentioned that Moscow had been informed through Khazanov and highly appreciative of his handling the prosecution of Píka. No written evidence was produced and no Soviet witnesses called in at the Vaš trial. However, the former prosecutor must have impressed his judges because he received a 'mere' life sentence, which was further commuted after 1956. He was subsequently released from prison and in 1963 fully rehabilitated: his Communist Party membership was restored, his military rank returned and he was to receive a substantial financial compensation.. From then onwards Vaš never stopped declaring his innocence with regard to his involvement in the Píka trial, referring to his rehabilitation in 1956 according to the principle that 'no one should be punished twice for the same crime'. In 1968, during the Prague Spring, General Píka's surviving son Milan and his defence lawyer requested a revision of the 1949 trial. A military court declared the dead general rehabilitated, but left Karel Vaš unpunished, which he has cleverly exploited as evidence that the Roman legal principle 'Ne bis in idem crimen iudicetur' must have been applied in his case.[25]

The Transition from one Totalitarian System to Another

The Postwar Retributions

The modern history of Czechoslovakia is full of paradoxes. Its judicial system is no exception. The notorious miscarriage of justice in the 1950s, effectively a replica of the 'Great Purges' in the Soviet Union, could have hardly taken place had it not been for its relatively smooth transition between May 1945 and February 1948, from Hitler's into Stalin's empire. Whatever remained in the judicial system that would be reminiscent of the enlightened and liberal framework founded and perfected during the late Habsburg monarchy was to be eroded during the two dictatorships. In the Píka case, for instance, we have already noticed the deliberate manipulation of evidence under Reicin, the exclusion of witnesses for the defence. Furthermore, we have seen Vaš, while dealing with the same case, switching his function from interrogator to prosecutor at the whim of his communist superiors, something that even the rumoured Nazi *Volksgerichtshof never* did.

Comparative assessments of the infamous political trials of the 1950s in Czechoslovakia have suffered from a number of unnecessary overstatements. One of the most glaring ones, from the pen of the perhaps most knowledgeable chronicler of the purges, Karel Kaplan, stands up when he had literally written that the great show trials in Czechoslovakia, even if they started later than in other East European countries, 'resulted in more deaths than the trials in all other popular democracies taken together'.[26] This statement has been uncompromisingly challenged by Muriel Blaive, a French sociologist, who has accused the 'regime historian' Karel Kaplan of distorting the facts, and the remainder of Czech historians for having produced inaccurate statistics concerning the key years of communist repression.[27]

Political scientist Jacques Rupnik believes that regarding its communist past the Czechoslovak case constitutes a double paradox. On the one hand, the decommunisation in Czechoslovakia (and since 1993 in its successor state, the Czech Republic) has gone further on both legal and rhetorical levels than in any other country of post-Soviet east-central Europe (perhaps with the exception of East Germany). On the other hand, the country still has one of the most conservative and unreconstructed Communist Parties of the former Soviet bloc, represented in the parliament and a faithful membership exceeding in numbers that of any other political party. Moreover, none one of the former communist leaders has been sentenced and sent to jail so far for the past crimes, including the charges of high treason for explicitly inviting the Warsaw Pact armies to occupy the country through that infamous 'letter of invitation', sent by a group of old communist die-hards to comrade Brezhnev and the Soviet politburo. The second paradox, still according to Rupnik, consists of the persistently wide gap between the persecution of historians during the 1970s and 1980s and the absence of a critical debate about the communist past among Czech historians. Paradoxically, the absence of a genuine Czech *Historikerstreit* does not seem to stop the prevalent legal decommunization.[28]

How Czechoslovakia accumulated so many paradoxes may be partially related to the close and rapid transition from one type of totalitarian system to another. In the pursuit of our subject it might be more instructive, rather than to start with the assessment of the political trials of the 1950s (as Muriel Blaive does), to look first at the earlier retribution period during the months immediately following the collapse of the 'Greater German Empire' in May of 1945.

Regulated retribution, according to the 'Great Decree No. 16', known as the 'Retribution Decree', which was to be primarily directed against Germans and their Czech collaborators, allowed Czechoslovakia to reach the contentious first place among European nations pursuing retribution at the time. Czechoslovakia is, for instance, comparable with France, the country that sentenced the highest number of collaborators to death but executed a mere 11 per cent of them (out of 7037 capital sentences there were 791 executions). Not counting Slovakia, where on the whole a milder judicial prosecution prevailed, the Czech provinces, with one-quarter of the French population, executed almost as many defendants as France, namely out of 723 death sentences 686 were carried out, by far the highest rate (95 per cent) in Europe (in Slovakia out of 65 sentences there were 25 executions).[29]

Regarding the customary judicial procedure the Czech Retribution Decree had already broken ranks when Beneš and his advisers conceived it in London. It was not produced under communist pressure. The president desired trials to be as short as possible and for defendants to have no right to appeal. Moreover, against the verdict of the Extraordinary People's Courts, handling the retribution cases, there should be no legal redress. Compared with other judicial systems in Europe, the Czech postwar court system developed into a something of an efficient killing machine – banning appeals, limiting the mitigating circumstances to a bare minimum and ruling that the death sentences must be carried out within two hours of the pronouncement of the capital verdict. In theory, the president had the right to grant the plea for clemency. If the president did not respond positively within the mandated three hours, the execution proceeded as planned. Frommer concludes that, aside from Bulgaria, where Stalinist justice had liquidated thousands before the war even ended, Czech retribution courts sent more defendants to death per capita than anywhere else in Europe.[30]

The picture of the passage from Nazi to communist dictatorship through a brief period of multi-party co-existence between the immediate end of the war and prior to the February 1948 coup, would not be complete without mentioning the darker side of the brief presence of the Red Army, which involved kidnapping and deportation of persons whom the NKVD considered particularly dangerous. These were, in the first place, members of the 'Russian Liberation Army', (ROA), raised by German military authorities from former Soviet prisoners-of-war. In the last days of the war they tried to reach U.S. troops in Western Bohemia by changing sides and fighting the Germans, to no avail. The U.S. Army handed them over to *Smersh*. Thousands of them were executed on the spot and the rest deported to Siberia. Their commander General Andrei Vlasov was taken to *Lublyanka*, the NKVD Headquarters, where he was summarily tried and executed in August 1946.[31] It is estimated that *Smersh* deported about a further 500 persons from Czech territory, of whom 300 perished.[32] About 6000 were abducted from Slovakia, of whom nearly half were Slovaks; about 2000 of them survived. Furthermore, from Subcarpathian Ruthenia, a former province of Czechoslovakia but since 1945 attached to the USSR, an estimated 40,000 persons were deported to Soviet labour camps.[33]

The Political Processes of the 1950s (1948–54)

When the communists took control of the justice sector, existing 'bourgeois' legislation was found inadequate to go after the omni-present 'class enemy'. The new Law no. 231/1948, promulgated on 6 October 1948, provided the communist regime with an instrument of terror to strike against every manifestation of anti-state activities, ranging from attempts to leave Czechoslovakia to spreading hostile rumours.[34] This law in fact introduced brutal terror, reminiscent of the worst excesses of the Great Terror period of the French Revolution with its dreaded *Loi des suspects (1793)*. In fact, as aptly characterized in a recent study, Law no. 231 legalised the conduct of civil (class) war by one segment of the society against the other.[35] The chief historian of the repression era, Karel Kaplan, estimates that, with regard to 'political crimes' specifically, the Czechoslovak courts sentenced 95,600 citizens during 1948–54 and in the following period, 1955–69, imposed a further 54,749 sentences. By contrast, 'a mere' 47,887 persons were sentenced during the 'normalization' twinge of 1970–72.[36] Between October 1948 and January 1953 the State Court passed 232 death sentences, of which 178 were carried out. Obviously, many more persons died in detention; Kaplan, puts the figure at 1157 persons.[37]

Further repression occurred through the labour camps, which absorbed over 22,000 persons. Unreliable soldiers and conscripts, almost 10,000 of them, were sent to special Construction Battalions ('*PTP*' for '*Pomocné technické prapory*'). A particularly brutal category were camps at uranium mines like Jáchymov, which had a very high death rate and were nicknamed the 'Czech Gulag'.[38]

In the early 1950s Czechoslovakia counted 32,638 prisoners of whom over 11,000 were serving sentences for anti-state activities, implied in the all-embracing article 231, but almost the same number, 10,000 were still 'retributionary' detainees, serving sentences for crimes of collaboration with the Nazis. A country with 12.5 million inhabitants had 422 labour camps and prisons.[39] Thus, the law-enforcing landscape of Czechoslovakia, a liberal democratic country following the western tradition until 1939, was modified by the early 1950s into one resembling the countries of the Soviet bloc. It was a gloomy landscape, excessively filled with military barracks and labour camps, one that men like Karel Vaš helped to reinforce and preserve.

If Muriel Blaive was right in criticising the exaggerated and blown-up Czech figures for communist victims in the 1950s as reflected in the works of the main 'regime historian' Karel Kaplan, she would certainly be less annoyed if she looked at the distribution of justice through both the wild and regulated retribution legislation during the period immediately following the end of the war. Here, perhaps, seems to be rooted one of the causes for the Czechoslovak paradox.

Around 90,000 Czechoslovak citizens were prosecuted for 'political crimes' during the period 1948–54; of 233 death sentences 178 were actually carried out.[40] According to a more recent source, during the five-year rule of the 'First Workers' President' Klement Gottwald (1948–53), 237 death sentences were passed, of which close to 190 were for alleged political crimes. Gottwald granted only 18 presidential pardons, one for a murder and 17 for those who committed 'anti-state' crimes. Under his both successors between 1953 and 1967, a further 181 death sentences were passed.[41] The last person who received capital punishment and was executed in June 1989 was a triple murderer. The Federal Assembly of the former Czechoslovak Republic abolished the capital penalty in May 1990.

Thus – to return to Muriel Blaive's charges against the superficial judgment of Karel Kaplan in both absolute and relative terms – these figures seem to be substantially lower than those for Poland and Hungary.[42] During the civil war in Poland that raged between 1944 and 1948, if not longer, between 8000 and 15,000 persons were killed; in Hungary it is estimated that between 500 and 700 were executed between 1948 and 1955.[43]

However, having tried to assemble many random figures in order to do justice to the prevalent method of quantitative comparison between various stages of totalitarian regimes in transition, we must not forget that too much of a concentration on quantitative analysis alone might easily lead to a kind of morbid accountancy, which can blur rather than help to identify the differences between communist victims on the one hand and non-communist on the other.[44]

Velvet Revolution and Velvet Justice: Persecution, Ostracism and Lustration

At first, it seemed as if the resumed rehabilitation of victims of the communist oppression that followed the 'Velvet Revolution' of November 1989, and which found its legal expression in Law no. 119/1990, resembled closely the rehabilitation legislation of the 'Prague Spring' (Law no. 68/1968). Rehabilitation would be the legal category into which correcting the miscarriage of justice in the case of General Píka should fall. But 'rehabilitation' could be also claimed, by the paradoxical twist of historical development in communist Czechoslovakia, by the chief perpetrator of injustice in the Píka case – his henchman, the former military prosecutor and judge, Lt Col. (rtd) JUDr and PhDr Karel Vaš.[45] Since the rebuilding of democracy was Czechoslovakia's central preoccupation after the fall of communism in 1989, in addition to rehabilitation the process of de-communisation, it had to find additional devices in order to verify a person's civil background and prevent former communists and their shadow collaborators from remaining in or reclaim position of power and influence. Such information, however, together with the real and coded names of the suspects, figured only in the hidden files of the Secret Police (*Státní Bezpečnost*, abbreviated as 'STB').

According to Law no.119/1990, most of the former victims, estimated at 260,000, who had been persecuted by the communist regime through the loss of freedom, employment, property, etc., were instantly rehabilitated, without even having to make a request at a tribunal.[46] Improvising through a brief period that one newspaper amply called the 'Wild Lustration',[47] the Czech legislature finally introduced on 4 October 1991 the so-called Lustration Law no. 451/1991.[48] While most other states with a communist past have sought political justice through direct criminal proceedings in the courts (but with very few convictions), the Czech Republic took a distinctly non-judicial approach, based on the criterion that any public official or civil servant, such as judges and university professors, must give proof that during the period between 1948 and 1989 he or she was not a collaborator or informer of the STB. To avoid revenge-seeking and legal retroactivity, lustration was sold to the Federal Assembly and the public as a defence mechanism for the fragile new democracy. It was not meant to serve justice or help the country come to terms with the past, as Kieran Williams correctly observed, but to prevent a repetition of the communist coup of February 1948.[49]

Until 1999 the Interior Ministry issued 426,000 lustration certificates. Obviously, the highest number of applicants turned up at the beginning: in 1992 over 209,000 people applied; between January and June 2005 no more than 3000. From 1991 to 1997 a total of 303,504 screenings took place, of which 15,166 (5%) resulted in positive certificates. Those were transferred to less sensitive jobs or retired. The overwhelming majority of applicants were therefore found not to be listed as informers or employees of the secret police.[50] There were gross discrepancies among the applications of course; the higher one studied the structure of public posts the bigger the gaps. No one was in fact surprised that the Lustration Law overlooked some of the top jobs in the country. The then Speaker of the Federal Parliament, Alexander Dubček, a living legend from Prague Spring of 1968, would probably not have been allowed to run a local post-office on the grounds of his multiple involvements with the Communist Party.[51] In the most sensitive areas, however, for which lustration was most expressly intended, sweeping purges had already taken place before the law came into effect. Thus most of the 8900 STB officers had already been dismissed from service in 1990. Its successor, the Federal Security Information Service (FBIS), established in July 1991, had among its 1000 employees less than 140 old STB hands, but their numbers dwindled over the next two to three years through recruitment and training rather than by lustration.[52]

Few pieces of 'velvet' legislation experienced so much confusion and disunity as lustration did. The World Labour Organisation, the Council of Europe, and the European Parliament, criticised the Czech Lustration Law and explicitly recommended its abrogation. The Communist Party, which is still sitting in the Czech Parliament with the support of votes from 15% votes of the electorate, went almost berserk when the Lustration Law was introduced. President Václav Havel, who had originally signed the law, changed his view when the Parliament extended its validity. The Lustration Law was to remain valid only until 1995, but – in spite of President Havel's opposition – was twice extended, in 1995 and again in 2000. On 7 December 2005, the Parliament voted for a third extension, which encountered 60 negative votes (all communist and left social-democrats) out of a total of 180. The results of the lustration are far from perfect. Muriel Blaive, a French sociologist known for her critical analysis of the love–hate relationship of the Czechs with communism, claims that no one has yet conclusively analysed the impact of the lustration laws on the contemporary Czech society. She has argued that those who felt unjustly 'purified' and went to court to prove the opposite usually won their cases.[53]

One still wonders, however, that the 'purification tests' brought up relatively modest numbers of people who had so actively supported the communist regime in Czechoslovakia – even taking into account the usual attrition due to retirement and withdrawal from politics. For instance, a figure of 150,000 persons is often quoted as having been informers for the STB between 1948 and 1968.[54] In 1992 a certain Petr Cibulka, a former dissident, described by some as a fanatical anti-communist, by others as an unbalanced crackpot, obtained from obscure sources and published a long list of approximately 160,000 alleged STB agents. What was suspect about the list was that it gave only names, dates of birth and agents' code-names. Judging by the follow-up discussion inside the Czech Republic, nurtured by Cibulka's periodical fits of pathological panic that a Bolshevik conspiracy was lurking round the corner, in which a certain communist agent called Václav Havel would play a chief role, one must admit that the post-velvet period of the Czech Revolution had its irresistibly exciting moments. There is also, however, the darker side of the lustration. Some people have complained that lustration under the threat of the Secret Police name register evokes parallels with the *proscriptiones* of the Roman dictator Sulla or those from the French Revolution and thereafter. In 1968 a couple of unmasked communist crime perpetrators were driven to suicide when ostracized. I am not aware of any suicide directly attributed to Cilbulka's ostracism. However, several individuals, among them the wife of the celebrated Czecho-Canadian writer Josef Škvorecký, were deeply disturbed by finding their names on Cibulka's proscriptions.[55] The Škvoreckýs sued the Ministry of the Interior, others went on trial to prevent further disgrace. The Interior Ministry felt challenged and at long last prepared its own official list that, however, failed to provide additional details on the persons accused of being police informers or worse. Exposed to constant public criticism, the Ministry produced a second list, which was even worse since a number of agents and conspirators disappeared from the list.[56]

In the absence of anything similar to the German 'Gauk Institute' or the Polish 'IPN' or the Slovak 'Ústav pamäti národa', founded by the last Czechoslovak federal (joint) Minister of the Interior, Pavol Langoš, the virtues and sins of also having such an institution in the Czech Republic are being discussed with no avail. The Bureau of Documentation and Investigation of the Crimes of Communism

[Úřad pro dokumentaci a vyšetřování zločinů komunismu = ÚDV], founded in 1991, has served a much narrower purpose, namely to prepare a list of top crime perpetrators who ought to be prosecuted. After 14 years of investigation the list has no more than 71 names. Out of these 51 were indicted, but a mere nine received sentences, and out of these only a very few were actually imprisoned. Sixty-four individuals are being still processed. Reluctant judges, coming from the *ancien regime*, make speedy prosecution impossible. Firmness was certainly lacking in the case of Alois Grebeníček, a notorious torturer, whose son Miroslav happened to be at the time the chairman of the Communist Party and a deputy in the Parliament. Grebeníček senior simply ignored court orders under the pretext of bad health, never turned up at trial and finally died.[57]

'Ecrasez l'Infâme'[58] – or How an anti-Commuunist Blogger Attempted to Take Justice into His Own Hands

Let us return to the bizarre case of Karel Vaš, which is central to this paper. Can one break the vicious circle of post-communist legal rehabilitation syndrome, with its endless delays and foul tricks and the sheer legal paralysis to bring real perpetrators to justice? Here is one example of a genuine Czech grass-root improvisation, which was successfully tested last year. After the mandatory ceremony at the General Píka memorial in front of the General Staff building in Prague on the 56th anniversary of General Píka's execution, a small group of uninvited anti-communist intransigents met. Their spokesman, the notorious Jan Šinágl, suggested that he would instantly pay a visit to the old invalid Karel Vaš (whose address he made available on his web site) to appeal to his conscience.[59]

> [A man stepped in one of the bedrooms of the old peoples' retirement home in Prague ... where a 90-year old man was resting undressed on his bed]
>
> Visitor: 'How are you, Mr. Vaš? I wish you a good day. I am coming from General Heliodor Píka'.
>
> Vaš: [frightened, confused]: 'Who are you?'
>
> 'I am a Czech patriot', answered the visitor, :'It is 56 years today since you had despatched a valiant man to death'.
>
> 'Leave me alone, I beg you'.
>
> 'Don't you wish to say anything? I am coming from the memorial service in front of the General Staff building where a valiant soldier was commemorated today'.
>
> 'Leave me alone', the old man repeated.
>
> 'How can you wear this burden on your conscience? Would you be prepared to recant?' That you regret what you have done in the past? Your dreadful crimes?

'None of the guests at the memorial service said what I am telling you now: Would you be prepared to express your regrets so that people knew what went wrong and keep their eyes open in the future to avoid such mistakes happening again? There are Communists in our country who are active again, in the parliament, and keen to usurp power.

If you do not express regrets and if you do not ask for forgiveness for what you have done in the past … that you sincerely regret – otherwise you might find dying difficult'.

…

'Can I take a picture of you? I don't know how many people you have sent to death. It is said that they were hundreds of them, thousands. God be with you'.

Corpus Delicti

The chief *corpus delicti* of communist prosecution that brought General Píka to the gallows, and for which Reicin and Vaš were directly responsible, is reproduced below. Since it is the only document in English in the huge bundle of protocols surviving in the archives,[60] the reader can assess for himself how communist justice operated and how the standards of the legal profession in Czechoslovakia declined after the war that such a piece of 'evidence' could even be admitted in a courtroom, let alone have a defendent sentenced to death. Some years ago I happened to inspect a huge bundle of protocols pertaining to the Píka case. Among the protocols, mostly by fellow officers who were forced to testify against their former colleague, I found one document which attracted my attention. It was the only one in English, but written in strange English with unusual grammatical errors and typos. Since it pretended to be an internal message from one British intelligence officer to another about General Píka's confidential conversation while visiting London in 1946, it certainly was idiomatically suspicious. None of the Czech forgers had the slightest idea how to replicate a British officer's jargon, let alone one from the special intelligence branch.

It is therefore hardly surprising to announce that this key document, allegedly intercepted by Czech agents operating in England, was in fact entirely manufactured inside Czechoslovakia. And indeed, it was Reicin's secretary, a certain Mrs Ludmila Uhlířová, who had seen him drafting the original Czech text, and who testified about the callous forgery during the first rehabilitation trial of General Píka in 1968.[61] When confronted with the forgery as a witness at the same rehabilitation trial of 1968, Vaš claimed that he did not know in 1948 that the key document used against Píka was a fake.[62] Why did Reicin need this extra proof so much that he would make an effort to use a fake of such low quality in order to compromise Píka?

Reicin's two previous scenarios had not been satisfactory. Even before Píka's arrest it was rumoured among the OBZ operators that Píka should be kidnapped and delivered to Soviet authorities in Austria, presumably for physical liquidation. This scheme, hastily concocted following a few hints from the NKVD resident Khazanov, had to be dismissed as unworkable since the OBZ could not find a Soviet counterpart at the Austrian border ready to cooperate so that the 'goods'

A FACSIMILE OF THE PROTOCOL

Opis agenturní zprávy - v procesu Píka,kterou Reicín sám sestavil a soudu podvrhl:

Our guest from Czechoslovakia,gen.Píka,seemed to be very pleased about my invitation and mostly impressed by what he learned at this commission,was very flattered when I told him that his war reports on the Russians have been so initiative and thorough,that sometime they served as the only ground of information for His Majesty Government showing us clear the true situation of our ally of the time.

I think that distinguishing him would mean a reward for his excellent service during the war.According to the eagerness and frankness whith which he accepted the distinguish,one may judge that he will be only too willing to further collaboration which he expressed also in our further debate.

His knowlidge in estimatting the USSR are remarkable for such modest a man and even more that he being an officer should be so well aquainted with those various matters.There were mostly his knowledge about the lability of the interiors state of affairs,the indescribable want,the longing of the people for a higher standar of life: at the same time he observed the attempts being made to increase the strength of the Navy of Russia.His knowledge of the russian building.......

My admiration for the courage and disire for the independence of the Czech people were accepted by our guest with firm assurance that the good relations of the Czech Army to his Majesty Forces are deeply rooted in our hearts and that every effort of a Russian hegemony are out of the question although the Russians trying very hard to achieve it.

Answering my question concerning the good relations of the Czech Army to the russian Army,my guest declared without hesitation that the previous illusions of the great part of the people after the acts of violation in 1945 and that a far as the Russian infiltration is concerned,the limits with the Czech have been reached already.Some of the most intelligent and strongest personalities amongst the Czech politicians,will be more and more maste of the situation. Theelections have schown a remarkable decline of communist influence since the culmination in 1945.The aversion against Russian unculture was most remarkable here,he said.As to teh russian mission in Prague our guest declared that one succeeded to limit its previous sence of unfiltration by soviet officers in a most remarkable way,and that at present it is doing only quite insignificant instruction work at the military schools.... Speaking about those of his seniors schowing dependance from the Russians he had no great sympathy with them, but avoid to speak about it.

As to my question whether the Czech Intaligence Service and NKGB were on good terms and how their collaboration worked,the guest replied that there is no such thing good relations between the two services-with the exception of a few by communists influenced persons -assuring me that it is not the Czech intaligence service that is taken a basis by the Russians but that of occupied Germany,our guest is very well aquainted with personalities of the NKGB though he met nobody in Prague,hau knows them from his stay in Moscow.Personally he knows only Mr Chichief and another insigdifisant man at the Consulat Mr Tichmov.He said.....

Expressing the hope that the relations between out two nations so good during the war shoud continue for being so I said good by to him.

Some furter remarks and information will be put forward to those departments concerned.

8 th June 1946   Razítko MNO   Originál souhlasí s kopii
                                              opis Nyč.

Figure 1.   The facsimile of the *Corpus delicti* presented at the Píka trial. Lt Col. Bohumír (Nitsch) Nyč, signed at the bottom, was one of Reicin's subordinates, who was instructed to manufacture the forged document against Píka.[64]

could be delivered without attracting attention. The second scenario, based on laboriously collected testimonies to prove that Píka compromised himself by working for British Intelligence during the war, since he maintained regular contacts with the British intelligence community as part of his official duties, did not seem to amount to death by hanging, which Reicin and Vaš by now understood was desired from their superiors both in Prague and – one could only speculate due to the absence of direct evidence – in Moscow as well. Even the communist propagandists found it difficult to dismiss the fact that Great Britain and the Soviet Union were allies fighting together against Nazi Germany. Thus, convincing evidence of Píka's continuing contacts with the British had to be found for the period after 1945. Hence the importance of Píka's official trip to London in May 1946 to celebrate the Victory Day. To quote again the witness Uhlířová, she claimed overhearing Vaš asking Reicin: 'Just tell me how much you need for Píka, fifteen years or the gallows, and the indictment can be manufactured accordingly'.

Having corresponded with the late British writer Edward Crankshaw, who during the war served as British intelligence officer in Moscow and remembered Píka, I sent him the text of the fateful 'document'. 'The document you sent me', Crankshaw replied in March 1983, 'is really the most appalling and most unimaginably inefficient bit of forgery I have ever come across. The whole European communist apparatus ... is lowered in my esteem if this is the kind of thing the Czech secret police, or whoever, is allowed to produce as fabricated evidence. I don't think I need elaborate on that', concluded Crankshaw. And this is my conclusion as well.

However, the unmasking of transparently forged evidence should be only the beginning in the restoration of the country's judicial system after 40 years of paralysis and decline. Given the internal haemorrhage of the judicial mechanism, there is little hope that relief will come from within the profession, stimulated by the wishes of the former victims wishing that justice should take its course by retrying and locking up those last surviving torturers and perpetrators of crimes, now in their eighties if not nineties. To anticipate, on the other hand, that the initiative for the retrial could come from the outside, more than half a century after the crime was committed, is delusive. Even a country that produced Václav Havel with his brilliant plays, cannot expect him to act like Thomas Masaryk in the Hilsner Affair.[63] The interventions by Voltaire, Zola and Masaryk in the affairs of Jean Calas, Dreyfus and Hilsner required a propitious moment for 'crushing the infamy' – and that cannot be staged at will like a drama.

Notes

1. When Karel Vaš was sentenced, I wrote a brief essay under a somewhat similar title, "Crime and Punishment in Prague", which was published in the *World Policy Journal* (Winter 2001/2): 93–6.
2. Two of the most brutal interrogators from the Slánský Trials, B. Doubek and V. Kohoutek, were arrested in 1955 and tried for applying "unlawful methods" while carrying out their investigations. To mitigate his nine-year sentence Doubek volunteered to write an account of his participation in the Slánský Trials. This 460-page testimony has been edited and provided with detailed introduction by Karel Kaplan: *STB o sobě. Výpověd vyšetřovatele B. Doubka* ["Secret Police about Itself. Interrogator B. Doubek Testifies] (Prague: Edition Svědectví, 2002). After 1990 enough evidence became available to charge Doubek with several cases of murder. However, with reference to his previous prison sentence he had received from communist judges in 1955, his lawyers successfully used the legal principle borrowed from Roman Civil Law, *Ne bis in idem crimen iudicetur* ["Not to be judged twice for the same crime"].

3. Dr Milada Horáková, member of the Parliament, figured as the chief defendant among a group of non-communist politicians, who had been accused of "anti-state activities". They were sentenced to death and executed in June 1950.

4. The Communist Party Secretary General Rudolf Slánský, the driving force behind repressions in Czechoslovakia, who pressed for General Píka's execution, was himself arrested in November 1951. Together with a group of high-ranking Czechoslovak Communists, he was accused of Zionism. Twelve months later Slánský and 10 others received death sentences and were promptly executed.

5. Karel Vaš, *Moje perzekuce v právním státě aneb epochální výlet české justice do 50.let XX.století* ["My Persecution in the Legal State OR a Fancy Journey of Czech Justice to the 1950s] (Prague, 2001). This brochure, in spite of its humorous title that is a literary pun in the Czech language, was in fact Vaš's appeal against the verdict of 15 June 2001. It was prepared with the help of his counsel Čestmír Kubát in December 2001 and distributed as a brochure. Antonín Benčík and Karel Richter responded with a critique, carrying even a longer title: *"Ukázkové zneužití demokracie – aneb Epochální pokus dvojnásobného doktora Karla Vaše a jeho obhájce JUDr.Čestmíra Kubáta o rehabilitaci uměle vykonstruovaného obvinění a zločinného odsouzení generála Heliodora Píky"* ["An Exemplary Abuse of Democracy – OR a Fancy Attempt of Dr Dr Karel Vaš and his Defence Lawyer Dr Čestmír Kubát to Save the Artificially Construed Indictment and Punishment of General Heliodor Píka"], published in *Přísně tajné – literatura faktu* 4 (2002), pp.116–33.

6. ČTK (Czech Press Agency), 22 June 2005. See also the interview of the legal historian Zdenk Vališ with *Mladá fronta – Dnes*, 27 June 2005, and his detailed internet article "Quid Iuri?" (www.Vas Karel ZV 0705).

7. See *The Prague Post*, 27 January 2002; http://muchr.radio.cz, 16 January 2002.

8. 'Vas' in Hungarian means iron. Vaš was born in Uzhgorod (Ungvár) where Hungarian was spoken.

9. Karel Richter and Antonín Benčík, *Kdo byl Generál Píka?* (Brno: Doplněk, 1997). For earlier accounts on Czechoslovak–Soviet cooperation in intelligence matters, see: J.Křen and V.Kural, "Ke stykům mezi československým odbojem a SSSR 1939–1941", in *Historie a vojenství* 3 (1967), pp.437–71, and 5 (1967), pp.766–70; J.Šolc, "Československá zpravodajská skupina v SSSR, duben–červen 1941", *Historie a vojenství* 5 (1997), pp. 51–52, 65–71; Col. F. Hieke-Stoj, "Mé vzpomínky z druhé světová války", *Historie a vojenství* (1968), pp. 581–619.

10. Bruce Lockhart, who was the Foreign Office representative and liaison with the Czechoslovak Government, used to translate Píka's highly valued dispatches into English for further circulation. See his *Giants Cast Long Shadows* (London: Putnam, 1960), pp.166–9; Kenneth Young (ed.), *The Diaries of Sir Robert Bruce Lockhart*, vol. II., 1939–65 (London: Macmillan, 1980), p.222.

11. Original documents have been compiled in 1968 for the rehabilitation trials of General Píka by his defence lawyer R. Váhala. This collection of 710 pages, entitled "Život a smrt gen.Heliodora Píky" ["Life and Death of General H. Píka"], has been available since 1985 in the Hoover Institution Archives, Czechoslovak holdings, Stanford, CA. Hereinafter referred to as the *Píka Dossier*. Píka's lawyer, Rastislav Váhala, has used the documents in his monograph, *Smrt generála* ["The Death of a General"] (Prague: Melantrich, 1992).

12. Consisting of President Gottwald and Central Committee members Zápotocký, Slánský, Kopřiva and Veselý. Reicin was also invited (*Píka Dossier*, note 11, pp.519–620; Váhala, note 11, pp.126–36).

13. A comprehensive synopsis of the Píka case, based on the *Píka Dossier* and other sources, was prepared for the rehabilitation trial by two experts, Antonín Benčík and Jaromír Navrátil: "O životě a smrti generála Heliodora Píky" ["About the Life and Death of General H. Píka"], whose shortened version was published as a documentary supplement in the popular weekly *Reportér*, IV/8, 27 February 1969.

14. The Protectorate of Bohemia and Moravia was the Czech portion of the former Czechoslovak Republic occupied since March 1939 by Nazi Germany. For details on Reicin see Benčík and Richter (note 9), pp.168–71; Benčík and Richter (note 5), 125; M. Lichnovský, "Bedřich Reicin a Československá armada", *Historie & Vojenství*, 1–2 (1994).

15. L. Svoboda, *Z Buzuluku do Prahy* (Prague, 1968); L. Svoboda, *Cestami života*. Prague: Naše Vojsko, 1971; V.V. Mariina, "Chekhoslovatskii legion v SSSR 1939–1941gg", *Voprosy Istorii*, 2 (1998), pp.58–73.

16. In fact Vaš prepared the main prosecution document himself since the nominal chief prosecutor, Colonel J.Vaněk, admitted on several occasions that he had no time to study the script and had to rely entirely on Vaš (*Píka Dossier*, note 11, pp.295, 600–2; 815–19, 829–32).

17. A special NKVD unit under Captain Bragin, whose task was to arrest and 'remove' unwanted witnesses, was closely cooperating with Vaš's unit. Cf. Benčík and Richter (note 5),pp.126–9; Vališ (note 6), pp.4–6.

18. Josef Bartovský, *Cesta až na dno zrady – Rub historie druhého zahraničního odboje* (Praha, 19490, p. 6.
19. Vaš (note 5), pp.3–4.
20. That is by Vaš himself, since he was the deputy to the chief military prosecutor, Colonel J. Vaněk, present at the main trial of Píka, from 26–28 January 1949. For Vaš's manipulation with Píka's dispatches, testimonies of the witnesses, see: *Píka Dossier* (note 11), pp.519–54; Váhala (note 11), pp.99–113, 126–136; Vališ, pp.14–15.
21. Vaš (note 5), 4. While imprisoned Vaš appealed several times. In the longest appeal of some 250 pages, dated 26 January 1956, addressed to the Minister of Justice, he described his activities in detail including his close cooperation with Soviet intelligence before and during the Píka Case (Vališ, p.8). At the age of 90, Karel Vaš agreed to give a four-hour interview to the Czech Radio, in which he emphasized over and over that he did not wish General Píka's death – despite the evidence, as he claimed, that Píka pleaded guilty to acts of espionage for the British. When urged by the reporter to be more specific, Vaš conveniently claimed weak memory and fatigue. The shortened version, which was broadcast on 18 June and 23 July 2006, is available on a diskette "Příběhy 20.století" ["Stories of the 20th Century"], Collection "Post Bellum" (further information: info@hrdinove.cz). I am grateful to Mikuláš Kroupa, interviewer and editor of the Czech Radio, for enabling me to listen to the unabbreviated version of the interviews.
22. At the time of Vaš's recorded enrollment with the Czechoslovak unit in January 1943, he was already 'directed' by the following NKVD officers: Kambulov, Myshin, Tokarenko, and from the autumn of 1945, Tikhonov. From the end of 1946 to the summer of 1950 it was indeed Khazanov (Vališ, pp.10–12).
23. Kaplan and Paleček, Paleček, *Komunistický režim a politické procesy v Československu*. Brno (2001), p.87; K. Kaplan, *Sovětští poradci v Československu, 1949–1956* ["Soviet Counselors in … "] (Prague, 1993); A. F. Noskova, "Moskovskie sovetniki v strankh Vostochnoi Evropy", ["Moscow Advisers in E.European Countries"], *Voprosy Istorii* 1 (1998), pp.104–13.
24. Named after Rudolf Slánský, secretary general of the Czechoslovak Communist Party, who spent the war years in Moscow. He was arrested in November 1951 and executed a year later.
25. The English Common Law refers to it as "Double Jeopardy". The European Convention of Human Rights protects against Double Jeopardy (7th Protocol, Art. 4), which has been ratified by all but six EU members (Czech Republic is not among the six dissenting members).
26. K. Kaplan, "Zamyšlení nad politickými procesy", [Political Trials Reconsidered …], *Nová mysl* 7 (1968), 15.
27. Based on Muriel Blaive's dissertation, *Le regime de terreur tchécoslovaque et l'année 1956 en Tchécoslovaquie*; Blaive, "1956 – Anatomie d'une absence", in F. Fejtö and J. Rupnik (eds), *Le Printemps tchécoslovaque 1968* (Brussells: Editions Complexe, 1999), pp.50–63; and also the Czech version: *Promarněná příležitost. Československo a rok 1956* (Prague, 2001), pp.187. Although Mme Blaive may be correct on Kaplan's deficiency in acquiring statistics on victims of political purges in the rest of eastern Europe, she is unfair in calling Karel Kaplan a "regime historian". It is true that Kaplan, who joined the CP as a teenager, served briefly prior to 1968 on a government commission for the investigation of the judicial crimes of the 1950s. However, after the crushing of the Prague Spring Kaplan was sacked, his research materials confiscated, and he himself compelled to leave the country in1972. He settled in Munich and thanks to the assistance of colleagues and West German foundations, Kaplan was soon able to resume his writing (e.g. K. Kaplan, *Die politischen Prozesse in der Tschechoslowakei 1948–1954* (Munich, 1986), Collegium Carolinum, vol. 48.
28. J. Rupnik on "Coming to Terms with the Communist Past", *Soudobé dějiny* [Contemporary History] IX/1 (2002).
29. The following statistics have been mostly drawn from Benjamin Frommer, *National Cleansing. Retribution Against Nazi Collaborators in Postwar Czechoslovakia* (Cambridge, 2005), p.91.
30. Frommer (note 29), pp.78–94; for the English translation of the "Great Decree", no. 16/1945, see pp.348–63. See also Karel Jech and Karel Kaplan (eds), *Dekrety prezidenta republiky 1940–1945*. Dokumenty (Brno: USD, 1995), p.179; an earlier monograph is K. Kaplan's, *Die politischen Prozesse in der Tschechoslowakei (1986)*, note 27.
31. Abbreviated from *"Smert Shpionam"* ("Death to Spies") were special NKVD units raised to deal with deserters and POWs recovered from captivity.
32. Among them were "White Russians", who emigrated from revolutionary Russia after 1918 and settled in Czechoslovakia, e.g. General Sergej Vojcechovsky, who belonged to the top generals of the Czechoslovak armed forces and one of the few senior officers convinced that the army should have fought in September 1938. When he was arrested by *Smersh* in 1945, President Beneš did nothing to save his life.

33. M. Borák *et al.*, "Perzekuce občanů z území dnešní České republiky v SSSR" ["Persecution of Czechoslovak citizens in the USSR"]. *Sborník příspěvků. Sešity ÚSD* 38 (Prague: USD, 2003), p.125.

34. During the Prague Spring of 1968, one of the most influential new political parties and most effective pressure groups, composed of former political prisoners sentenced by the Law no. 231/1948, called itself "Klub 231".

35. See Petr Blažek, "Politická represe v komunistickém Československu 1948–1989", in: *Moc verzus občan. Úloha represie a politického násilia v komunizme* ["Political Repression in Communist Czechoslovkia, in: "Power verus Citizen. The Role of Repression and Political Violence under Communism"] (Bratislava: Ústav Pamäti Národa, 2006), pp.8–22, here p.13. I am grateful to Mr Blažek for showing me an earlier draft of his paper, containing the most updated and comprehensive statistics of political repression in communist Czechoslovakia.

36. Blažek (note 35); Karel Kaplan and Pavel Paleček, *Komunistický režim a politické procesy v Československu* (Prague & Brno: USD, 2001), p.40.

37. Kaplan and Paleček (2001), p.42. Blažek (note 35, p.12) estimates that there were 240 'victims of judicial murder' by 1960.

38. V. Pacl, *Tajný prostor Jáchymov* (České Budějovice, 1993); L. Petrášková, "Vězeňské tábory v jáchymovských uranových dolech 1949–1961", *Sborník archivních prací* 44/2 (1994), pp.335–447.

39. Blažek (note 35), pp.13–14.

40. F. Gebauer et al., *Soudní perzekuce politické povahy v Československu 1948–1989* [Judicial prosecutions of political nature ...] (Prague: USD, 1993), p.64.

41. Recent figures published by the Bureau for Investigation and Documentation of the Crimes of Communism in 2006. Information broadcast by the Prague Radio News on 9 May 2006.

42. Blaive (note 27), p.52.

43. Blaive (note 27). The Hungarian figures do not include hundreds of further executions which had taken place during the suppression of the 1956 rising.

44. Françoise Mayer: "Vězení jako minulost, odboj jako pamět". ["Prison as History, Resistance as Memory"], *Soudobé dějiny* 9/1 (2002), p.45.

45. In addition to his doctorate in jurisprudence(1939), Vaš acquired a doctoral degree in history after his release from prison.

46. František Gebauer",Základní zásady zákona o soudní rehabilitaci č.119/1990", in: *Soudní perzekuce politické povahy v Československu 1948–1989* [Judicial Persecutions of Political Nature...] Prague, USD, 1993. For more accurate figures see Blažek (2006).

47. *Lidové Noviny*, 25.11.2005.

48. This law was after ten years modified by no. 107/2002 Law, allowing access to the police files to any person older than 18 years. The word *'lustration'* has two meanings. First, the obvious Latin root meaning a kind of a purifying rite associated with washing. The second meaning is that of extracting from declassified files information about cooperation with secret police.

49. Kieran Williams, "A Scorecard for Czech Lustration", *Central European Review* 19/1 (1 XI 1999).

50. Williams (note 49).

51. According to Jan Brabec and Jaroslav Spurný, "Lustrace: pro & proti", *Respekt*, 4 November 1991.

52. *Lidové noviny*, 10 February 1998.

53. Muriel Blaive, "The Czechs and Their Communism. Past and Present" (Vienna : IWM Conferences, 2005).

54. František Koudelka, *Státní bezpečnost 1954–1968. Základní údaje.* ["The State Secret Police ... Basic Facts"] (Prague: USD, 1993), p.68.

55. Zdena Salivarová-Škvorecká (ed.), *Osočení. Pravdivé příběhy lidí z Cibulkova seznamu* [The Vilification. True Stories of People from Cibulka's Proscriptions] (Brno, 1993 and 2000). See also her husband's novel, *Two Murders in my Double Life* (Toronto: Publishers 68, 1999). Cibulka's web site, containing a more or less complete list of STB agents of various categories and service assignments, is available at www.cibulka.com

56. See the weekly *Respekt*, 24 March 2003 and 7 April 2003.

57. *Respekt*, 7 July 1999. Author's consultation with sources inside the Czech Republic who prefer to stay anonymous.

58. I have borrowed this famous sentence from Voltaire, who applied it to the Catholic Church during the affair of Jean Calas, a Protestant citizen from Toulouse, accused of having murdered his son to prevent his conversion to Catholicism. When Calas was broken on the wheel (1762), Voltaire, livid with anger, took up the case and by his vigorous intervention obtained the vindication of the unfortunate Calas and the indemnification of the family.

59. The following is a tape-recorded conversation by Mr Jan Šinágl, who is known in the Czech media as the most active fighter for lost causes. He maintains an active web site

(www.jan.sinagl.cz), from which the reproduced conversation has been taken down and translated by myself.

60. See note 12 above. The protocols of interrogation of General Píka and the proceedings of the rehabilitation trial were copied in 1968. With the agreement of General Píka's son Milan and the surviving lawyer R. Váhala, one complete set was made available for the Hoover Institution Archives, Stanford, CA.

61. *Píka Dossier* (note 11), pp.288–98, 715–17, 835–8; *Váhala* (note 11), pp.40–47; Vališ, p.10.

62. *Píka Dossier* (note 11), pp.815–19; Benčík and Richter (note 5), pp.132–8; F. Hanzlík and J. Pospíšil, *Sluha dvou pánů* [Servant of Two Masters] (Vizovice: Lípa, 1999), p.221. Even today Vaš's counsel refers to the fake document below as "the alleged forgery" (cf.Vaš, note 5, pp.4, 29, 34). Under such circumstances trials and counter-trials can go on and on forever.

63. The Hilsner Affair of 1899 was the Austrian version of the Dreyfus Affair, in which Leopold Hilsner, a Jew, was accused of having performed ritual murder on a Christian virgin. Thomas G. Masaryk, a Czech university professor of philosophy, decided to involve himself in the affair. In response, he was hounded by students and the university put him on compulsory leave. There were several retrials and the affair dragged on until 1916 when Hilsner, whose death sentence had been meanwhile commuted to life imprisonment, was finally pardoned by the Emperor Charles.

64. Colonel Nyč figured as one of the witnesses at the rehabilitation trial in 1968. He supported the testimony of witness Uhlířová regarding the forgery, which according to her, Vaš knowingly accepted and incorporated in the indictment text. See *Píka Dossier* (note 11), pp.288–92, 792–8; Vališ, pp.10–14; Benčík and Richter (note 5), pp.133–6.

Cambodia Deals with its Past: Collective Memory, Demonisation and Induced Amnesia

DAVID CHANDLER

> Responses to collective violence lurch among rhetorics of history (truth) theology (forgiveness) justice (punishment, compensation, deterrence) therapy (healing), art (commemoration and disturbance) and education (learning lessons). None is adequate. (Martha Minow, *Between Vengeance and Forgiveness: Facing History after Genocide and Mass Violence*, p.147)

Introduction

At a press conference in Phnom Penh at the end of December 1998, the Cambodian Prime Minister, Hun Sen, welcomed Nuon Chea and Khieu Samphan, two leaders of the recently defunct Cambodian Communist movement, back into Cambodian society.[1] He had already offered them informal amnesties for anything they might have done between April 1975 and January 1979, under the regime of Democratic Kampuchea (DK), known in the West as the Khmer Rouge.

Both of them had been key figures in DK: Nuon Chea had been second in command of the country, just below Pol Pot, and Khieu Samphan had been the *de jure* chief of state. Their close affiliation with the policies and practices of DK made Hun Sen's seemingly off-the-cuff forgiveness difficult for many to accept. After all, in less than four years under DK, perhaps as many as 2 million Cambodians, or almost one in three, had died of malnutrition, overwork, misdiagnosed diseases or executions. Most of these deaths, and all of the executions (estimated at perhaps 1,000,000) can be traced to the ideas of the DK leadership, the commands they issued and the actions of perhaps as many as 50,000 loyal followers.[1]

Despite, or perhaps because of, the enormity of these statistics, Hun Sen enjoined people at the 1998 press conference to 'dig a hole and bury the past'.[2] As far as he was concerned the Khmer Rouge period, by coming to an end, was no longer a political issue and was therefore devoid of interest. The history of the movement, its rationale, the culpability of its leaders and followers and the traumas of survivors (including, perhaps, his own) had become irrelevant to his overriding concerns, which were to develop Cambodia and to maintain himself in power. At another level, he assumed that forgetting this particular segment of the past was the best route to national reconciliation.

As this is written (November 2007) Hun Sen's policy, although somewhat modified, remains in place. Cambodian school textbooks say very little about the DK era and no university courses cover the period in detail. A ninth grade school textbook printed in 1990, for example, dealt with the period very laconically:

> From April 25 to April 27, 1975, the Khmer Rouge leaders held a special general assembly in order to form a new Constitution and renamed the country 'Democratic Kampuchea'. A new government of the DK, led by Pol Pot, came into existence, following which the massacre of Khmer citizens began.[3]

The period is seldom revisited over government-controlled radio or TV – although this silence lifted in 2007 as the internationally sponsored tribunal to try surviving leaders of DK, discussed later in this paper, steadily gathered momentum.[4]

All of this officially enforced amnesia coexists uneasily alongside the voluminous documentation about DK still being produced by NGOs[5] and alongside the memories of DK that rest or fail to rest inside the heads of all Cambodians over 40 years of age. The Tuol Sleng Museum of Genocidal Crimes in Phnom Penh, established in 1980 on the site of a murderous DK facility, continues to operate and so do the so-called killing fields of Choeung Ek, east of the capital, where the remains of over 6000 victims of DK were unearthed in the early 1980s. At that time, the Cambodian government, responding to Vietnamese pressure, developed both sites as evidence of Khmer Rouge 'genocide'. They have since become tourist destinations visited by thousands of people every year. A third tourist site has recently been inaugurated at Anlong Veng, the last headquarters of the Khmer Rouge faction, where Pol Pot died in 1998.[6]

The hole into which the past is to be buried, in other words, has only been partially dug or partially filled in, and the years that followed Hun Sen's injunction coincided with a period of renewed international interest in punishing the leaders of the Khmer Rouge. A UN sponsored international tribunal that aims to indict Nuon Chea, Khieu Samphan, Ieng Sary and perhaps several other DK figures for crimes against humanity opened in Phnom Penh, after long delays, in early 2007. Whether the tribunal will produce closure, re-open a range of traumatic recollections or sink without a trace remains to be seen but with a budget of almost U.S. $60 million, provided almost entirely by foreign donors, it promises to be a significant operation.[7]

The idea that memories and history-writing can be stopped in their tracks by an order from above, as in December 1998, suggests how history-writing has traditionally been perceived among the Khmer, namely as something emanating from those in power.[8] Even so, there is a real disconnect between the silence enjoined by the regime and the memories of DK that flourish or fester in Cambodia and among Cambodians overseas. These memories become more abundant and more accessible every day. Alon Confino has pointed to a similar disconnect that occurred in France in the 1950s and 1960s, when official neglect of the Vichy regime contrasted with millions of unofficial memories, many of them sharp and unpleasant, and others more nuanced, that stayed alive among the populace and re-emerged with a vengeance later on.[9]

As I hope to show in what follows, there have been several official policies toward the Khmer Rouge in the quarter-century since DK was overthrown. A policy of encouraging hostile recollections *en masse* in the 1980s was replaced in the late 1990s, after the Khmer Rouge movement collapsed, by a policy of induced amnesia that remains partially in force. In 2005, however, Hun Sen's government changed tack again and reluctantly agreed to give support to a tribunal. In 2007, popular interest in this period of Cambodian history revived.

Dealing with DK, 1979–80

After DK was swept from power by a Vietnamese invasion in January 1979, the fledgling Peoples' Republic of Kampuchea (PRK) and its Vietnamese advisors faced enormous economic, organizational and social problems.[10] The 1978–9 rice harvest had been neglected and food was scarce. Under DK, money and markets had been abolished, schools had been closed, towns had been emptied and medical treatment had been derisory. After DK collapsed, hundreds of thousands of ragged, hungry people criss-crossed the country looking for relatives and trying to reoccupy their former homes. Tens of thousands fled to the Thai border, where the UN soon established refugee camps and where the DK army was reconstituted with aid from China and Thailand. By June 1979, a quarter of a million Cambodians, including military and civilian remnants of DK, were camped along the Thai–Cambodian border. In the meantime, PRK was trying to establish the rudiments of administration in the newly reoccupied capital of Phnom Penh.[11]

Markets in Cambodia soon reopened, but money was not printed until 1980, the country's infrastructure was in ruins and international aid, except from India and the Soviet bloc, and was very slow in coming. Moreover, the euphoria that had greeted the Vietnamese invasion began eroding after a few months, as Evan Gottesman has written, 'in part because of the desperate conditions in the country but also because of Vietnamese control and Communist ideology'.[12] In 1979–80 thousands of educated Khmer sought refuge overseas. Meanwhile, in New York, the UN General Assembly, dominated by the United States, China and their allies, voted throughout the 1980s to condemn the Vietnamese invasion of Cambodia and to accept the credentials of the DK delegation, which until 1989 represented Cambodia at the UN. These policies cut off the possibility of UN assistance reaching the PRK and forestalled UN support for a tribunal to bring the leaders of the Khmer Rouge to justice.[13]

In this period, the ostensibly socialist PRK also faced the problem of how the socialist DK period should be regarded. The leaders of the PRK, after all, consisted largely of defectors from DK like Hun Sen, Heng Samrin and Chea Sim, and Cambodian Communists like Pen Sovan, who had lived in Vietnam since the 1950s. These people had to be given biographies that papered over the 'genocidal'

Khmer Rouge movement (in which some of them had been active participants), while holding onto the tenets of Marxism–Leninism and giving credit to the Khmer Rouge for the 'liberation' of the country in April 1975. The readjusted narrative required Pol Pot's Communist Party of Kampuchea (CPK) to go off the rails immediately following its admirable military victory in 1975, only to be resuscitated by DK defectors in Vietnam three years later. As Viviane Frings has suggested, these contorted revisions of history involved a considerable legerdemain: 'some things had to be said, others could not be said'.[14]

The PRK, like all Cambodian regimes, linked history writing to its own priorities. In earlier times, those in power in Cambodia had also fitted historiography to their needs without much interference from outside the country or from ordinary people. In 1979–80, however, PRK officials found it hard to dictate the ways in which Cambodians should perceive and write about their recent past. The impact of DK and its radical form of socialism had been so severe, widespread and unprecedented (at least in living memory), after all, that many survivors now saw their nation's history as a collectively lived experience that could be remembered, spun and recounted in different ways. Some survivors began writing histories of the period by themselves.[15] Ironically, what people were told to think about DK in the 1980s and much of what was written about the Khmer Rouge under the PRK often coincided, in a pleasingly Manichean fashion, with what most people remembered later on, and with what was published about DK by expatriate survivors.

Much published writing about DK, unsurprisingly, has privileged these harsh personal memories over ostensibly balanced analyses of events. This may be due in part to the fact that many survivors' narratives are written by people who were children in the DK era and also because, as Michael Lambek suggests, because memory 'is seen as a privileged site of resistance to hegemonic narratives'[16] – although in the Cambodian case the hegemonic, demonising narratives of DK in the PRK period were seldom subverted by published memoirs, which were written almost entirely by people who had taken refuge in other countries. More to the point, perhaps, as Hodgkin and Radstone write, 'Memory because of its powerful pull toward the present and because of its affective investments allows more readily a certain evasion of critical distance'. The historiography of the Khmer Rouge period has barely begun to cool down.[17]

Memories of DK, and what was written about it, were channelled under the PRK to suit the demonising policies favoured by the regime and its Vietnamese mentors. Memories of positive experiences in the era, such as they were, were impermissible, and so was evidence of Vietnamese support for the Khmer Rouge movement before 1975. More recently, however, without discounting the horrors of DK, this demonised, hegemonic historiography has beginning to give way – autobiographically again – to something more nuanced, as the lines between perpetrators, bystanders and victims become blurred – sometimes a single person fits all three categories – and as contradictory memories, photographs and documents come to light.[18] What Paul Thibault has called the 'surgical Utopia' of separating good from evil with precision, especially when we talk of daily life under DK (which was not, after all, the same as daily life at Auschwitz) may have become inoperative with the passage of time.[19] Moreover, the fact that some Cambodians were relatively better off under DK – and these would include the poorest of the poor, who were highly favoured by the regime – does not make these men and women murderers, although they will never attract sympathy from Cambodians who are better off and who suffered disproportionately under DK. Indeed, nearly all the people who have published memoirs of DK belonged before 1975 to Cambodia's tiny bourgeoisie, and the historiography of DK in western languages has tilted in their direction.

The 1979 Trial of Pol Pot and Ieng Sary

Because the Vietnamese in Cambodia in 1979 had faint hopes that some members of the DK hierarchy might defect to Phnom Penh, and because they were unwilling to blame a large number of Cambodians for the conduct of the Khmer Rouge, they chose to demonise Pol Pot and his brother in law Ieng Sary, who had served as foreign minister of DK. Aside from Khieu Samphan, whose name was added to what the Vietnamese called the 'genocidal clique' in 1980, no other DK official was ever singled out by the People's Republic of Kampuchea (PRK). Instead, foreshadowing the policies pursued by Hun Sen in the 1990s, the PRK encouraged supporters of DK to defect and welcomed people who 'repented' their involvement in the previous regime. An April 1979 PRK document declared that

> Those who directly engaged on the massacres of people or signed such an order must stand before the post revolutionary power, ask forgiveness from the people, and fully recognize their crimes.[20]

Five years later, Hun Sen reiterated the policy, remarking, 'We will not close our eyes to those [defectors] who awaken in time'.[21]

Throughout the 1980s very few people were questioned about their activities under DK, even fewer were detained and none, as far as I know, was put to death.[22] PRK officials needed all the holdovers they could find. Throughout the 1980s, hundreds of ex- Khmer Rouge cadre held positions in the administration. Anecdotal evidence suggests that many of these men and women are still in place.

Still hoping for international recognition and seeking closure on the DK issue, the PRK and its Vietnamese mentors decided in early 1979 to indict Pol Pot and Ieng Sary for genocide. Legal experts brought from Vietnam worked with Cambodian colleagues to ensure that only these two men were indicted, that the Cambodian 'people's assessors' who would endorse the verdict were people with 'a profound animus vis a vis Pol Pot–Ieng Sary', that a relevant law to justify the tribunal was in place and that the international jurists, journalists and observers invited to the proceedings knew in advance what the outcome of the proceedings would be. PRK's Decree Law Number 1, issued on 15 July 1979, authorised the tribunal and set out its *modus operandi*. Cambodian attorneys named for the defence were told that they were not expected to defend Pol Pot and Ieng Sary, but were encouraged to extend the blame for genocide to DK's 'hegemonic' patrons in China.[23]

The tribunal convened in Phnom Penh on 15 August 1979. As Tom Fawthrop and Helen Jarvis assert, this was the world's first trial of people charged with genocide, although the definition of the term used at the tribunal was far wider than the one laid down in the UN Genocide Convention.[24]

Steve Heder has argued that the 1979 tribunal cobbled together aspects of French colonial jurisprudence, pre-revolutionary Cambodian practice and procedures in effect in Communist Vietnam. What was on display in the tribunal, as at

Nuremberg and Tokyo in 1945–6, was victors' justice, combined with an understandable desire on the part of the Khmer witnesses to express their anger and grief about what had happened to them and their loved ones under DK.[25]

The tribunal lasted for five days. Over 50 witnesses provided graphic evidence, often verified later by other sources, of the horrors of what came to be called the 'Pol Pot time' (*samay a Pot*). Toward the end of the trial, an African-American lawyer, Hope Stevens, made a statement on Pol Pot's behalf as an additional defence attorney. Stevens blamed China, the United States and Zionism for the crimes of DK, adding, 'It is now clear to all that Pol Pot and Ieng Sary were criminally insane monsters'.[26] After a 'short interval' following the concluding statements, the president of the court read out a lengthy verdict – guilty on all counts – and pronounced two death sentences, *in absentia*. The verdict and sentencing papers had clearly been prepared well in advance.

Many people nowadays would agree instinctively with the guilty verdict, but no evidence was brought forward at the tribunal that linked either Pol Pot or Ieng Sary to specific acts of murder or to the commission of genocidal crimes. Moreover, show trial aspects of the proceedings, the absurdity of the 'defence' and the absence of a genuine judiciary in the PRK, as well as generalised western animosity toward Vietnam in 1979, combined for many years to keep the evidence presented at the trial from gaining traction outside the PRK. As Steve Heder has argued, however, the trial has served as a template for Hun Sen in his protracted negotiations with the UN and others in the 1990s regarding an international tribunal.[27]

PRK Memorials of the DK Era

PRK officials and their Vietnamese advisors labelled the Khmer Rouge 'genocidal' and 'fascist' to encourage comparisons with Hitler's Germany and to downplay DK's socialist credentials. Similarly, the DK's interrogation and torture facility at Tuol Sleng, known in DK by its code name S-21, was quickly labelled an 'Asian Auschwitz'. Although nearly everyone entering both of these facilities was put to death, the analogy between S-21 and Auschwitz breaks down because the 'Jews' who were tortured, interrogated and put to death at S-21 – over 15,000 of them – were not only almost all ethnic Khmers, but were also overwhelmingly DK soldiers, CPK cadre and other loyal servants of the regime who were forced to 'confess' to a range of often fictional counter-revolutionary conspiracies and crimes. During interrogations at S-21 memories were created, manipulated and destroyed to meet the exigencies of the interrogations – namely, to find each prisoner guilty of a counter-revolutionary crime. As in Franz Kafka's novel, *The Trial*, prisoners at S-21 were not arrested because they were guilty, but were guilty because they had been arrested.[28]

The Vietnamese capitalised on the horrors of S-21 almost immediately after they arrived. In February 1979, a Vietnamese colonel named Mai Lam, who had designed the Museum of American War Crimes in Ho Chi Minh City and was fluent in Khmer, arrived in Phnom Penh to examine the archives of S-21, with a view to producing evidence for the upcoming trial of Pol Pot and Ieng Sary.[29] The archive then and later contained no 'smoking guns' linking Pol Pot and Ieng Sary to executions at S-21 or elsewhere, although documents at the prison and testimony by an S-21 survivor at the August 1979 trial established the connection between the murderous facility and the handful of men and women who had directed DK.

Until 1987, when he returned to Vietnam, Mai Lam worked with Cambodian colleagues to turn S-21 into a museum of genocidal crimes resembling the Holocaust memorials in eastern Europe. Mai Lam was eager not only to establish the links between DK and Nazi Germany but also to teach Cambodians about their recent past. In 1995, he told an interviewer that he had established the museum so that the Cambodians could study 'the war and the many aspects of war crimes'[30] – referring, it seems, to the war that DK had waged against Vietnam. Mai Lam believed that the Cambodians needed to be force-fed a lesson about themselves with the implication that blame for DK atrocities might extend far beyond the 'genocidal clique'.

The Tuol Sleng Museum of Genocidal Crimes opened to the public in July 1980. In that month alone, 19,060 Cambodians visited the museum, as did 720 foreigners.[31] Many of the Khmer were looking for relatives in the hundreds of mug shots of prisoners that were posted in the museum. Over 6000 of these often haunting photographs were cleaned and catalogued by an American NGO in 1994–5. Selections of the photographs were later published and exhibited in overseas museums.[32]

Over the years, despite occasional efforts to close it, the museum has been an important tourist attraction. It is a poignant memorial to the horrors of DK. A map of Cambodia composed of real skulls, with a blood-red Mekong river running through them, which was one of Mai Lam's macabre contributions, has recently been taken down and the exhibits have become more sophisticated, but its essential horror – 15,000 men, women and children questioned, tortured and put to death – lingers for every visitor to the site. As Judy Ledgerwood, an anthropologist who worked on the Tuol Sleng archives in the early 1990s has recalled,

> Over time, one begins to see the details. On stairway landings, for example, holes have been knocked in the walls so sloshing water down the staircase can clean the stairs. Below each of these openings on the building's exterior can still be seen stains of blood that ran down the sides, as if the buildings themselves had bled.[33]

S-21's archive of 'confessions', DK documents and administrative materials, of great interest to historians of DK and to more recently to people gathering evidence for the tribunal, was shifted to the Documentation Center of Cambodia (DC-Cam) in the mid 1990s.[34]

In early 1980, PRK teams excavated the killing fields of Choeung Ek west of the capital where at least 6 000 prisoners from S-21 were executed and buried between mid 1976 and the end of 1978. In 1986, an *ersatz* Buddhist stupa, filled with skulls visible through windows on all four sides was erected at Choeung Ek under what needs to be called insensitive Vietnamese supervision. As the anthropologist Charles Keyes has suggested, Choeung Ek is a place where ghosts are kept alive. For this reason, Choeung Ek makes many Cambodians nervous.[35]

The Anlong Veng tourist site, which has been developed recently by private interests, is in some ways even more macabre, and is the subject of Timothy Dylan Wood's ongoing research.[36]

Days of Hate

Throughout the 1980s, PRK and Vietnamese troops fought DK forces and those of their Cambodian allies along the Thai–Cambodian border. Thousands of soldiers on both sides died in these campaigns, and to justify their efforts the PRK strove to keep the horrors of DK in the forefront of peoples' minds. Starting in 1983, annual days of hate (*tvea chong komhung*: literally, 'anniversaries [for] holding onto anger') were staged throughout the country on 20 May, a date that had been chosen because DK had ordered the total collectivization of Cambodian life on 20 May 1976.[37] On these occasions, selected survivors of DK, as well as PRK officials, recalled their sufferings and the evils of 'the Pol Pot time'. The ceremonies reminded listeners that the legitimacy of the PRK rested on the fact that, with the assistance of Vietnam, Cambodians had driven the Khmer Rouge from power and 'saved Cambodia from genocide'. On 20 May 1986, for example, the PRK minister of the interior Chea Sim, a former DK cadre, told an audience that

> Those who died are reminding us to be vigilant, to strengthen our soli-darity and practice revolutionary activities we must be on the alert against the cruelties and poisonous tricks of the enemy, even though they try to hide themselves in multiple [political] disguises.[38]

Formal visits by school children, teachers and Buddhist monks to the Tuol Sleng Museum, Chhoeung Ek and 'killing fields' elsewhere in Cambodia were often scheduled for these days of hate,[39] which continued to be celebrated throughout Cambodia for several years after the Vietnamese withdrew their troops in 1989. Lower key Days of Hate were celebrated periodically in the 1990s, and on 20 May 2007 a low-key 'Day of Remembrance', resembling a Day of Hate, was celebrated in Phnom Penh and elsewhere in the country.

The Killing Fields and PRK Textbooks

In 1981 the PRK established a Genocide Research Committee empowered to gather oral evidence on a national basis about DK and also to exhume some 309 mass graves from the DK era, often associated with 158 detention facilities that had been located throughout the country. Over 19,000 grave pits dating from the DK era have also been identified.[40] DC-Cam forensic teams followed up these investigations in the 1990s.[41] The Genocide Research Committee collected data about regime-related deaths from thousands of survivors. Some 10,000 docu-ments produced for the Committee bear the signatures or thumbprints of over a million Cambodians who testified singly or *en masse* about their experiences under DK.[42] Craig Etcheson has argued that, although the data collections were methodologically faulty, the data themselves were often accurate and point to a higher total death count under DK – approximately 2 million – than the 1.7 million figure that had been generally agreed upon by western analysts.[43]

In a ceremony in September 1983, soon after the PRK National Assembly had approved the construction of a memorial tombstone, or *stupa*, in Kampot, the town's assembled inhabitants, in a petition to the Assembly, recited statistics that had been drummed into them, and into all Cambodians for several years:

> We ... would like to declare our approval of the accounts of crimes committed during 1975–1978 by Pol Pot, Ieng Sary and Khieu Samphan. *In accordance with our knowledge, we the citizens know exactly that during this brutal regime*, 3,147,768 innocent people were executed, leaving 141,848 disabled people, over 200,000 orphans, and hundreds of thousands of

widows … Scholars and clergymen were atrociously tortured. There were 25,168 Buddhist monks, 594 medical doctors and dentists, 18,000 teachers and 10,550 students, 975 lawyers, 191 journalists, and 1,120 artists murdered in many cruel ways.[44]

These figures are risibly precise, but the extent of genuine losses throughout Cambodia, the reality of the mass graves and the recurrent ventilation of personal experiences kept the traumas of the DK period in view for most Cambodians throughout the 1980s. Everyone's memories and attitudes were channelled in the same comforting Manichean direction and, as two psychiatrists who worked with Cambodian refugees in Thailand have written, 'It is always more comfortable to have a Manichean vision of the world, for that allows us not to ask too many questions or at least to have the answers readily to hand'.[45]

Unsurprisingly perhaps, no one in the PRK era publicly raised issues of individual or collective responsibility for what had taken place under DK. No one suggested that Marxism–Leninism as practiced in Vietnam and in a diluted form in the PRK might be as unsuitable (or as indigestible) for most Cambodians as its 'Maoist' form had been under the Khmer Rouge. No one remembered that the Khmer Rouge movement, until the early 1970s, had benefitted from extensive Vietnamese assistance and had attracted thousands of willing disciples. Finally no one dared to suggest that officials of the PRK who had served, in many cases, contentedly under DK should be held accountable for anything they had done in those years. Throughout the 1980s, thousands of men and women who had committed crimes against their fellow Khmer between April 1975 and January 1979 resumed their pre-revolutionary lives and in many cases were rewarded with administrative positions. Although former Khmer Rouge cadre lived all over the country, often alongside their victims, they were nowhere to be found. 'The Pol Pot time' was evil, but the men and women who had administered DK, except for a phantasmagoric 'genocidal clique' had disappeared. In other words, a hole had been dug, and parts of the past had been buried.[46]

Under the PRK, primary school textbooks, novels, poetry collections and books for adult literacy, cleared and subsidized by the state, were filled with gruesome verses, narratives and pen and ink drawings that demonised DK. A Grade 5 text from 1984, for example, carried a poem entitled 'Great Solidarity, Great Victory'. A drawing above the poem shows soldiers with PRK, Lao and Vietnamese flags bayoneting DK guerrillas on the grounds of Angkor Wat.[47] An earlier textbook, aimed at teaching literacy to adults, carried a sketch of DK soldiers pulling down a Buddhist *wat*; in the background women and children were being beaten and stabbed by Khmer Rouge cadre. An illustration in another text showed DK soldiers bayoneting a Buddhist monk, noting condescendingly 'the Buddhist religion was loved and respected in the past by many Cambodians'.[48]

A traditional aspect of these texts, of course, is that those in power had cleared or scripted them to suit their own priorities. Since 1993 government interest in the recent past has faded and, except for Days of Hate, amnesia has become the order of the day. Cambodia seems to have entered a phase of its history where officially sponsored historiography of the recent past has become intrinsically unimportant and irrelevant to those in power, some of whom could be tarred with the Khmer Rouge brush. Whether this means that history has been returned to people without power is an unanswerable question. [49]

Dealing with DK Since 1989

After the Vietnamese withdrew their troops from Cambodia in September 1989, the country renamed itself the State of Cambodia (SOC), but the KPRP remained in power and most of its leaders remained in place. A week before the Paris Peace Accords that were signed in October 1991, the Kampuchean Peoples' Revolutionary Party, which had ruled the country since 1979, changed its name to the Cambodian Peoples' Party (CPP) and abandoned its Marxist–Leninist orientation. The party's organization and its leaders were unchanged. Over the next few months, the welfare state in Cambodia collapsed and gaps between rich and poor, invisible or unimportant since 1975, reappeared and widened, especially in the towns.

Throughout the 1980s, fighting had continued between Phnom Penh forces and those arrayed against them. After the Vietnamese withdrawal, inhospitable parts of Cambodia's north and northwest fell to insurgents and pressures mounted outside Cambodia to impose a settlement on the country. These efforts culminated in the Paris Peace Accords of October 1991. To ensure Khmer Rouge participation and Chinese support for the peace process, the final declaration of the Accords failed to mention genocide or crimes against humanity, pledging only that Cambodia would not return to unspecified 'policies and practices of the past'.[50]

Under the United Nations Transitional Authority in Cambodia period (UNTAC, 1992–3) Hun Sen and his colleagues in the CPP resisted attempts to include the Khmer Rouge in the interim Cambodian government, as had been decided in Paris. Luckily for the CPP and probably for the Cambodian people, the Khmer Rouge failed to emerge from their bases, refused to disarm and boycotted the UN-sponsored elections of 1993. As the Khmer Rouge became guerrillas again, the movement slowly collapsed, in part because of amnesties offered by Hun Sen's government. As Cambodia opened up to journalists and tourists, international interest in the kingdom quickened, and so did the interest in a tribunal to try officials of DK for crimes against humanity.[51] In the early 1990s pressures developed, especially in the United States, to 'do something' about the Khmer Rouge.[52]

It is ironic but unsurprising that, by the time the Khmer Rouge ceased to be a serious politico-military problem for the Cambodian government (or a useful, undeclared ally for the United States), the idea of dealing with the movement in a juridical way became a matter of urgency for the UN, human rights NGOs and elements in the United States, especially those that were hostile to Hun Sen.[53]

In June 1997 Cambodia's two prime ministers, Hun Sen and Prince Norodom Rannaridh, for reasons that are still unclear, formally petitioned the UN for assistance in setting up a tribunal to indict the former leaders of the Khmer Rouge. Their letter asked for 'the assistance of the United Nations and international community in bringing to justice these persons responsible for genocide and crimes against humanity from 1975 to 1979'. Almost immediately afterwards, however, a political crisis engulfed Cambodia, in which Hun Sen presided over a *coup de force* against his coalition partners. The idea of a tribunal was set aside, but over the next few years, emboldened by the success of tribunals and truth commissions elsewhere, the UN, NGOs and foreign governments that had supported the tribunal pressed the Cambodian authorities to review the proposals and to establish an international tribunal to indict the senior leaders of DK.

Hun Sen and his colleagues resisted these pressures on sovereignty grounds and because they suspected that an internationally controlled body might extend the indictments beyond a handful of senior figures. Hun Sen was probably also encouraged to resist the proposals by China, whose government was reluctant to be shown to have supported the Khmer Rouge so enthusiastically for so long. The UN was also reluctant to place the tribunal in the hands of the Cambodian judiciary. However, by the end of May 2007 the tribunal appeared finally to be back on track[54] and a new era of remembering and dealing with Cambodia's recent past appeared to have begun. As this is written (November 2007), several leaders of DK, including Nuon Chea, Ieng Sary, Ieng Thireth (Ieng Sary's wife) and Khieu Samphan, have been formally charged with crimes against humanity and have been incarcerated awaiting trial.

Conclusion

Everyone in Cambodia over 40 years of age is aware of what happened, at least to them, under DK and, in the words of the Cambodian scholar Rath Many, 'Setting up a credible tribunal [can] help the dead gain peace. And alleviate the sufferings of the survivors'.[55] What the tribunal might accomplish, in other words, is something more complicated than exacting public vengeance on DK's surviving leaders or granting them some kind of judicial forgiveness.[56]

The tribunal that is now in place is bound to open up the people it indicts to scrutiny after what Rath Many has called a 'quarter century of drift in the fields of accountability'.[57] DK's reclusive, aging leaders will be dragged into public view, in circumstances that they will be unable to control. The effects of this exposure on these men and women and on Cambodians at large are impossible to determine, but surely for people too young to recall DK, as well as for survivors of the regime, the advantage of having access to a debate about those years will be more valuable than accepting orders that the period be forgotten and believing, as many young Cambodians apparently do, that the horrors of DK never even took place.

As a foreigner, I have no right to 'guide' Cambodians toward a decision that is pleasing to me or that suits my admittedly western notions of jurisprudence, but I feel strongly that the remnants of the 'genocidal clique' need to be called to account for what they did between 1975 and 1979. This needs to happen in a regulated public forum, rather than before a kangaroo court, as was the case in 1979. These aged people need to hear other survivors talk about what happened. They need to face the mass of documentary evidence about DK, and their own once concealed behaviour, that has piled up since 1979. Although, as in 1979, this may be victors' justice, in view of what happened under DK it is justice nonetheless.

The idea of personal accountability for wrong-doing resonates with Buddhist ideas of morality and justice, in a way that Judeo-Christian notions of vengeance and forgiveness do not, and holding these men and women accountable for some of the horrors that occurred between 1975 and 1979 does not run counter to Buddhist teachings or to Cambodian culture. I feel strongly that the men and women who held positions of responsibility under DK, and wrought so much damage on the Cambodian people, need to bear witness to a period of the recent past which haunts the minds of nearly all the men and women who survived it.

Whether the tribunal will bring peace of mind or closure to survivors individually or *en masse* is impossible to say, but digging a hole and burying the past, which is now impossible to do, would have done nothing to inform young

Cambodians about DK or to soften the memories which accost older people on a daily basis. For these people, to rephrase Primo Levi slightly, 'The pain of every day [is] translated ... constantly into our dreams, in the ever repeated dream of the unlistened-to story'.[58]

Notes

1. Seth Mydans, "Cambodian Leader Resists Punishing Top Khmer Rouge", *New York Times* 29 December 1998.
2. Mydans, note 1. Khieu Samphan at the time remarked that 'history should remain history' – whatever that means. Voting in the Cambodian national elections in 2003, Nuon Chea 'said he hoped Cambodians would forget the past'. *Phnom Penh Post*, 28 July 2003. To be fair to Hun Sen, similar amnesties had been granted in El Salvador, Uruguay and Zimbabwe. See Stanley Cohen, "State Crimes and Previous Regimes: Knowledge, Accountability and the Policing of the Past", *Law and Social Inquiry* 10 (1995), pp.7–50 at p.29.
3. Royal Government of Cambodia Ministry of Education Youth and Sports, Social Studies text-book, Grade 9, Lesson 12, p.169 (Phnom Penh, 2000). Text funded by UNESCO. Translation by Documentation Center of Cambodia (DC-Cam). A more detailed text intended for Grade 12, but never published, fails to mention the Marxist–Leninist orientation of DK. See also Khamboly Dy, *A History of Democratic Kampuchea (1975–1979)* (Phnom Penh: DC-Cam, 2007), a volume financed in part by the Soros Foundation which will be used in Cambodian high schools as a supplementary text.
4. The tribunal is called the Extraordinary Chambers of the Courts of Cambodia (ECCC). See Seth Mydans, "Proceedings to Open on Aged Chiefs of Khmer Rouge" *International Herald Tribune*, 4 August 2006 . See also John D. Ciorciari (ed.) *The Khmer Rouge Tribunal* (Phnom Penh: DC-Cam, 2006).
5. The most active NGO in Cambodia dealing with DK and with issues of trauma and memory is the Documentation Center Cambodia (DC-Cam) in Phnom Penh. Since 1997 its energetic and talented staff has collected, archived and disseminated a vast amount of information about DK and has conducted a vigorous popular education program. I am immensely grateful to DC-Cam's director, Youk Chhang, and his staff for their assistance to me over the years.
6. On Tuol Sleng, see David Chandler, *Voices from S-21: Terror and History in Pol Pot's Secret Prison* (Berkeley, CA: University of California Press, 1999). On Choeung Ek, see Peter Maguire, *Facing Death in Cambodia* (New York: Columbia University Press, 2005), pp.84, 160–61. The site was priva-tized in 2005. When I visited it on 19 May 2007, it was a smoothly running tourist destination. On Anlong Vong, see Timothy Dylan Wood, "Touring Memories of the Khmer Rouge", in Leakthina Chau-pich Ollier and Tim Winter (eds), *Expressions of Cambodia: the Politics of Tradition, Identity and Change* (London: Routledge), 2006, pp.181–93.
7. See Tom Fawthrop and Helen Jarvis, *Getting Away with Genocide? Elusive Justice and the Khmer Rouge Tribunal* (Sydney: University of New South Wales Press, 2005).
8. For a review of traditional views of history among the Khmer, see Claude Jacques, "Nouvelles orientations pour l'étude de l'histoire du pays khmer" *Asie du sud-est et le monde insulindien* (*ASEMI*) 13 (1982), pp.39–57.
9. See Alon Confino, "Collective Memory and Cultural History: Problems of Method" *American Historical Review* 5 (1995), pp.263–83 and Katharine Hodgkin and Susannah Radstone (eds) *Contested Pasts: the Politics of Memory* (London: Routledge, 2003), pp.1–21.
10. See Evan Gottesman, *Cambodia After the Khmer Rouge: Inside the Politics of Nation Building* (New Haven, CT: Yale University Press, 2002), pp.37–60.
11. Khmer expatriates, especially in the United States, still form a vocal anti-DK and anti-Vietnamese lobby.
12. Gottesman (note 10), p. 57.
13. For a helpful overview, see Fawthrop and Jarvis (note 7), pp.24–39.
14. Viviane Frings, " Rewriting Cambodian History to 'Adapt' it to a New Political Context", *Modern Asian Studies* 31/4 (1997), 8-7-46 at p.810. The 'Marxist–Leninists' in the PRK had no party of their own until 1981 when the CPK, to which many of them had belonged, was renamed the Kampuchean Peoples' Revolutionary Party (KPRP), sharing the acronym with a predecessor party, the Khmer Peoples' Revolutionary Party that had been organized in Cambodia in 1951 by Vietnam. See Margaret Slocomb, *The Peoples' Republic of Kampuchea: the Revolution after Pol Pot*

(Chiangmai: Silkworm Books, 2004), p.139. The ruling party in Cambodia today, the Cambodian Peoples' Party (CPP), traces its origins to the first KPRP but plays down its socialist past.

15. Ironically, a Khmer Rouge slogan pointed in the same direction: 'Only the people can construct the history of the world'. Henri Locard (ed.), *Pol Pot's Little Red Book* (Chiangmai: Silkworm Books, 2004), p. 292 (my translation).

16. Paul Antze and Michael Lambek (eds), *Tense Past: Cultural Essays in Trauma and Memory* (London: Routledge, 1996), p.252, note 14.

17. Hodgkin and Radstone (note 12). See also Irina Paperno, "Personal Accounts of the Soviet Experience", *Kritika* 3/4 (autumn 2002), pp.577–610, which refers (on p.584) to the 'privatization of history', adding: 'Soviet people use … catastrophic history as a justification of authorship and a source of personal significance – an instrument of subjectivization'.

18. P. LeVine, *A Contextual Study into Marriages under the Khmer Rouge: The Ritual Revolution* (PhD thesis, Monash University, 2007) analyses allegedly "forced" marriages under DK, and suggests a more nuanced picture of this aspect of the DK period, with none of the tragedy left out. See also Wynne Cougill et al. (eds), *Stilled Lives* (Phnom Penh: DC-Cam, 2005).

19. Paul Thibault, "Vichy: la culpabilité française", *Esprit* 24 (January 1991), pp.22–30 at p.26.

20. Craig Etcheson, *After the Killing Fields: Lessons of the Cambodian Genocide* (Westport, CT: Praeger, 2005), pp.180–81, quoting a PRK document cited by Steve Heder in an unpublished essay.

21. US Foreign Broadcast Information Service, Asia-Pacific, *Daily Reports*, 3 April 1984.

22. Two men imprisoned briefly in 1979 had been employed at S-21. Linton, *Reconciliation in Cambodia* (Phnom Penh: DC-Cam, 2002), p.58. One of them, Him Huy, was interviewed repeatedly by scholars in the 1990s and appeared in Rethy Panh's film about S-21 in 2004. Phephai Phear (alias Hor), a DK soldier who had fought against Vietnam, was arrested in June 1979 and imprisoned without charge for seven years. *Searching for the Truth* 14 (December 2001), pp.21–22. In his 2001 interview, he boasted about fighting the Vietnamese. If he had said this in 1979, it would have been his undoing.

23. Gareth Porter, *Vietnam: the Politics of a Bureaucratic System* (Ithaca, NY: Cornell University Press, 1993), p.172 points out that the position of defence counsel was abolished in Vietnam in 1975, and replaced with a socialist pleader 'who was not expected to present a legal defense on behalf of his client'.   .

24. Fawthrop and Jarvis (note 7), p.42.

25. See Steve Heder, "Hun Sen and Genocide Trials in Cambodia: International Impacts, Impunity and Justice", in Judy Ledgerwood (ed.) *Cambodia Emerges from the Past: Eight Essays* (De Kalb, IL: University of Northern Illinois Press, 2002, pp.178–223). Gottesman (note 10), p.62 ff; and Howard de Nike, John Quigley et al. (eds), *Genocide in Cambodia: Documents from the Trial of Pol Pot and Ieng Sary* (Philadelphia, PA: University of Pennsylvania Press, 2000).

26. Maguire (note 6), p.60.

27. Heder (note 25), p.206.

28. Chandler (note 6), especially pp.41–109.

29. On Mai Lam, see Chandler (note 6), pp.4–6 and Maguire (note 6), pp.85ff. See also Ong Thong Hoeung, "Le 30 novembre j'ai quitté Phnom Penh précipitamment", in C. Scalabrinio, (ed.), *Affaires cambodgiennes* (Paris: L'Harmattan, 1989), pp.121–8. Hoeung worked in the S-21 archive for several months in 1979.

30. Sara Colm's unpublished interview with Mai Lam, 24 May 1995.

31. See Judy Ledgerwood, "The Cambodian Tuol Sleng Museum of Genocidal Crimes: National Narrative", *Museum Archaeology* 21/1 (spring–summer 1997), pp.83–98 at p.85. The July 1979 statistics are from "Rapport sur les visiteurs du mois de juillet 1980", uncatalogued typescript, DC-Cam Tuol Sleng archives.

32. See Maguire (note 6), pp.17, 150–51; Doug Niven and Chris Riley (eds), *The Killing Fields* (Santa Fe, NM: Twin Palms Press, 1996), a collection of photographs from S-21; Rachel Hughes, "The Abject Artifacts of Memory: Photographs from the Cambodian Genocide", *Media Culture and Society* 25 (2003), pp.123–44; R. Hughes, "Memory and Sovereignty in Post-1979 Cambodia: Choeung Ek and Local Genocide Memorials", in Susan Cook (ed.), *Genocide in Cambodia and Rwanda: New Perspectives* (New Brunswick, NJ: Transaction, 2006), pp.257–79, and Vann Nath, *A Cambodian Prison Portrait: One Year in the Khmer Rouge's S-21* (Bangkok: White Lotus, 1998).

33. Bronwyn Sloan, "Can Cambodia Get Justice?", *Bangkok Post*, 12 April 2006, quoting a former S-21 guard whom she had interviewed: "The smell of the blood and death comes back to me as strongly as if it were yesterday".

34. See Rachel Hughes, "Nationalism and Memory at the Tuol Sleng Museum of Genocidal Crimes", in Hodgkin and Radstone (note 12), pp.175–92.

35. Charles Keyes, personal communication. On Choeung Ek, see Chandler (note 6), pp.136–40. On the Day of Remembrance on 20 May 2007, a bizarre charade was enacted at Choeung Ek, in the presence of Buddhist monks and Cambodian officials, during which 'victims' were 'executed' by people dressed as Khmer Rouge. On days of hate, see note 39, below.

36. See note 6, above.

37. Author's interview with a former PRK official, October 1990. See also *Cambodia Daily*, 21 May 1997. The decree that set up the ceremonies stated that 20 May 1976 was when DK 'began to carry out their policy of continuous genocide … throughout the entire country'. Fawthrop and Jarvis, note 7, p.74.

38. Unnumbered document from DC-Cam. Archive. See also Peoples' Republic of Kampuchea, *Okritikam reboh bang viet nei chuttapheapniyum Chen pekin nung boriva Pol Pot-Iengsary-Khieu Samphan knong onlong chnam 1975–1979* [The Crimes of the Hegemonic Gang of Beijing China and the Puppets Pol Pot, Ieng Sary and Khieu Samphan in the Epoch 1975–1979] (Phnom Penh: n.p., 1983), p.65. See Rachel Hughes, "Remembering May 20 – Day of Anger", *Searching for the Truth* 12 (December 2000), pp.39–41.

39. See Hughes, note 35, and p.177.

40. These statistics are from Kava Chongkittavorn, "The Khmer Rouge Trails Should be Shared", *The Nation* (Bangkok), 20 August 2006.

41. *Searching for the Truth* 22–24 (October–December 2001), pp.6, 11–12 and 16–20. Some mass graves contain the remains of a dozen people, others the remains of several thousand. See Rasy Pheng Pong, "Five Years of the Mapping Project", *Searching for the Truth* 20 (August 2001), pp.10–12. A government decree of 14 December 2002 ordered that killing fields throughout the country be maintained as memorials and tourist destinations. I am grateful to Craig Etcheson for this information.

42. Linton (note 27), pp.65–6.

43. Craig Etcheson (note 20), pp.117–18.

44. Unnumbered document from "Renakse" archive held in DC-Cam. Emphasis added. The figures match those in the tables printed in PRK, *The Crimes*, and pp. 16–12. The petition added: 'The whole assembly has agreed … that the compatriots should remember this event as a sad history and pass this knowledge onto the next generation'. A similar petition, dated September 1983, called for UN action against the 'genocidal clique' but closed with a pledge to 'follow the Party's political line', *Searching for the Truth* (third quarter 2005), p.5.

45. Jean-Pierre Hiegel and Colette Landrac, 'Les Khmers rouges: orthodoxie et paradoxe', *Les temps modernes* 523 (février 1990) pp.62–90 at p. 65 (my translation). Survivors' published memoirs, with rare exceptions, treat the DK era as evil, consistent and inexplicable. This Standard Total View (a term invented by the historian Michael Vickery in his *Cambodia 1975–1982)* responds to Manichean market demands, and perhaps to psychological ones as well. It also meshes nicely with generalized Cambodian memories of the Khmer Rouge period. On this issue, see Chandler (note 6), pp. 154–5.

46. But see Cougill et al. (eds) (note 18), in which relatives of low-ranking Khmer Rouge figures movingly relate their life histories, their losses and some positive experiences under DK.

47. PRK Ministry of Education (ed.) *Rien aksar tnak ti 5* [*Learning to Read, level 5*] (Phnom Penh: n.p., 1985), p.17. Buddhism was discouraged under the PRK.

48. PRK Ministry of Education, *rien aksar tnak ti 3* [*Learning to Read, level 3*]. (Phnom Penh: n.p., 1982), unn.

49. In a departure from the praxis of previous Cambodian leaders, Hun Sen places no iconic value on Angkor, seeing the site primarily as a source of revenue from tourism. His refusal to be mesmerized by Cambodia's past or by the sociology of victimhood are refreshing aspects of his harsh style of rule.

50. Gottesman (note 10), p.343.

51. See Diane Orentlicher, "Settling Accounts: the Duty to Prosecute Human Rights Violations of a Prior Regime", *Yale Law Journal* (1991), pp.2537–615. On NGO efforts and U.S. government foot-dragging in the 1980s, see Priscilla B. Hayner, *Unspeakable Truths: Facing the Challenge of Truth Commissions* (London: Routledge), pp.195–8.

52. See Stephen P. Marks, "Forgetting the 'Policies and Practices of the Past': Forum on World Impunity in Cambodia", *Fletcher Forum on World Affairs* 18 (1994), pp.17–35.

53. Linton (note 27), p.54 writes that U.S. suggestions at the Paris Peace Talks on Cambodia in 1991 to support a post-UNTAC genocide trial were blocked by several other participants.

54. See Seth Mydans, "Unwieldy Court Further Complicates Long Delayed Khmer Rouge Trial", *International Herald Tribune*, 25 January 2007 and Seth Mydans, "Cambodia Moves a Tiny Step Closer to a Khmer Rouge Trial", *International Herald Tribune*, 1 May 2007.

55. Rath Many, "Cambodian Khmer Rouge Tribunal and International Law", MA thesis, Monash University, 2004, p. 58. See also Fawthrop and Jarvis, note 7, pp. 232–54. However, as note 2, Cohen, "State Crimes of Previous regimes" p. 49 suggests, "Few nations anywhere have acknowledged their own historical victims".

56. On these issues, see Minow, *Between Vengeance and Forgiveness: Facing History after Genocide and Mass Violence* (Cambridge, MA: Harvard University Pres, 1999), especially pp.10-21. See also Fabienne Luco, *Entre le Tigre et le crocodile: approche anthropologique sur les pratiques traditionelles et nouvelles de traitement des conflits au Cambodge* (Phnom Penh: UNESCO, 2002), a brilliant analysis of the ways in which rural Khmer, deprived of access to the legal system, deal with issues of conflict and reconciliation.

57. Many (note 58), p. 55.

58. Primo Levi, *Survivor of Auschwitz* (New York: Touchstone, 1996, p. 160).

Neither Truth nor Reconciliation: Political Violence and the Singularity of Memory in Post-socialist Mongolia[1]

CHRISTOPHER KAPLONSKI

In the late 1980s, shortly before the democratic revolution of 1989–90, the Mongolian People's Revolutionary Party (MAHN), the ruling party under social-ism, began to allow public discussions of limited aspects of socialist-era political repression in *Ünen* [*Truth*], the party newspaper. Certain individuals, seen to have symbolic usefulness, were publicly rehabilitated.[2] Following the democratic revolution itself, political repression and its aftermath apparently have been freely discussed topics in Mongolia. In the mid-1990s, a museum commemorating the victims of the repressions opened around the corner from the Foreign Minis-try in downtown Ulaanbaatar, the capital. In 1996, 10 September – the night of the first mass arrests – was declared a day of commemoration by the government, who in 1997 unveiled a sculpture commemorating the victims of political repres-sion in front of the national history museum, next to the main government build-ing. After much debate, the *Ih Hural* [Parliament] passed a law on rehabilitating and compensating the victims of political repression in early 1998.[3]

Yet as I studied the issue of political repression and its aftermath over the course of a decade, starting in 1997 and continuing today, as I conducted inter-views and continued to read newspaper articles and books, and through daily conversations with a range of people, it became clear that, in many ways, political repression in Mongolia was a matter of deeply personal memory. It had the char-acter of a personal quest to find out what had happened to relatives who had disappeared decades earlier; it never developed into a more collective or social undertaking. Despite the apparent successes and openness alluded to above, there was a deeper ambivalence beneath the surface. It was easy to miss if you simply looked at what was publicly said and done by politicians, but once you stopped and listened, and more importantly, talked to people, it became clear that political repression was important, but only in certain ways and at certain times, all of which I argue reflect the personal nature of understanding political repression in Mongolia.

Most tellingly, despite the willingness – and it seemed at times, the need – for people to talk about what had happened to them or their relatives, Mongolia *as a society* never sought to come to terms with the political violence of the socialist period. People were willing to tell me what had happened to their relatives, and many were grateful that someone wanted to listen. Yet the museum to the victims of the repressions was chronically under-funded, and in informal surveys, most people could not tell me what the memorial sculpture in front of the history museum actually commemorated.[4]

As I reflected on this disparity, it struck me that the contexts in which issues surrounding political violence and its legacy were manifest were all ultimately linked to personal memory. Unlike South Africa or Chile, to give just two examples, the issue of political violence and how best to address it never spread into a wider social or political sphere. There was no Truth Commission, and far as I have been able to determine, one was never widely discussed. Lustration, the 'screening of bureaucrats and political leaders to ascertain who had collaborated with the Communist-era secret police', was apparently discussed, but quickly and decisively shelved.[5]

This is the question I ask in this paper: why have the memories taken on such a deep and personal character? Why have they not coalesced into a broader social narrative? In answering these questions, I also address the issue of why does Mongolia not have a truth commission and why has it chosen not to pursue the perpetrators of violence? Many of the conditions cited elsewhere (length of time passed, influence of the military, explicit negotiations between political parties, etc.) for avoiding the issue of political violence do not necessarily hold in Mongolia.[6] Mongolia is thus a theoretically interesting and important case because it argues that we need to pay attention to a completely different level than is often addressed in work on political repression.

While we cannot ignore the geopolitical context, which I will touch on here, to fully understand and appreciate the Mongolian case, we need to look to the realms of memory. I argue that the particularities of the Mongolian case can only be understood through a focus on the nature and importance of memory in different spheres of life in Mongolia. Specifically, the Mongolian case can only be appreciated by the realisation that there is what I call a surfeit of personal memory. For a number of reasons, there is a particular emphasis on personal memory at multiple levels in Mongolia. These reasons include not only state-sponsored suppression of public memory, but pre-existing concerns with the individual in the political realm.[7] In this particular context, I suggest that what have proven to be the key forms of memories dealing with repression are what I term 'singularities' – the points at which specifics overwhelm classification, where personal knowledge runs counter to the narrating of the event in a larger context.[8] These singularities remain the dominant form of remembering and talking about political violence in Mongolia. Singularities can encompass a variety of types of memories; I do not limit them here to mental recall. Body memory, spatial memory, mental recall and other associations may all be forms or types of singularities. The key contrast I am drawing here is the opposition and tension between a singularity and their incorporation into larger, over-arching – and, I argue, over-bearing – social narratives. I return to this distinction in more detail below.

Work on truth commissions and other means of 'coming to terms with the past' have largely taken the dynamics of memory for granted. Despite the free use of the term 'memory', even in the title of books the actual nature and function of memory remains largely unexplored.[9] While researchers have looked at competing narratives and issues of negotiated understandings of the past in their discussions of dealing with the legacy of political violence, the issue of the relationship of specific memories to the larger narratives remains unexplored.[10] The dynamics of how and why certain memories or events are recognised as important, how they are incorporated into or excluded from larger narratives of understanding and explanations, and, more fundamentally, how such memories and narratives interact, are seen as unproblematical. It is precisely these relationships and the ramifications they hold for broader understandings of the past that I am most concerned with here.

It is thus the topic of memory and narrative in general that I turn to next. I briefly lay out my argument in theoretical terms, highlighting the importance of what I term the singularity for understanding ways of remembering violence. I then move on to a discussion of the context of the political violence that took place in Mongolia, before turning to the specific ways in which the memories of violence have been manifested in Mongolia. Finally, I close by addressing the larger issues my work raises.

Memory, Events and Singularities

Allen Feldman, in his study of violence in Northern Ireland observes: 'The event is not what happens. The event is that which can be narrated. The event is action organised by culturally situated meanings'.[11] This distinction – between the event as narrative and the action which Feldman leaves unnamed, but which provides the material for the narration and I will call a *happening* – is what I draw attention to here. This distinction, often overlooked, is important to keep in mind. The narrative is not the memory. Although for most intents and purposes, memory/event as narrated is a palimpsest overwritten on the *happening*, in certain contexts, the *happening* remains accessible and relevant.

The philosopher Edward Casey has written of what he calls the 'quasi-narrative form' of many memories.[12] He uses this term, in part, to highlight 'the narrative-*like*, yet still not strictly narrative, nature of remembering'.[13] Casey here recalls us to a stricter understanding of narrative, narrative as story-telling, than the manner in which the term has often been used in academia of late.[14] This understanding is important in perceiving how memories differ from the larger narratives in which they are often embedded or through which they are encountered. A memory need have no beginning, middle or end, as narratives are want to. Casey also argues that they 'lack a distinct narrative voice'.[15] Casey does not particularly address the relationship between memory and narrative. It is a highly complex one, and one perhaps cannot fully separate out the two, as memories are understood and processed in terms of previous experiences and cultural norms. A recounting of a memory takes place in narrative form. Yet personal, particular, memory underlies the narrative that shapes and informs it. At times, personal memory even resists incorporation into larger narratives, for to incorporate it would be to extinguish it at some level. This, I argue, is what has happened in the case of political violence in Mongolia.

This memory that resists incorporation is what I have been calling the singularity – the overbearing of the personal at the necessary expense of a narrative constructed in the social spaces of a culture. It is this process, the transformation of the *happening* into the *event*, the enfolding of the singularity into the socially shared memory and narratives, that has not taken place in Mongolia. There is too much emphasis on personal memory for this to happen. The singularities themselves are too important for most people to lose sight of, to leave out of the individual, specific narration.

Veena Das, writing of the victims of the Bhopal disaster in 1984, has observed 'The more suffering was talked about, the more it was to extinguish the sufferer'.[16] As I read this passage, Das is reminding us that the more we talk about abstractions – suffering divorced from those who suffered – the more we lose sight of the people actually involved. The Mongolian case represents an acknowledgement of this, and the importance of specific memories set against more encompassing narratives is a reaction against extinguishing the memories of those who suffered and were killed.

For decades, all most people had to recall their relatives by were memories. These memories, furthermore, were often kept from children and relatives. They were not discussed even with other family members. The memories of individuals could not be constructed into even a modest family narrative, since the safest form of commemoration was silence. The sense of 'commemoration' as remembering or honouring a person was set against 'commemoration' as co-memoration, a shared act of memory.

At the time of the arrest, most property – including at times the *ger* (felt tent) itself, household items and children's toys as well as livestock – was confiscated. One man recalled that the men who arrested his father, after making an inventory of all their possessions, locked them in a chest (they would return later to take the items) and threatened to cut off the head of anyone who touched it. In a plaintive letter, a man who had been cleared of wrongdoing petitioned to have his confiscated property returned, listing 56 different items, among them, clothes, books, a tea kettle and a child's toy polar bear.[17] In such situations the specificities of the singularity are all that more important. When the state has undertaken an attempt at silencing, the retained memory itself takes on the status of a prized possession, and resists incorporation into larger, homogenising narratives.

As I noted above, all memory, including personal, is at some level shaped by narrative. At the most fundamental, a memory cannot be told without taking some form, without being narrated. Even a simple accounting of what happened is necessarily influenced by cultural understandings, literary tropes and expectations. A relatively straightforward statement: 'My father's brother was arrested in 1937' contains a number of cultural references and mediations. To cite only two, the category of 'father's brother' is a culturally constructed and socially loaded one, and even the verb 'arrest' calls into play cultural knowledge and linguistic expertise.

Yet I am contrasting personal memory here with what I will call 'social narrative' – the larger, overarching narrative that seeks to contextualise and explain *why* and *what*.[18] Why did the repressions happen? What were the larger issues that impacted the repressions? Personal memory, the singularity, is more concerned with *who*. It is the fact that it was *their* relative who was repressed that matters to a person. To some degree, these emphases are mutually exclusive. The construction of the social narrative necessitates a shift in emphasis from the singularity. It requires a form of forgetting. In organising the social narrative, a narrative constructed to talk about and understand what happened and why in structural or institutional terms, the specificity of the individual becomes suppressed. It is no longer 'my father's brother' who was repressed, but a person caught up in larger events who happened to be my father's brother. This is a significant shift, and one that is antithetical to how the victims of repression have been remembered and the repressions themselves often discussed in Mongolia. To a certain extent, the larger waves of repressions form a taken-for-granted background to individual stories of loss and suffering.[19]

Before I examine the ways in which these forms of memory have played out in the Mongolian case, and how this affects or inhibits the aims and goals of truth commissions and lustration, I outline the history of political violence in Mongolia. I then move on to a discussion of the ways and contexts in which political violence is talked about in Mongolia today before returning to underline the role of personal memory and the broader implications this contains for understanding the legacy of political violence.

The Destruction of the Old

Political violence in Mongolia remains perhaps one of the episodes of terror least understood and acknowledged by researchers of political violence. It is also largely neglected by scholars of socialism. As just one example, *The Black Book of Communism*, which claims to catalogue the atrocities of communism, completely ignores Mongolia.[20] Yet the destruction was overwhelming and almost inconceivable in scope. Aimed largely against the Buddhist clergy and Buryats – an ethnic minority accused of having been White Russian sympathisers during the Russian Revolution – the repressions were part of an attempt to not only consolidate the ruling Mongolian People's Revolutionary Party's hold on power, but also to destroy the old ways of life and belief. Prior to the socialist revolution in 1921, Mongolia had been a theocracy, ruled from 1911 to 1921 by the Eighth Javzandamba Hutagt, a high-ranking Buddhist reincarnation (often glossed as a 'living god'), and the Buddhist church continued to be a threat to the socialist government.[21]

Purges and politically motivated killings stretch back as far as the early 1920s, even before Mongolia officially became a People's Republic in 1924, but the vast majority of arrests and killings took place in a span of roughly 18 months, from September 1937 to the spring of 1939, closely paralleling the time frame of Stalin's Great Terror in the Soviet Union. For multiple reasons, the true number of people executed will never be known. Although many were arrested and prosecuted by tribunals, others were simply swept up as whole villages were cleared of their adult men, or herders were arrested simply to fulfil a quota. Extrapolating from fairly reliable lower estimates, based upon data from the Ministry of Internal Affairs (the secret police), D. Ölziibaatar, a historian of the repressions, suggests that about 35,000 people were killed during the period.[22] This figure, however, would not include those who were executed, but never officially tried. Other authors claim a higher number, one out of every eight adult males being killed.[23] This number, unfortunately plausible, translates into approximately 45,000 people being killed, at a time when the population of the entire country did not exceed 800,000 people.[24]

Coupled with the mass arrests and killings, the state moved against the Buddhist hierarchy. A large number of those killed were Buddhist lamas, and show trials were held against high-ranking lamas. These trials served to pave the way for further violence as well as to dissociate the people from the Buddhist hierarchy.[25] Excessive taxes were levied against monks and the monasteries, and tens of thousands of monks (by some estimates, close to 100,000 in all) were driven out of religious life during the 1930s. The destruction was levelled against material objects as well. The vast majority of Mongolia's more than 700 monasteries and temples were destroyed in the late 1930s, with only a handful surviving. Gandan, the main monastery in Ulaanbaatar, the capital, served for a time as the state archives and Dashchoilan monastery, only a few kilometres away, was turned into the headquarters and training grounds for the state circus.[26] Countless religious artefacts and other indicators of the 'old ways', such as family genealogies, were destroyed as well.

Political violence and repression were to continue throughout the socialist period, with another, smaller, wave of repressions taking place in the 1960s, although people continued to be arrested and charged for political reasons across the decades.[27] However, after the late 1930s, most of those repressed were sentenced to imprisonment and/or exile, rather than being executed. And while by no means excusing or justifying the repressions, it should be realised that most of those repressed after the 1930s were often victims of intra-Party political struggles, rather than people arrested for their occupational or ethnic backgrounds or simply at random. This made the later repressions a much more limited and, vitally, a delimited event. This ability to see them as a limited event was one of the reasons that publicly rehabilitating in the early 1990s the victims of the later repressions worked on a symbolic level. What had happened to them had limits and could be conceptualised, abstracted and remembered in a social context, the way the victims of the 1930s could not.[28] While it is clear that anyone could be – and was – arrested, the most prominent cases of the post-1930s years were limited to Party functionaries, arguably decreasing their random and unpredictable nature. With this in mind, I turn now to outline the ways in which the issue of political repression plays out in post-socialist Mongolia.

The Private in the Public

It is often – and no doubt accurately – said that every family in Mongolia has at least one repressed relative. The totality of the violence and the small population has assured that the impacts of political violence are not limited to a small section of society. At this level, political violence and its legacy are very important and immediate. As in other places across the globe, there is a need to know, a need not necessarily to understand why the violence happened, but simply what happened. There is a desire to understand what happened to one's relatives. Most people simply do not know. 'They showed my father a paper, and took him away' was a common description of the last time someone saw their relative. In the vast majority of cases, no further information was ever provided. While a few people seek to place blame for what happened to their relative, most do not. They simply want to know what happened, and in this context, it is irrelevant why it happened. In re-reading my interview notes, only a very few activists would bring up topics of blame and guilt without prompting. Even when explicitly asked, most people did not see much point in talking about such issues. It was the personal memory that mattered to them. (I see here certain parallels with the origins of the Mothers of Plaza de Mayo in Argentina. The organisation began as a result of mothers attempting to find out what had happened to their disappeared children. I do not want to draw the parallel too strongly, however, as the Mothers of Plaza de Mayo soon become a political force, which has not happened in Mongolia.) Very few people are interested in constructing narratives that draw in larger issues of responsibility and geopolitical justifications; they simply want to know what happened once their relative was taken away.

To illustrate the ways in which the private memory remains resistant to larger social narratives, I give two examples. The first involves a prominent public figure, a Prime Minister in the 1930s. This particular case is illuminating for the very reason that the most public guardian of his memory remained in many ways a private person.

P. Genden was a Prime Minister who was arrested and sent to Russia in the summer of 1937 and killed a few months later. Propaganda in the fall of 1937 implicated him in a number of counter-revolutionary plots. Although he was executed in November, 1937, this was never made public knowledge. While his family must have suspected what happened, they simply did not know for sure. At some level, hope remained. Nor did they know that Genden had, in fact, been rehabilitated in 1962. This was, for reasons unknown, never revealed until the opening up of Mongolian society and history in the late 1980s. Genden's daughter lived to find out what had happened, but his wife did not. The wife, I was told, had died in 1981, still waiting for her husband to return. Although G. Tserendulam, Genden's daughter, became a prominent activist and the founder of the museum dedicated to the victims of political repression, her anger and sorrow was more immediate, personal. Although an activist, she was not driven by larger issues – indeed, she derided another activist who did agitate for concrete steps to be taken against the ruling party during socialism as someone who did not understand repression and was only interested in money. Nor was she driven by a desire to seek revenge or compensation from MAHN, the ruling part at the time of the repressions. In fact, she was grateful to several key figures in MAHN who had helped obtain funding to establish the museum. She was interested in commemoration, not political activism. (I am here contrasting her concern with commemoration – remembering and acknowledging people – with a desire for political power or explicitly political ends. Commemoration is indeed a political act, but one that is agreed upon at some level by most public figures in Mongolia. It thus stands in contrast to more political goals in an instrumental sense.)

In the conversations I had with Tserendulam over the years, it seemed at times that her greatest sorrow and regret was that her mother had died not knowing what had happened. The contacts she had with other relatives of the repressed were all also deeply personal. She would constantly interrupt interviews I was conducting to reminiscence with the person I was talking to, or simply lend silent support by laying a hand on their shoulder. It was clear that, to her, the memory of the repressed relative was more important than legal action or similar steps.

The rehabilitation process in Mongolia was, in regard to personal knowledge and memories, both critical and deeply unsatisfying. It was critical in the sense that it served as an acknowledgement of a great wrong. The actual rehabilitation was an explicit recognition of a specific person and what had happened to him or her. It also provided a few additional scraps of information about the fate of a loved one. But it was deeply unsatisfying in that what information it provided was usually cursory. It is thus worthwhile to briefly examine this process.

The vast majority of people were not automatically rehabilitated; a relative (or potentially, a concerned stranger) had to apply to start the process. Only in a very few cases – those that the ruling party saw as having symbolic significance and use – were people rehabilitated at the instigation of the state. An application led to an investigation. Rehabilitation, even once initiated, was not guaranteed. The commission responsible for rehabilitation had to be satisfied by searches in various archives that a person had been in fact repressed – falsely accused.[29] The entire process was, in effect, an appeal. Indeed, at least one ruling exonerating victims that I am aware of notes that the plot they were accused of – a plan to overthrow the government – probably did exist, but that there is insufficient evidence to link the accused.[30] In this case, at least, the rehabilitated were not so much declared innocent, as 'not guilty' – an important legal distinction.

If the person in question met the criteria, an *ünemleh* [certificate] was issued. The certificate is physically small – less than 3 by 9 inches, although even this betrays the amount of white space it contains. The certificate simply states, in one long sentence with blanks to be filled in, that the person has been investigated and cleared. Others were more fortunate, and also received a page or two of sparse information on their relative, summarised from archival documents, which they themselves were not allowed to see. The amount of absolute information is pitiful. The preprinted text of the *ünemleh* merely reads:

> Upon inspection, _____, surnamed _____'s conviction in the year 19__ for a political crime was determined to be a false conviction and the ruling numbered ___ of ____ [day] of ____[month], 19__ of the Military College of the Supreme Court of the MPR [Mongolian People's Republic] invalidates [this conviction] and he is rehabilitated.[31]

Some people were keenly aware of this lack of information. A life had been taken unjustly, and all that they received was a slip of paper and a token sum of money.[32] Yet many people I talked to found some slight comfort in the fact that at last they knew something about what had happened. (Many, however, never knew the full details. The *ünemleh* merely admits that the person was repressed, not why. Many people to this day do not know the exact reason their relative was arrested.) There was sorrow in their voices when we talked, but seldom anger. It was the specific knowledge, however meagre, that mattered. People cried at the loss, but few expressed anger or a desire for revenge.

People were not interested in placing their relative in a larger political or geopolitical context. *Why* their relative had been killed did not matter. Most people were simply not interested in whether H. Choibalsan – the dictator of Mongolia at the time – was to blame, or if guilt should be placed on Stalin. Such topics did not come up unless I first raised the issue. Were the repressions an unstoppable force that rolled in from the Soviet Union, or where they a settling of scores by Choibalsan and the secret police? Just how much autonomy did Choibalsan and the Mongolian government have? These remain open questions, but to most people I talked to, they were also irrelevant ones. Such issues were too abstract. Intriguingly, when I asked about the issues of responsibility or guilt for the repressions, people answered in terms of specific individuals – either

Choibalsan or Stalin. There was not discussion of larger issues, and even the reduction of an entire system or state apparatus to a specific individual suggests to me the need to talk about what happened in terms that do not fit the patterns used in truth commissions and other ways of 'coming to terms with the past'.[33]

For 60 years people had lived with suppressed knowledge and memories. They knew their relative had been repressed, but could not talk publicly about this. In the 1990s, for some, the status of victim of repression (or relative of one) was almost a badge of honour – a claim to moral superiority.[34] Even here, to subsume the personal memory into a larger social narrative of impersonal causes and effects would, perhaps, be seen as diluting the claim to moral superiority, as it would suggest that the repressed person was a victim of circumstance, rather than repressed for particular reasons.

Under socialism to have a repressed relative was a mark of shame, one that could have tangible negative consequences, such as being barred from higher education or certain jobs. The memory of the repressed was thus kept private, suppressed, hidden from the public discourse. And this suppression of memory had very real implications, as is made evident in my other example.

For others – particularly those in the countryside – the situation was more complex. Manduhai Buyandelgeriyn, in an unpublished manuscript, has written movingly of the Buryats' search for answers to the misfortunes and difficulties of the post-socialist world.[35] In doing so, she argues convincingly that the very state suppression of memory that gives rise to *uheer* – a particularly virulent, unappeasable spirit – allows people to largely avoid the issues of responsibility for the violence through subscribing to the 'dominant rhetoric of protective nationalism'. In this view, the violence ultimately preserved Mongolian sovereignty. Through shifting the discourse to the geopolitical, and offering vague answers to Buyandelgeriyn's inquiries – all were victims, nothing could be done – people are responding to the state suppression of memory. Buyandelgeriyn also points out that people avoided explicitly placing blame and talking about the specifics of the violence because to do so would be to admit Mongolia's 'semi-colonial' status under socialism, and people's own powerlessness. In other words, the geopolitical context in which Mongolia existed, and in which it must continue to manoeuvre, has reinforced tendencies to avoid the construction of larger social narratives. Those narratives that are constructed, such as the overarching acceptance of the equation of *uheer* largely with relatives who died during the repressions, reinforce the singularity of the memory. The very problem is the lack of personal knowledge, of memories never transmitted.

These observations underscore the point I have been making. In not talking about the issue in order to deny their powerlessness, people are avoiding the larger issues of the social narrative. The memory remains personal and immediate. Answers are 'general and vague' not because people do not know, but rather they know too personally, and yet do not know enough. To the Buryats, even if not all of them know the fate of their relatives, the legacies of the repressions are real and immediate. *Uheer* – malevolent spirits – lurk everywhere, and forgotten ancestors bring curses and misfortune upon the living. There is no need – nor even, I would suggest, way – to create a larger narrative of memory when the personal memories exist as ancestors to bring misfortune and suffering. It is each ancestor/singularity that must be appeased, not some vague narrative of distant politicians. It is clear that it is the very inability to remember details that brings misfortune. Worshipping ancestors in general is not enough. Genealogies must be reconstructed, and it is only through getting the details right that (at least in theory) the misfortunes can be averted.

These two examples, of Prime Minister Genden's daughter and the Buryat's *uheer*, do not exhaust the range of experiences of the legacy of political repression. I next take up the political realm. Here I will limit my discussion to a rather narrow conception of the political. I am discussing politics as traditionally perceived – what is done by politicians, and what other people do in response to (or anticipation of) such actions – rather than the more expansive view usually taken by anthropologists. I do this as a shorthand to highlight how the issues under discussion are used by politicians, although I am aware such sharp bound-aries can not be sustained, particularly in a post-socialist society with little experi-ence of 'civil society'. The distinction between the social and political spheres made here is a highly artificial one, yet as a heuristic device and for the sake of clarifying my arguments, I retain the distinction.

In the political sphere, we begin to see the legacy of political violence wielded as a tool. Here we begin to see a shift in how the memories of violence are used, but it is important to observe that the type of memory people call attention to is still personal. Despite the political use, the larger social narrative has not been constructed and called upon. The legacy of political violence and the apportion-ing of blame have all been wielded for different, yet all ultimately political, ends. Yet rather than undermining the emphasis on the personal and individual nature of memory and repression, the ways in which political repression has been politicised reinforce it.

The Politics of Memory

Early drafts of the law on rehabilitating and compensating the victims of political repression (passed in 1998) included a few sentences apportioning blame. These were ultimately removed from the final version as MAHN – the ruling party under socialism – threatened to boycott Parliament, and bring the government to a halt, if the offending sections were left in. Yet the fact that they were there at all was an attempt to score political points by playing on people's memories of the repressions. In a similar manner, as already mentioned, even before the demo-cratic revolution, MAHN was distancing itself from the excesses of earlier years, publishing several pieces in *Ünen* ('*Truth*'; the MAHN party newspaper) on important people who had been repressed. In these articles, the full extent of the repressions was not addressed. Indeed, so important was the need to distance themselves that at the very Central Committee plenum that precipitated the hunger strike by protesters that led to the resignation of the government in March 1990, the Party still found time to publicly rehabilitate several people who had been repressed in the 1960s in two particularly famous incidents. The more general issues of repression, however, remained largely untouched. Even when alluded to, it was through a reference to individuals, such as the *Ünen* article, 'Repressed Buryat citizens: from workers' letters', which recounts the multiple stories of repression, but offers no commentary or larger context in which to place them.[36] It was not only the ruling party, however, who used the issue of repression politically. In early 1993, *Ardchilal* [*Democracy*], the newspaper of the Mongolian Democratic Party ran lists of the repressed, under the heading 'Memorial to the repressed' (*Helmegdegsdiin dursgald*). Less anyone miss the polit-ical intention of such a list, however, above the main title ran, in smaller type, the phrase: 'The red party's black sin' (*Ulaan namyn har hügel*), a clear reference to the role of MAHN in the repressions.[37] Yet again, the form that this political manoeuvre took is significant – they were lists of specific individuals, with information such as age, and on at least one occasion additional data such as ethnicity, profession and date arrested. The effect is to personalise the lists, to make what would otherwise be a mere list of names a list of people. One is invited to identify with them and their relatives, to imagine them as specific individuals, not merely statistics. Indeed, given the relatively small population and the importance of social networks and personal connections, it would be surprising if people reading the lists did not recognise at least a few names as belonging to relatives of friends and colleagues.

The use of political repression as a tool continues even up to the present. Ostensibly published in conjunction with the day of commemoration on 10 September (the date marks the first night of mass arrests in 1937), the 'Motherland – Democracy' coalition ran a photo of a recently uncovered mass grave of lamas. Across it was a headline: 'Don't forget … This repression shouldn't be repeated'.[38] Although no names were mentioned, none had to be. The fact that it was run by the coalition – whose name appears on the image – clearly marked it as being directed at MAHN. As much – if not more – than a commemoration to the victims of repression, the photo was an early shot in the Parliamentary elections that would follow in the spring of 2004.[39]

Despite possible appearances, what is happening with these examples is not the creation of social narrative. Rather it is the *utilisation* of personal memory.[40] In order for such tactics to function most effectively, the singularities must be present, and must remain as singularities. For the political tools to resonate with people, for them to be meaningful, the message they are conveying has to resonate at a personal level. Personal memories must be evoked. Abstractions, discussions of ultimate responsibility and structural constraints do not sway voters as well as reminders that the Party in power when your relative was killed would like you to vote for them. Or, conversely, that the Party has exhibited some remorse, and isn't really the same Party.[41] A similar action is suggested with the lists *Ardchilal* published in the early 1990s. To a certain extent, the publication of the lists was partly an explication, 'here's what happened'. It is, however, an explication at a very personal level. The lists are of individual names rather than discussions of geopolitical influences, or statistics of people killed. A discussion of geopolitical manoeuvring does not have the impact that calling to mind specific individuals does. My point here calls to mind a statement attributed, ironically, to Stalin: 'A single death is a tragedy; a million deaths is a statistic'. One does not feel towards a statistic the same way one feels towards a more personal story.

Individuals and the Social Sphere

If the political sphere represents the utilisation of personal memory, a making public of the singularity, we would perhaps expect to find something similar happening in the social sphere. This, however, has not been the case. Indeed, while there are exceptions, the legacy of political violence is largely absent from the social sphere. Even the exceptions highlight the individual and do not address the issue of a social narrative. There is a national day of commemoration, when politicians and various groups lay wreaths at a statue commemorating the victims of repression, and lamas read prayers for the dead at temples, but little else is done publicly. There is a Centre for the Rehabilitation of the Politically Repressed, but as Manduhai Buyandelgeriyn points out, it operates with little to no public or official support, and is tucked away, largely ignored, in the corner of an apartment building.[42] There is knowledge of at least the outlines of what happened, but little public discussion. And once more, the discussions focus on the victims, the memories of individuals as individuals.

In the early and mid-1990s, various politicians did apparently discuss opening the Ministry of Internal Affairs (secret police) archives, although this was never done.[43] I was told by some that this was because people felt that to do so would be too destructive. There is doubtless truth in this assertion. Given Mongolia's small population – today about 2.5 million people – the knowledge of who had spied and informed on whom would create deep fissures in Mongolian social relations. Yet there is more going on here than pure pragmatism. The answer must be sought, once again, in the singularity of personal memory.

Narrative, in this context, the creation of memory and events, is not 'one single code monolithically utilised, but ... a complex set of codes'.[44] It is more than chronology, a simple listing of events. '[A] narrative discourse performs differently from a chronicle'.[45] A narrative is a performance. Even if only recounted internally, a narrative has an audience, and shapes and is shaped by expectations and cultural understandings. This again moves us from singularities to the social narrative in a process of subsuming the particular under the general codes of the larger narrative. As noted earlier, to effectively include individuals in the social narrative, what is most unique about them must be downplayed or ignored. If one is to talk about the forest, you cannot dwell too much on particular trees. But precisely because this is what needs to take place, it has not. The emphasis remains on the individual. Most people are not concerned with whether or not ultimate blame rests with the Mongolian government of the time, the Soviet Union or a handful of specific individuals. To arrive at such conclusions – or even to consider them worthy of much debate – would require a depa deprivileging of the personal, and this is a yet another sacrifice people are unwilling or unable to make.

It is worth noting in this regard that the few people (only two or three) I have met who were not scholars but who have explicitly addressed the larger contexts are those who were victims of the later repressions. While at first this may seem counter to my argument on the importance of the singularity, it in facts reinforces what I am arguing. The victims of the later repressions were not killed.[46] They suffered arrest, exile and discrimination, but they remained alive. As people who themselves were arrested, they have no need to maintain the specificity of the memory of others. Their memories are memories of events that happened to them. While relatives of the victims of earlier repressions may have memories of the events, the singularities are of individuals. The transformation of a Buryat into an *uheer* may have been caused by an event or series of them (an execution, the inability to mourn), but the *uheer* – the singularity – itself is an individual. To subsume the memory of the individual into the larger social narrative is to risk losing a relative lost once already. No such risk exists for those drawing upon memories of their own experiences; their own physical existence is proof against the larger narrative.

This utilisation of the individual in the social sphere also carries through into the majority of what few books have been published on political repression in Mongolia. There are not many. Some, such as D. Ölziibaatar's *Yagaad 1937 on?*

[*Why 1937?*] deal with political repression in general, and examine the larger social narrative.[47] But these are swamped in numbers by various biographies, a particularly telling genre. Although still relatively few in absolute numbers, most publications dealing with political repression are biographies; that is, they deal with individuals. The focus remains on the personal. Some deal with only one individual, such as the series of short 'political biographies' published in the mid-1990s.[48] Others, such as the *Helmegdsen zaya* [*Repressed Fate*] series, are a collection of biographies under a single cover.[49] A more ambitious version of the collected biographies is the recent multi-volume *Uls töriin helmegdegsdiin namtryn tovchoon* [*Summary of the biographies of the politically repressed*].[50] This last project, like the political biographies, is explicitly labelled as a 'continuation' (*havsralt*) of the White Book, the official list of the repressed. Perhaps suggesting a reluctance to acknowledge the shear size of the repressions, the full White Book only resides in a few government offices and is not easily accessible to the general public.

Such collections, while drawing attention to the repressions, do so by underlining the impact of the repressions on individuals and their families. It is something immediate. They, like memories of political repression in the personal sphere, are a recital of singularities and happenings. What larger context is to be found in such works remains linked to the personal. The larger social narrative is invoked, but in the support of the personal. The social narrative is not wielded as an explanatory mechanism, but rather as stage-setting. The social narrative is relevant only to the extent that is impacts the individual. It is not the politics as such that matter, but that the politics led to a particular result. Such works, then, move specific individuals and what happened to them from the private realm to the public, but in doing so, they do not accomplish a similar translation from the personal to the collective realm.

Neither Truth nor Reconciliation

Truth commissions are predicated upon the idea that opening up the past for all to see, and foregoing vengeance or punishment, is the best way to further social reconciliation. Further, they assume that social reconciliation is the over-riding, most desirable goal. The individual subsumes his or her (possible) desires in terms of further larger social goals. The wounds must be cleaned and exposed to sunlight in order to heal. As David Crocker puts it, the chief virtue of truth commissions 'is discerning overall patterns, institutional context, and, to a lesser extent, the general causes and consequences of atrocities'.[51] This process requires a rethinking and subsuming of personal memory. 'Discerning overall patterns' and 'institutional context' requires that individual specifics are downplayed or ignored. Yet it is precisely the individual details that are all many Mongolians have to remember of their fathers, brothers and uncles.[52] It is the stark details – the knock at the door; the *chötgöriin gerel*;[53] how many soldiers were there; who carried rifles and who just sidearms; having to beg cups and a kettle for tea in the morning since the secret police had confiscated their own – that still seem sharp over seven decades of silence.

Truth commissions, policies of lustration and other approaches (for example, Poland's 'thick line' policy, which attempted to simply shut out the past) are, in Richard Wilson's terms, 'nation-building strategies'.[54] Such strategies require the singularity to be forgotten in favour of the social narrative.

> Truth commissions ... construct the national self with regard to the violent nation of the past rather than against other nations in the present, and they assert a discontinuity with the same past. The new national self is one which is forged in the suffering and violence of the past ... Truth commission hearings construct a new vision of the national self by inscribing the individual into a new national narrative on personhood.... Idiosyncratic and unique individual psyches disappear into the melting pot of a new official 'collective memory'.[55]

I am arguing here that Wilson's observation, while correct, is both too narrow and yet too encompassing. His comments about truth commissions and nation-building are merely a subset of the issue I am concerned with here. It is too narrow in that the issues of memory are broader than truth commissions alone. Similar questions are raised when considering if a policy of lustration should be pursued. Yet it is too broad in that it seems to assume all memory and identity processes are national and that the national level is the over-riding concern.

There are a number of intertwining reasons why Mongolia has not established a truth commission or pursued a policy of lustration. Some have already been mentioned – the pragmatics of a small population or Manduhai Buyandelgeriyn's reminder that geopolitics and shame at feeling powerless provided justifications for avoiding dealing directly with many aspects of the violence. Additionally, as I have argued elsewhere Mongolians have often historically employed the trope of exemplars – a model based on individuals – in the political imagination.[56] This also contributes to the privileging of the personal over the social narrative.

Yet even more fundamentally in this situation, the very attempts of the state to repress memory under socialism have encouraged the perpetuation of personal memory. Unable to construct large, sweeping narratives of social memory through open discussion under socialism, people were forced either to perpetuate memories in more subtle manners, or simply to preserve them as individual, specific memories.[57]

It is these memories – these singularities, where the individual overwhelms the social and that I have been exploring here – that are a key reason that Mongolia has not yet come to terms with the past as many other countries have done so. To construct a social narrative that would encompass larger issues would mean downplaying or denying the individual nature of the people who were repressed. To see your grandfather as one of 30,000 or 40,000 people who suffered a similar fate is to risk losing sight of him as an individual. This does not mean that people are incapable of understanding the larger contexts in which political violence took place. Rather, for most Mongolians it seems, the individual remains – for the time being at least – more important than larger discussions of geopolitical factors. Memory in all of its forms has been shaped around specific individuals and events.

It is often assumed that a failure to face the past will only lead to further social trauma and instability. As I already have noted, this is a fundamental working assumption of those that argue for truth commissions. Lustration works on a similar, if less explicit basis, invoking a necessary cleansing. Without lustration or truth commissions, wounds fester and sleeping dogs eventually awake. In an essay originally written almost 50 years ago, however, Adorno wrote '"Coming to terms with the past" does not imply a serious working through of the past ... It suggests, rather, wishing to turn the page and, if possible, wiping it from memory'.[58] Although he was writing of the German legacy of National Socialism, his observations are more widely applicable and worthy of notice. Adorno continues: 'One wants to be free of the past: rightly so, since one cannot live in its shadow, and since there is no end to terror if guilt and violence are only repaid, again and again, with guilt and violence. But wrongly so, since the past one wishes to evade is still so intensely alive'.[59] This first part is what truth commissions seek to pre-empt. Yet in doing so, they deny the 'intensely alive' past.

In the end however, for Adorno, to 'come to terms with the past' is to adopt the 'innermost principle' of the devil in Goethe's *Faust*: 'the destruction of memory'.[60] And this has one implication that cannot and should not be ignored. If this is the case, 'the murdered are to be cheated even out of the one thing that our powerlessness can grant them: remembrance.'[61] I thus close with a final observation: perhaps Adorno and the Mongolians have understood the core of dealing with the legacy of political violence better than most of us have: we must remember those who were imprisoned, exiled and killed. It is only through proper remembrance and commemoration that the *uheer* of Buyandelgeriyn's Buryats can finally find peace. Abstractions like reconciliation, social cohesion and understanding institutional contexts should be secondary. The best we can do is honour the dead by not forgetting them.

Notes

1. This paper is the outgrowth of reflections on fieldwork carried out since 1997. It is thus impossible to mention by name the various funders and numerous people who have provided information or informed my thinking on the general topic, but I am indebted to them all. Previous versions were given at the symposium, "Reckoning with the Past: Perpetrators, Accomplices and Victims in Post-Totalitarian Narratives and Politics", University of Wisconsin–Madison in April 2006 (which I was unable to personally attend) and New Directions in Post/Socialist Research Workshop, University College London in June, 2006. The participants in the latter provided useful comments. Rebecca Empson and Manduhai Buyandelgeriyn both offered helpful and insightful suggestions.
2. These figures usually were still alive, having been arrested in later waves of repression during the 1960s. For a discussion, see Christopher Kaplonski, *Truth, History and Politics in Mongolia: the Memory of Heroes* (London: RoutledgeCurzon, 2004), chap. 4.
3. For the debate, see Christopher Kaplonski, "Blame, Guilt and Avoidance: the Struggle to Control the Past in Post-socialist Mongolia" *History and Memory* 11/2 (1999), pp.94–114.
4. As I will return to below, the museum was largely the result of the work of one individual, Tserendulam, the daughter of a repressed Prime Minister. After her death, the museum was closed 'for renovations' for a few years. I was later told that there had been water damage due to a leak in the roof, and many of the museum's exhibits had been damaged or destroyed. When I visited the museum in the summer of 2006, the exhibition space was less than one-half what it had been in the late 1990s. By the summer of 2007, it had been re-expanded somewhat, and I was told that the damage had been intentional, not due to water damage.
5. Noel Calhoun, "The Ideological Dilemma of Lustration in Poland", *East European Politics and Societies* 16/2 (2002), pp.494–520 at p.494. At the present time, it is not possible to confirm this discussion. When I tried to get copies of the Parliamentary subcommittee minutes dealing with the issue, I was informed that they had been classified as secret and were unavailable.
6. I do not have the space here to examine all these issues, but I will raise two briefly. At first glance, the length of time since the greatest wave of repressions – 70 years – seems to argue that Mongolians have simply chosen to 'let sleeping dogs lie'. This, however, is not really the case. While this argument has indeed been raised by some, it is more significant that arguments against opening the archives and revealing publicly who had been informers for the secret police in fact run counter to this. Such secrets must remain secret precisely because they are too recent. Even if the perpetrators are dead, their children and grandchildren are still alive, and would suffer for the sins of their parents, the argument I heard time and again ran. It would also be possible to argue that the continuing influence of MAHN – the Mongolian People's Revolutionary Party, which has

been the single most dominant political party since 1990 – has precluded serious discussion of the issue. Certain elements seem to support this – the Party as a Party did not apologise until 2000, preferring instead to portray themselves as the greatest victim of the repression. Yet many people told me individually that at least N. Enhbayar – the current President of Mongolia and former Prime Minister – was sympathetic and helpful in a number of ways. As a key figure in MAHN throughout much of the post-socialist period, it seems he would have a vested interest in damping discussion and providing support. It is important to note, though, that it appears his support was at a personal and individual level.

7. See Christopher Kaplonski, "Exemplars and Heroes: the Individual and the Moral in the Mongolian Political Imagination", in David Sneath (ed.), *States of Mind: Power, Place and the Subject in Inner Asia* (Bellingham, WA: Western Washington University, 2006) pp.63–90.

8. I have chosen the term 'singularity' both with the intention to evoke somewhat the individual nature of these memories, but also another usage of 'singular', meaning 'remarkable' or 'unusual'. Additionally, the concepts of a singularity in physics and mathematics both imply a discontinuity or other 'special' aspect, which, while not strictly parallel, again hints at the nature of these memories when contrasted with more public narratives and memories.

9. For titles of books, see, for example, Alexandra Barahona de Brito, Carmen Gonzalez-Enriquez and Paloma Aguilar (eds), *The Politics of Memory: Transitional Justice in Democratizing Societies* (Oxford: Oxford University Press, 2001). These comments focus on the literature dealing with truth commissions and transitions from authoritarian regimes. Stern's work on Chile came to my attention only as I was finishing this article, and I have only been able to glance at it. I am unable to incorporate it here, but it appears to be an exception to my observation. See Steve Stern, *Remembering Pinochet's Chile: on the eve of London 1998* (Durham, NC: Duke University Press, 2006).

10. See for example, Sarah Nuttall and Carli Coetzee (eds), *Negotiating the Past: the Making of Memory in South Africa* (Cape Town: Oxford University Press, 1998).

11. Alan Feldman, *Formations of Violence; the Narrative of the Body and Political Terror in Northern Ireland* (Chicago, IL: University of Chicago Press, 1991), p.14.

12. Edward Casey, *Remembering: a Phenomenological Study*, 2nd edn (Bloomington, IN: Indiana University Press, 2000), p.43.

13. Casey (note 12), p.44.

14. Cf. Paul Ricoeur, *Memory, History, Forgetting* (Chicago, IL: University of Chicago Press, 2004) and Hayden White, *The Content of the Form: Narrative Discourse and Historical Representation* (Baltimore, MD: Johns Hopkins University Press,1987).

15. Casey (note 12), p.45.

16. Quoted in Vera Schwarz, "The Pane of Sorrow: Public Uses of Personal Grief in Modern China" *Daedalus* 125/1, pp.119–48 at p.120.

17. This list is drawn from a copy of a letter and list provided to me by the staff of the Museum for the Victims of Political Repression.

18. I use 'social narrative' in preference to 'national narrative' because, although the social narrative is often promoted by the nation and/or state in the interests of reconciliation or moving forward, it does not logically need to be allied to the state. Groups such as local communities are also capable of constructing social narratives.

19. I am indebted to Manduhai Buyandelgeriyn (personal communication) for suggesting the 'taken-for-granted' phrasing.

20. Stephane Courtois, Nicolas Werth, Jean-Louis Panne, Andrzej Paczkowski, Karel Bartosek and Jean-Louis Margolin, *The Black Book of Communism: Crimes, Terror, Repression* (Cambridge, MA: Harvard University Press, 1999).

21. I have transliterated this title from the modern, Cyrillic spelling of Mongolian, which more closely mirrors pronunciation. The title is often found as 'Jebtsundamba Khutuktu' in other sources.

22. D. Ölziibaatar, *Yagaad 1937 on?* (Ulaanbaatar: National Archive Office, 2004), p.294. Mongolians traditionally use only one name. An initial preceding it indicates the father's or mother's name, effectively a patronymic. Here I only use the initial the first time a name is mentioned.

23. D. Dashdavaa, *Manai Ulstöriin Helmegdegsdiin Ür Sadynhny Hohirol* (Ulaanbaatar: Urlah erdem, 2004).

24. Reliable demographic data simply does not exist for this time, but the population was between 750,000 and 800,000 in the 1930s.

25. Christopher Kaplonski, "Prelude to violence: show trials and state power in 1930s Mongolia", *American Ethnologist*, 35/2 (2008).

26. I am grateful to Ai Matsushima for reminding me of this latter point.

27. Scattered reports in the national historical archives make it clear that people were arrested for various political 'crimes' throughout most of the socialist period.
28. At a simple pragmatic level, there is the additional factor that the victims of the 1960s were, for the most part, still alive. This, however, was a double-edged sword, as accusations can be levelled as easily as gratitude expressed at the rehabilitation.
29. There are people who are ineligible for rehabilitation for unspecified reasons. One woman I know said her grandfather, who had been repressed but not killed, had been advised by both the military (he had been a commissar in the army) and the Ministry of Internal Affairs to seek his rehabilitation, but it was never granted. There are others for whom no documentation exists, leaving them in limbo. (The grandfather of my friend may well have been in this category, as the family was told that his files had disappeared.)
30. Decision Number 7 of the Supreme Court of the Mongolian People's Republic, 25 July, 1990.
31. The term I have translated here as 'rehabilitated' can also be translated simply as 'acquitted', highlighting the quasi-legalistic nature of the process.
32. The law passed in 1998 specified 1,000,000 *tögrög* – about $1000 at the time – for those who had been killed, and half of that amount for those who had been arrested. People who were rehabilitated before the law was passed sometimes received even smaller sums of money.
33. One could argue that this is merely a stylistic device – when one says 'Stalin' the entire Soviet system should be understood. This is a possible reading, but even the choice of such a device is, to me, telling.
34. See Christopher Kaplonski, "Morality and Violence: the Limited Good Revisited", paper given at the American Anthropological Association annual meetings, November 2003.
35. Manduhai Buyandelgeriyn, *Tragic Spirits: Shamanism, Socialism, and the Neo-liberal State in Mongolia* (Chicago, IL: University of Chicago Press, in press).
36. "Buriad irgediig helmegdüülsen n': hödölmörchdiin zahidlaas" *Ünen* 108/17325, 6 May 1989, p.4.
37. See "Helmegdegsdiin dursgald" *Ardchilal* 2/112, January 1993, p.2 and "Helmegdegsdiin dursgald" *Ardchilal* 7/117, March 1993, p.2.
38. In *Önöödör*, 212/1950, 9 September, 2003, p.2
39. Manduhai Buyandelgeriyn reports that this was made by the Center for the Rehabilitation of the Politically Repressed (personal communication). Even if this is the case, it remains significant that the research centre is not acknowledged, while the political coalition is. Indeed, this calls attention to the political intent all the more strongly.
40. I do not think that this was necessarily consciously designed to evoke such responses. Rather, I think the effect is symptomatic of the more general emphasis on singularities at the expense of broader social narratives.
41. This, in fact, underlines a repeated refrain from MAHN. They could not be guilty of the repressions since so many of the people killed were Party members. Surely they wouldn't repress themselves? In other words, we too suffered and were victims, just like you.
42. Buyandelgeriyn (note 35).
43. Indeed, from what I have been able to determine, the actual case files are apparently still classified as state secrets, and are to be treated as so for a period of 150 years.
44. White (note 14), p.41.
45. White (note 14), p.42.
46. It is widely believed that Tömör-Ochir, a Central Party member repressed in 1962, was killed by the security forces in 1985. Yet even if true, my point remains that – as far as I have been able to document – no one arrested and sentenced for political reasons was sentenced to death after the 1940s.
47. Ölziibaatar (note 22).
48. See for example S. Ichinorrov, *Dansranbilegiin Dogsomyn uls töriin namtar* (Ulaanbaatar: Mongolyn Shinehen tüüh, hünii erh sudlalyn töv, 1997).
49. See for example, B. Myagmarjav, Ts. Navagchamba and A. Dashnamjil, *Helmegdsen Zaya 17* (Ulaanbaatar, Mongolian Association of the Politically Repressed, 2000).
50. M. Rinchin, *Uls töriin helmegdegsdiin namtryn tovchoon* (Ulaanbaatar: Tsagaatgah Ajlyg Udirdan Zohion Baiguulah Ulsyn Komissyn Dergedeh Uls Töriin Talaar Helmegdegsdiin Sudalgaany Töv, 2004), three volumes.
51. David Crocker, "Truth Commissions, Transitional Justice, and Civil Society", in *Truth vs. Justice: the Morality of Truth Commissions*, Robert Rotberg and Dennis Thompson (eds) (Princeton, NJ: Princeton University Press, 2000), pp.99–121, at p.101. Richard Wilson argues that most truth commission reports 'did not write a serious structural or historical account' that incorporated a 'wider analysis of the causes of motivations of political violence'. Richard Wilson, "Anthropological studies of

national reconciliation processes", *Anthropological Theory*, 3/3 (2003) pp.367–387, at p.369. I would argue, however, that Wilson's recognition that 'new democratizing political elites went a step further than establishing salient truths about state terror' is akin to my distinction between the singularity and the larger social narrative (*ibid.*).

52. Although I have never seen hard statistical evidence, it appears that women were only a tiny fraction of those killed. My fieldnotes from 1999 note that, according to one display in the Museum for the Victims of Political Repression in Ulaanbaatar, '12 women (possibly 72?)' were killed. The same display listed about 21,000 people shot. While low, this figure probably represents the documented executions at the time of the display.

53. 'Devil's light' – a term some people used to refer to the flashlights wielded by the arresting officers, since flashlights were still uncommon in Mongolia in the late 1930s.

54. Wilson (note 51), p.369.

55. Wilson (note 51), p.370.

56. Kaplonski (note 7).

57. Kaplonski (note 2), pp.190–94.

58. Theodor Adorno "What does Coming to Terms with the Past Mean?", in Geoffrey Hartman (ed.), *Bitburg in Moral and Political Perspective* (Bloomington, IN: Indiana University Press, 1986), pp.114–129, at p.115.

59. Adorno (note 58).

60. Adorno (note 58), p.117.

61. Adorno (note 58).

Raising Sheep on Wolf Milk: The Politics and Dangers of Misremembering the Past in China

EDWARD FRIEDMAN

> A society of sheep must in time beget a government of wolves. (Bertrand de Jouvenal)

Overview

Mao Zedong died in 1976. By 1977–8, victims of Mao's purges, led by Deng Xiaoping, had taken state power. They knew that policies since 1949 had brought China a catastrophe. At least 35 million innocent people had died.[1] Since Mao had seized the reins of power, the poor villagers in his Yanan guerilla base area had experienced economic stagnation and decline. They were actually better off before the CCP conquered state power. Deng would abandon Maoist economics, dismantle parts of the Stalinist state, and open China up to the dynamism of the world economy. China would again become a great power. But the new rulers felt a need to embrace some of Mao's legacy to stabilise their hold on power. Might that choice again produce wolfish consequences?

Mao as Legitimiser

From 1977 Chinese party leaders, their aides and think-tank advisers deliberated on whether to reveal Mao's extraordinary crimes. The leaders and their assistants had family or friends who had suffered horrors as a result of Mao's wave after wave of crimes against humanity, people who were tortured, crippled, driven mad or died as a result of state policies that were legitimated in phrases such as 'leniency to the wolf is death to the sheep'. After prolonged debate, the CCP leaders decided to be soft on Mao, who they surely knew had acted as a wolf and taught the Chinese to act as wolves. Revealing Mao's crimes, however, would also expose his successors' roles as henchmen; Deng had led a 1957–8 anti-rightist purge to destroy a half million or so democratic persons who believed the Chinese would suffer less if the political system were democratic.

One hallmark of Maoism was that popular vigilantism, rather than a bureaucratically centralised secret police, was the preferred state instrument for controlling, crushing and doing away with purported class enemies, the real political targets. That meant that an unusually high number of Chinese had hands steeped in blood. The Deng regime committed itself to ending vigilante movement politics. The result would be a political transition to a system that worked something like a combination of Kadar's Hungary, an economically polarised Mexico under authoritarian PRI presidentialism and rapidly industrialising South Korea under military dictatorship.

But China's new ruling groups, in opening the country up to the world economy – seeking foreign investment, joint ventures and foreign tourist dollars – deprived post-Maoist rulers of the Mao era legitimation of anti-imperialist nationalism. The regime needed world market benefits but worried about its survivability if it lost the legitimacy of a passionate nationalism. It chose to bask in Mao's aura, keeping the dead tyrant's portrait hanging in Beijing's Tiananmen Square and building a mausoleum in the Square to display the embalmed corpse of a mass murderer, presented as the leader who re-united China, took China's seat on the UN Security Council and made China a nuclear power, a leader who was a great Chinese patriot.

The Deng regime defined itself as socialist which, to the rulers, meant, first and foremost, legitimating a Leninist party's monopoly of power as in 'the people's' interest, in contrast to a bourgeois democracy, which supposedly served the interests of the enemies of 'the people'. Chinese would learn to say that a democracy brought Hitler to power, a leader who discredited the nation. While abandoning Mao's view that Khrushchev's few, feeble economic reforms did more damage to socialism than had Hitler, Deng was anxious about political reform in Gorbachev's Russia, which seemed to open a Pandora's box, unleashing the loss of superpower status for the nation, the end of a colonial incorporation of non-Russian peoples, and a fall from power of the Communist Party. Consequently, post-Mao leaders treated an opening to democracy as an ultimate evil, a danger to the dictatorship which could return the nation to global glory.

The Imperative of Anti-Japanese Nationalism

This post-Mao CCP need to delegitimate a democratic alternative to an authoritarian single party dictatorship also produced a commitment to foster a nationalism[2] that could trump popular yearnings for democracy. The CCP would be presented as saving the innocent Chinese people from the inherently aggressive Japanese. The core patriotic passion ignited, starting around 1981–2, was hatred for the Japanese.

That CCP policy switch ended Mao's policy of détente with Japan which had begun in 1972. Mao had courted Japan as a partner against the USSR. Mao had not demanded reparations for Japan's crimes and devastation in China. He had responded to private Japanese apologies for the massive crimes against humanity committed in China from 1937 to 1945 by Hirohito's imperial military by saying that he, Mao, actually should thank the Japanese because, without their invasion of China, Mao's CCP could never have conquered state power. Even earlier, while Mao's civil war opposition, the National Party led by Chiang Kai-shek, had executed numerous Chinese for collaboration with Hirohito's invaders, Mao's CCP had not. Mao's CCP also blocked those Japanese who sought access to Chinese materials so that they could discredit holocaust deniers in Japan. As he wooed American President Richard Nixon, so Mao courted Japan's conservative ruling party. He would not embarrass it.

Mao promoted friendship with Japan. Alternative views were suppressed; 'Historical problems were treated as just history'. The view was that 'The Japanese people are good. Only a small clique of militarists were reactionary. Into the beginning of the 1980s, no nastiness toward Japan was allowed to undermine a "honeymoon" atmosphere'.[3] That all ended in 1981–2 when the Deng regime chose to bask in Mao's aura, and promoted a new nationalism to destroy the depiction of a friendly Japanese people by mobilising anti-Japanese passions in China that Mao had mostly suppressed.

Given these two major policy decisions of the post-Mao regime led by Deng, both to hide the enormity of Mao's crimes against the Chinese people and also to hype and revive consciousness of the enormity of Hirohito's crimes against the Chinese people, this study explores the impact on Chinese politics and policy of what was to be misremembered and what was to be remembered. CCP leaders tend to believe that the compromises hammered out soon after Mao's death, in 1977–81, have facilitated relative political stability for the ruling CCP, extraordinary economic growth for the nation, and a happy return to global power for China.

Actually anti-Japanese nationalism was not quite new. While a racialised Han nationalism goes back to the late Qing era struggle against the Manchu monarchy and for a Han-dominated Republic of China (ROC), an anti-Japanese core to Han Chinese racism had grown in the Kuomintang (KMT) era of resistance to Japan. The KMT saw nearly 60 per cent of the ROC as territory dominated by non-Han peoples – Manchu, Mongol, Tibetan, Turkic, etc. – who were susceptible to Japanese appeals to 'cast off Han oppression'. In response, KMT racist theorists claimed that since ancient times, going back to the pre-historic Yellow Emperor, the Chinese race had infused all these other people. Contemporary Han modernisers headed a Chinese blood-bound family with ancient roots. Great scholars such as Gu Jiegang, who argued against worship 'of the "idol of race"' lost out, although many tended to agree that 'the virility of the frontier minorities' could strengthen Han blood. 'Chinese consanguity was transformed into official policy'. Only traitors who did not care about 'the loss of the state and the extermination of the race', supposedly would not welcome this blood racism which needed to be invigorated by the feral non-Han.

Although Mao's internationalism had abjured this racism, and although he outlawed worship of the Yellow Emperor, the post-Mao 'PRC discourse on national unity remains the same' as in the KMT era.[4] Consequently, post-Mao historiography has elided the pro-Japan, anti-Han behaviour of non-Han peoples[5] and celebrated non-Han Manchu expansionism starting in the seventeenth century, which doubled the size of the previously Sinified Ming empire, 'as consolidating the "national unity" of China'. The expansionist post-Mao racism, which continues and intensifies the KMT's fascist racism, is 'anti-Japanese historiography'. A racist anti-Japan narrative is a 'fabrication' whose 'significance lies in discouraging minorities from resisting [Han] settler colonialism and in encouraging them to develop friendships with their [Han] oppressors and colonisers, ignoring, that is, the history of [Han] oppression'. Resistance to Han 'colonization becomes treason'.[6]

This study depicts how the post 1977–81 policy consensus fed the Chinese people wolf milk, with the political target being first and foremost the Japanese people, portrayed as uniquely evil enemies of a singularly victimised Chinese nation – sheep. Chinese compete to prove themselves patriots who stand up to even imagined slights to the national escutcheon such as denouncing a Chinese actress who kissed a Japanese actor in a film, or refusing to eat crawfish because crawfish supposedly ate Chinese who were killed by the Japanese and then dumped in rivers in the 1930s. A dangerously vengeful racism had been unleashed. Hence when, in spring 2006, a Chinese student at MIT came across a university website with an email address with a Japanese-sounding surname on which pictures were posted on Meiji history during the 1894–5 Sino-Japanese war, his rage exploded. Basically what had angered him were two depictions of Chinese soldiers being defeated by Japanese soldiers, whose accompanying text actually carefully deconstructed and exposed Meiji state propaganda that legitimated the wartime killing.

The Chinese student, nonetheless, rose up to denounce a 'F—king Jap who thinks killing Chinese is beautiful'. Many Chinese demanded that the web site be taken down, that the person with the Japanese-sounding name be fired (even though the text was written by John Dower, a Pulitzer Prize winning historian famed for showing how states use racist stereotypes to get their people to hate and kill other people). Chinese blogs and newspapers spread the distorted story. Death threats were phoned in and emailed to the two MIT scholars. It became a police case. Even nastier anti-Japanese expressions of racist hate have been manifest in China, from north to south.

The Path not Taken

Since many tens of millions had suffered so cruelly from Mao's crimes against humanity, and since CCP members themselves had suffered and then debated how to respond to Mao's crimes, voices emerged in China that insisted on the political importance of remembering the truth about the ruling party's crimes. Literature was published exposing these massive abuses of basic human rights, known as Wound Literature or Scar Literature. Xu Liangying, a respected historian of Einsteinianism in China, called for a museum to remember the crimes and victims of the 1957–8 anti-rightist campaign – democratisers and pro-democracy political parties. Ba Jin, one of China's most famous writers, supported by Feng Jicai, a younger author, called for a museum to remember the crimes of Mao's decade-long, 1966–76, Cultural Revolution (CR). Ba Jin's wife had died in the CR after being denied medicine. Ba Jin, it was said in the CR, 'deserves to die ten thousand deaths'.

Castigating himself for prior cowardice and mendacity, Ba Jin's writings highlighted the 'self-abasement and mutual slaughter' of the CR. Worried that many Chinese acted as both sheep and wolves, he called for truth and repentance embodied in a CR museum.[7] His goal was that China be 'spared another holocaust'. In the Mao era, CR activists were more likely to be rewarded if acting 'rapacious as a wolf and savage as a cur'.[8] The purpose of 'a CR Museum' was 'to leave a monument to the harrowing lessons of the past', so that Chinese could 'see clearly' and 'remember fully' 'terrifying events', 'degradation and torture', 'violent and ruthless murders'. 'Only by remaining mindful of the CR will people be able to prevent history replaying itself'. 'It is extremely important that we build this Museum, for only by remembering the "past" can we be masters of the "future"'.[9]

China is not unique in not building a museum to remember the ruling party's crimes against the people. In comparison to other former Leninist states, clearly the CCP regime has not done as well as those that have democratised. Neighbouring democratic Mongolia has rehabilitated and compensated victims and built a museum to tell the story of Stalinist repression. Lists of victims have been published. Photographs of atrocities have been circulated. But Mongolia did not have a truth commission, an opening of archives, and trials for the executioners. Victims can still feel ignored, forgotten and stigmatised.

Post-trauma Cambodia has erected memorials to the victims of the mass slaughter of the Khmer Rouge dictatorship. But this occurred because Vietnam invaded Cambodia, toppled Pol Pot, and sought evidence to discredit the Khmer Rouge mass murderers.

One could conclude, however, that in comparison to neighbouring Vietnam or North Korea, which have not democratised, authoritarian China has done better in confronting the crimes of the Mao era. There have been rehabilitations and some compensation. Fiction and biographies of the era of mass repression have been published. There has been at least some discussion of a memorial museum, and even of removing Mao's picture and corpse from Tiananmen Square.

But in China, as in Mongolia and other countries which have left a traumatic era for a more normal politics, people do not want to be thought of as having been stupid dupes or monstrous criminals for their behaviour in the Leninist era. Therefore, it is not easy to honestly explore the previous, traumatic era. Indeed, late 1970s stories of suffering Chinese sheep who were victimised were quickly replaced by a literature that lionised those Chinese who had volunteered for Mao's campaigns. Rather than being wolves with blood dripping from their fangs who had done evil, they were re-imagined as people with high ideals, comrades who sacrificed themselves to make China a better place.

Such a consciousness rejected an image of Mao and the Cultural Revolution as bloody wolfishness. Mao's 'Leap' famine, which cost the lives of at least 30 million innocent Chinese, mostly poor villagers, became thought of as a test of character in which Mao measured up. He shared weal and woe with the Chinese.[10] Young people who, under pressure, 'volunteered' to serve in the poorest countryside, were not imagined as dupes or wolves or victims. They became idealistic heroes.

In the post-Mao era, the hunger of the three bad years following Mao's murderous Leap, was commemorated in new Mao-style restaurants, a feature of the new commodity culture. Adorned with memorabilia to induce nostalgia, these Mao nostalgia restaurants offered customers well-prepared food mimicking the poor food of the era of mass hunger. Ignoring the actual 'ubiquitous' subsequent suffering of urban youth sent to the countryside in the CR, which Mao had acknowledged, the 'numerous crimes of assault, illegal imprisonment, and rape of rusticated youth',[11] the Chinese now focused on, 'memories of ... eating communally and ridding themselves of bourgeois liberalism'.[12] Family separation caused by arbitrary and unaccountable CCP power was remembered as the 'idealism' of a 'self-denying generation'.

The post-Mao CR theme restaurants serve as 'mini-museums'. They produce wistfulness for a time of ideals. This 'revolutionary chic' is made 'possible by a national-level accounting that alternately posits the CR in 'excessively romantic' terms, or as a period of loss and chaos, or nearly pretends it never happened'. In short, 'Nobody is telling the next generation what the CR was all about'. Instead of exploring how Mao's policies and commitment to power starved 30 plus million Chinese to death in his Leap era famine, customers are told about Mao's 'simple eating habits'. Yet one nostalgic Mao restauranteur contends that his restaurant partially fulfills Ba Jin's wish for a holocaust memorial, somehow reminding customers 'not to commit the same mistakes'.

CR era rusticated youth, now doing well, build connections at these eateries and remind each other of how wonderful they were in surviving Mao era hardships. They imagine themselves as having 'worked hard to help China'. They, supposedly in contrast to today's rural poor, developed character and entrepreneurial talents. They, in contrast to today's suffering poor, deserve their wealth.[13]

With a government promoting lies about the CR, by the 1990s the Mao era was increasingly looked at as a time 'of hard work, shared sacrifice and dedication'. Whatever the suffering, the experience 'built character'. The virtues developed could be harnessed for entrepreneurial efforts. Formerly sent-down youth remembered their efforts as 'meaningful'. Others knew the volunteers did no good in the backward countryside and were grateful to the post-Mao leaders for at least bringing them back from the poor rural areas. Most were either nostalgic or uncritical.

Writer Feng Jicai, who had promoted building a museum to memorialise the victims of the CR, inveighed against the nostalgia as an uncritical emotion which took a bad thing and treated it 'as beautiful … This is a very frightful and terrible thing … That the Cultural Revolution didn't go into a museum, but first went into restaurants, is a great tragedy for the Chinese'.[14] The popular post-Mao discourse obscures the wolfish behaviour that Feng, Ba Jin and Xu Liangying believed needed to be confronted so that the Chinese people would never again behave as sheep and wolves. No one would remember a question asked of prospective CR era red guards, 'Got enough guts to beat the shit out of people?'[15] Indeed, by the twenty-first century, some Chinese New Leftists still saw a great power China as too weak and too conciliatory to its neighbours to possibly seek a future of Han wolfishness. But against whom? Only Japanese?

Xu Youyu a professor of philosophy at the Chinese Academy of Social Sciences found that, 'young Chinese have no memory of the horrors of the CR. Nor are they allowed to remember'. Peking University history professor Yin Hongbiao worried. 'If younger people lack education about this then such extreme behavior could reappear'. A former Beijing Red Guard leader, Li Dongmin, agreed. 'If people cannot speak out, then one day China could explode again'. Social critic Liu Xiaobo agreed that the cover up and the lack of remorse were fostering a 'social crisis' that makes it difficult 'to avoid the repetition of this type of tragedy'.[16]

Saving the Chinese People

After the 1977–81 debates and decisions, anti-Japanese racism spread all over China. 'More and more Chinese people have come to hold belligerent emotions about the entire Japanese nation'. Indeed, 'assertive nationalism now underpins the communist regime's legitimacy'. The Hirohito era invasion of China was 'attributed ... to the Japanese national character and traditional culture'. The 'entire Japanese nation ... was brutal, aggressive, and unrepentant'. Since 'Japanese had no conscience but only greed and barbarism', 'To be a hero is to fight the Japanese'.[17]

In all walks of life the Chinese competed to prove themselves as the most anti-Japanese. A quality inspection official demanded, 'Have there been any complaints directed against Sony or Matsushita? Get everything you have on them – tvs, fridges, sound systems, the lot. We need all the evidence we can muster because the focus is on Japan at the moment, and we have to give it to them good'.[18] At colleges, on web sites, in films, at football matches, in the press, Chinese invented Japanese insults to incite Chinese rage, leading, in 2005, to a slew of anti-Japanese race riots.

Of course, actual Japanese atrocities from 1931 to 1945 and pre-1981 anti-Japanese nationalism in Mao era China provided plenty of kindling for the post-1981 fires of hatred. Mao's Red Army sang, 'Don't forget your hatred of Japan'. CCP propaganda presented its civil war against Chiang Kai-shek's Nationalist Army as a patriotic struggle against the Japanese, claiming that 'Chiang Kai-shek did not lift a finger against them'. The CCP had declared that 'it cannot allow the Nationalist traitors to pawn the whole of China; it cannot tolerate the wholesale butchery and rape of the Chinese people by Japanese Imperialists'.[19] Actually, while local guerrillas tied to the CCP did nip and bite at the heels of Hirohito' military, almost all the fighting by regular armies against the invaders from Japan was actually carried on by Chiang Kai-shek's Nationalists and other non-CCP military forces. According to Oxford's Steve Tsang, a leading historian of the Chinese military, in the entire war, from 1937 through 1945, the Red Armies destroyed less than 100 Japanese tanks and armoured vehicles. The one time that Nationalists and Communists cooperated against Hirohito's military, the major Nationalist effort was written out of CCP history texts. Zhongshan (Sun Yat-sen) University Professor Yuan Weishi got into trouble in 2006 for pointing this out.

While Mao in power primarily attacked counter-revolution, the basic crime of the counter-revolutionaries had been portrayed as allowing Hirohito's military to conquer, occupy and pillage China. The Museum of the Chinese Revolution established in 1961 in Tiananmen Square had two purposes, 'To legitimize the CCP's rule' and to highlight 'the pivotal role played by Mao'. Since 1961, the museum in Tiananmen 'exudes a strong sense of nationalism', highlighting 'struggles against foreign aggression', especially Japan's.[20]

Families told their children of Japanese atrocities. Red Guards, during Mao's CR, were shocked to learn that Mao had thanked the Japanese for invading China, facilitating thereby the conquest of power by Mao's CCP. Anti-American sentiment was raised to white-hot levels in the postwar era by treating the Americans as promoting Japanese revanchism.[21] During the CR, Han Chinese protected historical treasures against rampaging Red Guards out to destroy so-called feudal relics by asking the marauding youngsters not to repeat the anti-Chinese crimes of Hirohito's imperial military. Post-1981 anti-Japanese racism in China had reagents to work from.

> Chinese school textbooks in the 1950s–60s praised the CCP as the sole leader of the 'Great Chinese War of Resistance Against Japanese Aggression' and highlighted the heroism of the CCP-led resistance campaigns ... they accused the KMT of kowtowing to and actively

collaborating with the Japanese aggressors, blamed the U.S. for conniving with the Japanese.[22]

Although CCP rulers in the post-Mao era are, at times, willing to acknowledge that Chiang Kai-shek's Nationalist armies did fight the Japanese, the CCP concedes this in order to legitimate that Taiwan, the island 100 miles off the coast of Mainland China to which Chiang fled with his defeated army, is part of an anti-Japan China. The popular narrative still held, however, is that the 'Chinese Communist Party was the hope of the Chinese people for national salvation'. 'China's role in defeating Japan was, in fact, greater than America's', Chinese believed. 'The Chinese people were *the key* determining influence in defeating Japanese influence'.[23] Such a popular narrative allowed PRC President Hu Jintao, in September 2005, commemorating the sixtieth anniversary of the surrender of Hirohito's Imperial military which brought World War II to an end, to tell a national television audience how Mao's Communists defeated Japan. 'By winning the War of Resistance against Japanese aggression, the Chinese people thoroughly foiled the attempts of Japanese militarists to destroy China'.

Japan's surrender actually occurred on the U.S.S. Battleship Missouri. It was presided over by U.S. General MacArthur who led the coalition that actually defeated Hirohito's military. That historical basics, the defeat of fascist Japan by a coalition largely of democracies, are forgotten 'seems aimed at buttressing the legitimacy of the CCP's power'.[24] What is commemorated and what is forgotten are very political decisions, 'Chinese nationalism is essentially a state nationalism sponsored and manipulated by its party-state'.[25] The propaganda message is that the concentrated power of the CCP is the only salvation of the Chinese people.

Remembering an Atrocious Japan

By 1982, and then with renewed energy after the 4 June 1989 CCP massacre in Beijing of supporters of a nationwide democracy movement that had been headquartered in Tiananmen Square, the CCP chose to trump democracy by revving up nationalism, especially anti-Japanese nationalism. In the post-Mao era, the number of museums in China grew from a couple of hundred to a couple of thousand. Their focus has been to glorify the CCP and remember national humiliations. This is not new.

In the post-Mao era, after the 1977–81 debates and decisions, Japan is the main target of war museums and memorials all over the country, in Shenyang (the September 18 History Museum),[26] the Memorial Museum of the People's Resistance to Japan, Shanghai's Longhua Martyrs Memorial Park, the Nanjing Massacre Memorial Hall, two museums on the 1894–5 Sino-Japanese War in Weihai and the Unit 731 Crimes Museum in Heilongjiang,[27] which exhibits near life-size portrayals of Japanese atrocities. As memorialised, Chinese are but victims and martyrs.[28]

The most famous memorial commemorates the victims of the Nanjing massacre of December 1937 to January 1938.[29] Mao had actually not mourned these dead. Apparently, to Mao, Nanjing was essentially the capital of the counter-revolutionary enemy, Chiang's Nationalist Government. The innocents murdered in Nanjing were, from a Leninist–Stalinist perspective, enemies of the Chinese people. Mao never bemoaned the death of any opponents of his revolution, so-called counter-revolutionaries. The post-Mao recognition of the victims of

Nanjing as part of the Chinese nation reflected a shift from Mao's promoting of class war to his successors' promoting of a strong China. The new project required a new nationalism. Even Mao era class enemies could become patriotic heroes in the post-Mao era, that is, if they killed Japanese. So it was in Yu Hua's 1992 novel, *Death of a Landlord*. In the story, a landlord family member, a person in the Mao era who was the worst of exploiters of the Chinese people is lionised for sacrificing his life to guarantee the death of purportedly subhuman Japanese soldiers.[30]

A Chinese writer, Chen Shoumei, using the pen name Ah Long, served as an army officer defending against the Imperial Japanese military in Shanghai, the prelude to the march on Nanjing of Hirohito's Imperial Army. Chen was wounded. He eventually evacuated to the Red Army's headquarters in Yanan where, in 1939, he wrote novel-style reportage about Chiang Kai-shek's National Army's preparations to defend Nanjing. Titled *Nanjing*, Chen's work won a prize for the manuscript, but the book was not published, supposedly because he continued to work as a mole for the CCP in Chiang's army. However, after Mao's side conquered state power, the novel was still not published, perhaps because it showed Chinese civilians so hating the destruction caused by the Chinese army of Chiang Kai-shek that many preferred to just wait for the Japanese to take over, a portrayal 'lessening the perceived severity of the massacre'.[31] Trying to court the KMT on Taiwan, the CCP insisted on portraying all Chinese as fighting Japan. Therefore, the CCP would not allow publication of material showing how the behaviour of the KMT military in the Nanjing area facilitated the Japanese victory.[32] Unpublished, Chen died in a Mao prison in 1967, one of the many millions of innocent Chinese victimised by the CR. In the post-Mao era of promoting hatred toward and vengeance against Japan, however, the manuscript was published, but only after it could be revised to depict a *Nanjing Blood Sacrifice*.

At Nanjing, the Japanese military, with the fascistic underpinnings of a cult of death,[33] slaughtered about 100,000 of the city's 400,000 population,[34] a Pol Pot level of mass murder. Yet the CCP, in the post-Mao era, reported the number of Chinese killed as 340,000. This extraordinary exaggeration helps the cause of holocaust deniers in Japan. According to material translated by Peter Gries,[35] the CCP goal is to not recognise Japanese suffering at the hands of American atomic weapons by presenting the number of Chinese victims at Nanjing as 'more than the death toll at Hiroshima and Nagasaki combined'. In the post-Mao CCP nationalistic narrative, no great people could possibly suffer more than the Chinese.

In a similar exaggeration, whereas the consensus at the end of World War II was that Hirohito's imperial military in China was responsible for 10–11 million Chinese deaths,[36] a holocaust level of inhumanity, in the post-Mao era, the CCP, seeking to obscure how the CCP state behaved as a killing machine, according to Gries's translation of Chinese material, raised 'the number of [Japanese era] war casualties ... to 35 million', a tally supposedly larger than that of innocent Chinese who died as a result of the policies of Mao and the CCP dictatorship.[37] Japan was portrayed as the worst evil, with the CCP state as the only protector of the Chinese people against that evil.

Post-Mao Chinese history texts, museums and annual commemorations demonise Japan, minimise democratic America's role in the Pacific War, and mythologise the dictatorial CCP as the saviour of the people.[38] A 15-year-old school girl emerging from Beijing's Anti-Japanese War Museum, which features atrocities, rapes, disemboweling, and corpses of children stacked like wood, commented, 'After seeing this, I hate Japanese more than ever'.[39]

The Chinese people would, through CCP propaganda, be helped to forget the horrors which Xu Liangying, Ba Jin and Feng Jicai believed the Chinese people needed to remember if their future was not again to be threatened by a CCP state. In China, the legitimacy of the CCP is bound up with its perceived role as the stalwart defender of national interests during the war with Japan. 'The deference the party derives from that legacy grows ever more important to sustaining its rule as social inequities … increase'.[40] Whatever 'mistakes' the CCP may have made, they paled into insignificance when compared with its contribution in leading the sacred cause of resisting purportedly barbarous Japanese invaders.

CCP propaganda aimed at getting the Chinese people to hate the Japanese is pervasive. A film made in 2005 tells of a 12-year-old Chinese boy who witnesses his mother shot in the back by the invaders. He joins the Red Army to seek revenge. Upon blowing up a trainload of Japanese soldiers, he is handed a pistol with which to kill more Japanese. Chinese writer Liu Xiaobo explains, 'Reviving war memories keeps the nation united against Japan and for the party'.[41]

Proud Chinese patriots have been socialised to imagine the CCP as the sole entity protecting the Chinese people from bestial Japanese, with Japanese militarism revived since the end of World War II and continually reviving thereafter, such that the endangered Chinese people more and more need an unconstrained CCP to protect them from a supposedly threatening Japan. Unaware of how distorted their understanding of history is, patriotic Chinese rage at the Japanese for overlooking Japan's ugly past. Many Chinese angrily demand that Japan rewrite its history books to tell the truth about the crimes committed by Hirohito's military against the Chinese nation[42] and stop Japan's premier from visiting Yasukuni Shrine, which houses all Japan's modern war dead, including war criminals.[43]

Members of the Chinese left, imagining China as the natural leader of Asia, may, in the twenty-first century, actually be trying to co-opt the Yasukuni narrative to deepen the notion of China as victim. The Yasukuni shrine myth features Indian Judge Pal's dissent at the Tokyo War Crimes Trials. Pal held that Japan was completely innocent and America and Britain were guilty of crimes against humanity – firebombing Tokyo, dropping atomic weapons on the people of Hiroshima and Nagasaki, torpedo bombing a boat carrying 775 children from Okinawa to the main Japanese islands, bombing a ferry between Taiwan and Japan killing 844 people, etc.[44] In the Chinese New Left story, Americans are anti-Asian racists and China leads Asia against American racism.

A Dangerous Chinese Future

Chinese invaders of Vietnam, the CCP regime believes, should be forgotten. When an Indian official called attention to the autumn 1962 war the PRC initiated against India in disputed territory, the Chinese ambassador snapped back, 'Whatever happened in the past is history, and we want to put it back into history'.[45] The CCP policy is to look to the future and not closely examine the crimes of the Mao era as would Xu Liangying, Ba Jin and Feng Jicai.

In contrast, the CCP demands that today's democratic Japan should remember the pre-1945 evils of an authoritarian and imperial order. Of course, it would be wonderful if the Japanese people could be shamed into confronting the crimes in their past. Each of us should in our countries remember the evil our governments have done in our name.[46] If the Chinese care about protecting their fellow citizens from gross abuses of fundamental human rights, then it is CCP historiography which requires rethinking. The CCP, however, would have no interest in displaying the moving exhibition of the U.S.-headquartered Laogai Research Foundation, which it can ship overseas, displaying Chinese victims of the CCP, including prisoners forced into slave labour, the brainwashing of juvenile prisoners and mass executions.

In a Nazi concentration camp, a person who survived by assisting with the killing could, when the opportunity arose, sacrifice his life in an uprising against the killing machine. By treating one's people as pure and not facing up to one's own people's inevitable complicity with evil, by not seeing that modernisation and strength need not always be antithetical to colonialism and inhumanity, by dismissing survivors as evil collaborators, by not seeing the nation state as a killing machine, one makes more likely that one's own nation's purist, chauvinistic passions can be mobilised in the future for bloody ends.[47]

Professor Yuan Weishi, turned into a political target by the CCP in early 2006, had argued that it was important to end the CCP's lying about history, making everything Manichean, scapegoating foreigners and obscuring the need to reform China. In the CCP demonisation of Japan, China is pure innocence and suffering comes from a Japanese aggression, an attack on the Chinese nation by a cruel and unrepentant Japanese race going back at least to the late nineteenth century. The CCP ignores Professor Yuan's request that complications should be grappled with to help Chinese people understand how the Chinese created China. Modern Japan has not been the only enemy of the Chinese people.

The 1894–5 Sino-Japanese War,[48] an intra-imperial conflict between the Manchu empire and the Meiji empire was fought in and around Korea. At that historical conjuncture, imperial expansion was considered normal behaviour. That is, all powers did it. Chinese patriots led by Sun Yat-sen rooted for Japan's Meiji against the Manchu whose reactionary rule in Han China was imagined as the illegitimate fruit of a seventeenth-century invasion which included genocidal Manchu acts against the Han race. Sun Yat-sen and his fellow Chinese patriots supported a modernising Meiji Japan against the reactionary and murderous Manchu conquerors of China. To Sun, Japan was not the enemy.

Likewise, in no way reflecting CCP historiography in which an evil Japan acts and an endangered Asia is victimised, in 1905 the dynamic Meiji fought the reactionary rulers of the Tsarist empire largely for influence in the Manchu homeland north of Korea. (The Manchu's Qing dynasty empire consisted of four relatively equal geographical parts, the Manchu homeland, i.e., Manchuria (the northeast), a Mongol-Turkic region (the west), a Tibetan-hill minority region (the southwest) and Han China (the southeast).) Japan defeated Russia. Politically conscious people all over Asia celebrated the Japanese victory as a defeat of imperialistic white Europeans. Japan was on the side of Asia for the Asians. Japan's expansion was not the target of a mass anti-imperialist movement.[49] Besides, the major imperialist power in China was Great Britain, the narco-traffickers who instigated the Opium War.

The context of international behaviour changed as a result of World War I, the Great War, what Asians then referred to as the European Civil War. In the new era, imperial expansion would become immoral and indefensible. Lenin's Bolsheviks carried out a coup that toppled the Russian democracy that had ended the Tsarist regime and then, in power, Lenin's Communists promoted, at least verbally, anti-imperialism. Among the World War I Allies, American President

Woodrow Wilson promoted de-colonisation. Imperial expansion was no longer acceptable behaviour. Chinese nationalism targeted the major colonial power infringing Chinese sovereignty. That was Great Britain. It had seized Hong Kong and dominated Shanghai.

The 1920s, the Taisho era in Japan which followed the death of the Meiji Emperor, was in many ways similar to the Weimar era in Germany. A Japanese regime of parliaments and multiple parties tried to live by new norms. With Britain being the dominant imperial power in the region, many Chinese and Japanese hoped for China–Japan cooperation,[50] but the Great Depression hit, international trade dried up, and an expansionist military seized power in Japan with the blessing of the Showa era emperor, Hirohito, succeeding the Taisho Emperor.

Brutal Japanese military expansion was subsequently resisted and resented by patriots in Korea, China, Vietnam, the Philippines and Indonesia, but fighters for independence against British imperialism in Burma and India sided with Japan against the British Empire. Even many on the anti-imperialist Japanese left would defend Hirohito's regime as patriotic and liberating. The Burmese and Indian anti-imperialist leaders, Aung San and Subas Chandra Bose who cooperated with the Japanese military would long remain anti-imperialist heroes to their peoples. Elsewhere in Asia, post World War II movements for independence were aware that Japan's weakening of colonial rule by the French, Dutch and British facilitated their people winning independence after the war was over.

Those Japanese who, in the post-World War II era, comprehend Showa era military expansion as an idealistic Japanese people sacrificing themselves to liberate Asians from white Europeans, however, prettify what is ugly. They omit horrors. Hirohito's Japan carried out all the evils of Nazi Germany, except for ethnocide. Apologists construct a myth, but they do so out of shards of reality, none of which is apparent to Chinese patriots who see the Japanese after 1895 as a one-dimensionally evil people inherently doing horrible things in China and the rest of Asia.

Descendants of the 3 million or so Japanese who died in selfless service to the nation during World War II naturally want to believe that their ancestors died for a worthy cause. American heirs of the pro-slavery Confederate army are the same way. So are Chinese survivors of Mao's CR. They each and all remember that earlier time as an era of selflessness and idealism. In the post Mao era, many Chinese patriots remember the murderous Mao period pretty much as Japanese remember the Showa era. They forget the crimes against humanity. A dangerous politics of very purposeful selective forgetting seems ubiquitous.

China's Unique Victimhood

Chinese in exile who work to compile personal accounts of victims of Mao's Cultural Revolution and subsequent CCP massive abuses of basic human rights are mainly seen by patriotic Chinese in China as traitors. If one points out how the Chinese people suffered massively and egregiously in Mao's CR,[51] one will frequently be told by such patriots that that is not how they remember the era. They instead recall the camaraderie and the noble purposes to which people gave themselves. They critically call attention to post-Mao materialism, corruption and unfair polarisation. They say that if you see the past in terms of blackness and blankness, you deprive good people of the sources of their ideals which are needed to counter today's evils of an out-of-control commercialisation. To tell the truth about the Mao era could strengthen a cynical view that the Chinese people can do nothing to better China. What a slander on the great resources of Chinese history and culture it is to believe that, unless Chinese deny Mao's holocaust, they will lack the resources to build a better China!

Besides, Chinese were not mere victims. They volunteered with enthusiasm. They were both wolves and sheep. How can the Chinese face this truth when the same CCP in whose name Mao persecuted so many remains in power and still uses the aura of Mao to legitimate itself? It would take extraordinary courage for Chinese seeking to get ahead to face their wolfish past when a vision of Chinese as merely innocent lambs or idealistic heroes legitimates a brighter future for them in CCP China. Hating a uniquely and inherently evil Japan whitewashes the CCP record. In fact, by the twenty-first century, members of China's New Left openly promoted as a symbol for a China actively righting historic wrongs a wild and feral wolf. They, 'advocate a new national totem of the wolf and the wolf pack's blood thirsty, aggression-oriented, force-worshiped spirit of predators as the essence of a renaissance of Chinese civilisation'.[52]

Today's Chinese equivalents of holocaust deniers sound very much like conservative Japanese who, in proto-fascist ways, idealise cultural virtues to challenge a modern materialistic project. Given the rapid pace of post-World War I and II modernisation, which brought spiritual discombobulation, many Japanese would almost naturally come to contrast an earlier era of shared purpose and sacrifice with postwar greed, materialism, selfishness and individualism. This mind-set facilitated the 1930s neo-fascist polity. Then, in the 1960s, the conservative *Yomiuri* newspaper offered to the Japanese people the sacrifices which Mao demanded of the Chinese people as superior to Japan's materialism, denounced as Westernisation or Americanisation. Maoist China, imagined as an ethical good, seemed similar to ancient Japanese virtues as preserved in the imperial authoritarian era. Older Japanese verities were reinforced by commemorating into the 1970s the World War II era soldiers who had long hidden in distant jungles. Memorialising these 'living war dead' kept proto-fascist, communalist virtues alive.[53] Perhaps, given a similar Chinese nostalgia for the Mao era, there is something insightful in the democratic perspective which imagines CCP China as feudal Fascism or feudal Socialism, the enemy of liberal rights-based practices which protect the individual, create realms autonomous of the state, and promote market-oriented behaviour.

By the 1990s, the New Left in China sounded very similar to the old right in Japan. China's leftists longed for the ethical warmth of ancient traditions. They contrasted the Mao era, treated as a time of shared sacrifice for the common good, as congruent with their romanticised notion of their inherited tradition. They did not want to hear about the crimes of the Mao era. They did not want their children brought up on the facts that would fill the museums called for by Xu Liangying, Ba Jin and Feng Jicai.

The message that did fill the post-Mao patriotic museums of China was that Japan was evil personified. The goal was to make the people feel that the CCP was the Chinese people's only defence against that Japanese evil. The Crime Evidence Exhibition Hall of the Japanese Imperial Army Unit 731 in Pingfang in Heilongjiang presented those Japanese as, 'the cruelest fascist war criminals in the history of humankind'.[54] A feature film did the same.

One would never know that more Chinese in the prewar era went to Japan to study than to any other country because Japan was the accessible model of the modernity Chinese patriots sought. Some Chinese long remained pro-Japan.[55] Some Chinese had seen collaboration with Japan as superior to helping Chiang's Fascists or Mao's Stalinists.[56] Some found life in Japanese-occupied Manchuria, to which millions fled during the war, as superior to life under Chiang or Mao. Cultural life in Japanese-occupied Shanghai had flourished.[57] Demonising Japan obscures China's complex history so that the CCP can damn all its rivals as traitors.[58] Legitimating the post-Mao CCP involves stigmatising both Japan and also those Chinese who had sought or seek peaceful conciliation with Japan. That is, China's way of memorialising China–Japan relations keeps fires burning that could ignite a future conflagration.[59] The discourse is not one of national strength and human dignity, which would be natural, but of vengeance and hatred.

Japanese conservatives stress how Japanese colonialism hastened modernisation in Taiwan, South Korea and Manchuria, the north-eastern provinces of China. In fact, in the immediate post-Mao era, Chinese in the north-east romanticised the Japanese colonial era in contrast to what they had just suffered under Mao, and raced to Japan for better economic opportunities. Consciousness of this pro-Japanese sentiment was an impetus to the post-1982 CCP policy of building new monuments to focus on the brutalities against the Chinese nation of the Japanese occupation. The Chinese would learn to hate Japanese.

But the CCP portrayed the Chinese *nation* as the victim and did not dwell on Hirohito era crimes against *humanity*. The language of human rights abuses could legitimate democratic constitutionalism, something the dictatorial CCP abhorred and abjured. The language of human rights abuses might call attention to the crimes against Chinese humanity perpetrated by the CCP. Therefore, Japan was portrayed as the enemy of the Chinese nation and the CCP as the defender of the nation.

In her meditation on the holocaust that was the CR and on the 4 June 1989 Beijing Massacre, Vera Schwarcz is not sure that memory of actual history will triumph.[60] When the Romans seeded the soil of Carthage with salt, its civilization could not again be nurtured.[61] Ever more, Chinese seem to be holocaust deniers when it comes to the murderous crimes of the ruling CCP.

In contrast, democratic Japan, despite whitewashing by chauvinists and rightists, facilitates memory of Hirohito era atrocities in ways which are impossible in an authoritarian CCP state that works so hard to forget the crimes of Mao and the CCP. Polls show most Japanese are aware of the crimes of that earlier era. Books detailing the Nanjing Massacre have been best sellers. TV talk shows feature Japanese scholars who accurately describe the inhumanities of the Imperial Army while in China. Members of a left-wing union, Japanese teachers, almost never teach the right-wing programme promoted by the chauvinists in Japan's Ministry of Education. No such critical independence is possible in authoritarian China. The history museum in Mao's birthplace is silent on 'the disasters of the Great Leap and the CR'. All that is shown of the CR is Mao making China 'an equal in the international order'.[62]

Blind to their own lies about the murderousness of CCP history, the Chinese have learned to hate the Japanese as holocaust deniers. University of Chicago Professor Wang Youqin has established a Chinese Holocaust Memorial website (www.chinese-memorial.org/). There is also a web Virtual Museum of the Cultural Revolution in English (www.cnd.org/CR/english/). With such sites blocked in China, 'terror, indoctrination and distortion of history, combined with the analgesic effect of prosperity and personal profit, has effectively washed away national memory'.[63] The result, according to Yongyi Song is a China which, 'lacks the most basic capacity for self-reflection, is incapable of facing up to a dark period in its own history, and is capable only of accusing others and producing venom-spewing hyper-nationalistic youth, or rather "patriotic thugs"'.[64]

Chinese democrats in exile find that Mao and the CCP have much to apologise for, including carrying out 'a literary inquisition and book burning in the style of Qin Shihuang or Hitler',[65] mistreating political targets by 'brainwashing and the threat of violence to strip them of their human dignity and ideals, to turn them into walking corpses', at times even going beyond Nazi evil. Everyone knows 'that in Nazi concentration camps there was no "political study"'.[66] In China, there was. Victims had to learn to be grateful to the executioners.

Comparing the terror of life in the Mao era with the holocaust, Schwarcz comments that 'Mao Zedong demanded that his adherents ... cling to the "sweetness" of the present ... The CR ... pushed into the depths of the soul. Each person had to go through repeated confessions ... "combating selfishness" ... a war against the self'. People had to be wolves and sheep at the same time. An accused mother tried to save herself by turning on her son. He was then sentenced to 20 years. But the mother, despite proving that she so loved Chairman Mao and put Mao above family, was still found guilty. She went mad and committed suicide.[67]

Wang Youqin tells of one victim of the Mao's Red Terror, Li Jie. As a young girl Ms Li fled from an arranged marriage to succour in Japanese-occupied territory. She got involved with a Japanese national and gave birth to his baby. When the CCP came to power, poor Li Jie had to confess her 'crime'. In Mao's Cultural Revolution, this powerless 'class enemy' was again and again brutally beaten by young people, eventually rupturing her spleen and causing her death.[68]

There is much blood on Chinese hands because of CCP-induced hate-mongering. Instead of ever admitting to Chinese inhumanity, the Pingfang memorial features a monument donated by Japanese to thank Chinese who raised Japanese war orphans.[69] Actually these good Chinese became political targets in Mao's CR. One such young man, He Haishan, had saved a 12-year-old Japanese orphan girl. He Haishan was warned by neighbours he would be killed by the CCP for his humanity. He and the girl eventually married and had eight children, but they suffered cruelly in Mao's CR. When it ended, they moved to Japan, which they found 'wonderful'.[70] No such Japan is imaginable in China. To suggest it is is to prove yourself a traitor or an apologist for mass murders.

To Professor Wang, 'the persecutions in China were more serious than in Russia because of the vigilante campaigns induced by the CCP. In Russia, Stalin had "show trials" ... but ... Mao ... did not even bother with trials', instead unleashing vigilantes who caused 'greater terror ... [and] even deep fear and psychological scars'. Political targets had to sing 'I am guilty, I am guilty ... .May you beat me and smash me, Beat me and smash me'.[71] Torture and murder became a competition in proving loyalty to Mao. Yet memory has been shaped so Chinese patriots treat the ruling CCP as their saviours. That party system holds power and remains unaccountable.[72]

China is suffused with memory of a particular political kind. Post-Mao China is replete with memorials, commemorations and new museums. CR museums exist in various provinces. All use relics and pictures to trigger nostalgia. One 'is intended to "bring back the memories of ... eating communally and ridding themselves of bourgeois liberalism"'.[73] Post-Mao museums staged exhibits on the experience of urban youth sent to the countryside during the CR. Travel agencies made real money running tours to former Red Guard villages of the CR. As with

Tara and the Ku Klux Klan in the USA, an inhumanely forgetful nostalgia was commercialised in China.[74] Ironically, the commodified pro-Mao myth and Mao nostalgia that flourished were felt by its embracers to criticise contemporary commercialisation. Apologists persuaded themselves that their romanticisation of reality, which actually helped stabilise the system, was a 'counter-hegemonic discourse'. They wanted to remember in a way that made them feel good about themselves.[75] The CCP, strengthened by such a discourse, allowed it to spread.

The CR museum in Shantou, Guangdong, which opened in 2005, according to Kirk Denton, although part of a tourist site and Buddhist temple, does contain 'numerous memorial steles to important figures who died during the CR'. But photographic nostalgia is the dominant theme. There is a CR memorabilia shop in Shanghai. A museum just outside of Chengdu has a CR Porcelain Art Hall. But the focus is on local heroes, folklore and the anti-Japanese war. The Museum of Modern Literature in Beijing just omits the CR, a time when Chinese writers suffered from cruel human rights abuses, including persecution to death.

Dignity, however, insists on memory. In a poor mountain area just north of the Burmese border, acting on Mao's instruction to knock down everything counter-revolutionary, Red Guards in Mao's CR had desecrated the Buddhist temple of the Tai Lue villagers. The young rebels had 'destroy[ed] texts written in Tai Lue language, and burn[ed] the old, gold-covered image of the Buddha … The Red Guards … scraped off the old Buddhist murals, replacing them with Maoist slogans'. After Mao died and some semblance of normality returned, villagers 'carved and painted a new wooden Buddha statue and scraped off the desecrating slogans. But they left a few [Maoist] slogans up … so that they wouldn't forget'.[76] Such memorials whose meaning is clear to locals help them not to forget.

Australian analyst Kevin McCready reports on a Chinese website of pictures on the CR run by Li Zhengsheng. But while the images are mainly, 'of peasant women at work on an irrigation project and a gathering of Communist party officials who met to mourn the death of Chairman Mao', some CR horrors are shown. The non-official CR museum in Shantou was initiated by a victim of the CR who wants Chinese, 'to face this period of history squarely' so 'they will never do anything so stupid again'. The initiator, however, understands that he cannot call attention to structural or ideological problems that would 'undermine the party's credibility', just its stupidities.[77] Even these small steps in the direction of truth took courage. For most, it is as if the Mao era holocaust never happened.

One of the two most popular post-Mao novels written by and for the CR sent-down youth generation was produced by a returned student from the United States, Wang Xiaobo. His story, *Golden Age* (*Huangjin shidai*), highlightes profane sex and mocks sublime ideals. At first, Wang could only get published in Taiwan. The book was eventually published in China in 1994. It was ignored. But then in 1997 Wang died suddenly of a heart attack. His work became popular. As writer Feng Jicai noted, Wang was critical of the 'narcissistic nostalgia' of the sent-down youth. Instead of anesthetising 'the ugliness of the past', Wang thought Chinese should each say, 'I admit I was an asshole'. He spoke 'unabashedly of the absurdity and stupidity of his years in the CR countryside'. But what made *Golden Age* popular was its descriptions of sex as a physical act, supposed proof of being alive. The tale was a paean to a need for a feral, animal-like Chinese people. The book criticises Han civilisation as 'domestication and castration'. It celebrates the Dai people for being 'savage'.[78] It is a statement that Chinese need to be nourished on wolf milk.

Japan's post World War II forgetting is abominable; sadly, it is not unusual.[79] Yet, the CCP's obsession with Japan as evil 'can only create a distorted vision of the past'. Indeed, it is possible that in demonising Japan, the CCP is making a future bloody war more likely. Unconscious of how CCP propaganda has shaped their view of Japan, a 1999 poll in Beijing on who was responsible for strained China–Japan relations found over 90 per cent singularly blaming Japan, which was imagined as harbouring hostile military intentions toward China.[80] CCP liberal general secretary Hu Yaobang was dismissed on 1 January 1987 and pilloried for trying, 'to forge close links of friendship and cooperation with Japan'. Premier Zhao Ziyang, who would have compromised with the great 1989 democracy movement rather than slaughtering its supporters, was ridiculed for playing golf with Japanese.[81] '[D]emocratic groups in China have been constrained by a racially defined nationalism'.[82]

Remembering Japan with hatred plays into the hands of CCP hard-line, militarist chauvinists. The war 'may truly be over only when' the victims of the attack stop denying the aggressors 'their stories of suffering and loss'.[83] This is not an easy lesson for the heirs of victims. Instead they make invisible the need to constrain the CCP state with cries for vengeance against Japan.

I wish well to critically minded Japanese like conservative media baron Tsuneo Watanabe, who pillories Premier Koizumi for going to the Yasukuni Shrine which honours the war criminal, General Tojo, who Watanabe equates with Hitler. Watanabe urges the Japanese to re-think their wartime conduct so that instead of seeing kamikaze pilots as loyal self-sacrificers, one sees them as unwilling sheep led to a slaughter.[84] Peace and reconciliation require more such voices in both Japan and China.

Although Ba Jin is now dead, other Chinese still cry out for a rethinking of how Mao devastated China in an era when the Chinese people vied with each other in vigilante inhumanity, acting as both wolves and sheep. In early 2006, 48 writers and scientists appealed to the government to build a Cultural Revolution Museum so that the Chinese people would never forget the crimes against humanity of the late Mao era. However, a Hong Kong writer commented, given the official policy line in 2006 China, such a government museum would end up actually celebrating Mao and the CR.[85] The best one could hope for in China's political atmosphere of nostalgic memory and political repression is the scattered private efforts which do not fully subscribe to the official story.

'Jiang Rong, author of *The Wolf Totem*[86] writes that there are two ways to be a Chinese – a wolf or a sheep … '.[87] Professor Yuan Weishi depicts the CCP regime as still feeding children 'wolf milk', thereby nurturing wolves. As in the Cultural Revolution so, too, today the state ignites fury against its enemies. In the post-Mao era, that means foreigners, and especially the Japanese. The CCP claims that China is behind singularly because of what evil Japan did to China, and not at all because Mao and the CCP carried out destructive and counter-productive policies. Children play games based on killing Japanese. Chinese leave the memorials built to remember the innocent victims of Japanese atrocities swearing hatred against Japan, and wishing for vengeance premised on strength.

Practical, modern Chinese cannot believe there is anything dangerous in this vengeful xenophobic discourse. It is patriotic and righteous. Similarly, teachers in the CR, 'were astounded by the visceral fury of the young rebels'. But, asks a former Red Guard, 'Why should they have been so surprised that we reacted like wolves … After all, we had been fed on a constant diet of wolves' milk … '.[88] They still are.

Notes

1. Estimates reach to twice this number.
2. On the construction of this nationalism, see William Callahan, "History, Identity, and Security", *Critical Asian Studies* 38/2 (2006), pp.179–208.
3. "China and Japan 60 Years Ago", *Dushu*, March 2006, a symposium featuring analysts from the Chinese Academy of Social Scientists. Cf. Xuanli Liaó, "Foreign Policy Think Tanks and China's Coping with the History Issue", in *Chinese Foreign Policy Think Tanks and China's Policy Toward Japan* (Hong Kong: The Chinese University Press, 2006), ch. 5.
4. James Leibold, "Competing Narratives of Racial Unity in Republican China", *Modern China*, 32/2 (April 2006), pp.188, 194, 196, 202, 212.
5. Even in 2006 ethnic Mongols abroad, seeking to protect the rights of Mongols in China, looked on Japanese as an ally against the Han. (Katsuhiko Shimizu, "Ethnic Mongols from China See Ally in Japan", *Asahi Shimbun* 19 April 2006.)
6. Uradyn E. Bulag, "The Yearning for 'Friendship'", *The Journal of Asian Studies* 65 (February 2006), pp.27, 25, 20, 19.
7. "Ba Jin was Lu Xun's Spiritual Heir", www.people.com.cn/GB/32306/32313/32330/378095.html. Yet Ba Jin was silent about post-Mao victims of CCP repression.
8. Joseph Esherick, Paul Pickowicz and Andrew Walder (eds), *The Chinese Cultural Revolution as History* (Stanford, CA: Stanford University Press, 2006), p.132.
9. Ba Jin, "A Culture Museum", in Geremie Barmé and John Minford (eds), *Seeds of Fire: Chinese Voices of Conscience* (New York: Hill and Wang, 1988 [1986]), pp.381–4. However commendable the calls to eternally memorialise these many millions of Mao's and the CCP's victims and to identify the victimisers, memory will not check state power. Only democratic institutions can hope to do that.
10. There has been no call to remember the 30 million plus rural dwellers who died in the wake of Mao's 1958–60 Great Leap initiatives. Indeed, in 2001, commemorating the eighteith anniversary of the founding of the CCP, exhibitions in Beijing's Museum of Revolutionary History hyped the Leap as proof of Mao's genius.
11. Esherick et al. (note 8), pp.217, 218.
12. Jennifer Hubert, "Revolution is a Dinner Party", *The China Review* 5/2 (Autumn 2005), p.148.
13. Hubert (note 12). Investment banker Ying Fang, formerly a Red Guard, gave voice to these cliches. 'The 6 AM starts and the intense training taught me valuable lessons such as discipline, the need to set and achieve targets, and not to fear, that I could conquer all'. (Sundeep Tucker, "China's Corporate Revolutionary", *The Financial Times*, 31 July 2006.)
14. Hubert (note 12).
15. Ming-Bao Yue, "Nostalgia for the Future", *The China Review* 5/2 (Autumn 2005).
16. Liu Xiaobo, http://www.obserrechina.net/info/artshow.asp?ID=39008+ad=5/10/2006
17. He Yinan, "National Mythmaking and the Problems of History in Sino-Japanese relations", in Lam Peng Er (ed.), *Japan's Relations with China* (London: Routledge, 2006), pp.76,79–80 and 81.
18. Sang Ye, *China Candid* (Berkeley, CA: University of California Press, 2006), p.143.
19. Sun Shuyuian, *The Long March* (London: Harper Press, 2006), pp.220, 219.
20. Chang-tai Hung, "The Red Line: Creating a Museum of the Chinese Revolution", *China Quarterly*, 2005, pp.914–33.
21. Edward Friedman, "Preventing War Between China and Japan", in Edward Friedman and Barrett McCormick (eds), *What If China Doesn't Democratize?* (Armonk: M. E. Sharpe, 2000), pp.99–128; Friedman, "Still Building the Nation", in Shiping Hua (ed.), *Chinese Political Culture 1989–2000* (Armonk: M. E. Sharpe, 2001), pp.103–132.
22. Yinan He, "The Clash of Memories: National Mythmaking and the Sino-Japanese 'History Issue'", in press. In the mid 1950s, the CCP courted Japan so it would not support America's containment policy against Cold War China allied with the USSR. The PRC gave Japanese war criminals humane treatment while demonising the United States, claiming that the American missionaries in Nanjing who created a safety zone to save Chinese lives actually were 'more concerned with preserving American property' and 'were responsible for the Japanese atrocities'. The safety zone was denounced as a 'plot between American and Japanese devils to destroy Chinese patriotic resistance' (Yoshida Takashi, *The Making of the "Rape of Nanking"* (New York: Oxford University Press, 2006), pp.68, 70). The CCP presentation of the Nanjing Massacre has invariably distorted the truth to serve the party line of the moment.
23. Peter Gries, *China's New Nationalism* (Berkeley, CA: University of California Press, 2004).
24. Antoaneta Bezlova, "China Makes Mileage from Japan's Defeat", *Asia Times*, September 2006; www.atimes.com/atimes/China/GI07AD02.html/

25. Baogang He and Yingjie Guo, *Nationalism, National Identity and Democratization in China* (Aldershot: Ashgate, 2001), p.192.
26. The date 18 September 1931 marks the Manchurian incident beginning Japan's full colonisation of Manchuria and the end of the League of Nations.
27. Unit 731 carried out torturing, murderous medical experiments on humans.
28. Kirk Denton, "Museums, Memorial Sites and Exhibitionary Culture in the People's Republic of China", *China Quarterly* (2005), pp.565–86; Denton, "Horror and Atrocity: Memory of Japanese Imperialism in Chinese Museums", in press.
29. It was visited in 1995 by the Japanese Prime Minister 'to show his determination to handle the history issue properly', Kuang-Sheng Liao, *Antiforeignism and Modernization in China*, (Hong Kong: Chinese University of Hong Kong Press, 1984), p.179.
30. Steven Riep, "Rethinking History", a paper presented to the 9 April 2006 meeting of the Association of Asian Studies.
31. Michael Berry, "Writing Atrocity between New Culture and New Life", paper presented to the annual meeting of the Association of Asian Studies, 8 April 2006.
32. Takashi (note 22), pp.105–10 and 154–63.
33. David Earhart, "All Ready to Die", *Critical Asian Studies* 37/4 (2005), pp.569–96.
34. For data supporting the 100,000 figure, see David Askew, "New Research on the Nanjing Incident", *JapanFocus*.org. Jean-Louis Margolin, "Japanese Crimes in Nanjing, 1937–38", *China Perspectives* 63 (January–February 2006), pp.2–12, finds a minimally smaller number more likely. In 1997, six of the seven Japanese texts available to junior high students estimated the death toll as 100,000–200,000 (Takashi, note 22.)
35. Gries (note 23).
36. The Nazi death toll in Europe is believed to be around 18 million. A comparison of German and Japanese war-time atrocities cannot possibly make Hirohito's forces more murderous than Hitler's.
37. The CCP claims of war dead have gradually kept rising, soaring in 1991, in the wake of the CCP's 4 June massacre in Beijing of Chinese who peacefully supported a transition to democracy, from 21 plus million to 35 million. (Takashi, note 22, p.156.)
38. The political nature of the anti-Japan propaganda was again revealed after the CCP's 4 June 1989 massacre of supporters of democracy in Beijing. To court Tokyo not to stay with OECD sanctions on the murderous CCP, 'The history issue disappeared from the Sino-Japanese political agenda in the early 1990s, largely due to the impact caused by the 1989 "June 4th incident"'. (Liao, *op. cit.*, p.175.)
39. Matthew Forney, "Why China Loves to Hate Japan", *Time*, 10 December 2005.
40. Kent Calder, "China and Japan's Simmering Rivalry", *Foreign Affairs*, 85/2 (March/April 2006), p.133.
41. Forney (note 39).
42. Actually, even the worst Japanese textbook acknowledges that 'the people of China fell victim in large numbers to the invasion by the Japanese military'. (Mitzuru Kitano, "The Myth of Rising Japanese Nationalism", *International Herald Tribune*, 12 June 2005.) The cover-up of CCP murderous atrocities is far more thorough in Chinese school texts.
43. Many have suggested that yet another memorial, a secular commemoration of those who died in Japan's wars, one excluding the war criminals, could ease China–Japan tensions. But the suggestion, however wise, ignores why the CCP has fostered tensions with Japan. The key is political will in the CCP, not Japanese memorials. However, the priests at the Shrine aver that, once the body has been apotheosised, it cannot return from the spirit world to the corporal one. Therefore, there is nothing to move. In addition, the shrine is a private institution. Given the constitutional separation of church and state, the government has no power to order the priests to do anything. Nonetheless, to me, it would be better if Japanese leaders kept away from Yasukuni, whose museum is a lying paean of praise for Hirohito's brutal, military expansionism.
44. A similar narrative of wartime Germany as a victim has been spreading in Germany. The standard distinction between repentant Germans and unrepentant Japanese ignores the many, many repentant Japanese who have erected memorials to Chinese and Korean victims of Hirohito era inhumanity. The CCP presentation of a homogenous and evil Japanese people is mendacious racism.
45. Brahma Chellaney, "Beijing's Historical Fantasies", *International Herald Tribune*, 12 December 2005.
46. I was not proud to be an American when, on visiting the Red Crag camp in Chungqing, where communists were tortured and murdered with American assistance, I read the etched ID on the steel shackles which held victims: 'Made in Youngstown, Ohio'. It is shameful that the American south is full of statues of the Confederate general who founded the KKK and none to the general who backed full citizenship rights to Americans of African descent.

47. Charles Maier, "Europa, Europa", *The Nation*, 9–16 January 2006, pp.23–6. Cf. Arkady Ostrovsky, "Russian Liberals fear the Rising Threat of Nationalism", *Financial Times*, 30 December 2005.
48. Some Chinese tell the story of Japan as an aggressor and China a victim going back to the Ming dynasty. (Shaohua Hu, "Why the Chinese are so Anti-Japanese", *JPRI Critique* 13 (January 2006).)
49. I do not believe that such motives actually defined expansionist Japanese politics. As a needy population makes heroes of bandits to make rulers seem yet worse criminals, suffering others in Asia re-imagined Japanese militarism to serve their own local purposes.
50. Akiva Iriye, *China and Japan in the Global Setting* (Cambridge, MA: Harvard University Press, 1992).
51. Wang Youqin, *1966–1976 wenge shounanzhe* (victims of the 1966–1976 Cultural Revolution), Hong Kong, Kaifang Magazine Press, 2004 details the experiences of 659 victims.
52. Fei-Ling Wang, "Heading off Fears of a Resurgent China", *International Herald Tribune* 10 April 2006.
53. Beatrice Trefalt, "War, Commemoration, and National Identity in Modern Japan, 1868–1975", in Sandra Wilson (ed.), *Nation and Nationalism in Japan* (New York: Routledge, 2002).
54. Quoted in Denton, "Horror and Atrocity" (note 28).
55. Lu Yan, *Re-Understanding Japan: Chinese Perspectives, 1895–1945* (Honolulu, HI: University of Hawaii Press, 2004).
56. Gerald Bunker, *The Peace Conspiracy* (Cambridge, MA: Harvard University Press, 1972).
57. Nicole Huang, *Women, War, Domesticity: Shanghai Literature and Popular Culture of the 1940s* (Leiden: Brill, 2005); Christian Henriot and Wen-hsin Yeh (eds). *In the Shadow of the Rising Sun: Shanghai under Japanese Occupation* (Cambridge, MA: Cambridge University Press, 2004).
58. Timothy Brook, *Collaboration: Japanese Agents and Local Elites in Wartime China* (Cambridge, MA: Harvard University Press, 2005).
59. Former Malaysian Prime Minister Mahatir worries about the way Chinese fixate on Japanese atrocities, since 'if we all just look to the past we will never talk to each other'. "Interview", *Far Eastern Economic Review*, March 2006, p.53.
60. Vera Schwarcz, *Bridge Across Broken Time: Chinese and Jewish Cultural Memory* (New Haven: Yale University Press, 1998).
61. Michael Ignatieff, "Whispers from the Abyss", *The New York Review*, 3 October 1996, pp.4–6.
62. Hubert (note 12), p.133.
63. Liu Xiaobo, "Remembering June 4th for China's Future", *China Rights Forum* (2005), p.19.
64. Yongyi Song, "The Cultural Revolution and the War Against Fascism", *China Rights Forum* 4 (2005), p.23.
65. He Qinglian, "On State Crime and Public Responsibility", *China Rights Forum* 4 (2005), p.15.
66. Chen Xiaoya, "Emerging from under the Shadow of Mao", *China Rights Forum* 4 (2005), p.28.
67. Schwarcz (note 60), pp.78, 98.
68. Wang Youqun, "Penitence for the Death of Li Jie", *China Rights Forum* 4 (2005), pp.46, 67.
69. Denton, "Horror and Atrocity" (note 28). In like manner, Meiji era depictions of the 1894–5 Manchu-Meiji war depict the Japanese military saving Chinese children.
70. Ichikawo Miako, "Child Survivor of Mass Forced Suicide in Manchuria Still Loves Hero who Saved Her", *International Herald Tribune/Asahi Shimbun*, 15 August 2005.
71. Wang Youqing, "The Past is Another Country", *China Rights Forum* 4 (2005), pp.49–51.
72. The independent writer Yu Jie recounts the words of a plainclothes security officer's tirade at him in a small room at a police station in December 2004. 'Don't you start quoting the law to us. We in the Communist Party have never abided by the law … we Communists were hooligans from the outset. The blood of innumerable people was shed to establish our regime … What's our job as policemen? Defending the state power of the Communist Party … I could send you to a criminal prison … and have them beat the living daylights out of you. We can make you disappear and say that you died in a car accident. We're more ruthless than the KGB … We can also destroy your family'. (Yu Jie, "An Open Letter to My Police Readers", *China Rights Forum* 4 (2005), p.53.)
73. Hubert (note 12), p.148.
74. 'The Jefferson Memorial … proclaims Jefferson's boast, "I have sworn eternal hostility against every form of tyranny over the mind of men," without ever mentioning his participation in racial slavery'. Yet, 'Even the Museum of the Confederacy in Richmond has mounted an exhibition on slavery that does not romanticize the institution'. It 'included chains, torture devices, and a catalog that did not minimise the inhumanity of the institution'. In a democracy, the struggle over accurately depicting one's evil past truthfully has a far higher likelihood of success. (James Loewen, *Lies My Teacher Told Me* (New York: Touchstone, 1995), pp.149, 143, 277.)
75. Ming-Bao Yue (note 15).
76. Sara L. M. Davis, *Songs and Silence* (New York: Columbia University Press, 2005), p.5.

77. Edward Cody, "Gingerly, a New Museum Revisits the Cultural Revolution in China", *Washington Post*, 5 June 2005.
78. Liyan Qin, "The Sublime and the Profane", in Joseph Esherick, Paul Pickowicz and Andrew Walder (eds), *The Chinese Cultural Revolution as History* (Stanford, CA: Stanford University Press, 2006), ch. 9. The other popular novel is pure Maoist nostalgia, as described in this chapter.
79. In the United States, a century after the start of the Civil War that abolished human slavery, textbooks presented the war as unnecessary, as caused by abolitionist extremists, and as ending with a return to power by white southerners because southern blacks and northern whites were incompetent and corrupt.
80. Minxin Pei and Danielle Cohen, "A Vicious Sino-Japanese Cycle of Rhetoric", *Financial Times*, 21 December 2005.
81. Geremie Barmé, "Mirrors of History: On a Sino-Japanese Moment and Some Antecedents", *Japan Focus.org*, 14 December 2005.
82. Baogang He and Yingjie Guo (note 25), p.170.
83. Mark M. Anderson, "Crime and Punishment", *The Nation*, 17 October 2005, pp.31–8.
84. Norimitsu Onishi, "Publisher Dismayed by Japanese Nationalism", *International Herald Tribune*, 10 February 2006.
85. Liu Zili, "What Kind of Cultural Revolution Museum?", *Guancha* (Hong Kong), April 2006.
86. Lang Tuteng, *Changjiang wenyi chubarshe* (2004).
87. Sharon Hom, "A Second Kind of Optimism: An Interview with Guy Souman", *HRIC* 2 (2006), p.85.
88. Rae Yang, *Spider Eaters* (Berkeley, CA: University of California Press, 1997), cited by Geremie Barme, "Historical Distortions", *The Australian Financial Review* (March 2006).

How to Deal with the Past?

ANATOLY M. KHAZANOV and STANLEY G. PAYNE

The dictatorships of the twentieth century left in their wake a legacy of destruction and suffering unprecedented in modern history, so it is not surprising that coping with such a legacy also became a significant problem. This became yet more vexatious once contemporary culture entered the postmodern era of relativism and rejection of 'judgmentalism'. As Torney noted with not unreasonable concern,

> It is correct to say that in calling systems totalitarian we in effect condemn them. However, what is curious is that at the end of a century in which states have made it official policy to burn people in ovens, to condemn whole races and peoples to death, to rob and loot on a mass scale we should be worried that in the process of distributing regimes we find ourselves judging them at the same time.[1]

We would say that this situation is more regrettable than curious if one takes into account the fact that the number of victims of modern repressive regimes is unique in human history, and that they have managed to implicate whole societies in the repressive process.[2]

I. Relevance to the Present

The themes addressed in this volume are not antiquarian or merely academic issues. They are relevant to the contemporary life and democratic politics (or limitations thereto) in every post-totalitarian society of the former Soviet Union, East Central Europe and the Balkans, and in quite a number of other countries as well. They are not yet the dead past even in the countries that experienced totalitarian or authoritarian rule long ago and have subsequently achieved successful transitions to liberal democracy, as in the cases of Germany, Austria and Japan, as well as Spain and Portugal, and even France and Italy. In some Latin American countries the transition from authoritarian rule took place quite recently and with uneven success.

Nor is the age of dictatorship by any means over. To follow William Faulkner's saying, in Cuba, China, North Korea, Vietnam or Kampuchea the past is not dead; it is not even past. In this regard, one may doubt that Hobsbawm's 'short twentieth century'[3] really came to an end in 1991. While some authoritarian/totalitarian regimes have already receded into history, new ones are emerging on different continents. Thus the issues discussed in this volume have been highly relevant to the character and quality of democracy, civil society, political culture, law, historical memory and international relations in the postwar period and remain so in the twenty-first century.

In France and Italy, a myth of mass resistance created and propagated by the political elites in the aftermath of World War II contributed to the success of communist parties that presented themselves as the main protagonists of that resistance. Only their decline made it possible to acknowledge the true dimensions of domestic fascism, collaboration and participation in the Holocaust in these countries.[4]

The election of Kurt Waldheim as president of Austria[5] and, later, in 1999, the formation of a coalition government that included Jörg Haider and his Freedom Party caused serious damage to that country's international reputation. For a short time, the Haider controversy almost ostracised Austria within the European Union, and the government had to undertake urgent measures to improve its image. Unwillingness by Japan to admit crimes against humanity (ranging from biological warfare to the widespread practice of sex slavery) committed by the country during World War II aggravates its relations with many Asian countries to this very day.

Turkey's unwillingness to take responsibility for the genocide of the Armenians, the very existence of which it denies, complicates its relations with European countries and creates another obstacle to admission to the European Union. At the same time, the Orhan Pamuk affair clearly demonstrates that it is very premature to consider the country a liberal democracy. Similarly, Holocaust denial by the Iranian president Ahmadinejad has made his country a rogue state no less than have its nuclear ambitions. Putin's refusal to accept any responsibility for the Katyn tragedy strains Russia's relations with Poland, while the desire of Latvia, Estonia or Ukraine to somewhat whitewash the reputations of their collaborators with Nazi Germany does not improve their relations with Russia, or contribute to their international reputations.

On the other hand, the influence of external factors and agencies may be currently greater than ever before. The belated and still incomplete and inconsistent admission of Austrian guilt in Nazi crimes that the country embarked on after 1985, when Austria was dubbed 'Naziland', was connected with international public opinion no less than with its internal situation. In post-communist Romania, attempts at rehabilitation and glorification of Ion Antonescu, despite his direct involvement in the Holocaust, stumbled upon the much stronger desire to be admitted to NATO and to the European Union.

Still, even in this regard the picture is far from rosy. It is true that no mainstream public figures, academics and mass media in the West would dare to try to rehabilitate Nazism and fascism, or to diminish their crimes. But not infrequently, with regard to communism and its crimes, attitudes are more ambiguous. It is still shameful to be an ex-fascist or ex-Nazi, but much less to be an ex-communist. Even worse, many post-communist governments themselves still lack moral clarity on this issue.

II. Approaches to Dealing with a Totalitarian/Authoritarian Criminal Past

Different approaches to dealing with a troubling past have a great impact on political development and societal fabric in countries that have experienced totalitarian or authoritarian rule, as well as on peculiarities of their political transitions. Since 1945, different countries have dealt with this, and continue to do so, in quite varying ways.[6] It is nonetheless possible to identify the most common approaches.

The first consists in an honest reckoning and repentance, with extensive consequences that may include judicial prosecution and political cleansing of the culprits, official apologies, reparations, restitutions and compensation to victims, and corresponding commemorative practices. Apparently, this is the most difficult and rare way, but West Germany eventually proved that under certain circumstances this can be carried out with success.

The second approach is reconciliation and forgiveness without forgetfulness. So far this policy, first developed in Latin America, has been successfully implemented only in South Africa, where the Truth and Reconciliation Commission offers amnesty for confession. Similar approaches undertaken by several other countries have been less successful. This is not surprising, since there are at least two preconditions for success. First, the situation must have been one in which the crimes were committed against a country's own citizens, not citizens of other states. Second, there should be a political consensus about a country's past, and even more so about its present and future. Otherwise, the legitimacy of the right of forgiveness may be challenged. Even in South Africa decisions about parameters and limitations of transitional justice were made within the context of political struggle and negotiation. The most poignant issue of amnesty for human rights offenders was not made subject to public discussion, but was decided by a direct political deal between the African National Congress and the National Party.[7]

Amnesties practiced by some European countries in the postwar period were, at best, dictated by considerations of *Realpolitik*, but their very legitimacy was contested, and they did not heal the wounds of victims. In the Soviet Union and other communist countries, victims of the Stalinist repressions did not forgive their persecutors. Another problem was that the rulers were not interested in their opinion, and nobody was looking for their forgiveness.

The third approach is to draw a line between past and present which, without denying the past, leaves it to the work of historians. The transfer of power in such cases is peaceful and negotiated. This is what Spain has done, since 1976, and also what Poland and some other countries of east central Europe have tried to do since the collapse of communism, though with less success. Drawing the line takes place in a specific political climate aimed at encouraging the painless transition to liberal democracy, but being, as a rule, politically negotiated, in order to be successful it must also enjoy significant public support. Otherwise, it may later backfire, for neglecting wounds is not the best way of healing them.

In Spain, with exception of the Basque region, the policy of drawing a line was based on a national consensus which preferred reconciliation, peaceful dialogue and negotiation to confrontation. It also implicitly recognised collective guilt for the Civil War and collective culpability for crimes committed by both sides. In such a political climate, there was no widespread popular demand or political will for the prosecution of those responsible for the human rights violations committed by the Francoist regime.[8]

Support for drawing a line may be only temporary, and unsettled scores of the past may later become an issue in political struggle. This is just what one is witnessing at the moment in such different countries as Poland, Hungary and Mongolia. In Spain a formal condemnation of the dictatorship of Francisco Franco and the passage by parliament of a Law of Historical Memory in 2007 provided new recognition and some compensation to leftist victims of the Civil War of 1936–9, and ordered the removal of all symbols of the Francoist regime from public buildings, but ignored the victims of the Left. It was inspired not only by desire for moral justice but also by more mundane partisan considerations of José Luis Rodríguez Zapatero's Socialist government, which hoped to stigmatise the democratic centre-Right opposition by trying to identify it with the Franco regime. About 20 years earlier, the first democratic Socialist administration of Felipe González had taken the opposite approach, declaring that the Civil War was finally history and no longer played any role in Spanish affairs.

In Poland, the first non-communist Prime Minister, Tadeusz Mazowiecki, solemnly proclaimed to the parliament: 'We draw a thick line [*gruba linia*] under the past'. The subsequent development of Polish affairs, however, demonstrated that such a promise was premature. Many in Poland, including influential political forces, were not satisfied with pre-emptive forgiveness, and in 1997 the Polish parliament passed a lustration law, although quite moderate in character.

Still another approach is intentional forgetting of the past or forging a new and false past. In the master narratives of Austria, France, Italy and Japan the dark chapters of World War II and/or their collaboration with the Nazi Germany were sanitised, deleted, or simply denied.[9] For several decades, the master narrative in France was based on the myth of mass resistance and self-liberation, while collaboration with the German occupants, support for the Vichy regime and its participation in the Holocaust were all played down. The Italian master narrative was similarly based on distortion of the truth. The extent of the anti-fascist resistance movement was blown up out of real proportion, ignoring the fact that it emerged late, was somewhat limited in scope and was confined to the northern part of the country. Other realities, such as Italian imperialism, racism, war crimes in Ethiopia and the Balkans, the anti-Semitic laws of 1938 and the deportation of Jews in 1943 sank into oblivion. Until 1997, fascism and the war were absent in school curricula.

In contemporary Russia, the vast majority of people do not want to listen anymore about the crimes committed by the Soviet regime against its own citizens, and even less about those against other countries. They prefer that the skeletons of the past be tightly locked in the closet. The policy of drawing a line that prevailed in the Yeltsin period turned out to be completely inadequate, since it was not based on political or public consensus. It was possible, for example, not to perceive the Civil War of 1918–21 in black and white terms, to consider it fratricidal, and even to claim that the leaders of the Whites were patriots in their own way. Thus Putin's government treats the memory of such leaders of the White movement as Admiral Kolchak or General Denikin with demonstrative respect; the latter was recently reburied in Moscow with military honours. This is possible because the Civil War already belongs to distant history. The Soviet period, even the Stalinist one, is a different matter, about which the current Russian leadership is successfully fabricating another Soviet past. This past presents the Soviet period (and even Stalin) in a perverted, predominantly positive way, while its dark chapters are either relegated to oblivion, or are whitewashed and presented as not so dark after all. The main agency of the Soviet repression, the KGB, never discredited in mass consciousness, is glorified and romanticised again, and is held in high esteem by the majority of Russians.

However, when scores remain unsettled, national narratives distorted, and collective memories sublimated, they may later re-emerge with surprising and unpredictable consequences. In the early 1990s, even those few who, like one of the authors of this paper,[10] were rather pessimistic about the possibilities of Russia's successful transition to liberal democracy, would never have predicted that in less than 15 years the country would be run by the political police officers, and that they would acquire even more power than in the Soviet period. A past which is not overcome, which is still relevant, has not passed away; it is not even past yet.

Historical Distance

Different approaches to the past are often connected with the impact of historical distance, whose role may have one of at least three different kinds of consequences. On the one hand, an honest reckoning with a shameful past may be extremely difficult, perhaps even impossible, when a majority of the active population in one way or another may be considered as accomplices. Therefore, in some cases, historical distance facilitates the construction of critical narratives, since those who were born after crimes had been committed do not bear personal responsibility for them.

In the 1940s and 1950s, most West Germans did not want to talk much about their recent past; critical inquiry into it and public debate about it tended to be discouraged. *Vergangenheitsbewältigung*, mastering the past, began only in the 1970s. Only then emerged a new master narrative of German history which emphasised the mass support for the Nazi regime, the virtual absence of any German resistance to it, and the crimes committed by Germans. It is hardly accidental that it was mainly promoted by those historians, and accepted by those ordinary citizens, whose formative years took place in the postwar environment. The *Wehrmacht*'s involvement in war crimes was not admitted until later yet, and is still a matter of hot debate.

It is also remarkable that at present, in East Germany, exhibitions devoted to the Nazi past attract more public attention than those which expose the crimes of the *Stasi*. To those who attend such exhibitions, the Nazi period is apparently already history, and they bear no responsibility for it. The communist period is quite different, as many living East Germans were its voluntary or involuntary accomplices.

It is said that in Germany the children of the postwar era asked their fathers what they had done during the war; in Austria those who first asked this question were already grandchildren. Only in the 1990s did the Austrian master narrative undergo substantial change from the 'first victim thesis' to the 'co-responsibility thesis'. The latter acknowledges that the Nazi period was a part of the country's own history and, therefore, that Austria is responsible for its own share of the crimes committed during the years 1938–45.[11]

In France, the demythification process started by installments only in the late 1960s, and just as in Germany, was to a large extent an act of defiance against the wartime generation.[12] Still, the process can hardly be considered as completed.[13] President Mitterrand was not ashamed to place annually a bouquet of flowers on the tomb of 'the victor of Verdun', Marshal Pétain. This should not be very surprising, considering his own collaborationist past and his protection of such notorious people as René Bousquet, the Vichy chief of police responsible for the hunting and deportation of French Jews to the German extermination camps. Jacques Chirac publicly admitted a 'collective sin' – the assistance of the Vichy regime in carrying out the Holocaust – only in 1995.

In other cases historical distance may facilitate drawing a line. A comparison of this approach to the past in such countries as Spain and Poland demonstrates that drawing a line is easier when most of the culprits and victims are already dead, or, at least, departed from the political arena. In Poland, however, a significant number of citizens, as well as notable political forces, want neither to forget the communist past nor to forgive those whom they consider the culprits. And many alleged or real culprits are still alive, and even are active participants of the political process.

Historical distance, however, also increases the danger of historical amnesia. In the nineteenth century, Ernest Renan noticed that it is of the essence of a nation that all individuals should have much in common, and further should all have forgotten much.[14] In fact, such amnesia is never 'natural'; it may serve the interests of particular political groups and forces. This is particularly true with regard to non-democratic countries in which alternative sources of information are limited or non-existent and counter-narratives are suppressed. Still, distance facilitates their goals. Even in democratic countries, the state always influences the process of forgetting though school curricula, text-books, mass media and many other means, and has a strong voice in what should be remembered and commemorated, and what should be forgotten. The Germans certainly knew what they were doing when, by creation of the Federal Authority for the Records of the State Security Service of the Former German Democratic Republic (Gauck Authority), they made a serious attempt at institutionalising memory and, thus, preventing it from sinking into oblivion.

Historical distance and amnesia may also facilitate historical revisionism. In Russia, the general public, especially the younger generation, knows very little, if anything at all, about the crimes of communism, be they the horrors of collectivisation, Stalin's purges, the ethnic cleansings, suppression of the Hungarian revolution in 1956 and of the Prague Spring in 1968, or many others. Opinion polls reveal that only 12 percent of Russians today know about the partition of Poland in 1939, or about the Katyn massacre.[15] Mass lootings and rapes committed by Soviet troops at the end of the war remain virtually unknown. Recent opinion polls reveal that today one-third of Russians would like to live again under Stalin's rule. Under the circumstances, it is not very difficult for new school curricula developed by Putin's personal order to present the Soviet past in a predominantly positive way.

Identification of Perpetrators, Accomplices, Bystanders and Victims

To some extent, their very identification is connected with specific details of the transition, as well as the character of the previous regimes. The very criteria of identification are also politically charged, and, apparently, this could not be otherwise. Not only in the past, but also today, people of different political allegiances and ideological persuasions have, and apparently will have in the future, different opinions on who exactly were perpetrators, accomplices or victims, who should be condemned or exonerated, what circumstances should be taken into account as mitigating or aggravating, and who was ultimately responsible for what had happened under totalitarian/authoritarian rule. Strict and indisputable rules of international law are hardly applicable, for such law itself is an outcome of postwar developments, and is hard to apply retroactively to specific situations. Thus the debate is not primarily about judicial rulings but mainly about historical justice, not about retribution but about moral guilt in Karl Jasper's terms.

It is easier to identify victims than accomplices and sometimes even perpetrators, especially when the former are the Other: Jews, Roma, homosexuals, mentally retarded people in the Nazi case, some ethnic minorities, members of 'wrong' classes or 'wrong' parties, or dissidents in the case of the Soviet Union and other communist countries. However, just because they represent the Other, their sufferings may not get sufficient attention or are played down by the society at large. Even in western European countries, immediately after the war surviving Jews were at best treated like other inmates of concentration camps, or POWs. In many East European countries, they faced open hostility. The Kielce pogrom of 1946, in Poland, is only the most extreme example of this kind. In contemporary Russia, just as earlier in the Soviet Union, the 'punished peoples' did not enjoy much sympathy and understanding; on the contrary, they were often confronted with open hostility.

One's own victims often received more attention, but even in western European countries it was far from clear who exactly was a victim. Fallen resistance fighters, POWs and hostages were obvious victims, but even aside from the Austrian case, can the same be said about the population at large in countries occupied by Germany and the other Axis countries, if one takes into account the numerous collaborators or purely passive by-standers? And what about people in countries like Hungary or Romania that allied with Germany and had to pay for this choice? Last but not least, what about ordinary Germans or Japanese? The suffering and deprivation of the civilian population in those countries is an indisputable fact. Should they be considered simply more victims of the totalitarian regimes? This is how many people in those countries would like to be perceived, but to what extent is this self-perception convincing, considering the mass support or compliance their totalitatian/authoritarian regimes had enjoyed?

In many post-communist countries the problem had further twists. First, the real and fabricated anti-fascist purges which took place there in the first postwar years – it is far from always easy to discriminate between the two categories – were conducted in an arbitrary way, without due legal procedures and without proper discrimination between perpetrators and accomplices. In addition, many people responsible only for anti-communist actions and views were persecuted as well. Thus, in Hungary, more than 100,000 people suffered some kind of punishment during the immediate postwar years. Not only Ferenc Szalasi and some other leaders of the Arrow Cross party, but also four former ministers, two ministers of the interior, a minister of finance, and six other former ministers under the

Horthy regime were executed.[16] In Romania the anti-fascist purge was perhaps even more extensive.

Furthermore, considering the dubious past of many of those who were persecuted, shall they be exonerated as a group, or, at any rate, evoke our understanding and sympathy for the consequences of the choices they made? And how many of their compatriots were capable of understanding the issues divorced from ideological bias and abuse?

Moreover, in some cases notorious perpetrators later fell victim to the same criminal regimes which they had served. Many communist leaders, such as Zinov'iev, Kamenev, Bukharin and Tukhachevsky in the Soviet Union, Rajk in Hungary, Traicho Kostov in Bulgaria, Slansky and Clementis in Czechoslovakia, and others like them, who had been directly responsible for mass repression, were later executed. All charges against them were fabricated, and they were rehabilitated posthumously, but can they be considered real victims? Some of those in this category who suffered torture and imprisonment but not execution, like Janos Kadar in Hungary and Gustav Husak in Czechoslovakia, survived to become perpetrators again.

This problem is perhaps most complex in the case of authoritarian regimes stemming from genuine civil wars or major counterterrorist operations. In the cases of the civil wars in Spain, Greece and Croatia, insurrections were launched against systems that were not genuinely democratic, or, in the case of Croatia, against a regime that was highly authoritarian. The winners in Spain and Yugoslavia then established their own authoritarian regimes. Both sides committed many crimes and atrocities. Similarly, in several South American countries authoritarian systems were introduced under the pretext of combating large-scale terrorism. This led to the creation of numerous innocent victims, but the terrorists and their accomplices who were punished were simply perpetrators and accomplices, not true victims.

Transitional Justice

Prosecution of perpetrators, especially war criminals, proceeded most successfully when their countries were militarily occupied. In this regard, it is possible to speculate about the advantages gained by total defeat and unconditional surrender. One may have many doubts that the Nuremberg Trials or the Tokyo War Crimes Tribunal would ever have taken place, at any rate on the same scale, if the Allies had not taken the matter into their own hands. In the cases of governments allied with Germany, the Allies stipulated the prosecution of major perpetrators among the surrender clauses. The negative side of the Nuremberg and Tokyo trials was that a significant number of Germans and Japanese doubted their legitimacy and fairness, calling them 'victors' justice'. Still, by introducing a new legal category – crimes against humanity with no statute of limitation – these trials set certain criteria of criminal behaviour by individual regimes and, in principle, opened the way for international intervention in cases where such crimes are committed.

Even in the very rare cases of international intervention, however, justice is often delayed if it happens at all. The International Criminal Tribunal for the former Yugoslavia and especially the International Criminal Court for Rwanda, both created by the United Nations, are very expensive, not very efficient and prone to political pressure. One of the authors of this paper had an opportunity to observe the Court for Rwanda, in Arusha, Tanzania, leading to the impression that some judges of that court were more interested in maintaining their luxurious life style in an impoverished city than in energetic persecution of the culprits. No wonder that both Courts are reluctant or unable to deal with anything more than crimes committed by a few particularly notorious individuals. Likewise, the World Court (formally the International Court of Justice) is hardly truly independent, since some of its judges are prone to pressures from their non-democratic governments.

In Spain, which has become the new world leader in political correctness (as in 1936 it purported to be the world leader in ongoing violent collectivist revolution), the Constitutional Court in 2005 authorised Spanish tribunals to prosecute alleged perpetrators of crimes against humanity, regardless of whether or not these purportedly involved Spanish citizens. This merely authorised politically capricious freelancing by Spanish magistrates, particularly in the case of the grandstanding judge Baltasar Garzón, whose quest for publicity and notoriety feeds an immense ego but is counterproductive for serious jurisprudence.

The outcome is even more discouraging when justice remains in the hands of independent national governments. In Austria, the responsibility for the de-Nazification and prosecution of the culprits was assigned by the Allies to the Austrian government. However, from the very beginning the treatment of former Nazis was influenced by opportunistic politics and exploited for partisan political ends, which almost from the outset resulted in a noticeable desire to exonerate and to appease them. As early as 1946, 90 per cent of the 550,000 members of the NSDAP in Austria had been amnestied and reinstated in their jobs; the remaining 42,000 were amnestied a few years later.[17] Soon afterwards, former Nazis even began to be seen as victims of the de-Nazification demanded by the victors. In 1957, de-Nazification was officially terminated. The National Socialists Law not only included a general amnesty for almost half a million 'little Nazis', euphemistically called 'fellow travellers' (*Mitläufer*), but also entitled those who had been de-Nazified to reclaim their properties.[18] Under the influence of Adolf Eichmann's trial in 1961, a series of trials (the 'Auschwitz trials' of 1963–6) took place in West Germany, and several former SS officials were convicted of war crimes. Similar trials in Austria usually ended in 'not guilty' verdicts after witnesses for the prosecution had been ridiculed and intimidated.[19] Conversely, much more extensive prosecution of collaborationists was carried out by small West European democracies such as Belgium, Holland and Norway, but the most deadly punishment was meted out not by the courts but by vigilante action in France and Italy immediately following liberation, amounting to at least 7306 killings in France[20] and perhaps 3000 in Italy. In Italy, especially, this was done by communists, experts in killing, and sometimes targeted anti-communists rather than fascists and collaborators.[21]

With the Cold War, the quest for justice in West Germany at first vanished. War criminals received reductions in their sentences or were not prosecuted at all. In Italy, purges of fascists and collaborators took place only between 1946 and 1948, but were very limited and mainly symbolic in nature. Most of the administrative, judicial and even police apparatus was effortlessly integrated into the new Republican order.[22]

The Japanese never brought their war criminals to justice, not even in the cases of the doctors of the notorious biological warfare Unit 731, who after the war pursued successful careers. Another example is Kampuchea, still dragging its feet and showing great reluctance to prosecute Khmer Rouge leaders and their henchmen, and there are many other similar cases.

In post-communist countries, there was no strong public demand for retribution and almost no legal prosecution of culprits of the communist period, with the exception of a few particularly notorious individuals.[23] Lustration adopted by some countries was basically not revenge, but rather a protective measure by nascent and fragile democracies. In other respects, the problem of responsibility and guilt was left to historical and public discourse.

Four circumstances contributed to such a turn of events. First, there was no external power capable of imposing punitive policies. Second, the worst repression took place mainly in the years 1945–53 (and in Hungary also in 1956–8). By the early 1990s, many perpetrators and victims of that time were already old or had passed away. Third, the transition did not directly overthrow but rather was negotiated with the old communist elite. Had the latter faced certain prosecution they would not have handed over power so easily. Fourth, the transition began in conditions of political and moral disorientation, in which it was often declared that discrimination between perpetrators, accomplices, bystanders and victims would pose an insoluble dilemma. Amongst others, Tina Rosenberg has formulated well its essence: 'Who is guilty in societies where almost everybody collaborated with the system in some way?'[24] In communist countries, it was almost impossible not to be a direct or indirect accomplice, conformist or at least passive by-stander. Without a certain amount of accommodation and compromise with the existing order, one would simply not have been able to survive. Even many famous and courageous dissidents at one time in their life were conformists.

Still, preemptive forgiveness, first advocated by Vaclav Havel, Adam Michnik and some other dissidents, carries a danger of impunity, since it permits the avoidance of any individual accountability. If everybody was guilty, then nobody in particular was guilty. In such a case, the absence of judicial responsibility may be confused with lack of moral accountability, and this, in turn, may contribute to societal disorientation and cynicism. It is true that almost everybody in the communist countries had to be a conformist, but relatively few were perpetrators, torturers and executioners; far from everybody, even under pressure, agreed to become a secret police informer, and far from everybody strove to be the first student in his class. In the final analysis, this problem is better left to citizens of post-communist countries themselves. The former dissidents have the moral right to insist on forgiveness, whether this approach is expedient or not, but there is something repugnant when it is preached by certain western scholars and human rights activists, who were never victims of repressive communist regimes but are arrogant enough to believe that they can decide what is best for their former victims.

In countries in which the former communists remained in power in the beginning of the transitional period there was virtually no retribution at all. In Romania, from the outset President Ion Iliescu rejected demands by the opposition and announced that there would be no lustration, and that ordinary citizens would not be prosecuted for past collaboration with the *Securitate* or for crimes from the Ceausescu period. Later, only a few of the dictator's close associates were prosecuted, but their sentences were light and they were often paroled.[25] In Slovakia, nobody was prosecuted at all, and the Lustration Law remained on paper only.

In nearly all other post-communist countries, justice was more symbolic than real. In the Czech Republic, which showed greater concern than most, less than ten thousand people were seriously affected by lustration, and of these fewer than ten were taken to court, found guilty, and imprisoned. All were later paroled 'for good behaviour'.

It seems that East Germany is the only exception. There, however, justice was carried out by external force, the expanded Federal Republic of West Germany, with its judiciary and administrative apparatus. Moreover, aside from a thorough administrative purge and a process of de-Stasification, the ratio of convictions to investigations was extremely low. More than 20,000 people were investigated, but less than 1000 indicted, and only about 150 were actually convicted.[26]

After the disintegration of the Soviet Union, nobody in Russia and most other successor states was prosecuted for crimes committed in any period. The partial exceptions were the Baltic countries, where only a few people, all of them Russians, were prosecuted for crimes committed against the indigenous population during the Soviet years.

One may come to the conclusion that transitional justice should not be postponed or delayed until the transition has been fully accomplished and consolidated, if the real goal is the punishment of perpetrators. To what extent this facilitates the transition itself is a more difficult question, which can hardly be given an unambiguous answer applicable to all countries and situations. As Jan-Werner Müller has argued, 'Despite the numerous efforts at general prescriptions for 'transitional justice', it seems exceedingly difficult to make general prescriptions'.[27] It seems that dismantling the institutions of power and the support base of repressive regimes, and simply bringing past crimes to light, are more important for successful transition than revenge.[28]

III. National Narratives

The past may also be divisive: (1) when different groups within a state have conflicting opinions on its past; and (2) when other states have opinions on the past of an individual post-totalitarian or post-authoritarian state that is significantly different from its own self-perception. Many post-communist countries may serve as an example of the first case, since their societies lack consensus on the prewar, war-time and communist periods of their history. Many Hungarians oppose attempts to rehabilitate the interwar authoritarian regime of Miklos Horthy, who received a solemn reburial in 1993. In Slovakia, influential political groups have reemerged that want to rehabilitate Monsignor Tiso, executed in 1947 for his collaboration with Hitler, while to other Slovaks he remains a despised villain. Many Latvians and Estonians perceive their compatriots who collaborated with the Nazi and even served in the Waffen SS against the Soviet Union not as villains but as freedom fighters. This situation is not limited to eastern Europe, for divisions may still be found in western European countries such as Italy and Spain (and perhaps to a very slight degree in France).

In Ukraine there exists a division between its western and eastern parts with regard to the Organisation of Ukrainian Nationalists (OUN) and the Ukrainian Insurgent Army (UPA), the West Ukrainian nationalist organisations that fought the Soviets but at one time collaborated with the Nazis and committed mass murder and numerous atrocities against Poles and Jews. While to many East Ukrainians, especially veterans of the Soviet Army, these people are criminals, West Ukrainians hail them as freedom fighters and national heroes. Many streets in Lviv, Ivano-Frankivsk and Ternopil are renamed to honour leaders of the OUN and UPA, such as Stepan Bandera and Roman Shukhevych, or even the SS Galicia division.[29]

In the second case, those states which in the past committed crimes against other countries and peoples often tend to deny them or play them down. At best, they sometimes resort to paying lip-service. On a few selected official occasions their leaders ostentatiously apologise for past injustices, but do this in a way that leaves many doubts about their sincere repentance, especially if these apologies contradict the official versions of national history propagated at home.

The neighbours of Japan are certainly not satisfied with the few seemingly reluctant and strictly pro forma apologies pronounced by its leaders during their visits abroad, particularly when such apologies are compared with the prominence of the ultra-nationalist Yasukuni shrine or the difficult struggle to achieve revision of history text-books. Russia's east central European neighbours are of the opinion that the few occasional words of regret expressed by Yeltsin were a completely inadequate apology for Soviet imperialism and its atrocities, especially because Putin refuses to confirm them.

Moreover, a divisive past may be much more detrimental to the transition to liberal democracy when it is somewhat whitewashed in national narratives. In postwar Germany, no mainstream politician dared to say anything positive about the Nazi period and Hitler. But recently certain Ukrainian politicians have not hesitated to fuel nationalist passion in order to acquire additional votes. President Yushchenko, in a vain hope to bring the nation together, calls for a law recognising Ukrainians who fought alongside the Nazis that would grant them rights equal to those of Soviet Army veterans. On 12 October 2007, he posthumously conferred the title of hero of Ukraine on Roman Shukhevych, a Waffen SS officer in charge of the notorious Nachtigall battalion and the commander-in-chief of the UPA from 1943 to 1950. Consequences ensued almost immediately. Two days later, when Ukraine for the first time officially commemorated the anniversary of the OUN–UP, people wearing swastikas marched down the streets of Kiev along with columns of Ukrainian nationalists. In contemporary Russia, Putin's leadership still presents the Soviet Union and even Stalin in a fundamentally positive way.

Victimhood as the Poetics of National Narratives

Aristotle in the *Poetics* stated that poetry is superior to history, since poetry denotes what ought to be true, rather than what is really true. It seems that many national narratives follow this line, exploiting the past exclusively for partisan purposes.

The status of victimhood was clearly recognised immediately after World War II, with respect to the victims of the Axis, but its meaning was changed and expanded later in the twentieth century as the new ideology of political correctness replaced the class struggle with its own categories of victimisers and victims. Meanwhile, quite apart from the 'victimist ideology' of political correctness, a constant revision of national narratives has taken place, with an ever-growing concern to achieve victimhood status, even on the part of countries that historically were primarily victimisers. Whenever possible, historical perpetration is downplayed, while, conversely, new claims of victimisation of quite a different order acquire growing importance.

In this regard, Austria may once more serve as a good example. Beguilingly, a corner-stone of later national myth was already laid down in 1943, at the Moscow meeting of the Allied foreign ministers, when they declared Austria the 'first free country to fall a victim of Hitlerite aggression'. It is true that the same Declaration also stated that Austria bore responsibility for taking part in the war on the side of Hitler's Germany, but this was conveniently ignored. For the next 40 years and more, the official Austrian narrative claimed that in 1938 the country had been occupied and annexed by Nazi Germany against its will, and was liberated in 1945 by Austrian resistance fighters and the Allies. This myth was perpetuated even in the national emblem, the eagle that after the war was additionally provided with broken chains symbolising liberation from foreign oppression. By 1949, the myth of victimhood reigned supreme and was adopted by the vast majority of citizens; Austria became a nation of 'victims'. It was a consensus built on a lie; nevertheless, it was a very successful consensus and the emerging Cold War facilitated its perpetuation. Little wonder that in 1953 the Committee for Jewish Claims was told that all sufferings were inflicted not by Austrians but by Germans, and therefore that Austria would accept no claims for compensation.[30] In a somewhat similar manner, the new master narrative in Italy reflected the attitude of a public that wanted to perceive itself as victims of *nazi-fascismo*, and especially of the German occupation, thus bearing no responsibility for its own fascist past.[31]

Communist East Germany also rejected any responsibility on the part of its citizens for Nazi crimes. The culprits were the Other, the West Germans living in the country of 'capitalists and imperialists', but not the workers and farmers of the DDR, inheritors of the glorious 'anti-fascist tradition'. Meanwhile, many low-ranking Nazis continued to loyally serve the new totalitarian regime in the bureaucracy and even in the police.

After World War II, Japanese nationalists portrayed their country not as an aggressor, but as a victim. Japanese nationalists still view the war of aggression in Asia and the Pacific as a patriotic war against western imperialism. Massive crimes, such as the 'rape of Nanking', vivisection of prisoners of war, and many others, are ignored. At the same time, the memory of Hiroshima and Nagasaki and the dropping of the atom bomb are stripped of all historical context and manipulated to fuel the myth of Japanese martyrdom. The Japanese Society for History Textbook Reform, formed in 1997, regards the prevailing narratives as far from balanced, as too negative and 'masochistic', and proposes to introduce more 'balanced' texts.[32] Japanese governments pander increasingly to such an attitude.

Even in Germany, there are some indications of a shift in the national master narrative from guilt and responsibility to more attention to Germany's own suffering and losses. Although the attempt of conservative historians, such as Erich Nolte, Andreas Hillgruber and Michael Stürmer, to present Nazism as a defensive reaction against the Soviet Union and the communist threat did not achieve all its goals during the *Historikerstreit* of the mid-1980s,[33] it reflected a certain revisionist mood in the country. The desire to lighten the burden of guilt still provokes contradictory reactions in Germany, but is expressed by protests against an exhibition about the crimes committed by the *Wehrmacht*, or the debate reawakened in 2002 by publication of Guenter Grass's novel *Crabwalk*, on the sinking of the *Wilhelm Gussloft* in 1945, and *The Fire*, Jörg Friedrich's book on the bombing of Dresden. It is noteworthy that those who consider the destruction of Dresden a war crime rarely acknowledge any connections between the Dresden bombing and German air strikes on Dutch, Polish and British civilians.[34] On the contrary, attempts to establish the equivalence of German victims with the victims of the Germans are quite evident. It seems that nowadays many Germans, both on the Right and on the Left, are more interested in the suffering of expellees from Poland, Czechoslovakia and East Prussia than in their previous mass support of the Nazis.

The post-communist countries of east central Europe tend to present themselves as innocent victims of Soviet imperialism. As Timothy Garton Ash aptly noticed, 'Instead of exploring what Poles did to Poles, Czechs and Slovaks to Czechs and Slovaks, Hungarians to Hungarians, each nation dwells on the wrongs done to it by the Soviet Union'.[35] For the sake of objectivity, however, we would like to add that in honest historical reckoning one subject should not exclude another, especially since they are to a large degree intertwined.

In all post-Soviet countries, with the partial exception of Russia, new historiographies have embraced the rhetoric of victimisation. A lot of attention is paid to real or perceived historical injustices for which the Russians, as the embodiment of Soviet rule, are mainly blamed. In Uzbekistan, the Museum of the Victims of Repression (Tsarist and Soviet) was opened in 2001, and in Kazakhstan, along with several monuments, the Museum of the Victims of Soviet Oppression was opened in 2003, in Almaty. In May 2006, the Museum of Soviet Occupation was opened in Tbilisi, the capital of Georgia. In November 2006, the Ukrainian parliament adopted a law defining the famine of 1932–3 as a genocide of the Ukrainian people. The Russian government vigorously rejects this definition, preferring the term 'tragedy', since the law implicitly holds Russians responsible for the famine.

In the cases of countries which have undergone major civil wars or experienced authoritarian counter-terrorist regimes, it has been in every case the losers who have claimed victim status during the twenty-first century. This is understandable in so far as it was the losers who were subsequently subjected and victimised for a greater period of time, but they have fashioned their own master narratives which exclude the possibility of ever having been victimisers. Violent revolutionaries and terrorists responsible for much suffering and in some cases many thousands of innocent deaths are whitewashed as 'fighters for democracy' who may merely have committed a few excesses in time of emergency. As has been pointed out earlier, it is very hard in these situations to fully disentangle victimisers and victims, though reparations to some extent were made to the victims of revolutionaries and terrorists by the counter-revolutionary and counterterrorist regimes, and those who suffered under the latter, whether innocent or perpetrators, can with some logic claim recognition and compensation.

Collective Memory, Selective Memory

During the late twentieth century the field of memory studies became increasingly popular in the humanities and the social sciences, while more or less simultaneously the concept of collective memory or historical memory began to be embraced by political groups as an important tool with which to advance their causes.[36] This led to a great deal of confusion in certain countries. The concept of 'collective memory' is fundamentally misleading, since, strictly speaking, no such thing exists. The only genuine memory is that of individuals, not groups, since no group possesses a common mind capable of direct memory.

This problem was to some extent initially recognised by the first scholars in the field of memory studies. Maurice Halbwachs, in his path-breaking *Mémoire collective*, published in 1925, pointed out that what would be called historical memory was in fact anti-historical, since it always oversimplified, 'essentialised', rejected ambiguity and critical distance, and represented the influence of the present on the idea of the past, rather than vice-versa.[37] Collective or historical memories are in fact constructions, very often fabrications, by elites, whether of states, political interests or the media. Not surprisingly, scholars will tend to dismiss them as, at best, myths. Historians reject collective or historical memory as a basis of historical knowledge, though they study it as phenomena in cultural or political affairs. And when historians engage in oral history, they deal exclusively with individual memories. Attitudes or interpretations that are considered collective memories have been extensively studied by historians in recent years, but as political or cultural concepts, not as a guide to history itself. It is only in this sense that we have used the term in this conclusion.

Political groups, particularly, seek to formulate attitudes or ideas about the past that serve their causes and are accepted as collective memories. In the twenty-first century this ambition has been most extensively developed by the Left in Spain, with the passage of the Zapatero government's Law of Historical Memory, as well as its successful initiative in the European parliament in February 2007 to set up an international 'truth commission' on the Franco regime, in order to generate some sort of international validation of certain of its political schemes. This raises the question of how a body composed primarily of professional politicians, none of whom is an active professional historian or an investigative judge, can competently assess deeds of half a century ago.

A major argument on behalf of this initiative was that the introduction of democracy in Spain during 1977–8 supposedly took place under restricted conditions that imposed a 'Pact of Silence' or of 'Forgetting' about the Civil War and Francoism. Such a contention constitutes a serious distortion of political reality, as leading historians such as Santos Juliá[38] and the late Javier Tusell,[39] among many others, have pointed out. The introduction of democracy was instead based on a consensus that remembered the past very well, and was aware that both sides had been guilty of serious abuses. Consequently it sought a new consensus on the basis of liberal democracy for all. The most serious crimes had taken place more than 30 years earlier, the great majority of the major perpetrators were dead and their exposure was publicised at great length by a continuing series of historical and journalist studies from the 1970s to the present, which demonstrated that in no country in the world was there any greater awareness of contemporary history than in Spain. Amnesty and consensus was even more in the interest of the Left than of the Right. The leader of the Communist Party, Santiago Carrillo, was the only extant mass murderer from the Civil War (given his longevity), and would not have been able to participate in the political democratisation without general amnesty for past crimes. Leaders of some of the leftist parties were happy to accept the consensus formula of the Spanish democratisation, in part to gain democratic credentials for themselves or their organisations that in fact they had lacked in the past.

Against this historical reality the Law of Historical Memory proposed to establish by legislative fiat how Spaniards are to understand and define the issues of the Civil War of 1936–9, re-baptising Stalinists as 'democrats'. A research study which revealed the falseness of much of Zapatero's own claims about his grandfather in the Civil War managed to find a publisher, but has been completely ignored by scholarly reviews and the media (except for independent radio), partly for fear of political reprisals.[40] Thus the issues in Spain have been neatly reversed in the most extensive and successful application of political correctness ideology in any western country.

The constructions of so-called 'memory', that is, ideas and contentions about history, are endless, and are mobilised and targeted in almost every conceivable direction.[41] If the past is divisive, memory will be equally divided and divisive. The past can only be dealt with seriously and truthfully, however, on the basis of rigorous historical study, not the projections of political partisanship. The past should never be forgotten and should constantly be subject to serious investigation, but national reconciliation can never be achieved be achieved if present politics are based on past divisions.

V. The Limits of Retribution and its Role in Successful Democratisation

The experience of many different countries has clearly demonstrated that the goal of building liberal democracy may require a distinction between democratisation and complete judicial retribution. In the case of Austria, Pelinka has made the point that 'the domestic appeasement of former Nazis made it possible to gradually integrate a large portion of these former Nazis into the basic consensus of the Second Republic'.[42] A similar policy was pursued by Konrad Adenauer in Germany during the 1950s. In Italy, the state apparatus, which consisted mainly of former Fascists, continued to function after the end of the war, and in Italy, it was Palmiro Togliatti, the leader of the Italian Communist Party, who drafted the amnesty law that ended judicial purges, which had been very limited in any case.[43]

In France, after the liberation courts examined 160,287 cases, only about 24 per cent of them ended in prison terms, and another 25 per cent in national dishonour and the loss of civil rights.[44] Many prominent Vichyites escaped punishment, and, as in other countries, for practical reasons many Vichy bureaucrats continued to serve under postwar administrations. The first amnesty law was enacted in 1951, and in 1953, for the sake of '*la paix civile*', the country approved amnesty laws for treason and collaboration with the Nazis. Crimes against humanity were recognised by French law only in 1964, but the new measures were aimed mainly at Nazi criminals. The case against a major French perpetrator, Paul Touvier, was a rather collateral and lukewarm consequence of this law.[45]

In Japan, the political purge initiated and conducted by the U.S. occupation administration was aimed at those responsible for the policies of the old regime. However, established party politicians, big businessmen and, especially, career civil servants became the new ruling elite, thus providing a certain continuity with the previous one. Largely spared by the purge of the postwar period, the bureaucracy acquired and still holds more influence and power than before and during the war.[46]

It seems that in a transitional period civil administrations and bureaucracies cannot function effectively without making use of many of those who served under the previous totalitarian/authoritarian regimes, even though many of the latter may have been at least accomplices in preceding injustices. This is true not only with regard to the fascist and Right authoritarian regimes but also with regard to many post-communist countries of east central Europe. Such continuity did not prevent successful transformation. On the other hand, the example of Russia in seemingly choosing a similar path is clearly disappointing.

Apparently, the difference is not in continuity of the bureaucratic apparatus *per se*, but in other procedures. Institutional change is more important than a change of personnel. The successful transition depends on development and implementation of new rules of the game and procedures, such as the rule of a state of law, a multi-party system, free elections, separation of powers, checks and balances, and certain others. At the same time, it is also indispensable that the totalitarian/authoritarian regimes also be discredited in political, judicial and moral terms. This never happened in Russia, despite a few timid and inconsistent attempts at the beginning of the transitional period that were completely abandoned and even reversed after Putin's ascendancy to power.

The dismantling of repressive agencies and an apparatus of ruling totalitarian parties, as well as expelling the chief personnel of the latter, are more important than thorough punishment of individual culprits. One of the first measures undertaken by most post-communist governments was the dismantling or radical reform of the secret services. In Russia, on the contrary, timid and inconsistent attempts by the Yeltsin leadership to reform the main repressive agency, the KGB (at present, the FSB), have failed completely. In 1993, Yeltsin warned that the system of political police might be resurrected, and his words were prophetic. Shortly before Putin took power, the new president joked in the company of his former colleagues that FSB operatives 'dispatched under cover to work in the government of the Russian Federation were successfully fulfilling their task'. This jest was made public, because in fact it was not a joke. Nowadays, the FSB controls the government, administration, judiciary, economy, mass media and most other spheres of public life. Three out of four senior officials in the country were once affiliated with the KGB/FSB or with a military that has not been not reformed either. Preventive repression and the arbitrary abuse of administrative powers have once again become the order of the day.

In some cases, reform of the army should also be a precondition for successful transition. This was not the most urgent concern for post-communist countries, for there the army had not been an independent institution, and the military had been under strict party surveillance and control. But in postwar Japan, generally characterised by considerable institutional continuity, the armed forces were an exception, because the Allies made the military leadership the main targets.

In addition, the legitimacy of the emerging democratic order becomes stronger if the new political elite have genuine democratic credentials at the highest level. Political regimes are created, supported and changed not by blind political forces but by human beings responsible for their actions and inactions. If, so to speak, the equivalent of a dedicated atheist suddenly becomes a cardinal without living a day as an ordinary parishioner, this may compromise the fairness of the transition, even if it does not frustrate its ultimate goals. The founding fathers of the West German state and the Second Republic in Austria had in no way been implicated in Nazi crimes; some of them had been victims. In France, the composition of the upper echelons of the political class changed significantly in the aftermath of the liberation. The credentials of De Gaulle and many other members of the first postwar governments were impeccable.

Similar claims may be made about some, but far from all, of the new elites in post-communist countries. In Poland and Hungary former communists (many of them old regime reformers), who converted to social democracy, had to wait for their turn, although sometimes not for long. In Czechoslovakia, and then in the Czech Republic, they never returned to power at all, but in Romania, Slovakia and Bulgaria they did not have to wait; they led the first transitional governments. In any case, those who returned to power did not belong to the top echelons of the former ruling elites during the communist period and were, at worse, accomplices but not perpetrators. There is also another circumstance that should be taken into account. In many East Central European post-communist countries one witnessed not only a certain turnover of the ruling elites but – and this is more important – an institutional and ideological break with the communist past. In Poland and Hungary, those has-beens who had remained in the political elites or returned to power were unable to operate anymore as representatives of the *nomenklatura* class because this class and its power base to a large extent had ceased to exist. Last but not least, the construction or reconstruction of civil society and a degree of economic success are also important for successful transitions. Only then do people become convinced that, in accordance with Winston Churchill's famous saying, democracy is the worst form of government, except for all the others.

This is what was successfully accomplished in the West European countries after the war, in Southern Europe during the 1970s, and more or less successfully in east central European countries after the collapse of communism, but not in Russia, or in most post-Soviet countries. In Russia, the old nomenklatura remains in power. Granted, it has incorporated some new members, and the balance of power between its different groups has changed, just as the legitimisation of its power, but it continues to exercise excessive and arbitrary control over the society and economy.[47]

Our conclusion may seem disappointing and even repugnant from the moral point of view. As human beings we are not happy with it either, but as scholars we must admit that it is based on numerous facts. Consistent and large-scale prosecution of perpetrators is not indispensable and sometimes is even detrimental for the success of the democratisation process, since it may have destabilising effects. The postwar situation in western Europe was exceptional. There are other ways of dealing with a repressive past: free and open historical reckoning, public debate, commemoration of victims. In many countries, victims are fated to live beside unpunished and sometimes unrepentant perpetrators and their accomplices, who by no means are considered as such by a great number, sometimes even by the majority, of their compatriots. This is regrettable and unfair, but in such cases justice and fairness often resemble a train that arrives at the station too late, if it arrives at all.

It seems that a repressive past cannot be overcome completely until it becomes more distant history. Otherwise, the point of closure becomes impossible. Although failure to rectify past injustices may undermine the legitimacy of new states,[48] it is said that only victims have the right to forgive, and most victims are already dead. What remains is guilt or its denial. The examples we have dealt with clearly demonstrate that 50 or 60 years' historical distance is not enough for the atrocities, crimes, and repressions of the twentieth century to be forgotten or forgiven. And there is also a danger that this past may be revised and manipulated by partisan political forces.

Notes

1. Simon Torney, *Making Sense of Tyranny. Interpretations of Totalitarianism* (Manchester: Manchester University Press, 1995) p.187.
2. Juan. J. Linz, *Totalitarian and Authoritarian Regimes* (London: Lynne Rienner, 2000), pp.102–7.
3. Eric Hobsbawm, *The Age of Extremes. A History of the World, 1914–1991* (New York: Vintage, 1996), p.ix.
4. Tony Judt, "The Past is Another Country: Myth and Memory in Postwar Europe", *Daedalus* 121/4 (1992), pp.83–118.

5. Richard Mitten, *The Waldheim Phenomenon in Austria: The Politics of Anti-Semitic Prejudice* (Boulder, CO: Westview, 1992).

6. For a survey of post-fascist countries in this regard, see István Deak, Jan T. Gross and Tony Judt (eds), *The Politics of Retribution in Europe: World War II and its Aftermath* (Princeton, NJ: Princeton University Press, 2000), and, for post-communist countries, Timothy Garton-Ash, "Trials, Purges and History Lessons: Treating a Difficult Past in Post-Communist Eastern Europe", in Jan-Werner Müller (ed.), *Memory and Power in Post-War Europe. Studies in the Presence of the Past* (Cambridge: Cambridge University Press, 2002), pp.265–82.

7. Richard A. Wilson, "Justice and Legitimacy in the South African Transition", in Alexandra Barahona de Brito, Carmen González-Enríquez and Paloma Aguilar (eds), *The Politics of Memory. Transitional Justice in Democratizing Societies* (Oxford: Oxford University Press, 2001), pp.190–217.

8. Paloma Aguilar, *Memory and Amnesia: The Role of the Spanish Civil War in the Transition to Democracy* (New York: Berghahn, 2002); Stanley G. Payne (ed.), *The Politics of Democratic Spain* (Chicago, IL: Chicago Council on Foreign Relations, 1986); Paul Preston, *Revenge and Reconciliation: The Spanish Civil War and Historical Memory*. Working Paper of the Center for European Studies, Harvard University, Cambridge, Massachusetts, 1999; José Félix Tezanos, Ramón Cotarelo and Andrés de Blas (eds), *La transición democrática española* (Madrid: Sistema, 1989).

9. See, for example, Heidemarie Uhl, "From Victim Myth to Co-Responsibility Thesis", in Richard Ned Lebow, Wulf Kansteiner and Claudio Fogu (eds), *The Politics of Memory in Postwar Europe* (Durham, NC: Duke University Press, 2006), pp.40–72; Henri Rousso, *The Vichy Syndrome: History and Memory in France since 1944* (Cambridge, MA: Harvard University Press, 1991); Claudio Fogu, "*Italiani brava gente*: The Legacy of Fascist Historical Culture on Italian Politics of Memory", in Lebow et al. (eds), *The Politics of Memory in Postwar Europe*, pp.147–76; and Ian Buruma, *The Wages of Guilt: Memories of War in Germany and Japan* (New York: Farrar Strauss Giroux, 1994).

10. Anatoly M. Khazanov, *After the USSR: Ethnicity, Nationalism, and Politics in the Commonwealth of Independent States* (Madison, WI: University of Wisconsin Press, 1995).

11. Uhl (note 9), pp.40–72.

12. Richard J. Golsan, "The Legacy of World War II in France: Mapping the Discourses of Memory", in Lebow et al. (eds) (note 9), p.80.

13. Robert Gildea, *Marianne in Chains: In Search of the German Occupation, 1940–1945* (London: Macmillan, 2002).

14. Ernest Renan, "What is a Nation?", in Omar Dahbour and Micheline R. Ishay, *The Nationalism Reader* (Atlantic City, NJ: Humanities Press, 1995), pp.143–55.

15. Lev Gudkov, *Negativnaia identichnost'* (Moscow: Novoe Literaturnoe Obozrenie, 2004).

16. Laszlo Karsai, "The People's Courts and Revolutionary Justice in Hungary, 1945–46", in Deak et al. (eds.) (note 6), pp.233–51. For the case of Czechoslovakia, where more than 100,000 perpetrators and collaborators were prosecuted, see Benjamin Frommer, *National Cleansing: Retribution against Nazi Collaborators in Postwar Czechoslovakia* (Cambridge: Cambridge University Press, 2004).

17. Heidemarie Uhl, "The Politics of Memory: Austria's Perception of the Second World War and the National Socialist Period", in Günter Bischof and Anton Pelinka (eds), *Austrian Historical Memory and National Identity* (New Brunswick , N.J: Transaction, 1997), pp.64–94, and, for the broader contrast with Germany, David Art, *The Politics of the Nazi Past in Germany and Austria* (Cambridge: Cambridge University Press, 2005).

18. Brigitte Bailer, "They were all Victims: The Selective Treatment of the Consequences of National Socialism", in Bischof and Pelinka (eds) (note 17), pp.103–15.

19. Simon Wiesenthal, *Doch die Mörder leben* (ed. Joseph Wechsberg) (Munich: Droemer Knaur, 1967).

20. This is the calculation first made by Peter Novick, *The Resistance versus Vichy* (London: Charles and Windus, 1968), and generally confirmed by the more detailed investigation synthesized by Marcel Baudot, "L'Épuration: Bilan chiffré", *Bulletin de l'Institut d'Histoire du Temps Présent* 35 (1986), pp.37–53. The legal prosecution of collaborators was proportionately less extensive in France than in the democracies to the north, amounting to indictment of approximately 163,000 alleged collaborators. Of the 7037 death sentences, however, 791 were carried out. There were 2777 life sentences, 10,434 condemnations to forced labor and 26,289 other prison sentences, as well as many other smaller penalties. Philippe Bourdrel, *L'Épuration sauvage*, 2 vols (Paris: CNRS Éditions, 1988).

21. Giorgio Pisanò, *Il triangolo della morte: la politica della strage in Emilia durante e dopo la guerra civile* (Milan: Mursia, 2003).

22. Hans Woller, *I conti con il fascismo: l'epurazione in Italia, 1943–1948* (Bologna: Il Mulino, 2004) and Claudio Fogu, "*Italiani brava gente*: The Legacy of Fascist Historical Culture on Italian Politics of Memory", in Lebow et al. (eds.), (note 9), pp.147–76.

23. John Borneman, *Settling Accounts. Violence, Justice, and Accountability in Postsocialist Europe* (Princeton, NJ: Princeton University Press, 1997).
24. Tina Rosenberg, *The Haunted Land: Facing Europe's Ghosts after Communism* (New York: Vintage, 1996), p.xxi.
25. Mary Ellen Fisher, "Romania: The Anguish of Postcommunist Politics", in Fisher (ed.), *Establishing Democracies* (Boulder, CO: Westview, 1996), pp.178–212.
26. Jan-Werner Müller, "East Germany: Incorporation, Tainted Truth, and Double Division", in Barahona de Brito et al. (eds), *The Politics of Memory* (note 7), pp.248–74.
27. Jan-Werner Müller, "Introduction: The Power of Memory, the Memory of Power and Power over Memory", in Müller (ed.) (note 6), pp.1–35.
28. For futher discussion of transitional justice, see Neil J. Kritz, *Transitional Justice*, 3 vols (Washington, DC: United States Institute of Peace Press, 1995), James A. McAdams (ed.), *Transitional Justice and the Rule of Law in Democracies* (South Bend, IN: Notre Dame University Press, 1997), Eleazar Barkan, *Guilt of Nations: Restitution and Negotiating Historical Injustices* (New York: W. W. Norton, 2000), Claus Offe, "Coming to Terms with Past Injustices", *Archives Européennes de Sociologie* 33/1 (1992), pp.195–201, Jon Elster, "Coming to Terms with the Past. A Framework for the Study of Justice in the Transition to Democracy", *Archives Européennes de Sociologie* 39/1 (1998), pp.7–48, and Jon Elster, "Justicia transicional", *Claves de razón práctica* 169 (2007), pp.4–12.
29. Omer Bartov, "On Eastern Galicia's Past and Present", *Daedalus* 136/3 (2007), pp.115–18.
30. Uhl, "The Politics of Memory", in Bischof and Pelinka (eds) (note 17), pp.66, 72.
31. Claudio Fogu, "*Italiani brava gente*", in Lebow et al. (eds) (note 9), p.147.
32. Yoshio Sugimoto, "Nation and Nationalism in Contemporary Japan", in Gerard Delanty and Krishan Kumar (eds), *The SAGE Handbook of Nations and Nationalism* (London: SAGE Publications, 2006), pp.472–87.
33. Richard J. Evans, *In Hitler's Shadow. West German Historians and the Attempt to Escape from the Nazi Past* (London: I. B. Tauris, 1989).
34. Jeffrey K. Olick, "What Does it Mean to Normalize the Past? Official Memory in German Politics since 1989", in Jeffrey K. Olick (ed.), *Continuities, Conflicts and Transformations in National Retrospection* (Durham, NC: Duke University Press, 2003), pp.259–88.
35. Timothy Garton Ash, "Trials, Purges and History Lessons: Treating a Difficult Past in Post-Communist Europe", in Müller (ed.) (note 6), pp.265–82.
36. See, for example, Luisa Passerini, *Memory and Totalitarianism* (Oxford: Oxford University Press, 1992), David E. Lorey and William H. Beezley (eds), *Genocide, Collective Violence, and Popular Memory: The Politics of Remembrance in the Twentieth Century* (New York: W. W. Norton, 2002), Andrei S. Markovits and Simon Reich, *The German Predicament: Memory and Power in the New Europe* (Ithaca, NY: Cornell University Press, 2003), Antonio Gómez López-Quiñones, *La guerra persistente. Memoria, violencia y utopia; representaciones contemporáneas de la Guerra Civil española* (Madrid: Iberoamericana, 2006), and Ulrich Winter (ed.), *Lugares de la memoria de la Guerra Civil y el franquismo. Representaciones literarias y visuales* (Madrid: Iberoamericana, 2006).
37. The distinction was also recognized by the leading contemporary specialist in the field of memory study, Pierre Nora, in his *Realms of Memory: The Construction of the French Past*, ed. L. C. Critzman (New York: Columbia University Press, 1996–8), vol. I, pp.xv–xxiv, 1–23, as noted in Steve J. Stern, *Remembering Pinochet's Chile: On the Eve of London 1998* (Durham, NC: Duke University Press, 2004), pp.xxvii–xxviii, 163. The issue is well addressed by Enrique Gavilán, "La imposibilidad y la necesidad de la memoria histórica", in Emilio Silva, et al. (eds), *La memoria de los olvidados: Un debate sobre el silencio de la represión franquista* (Valladolid: Ámbito, 2004), pp.55–65, and is also addressed by Wolf Kansteiner, "Finding Meaning in Memory: A Methodological Critique of Collective Memory Studies", *History and Theory* 41 (2002), pp.179–97.
38. Santos Juliá (ed.), *Memoria de la guerra y del franquismo* (Madrid: Taurus, 2007), and "Memoria y amnistía en la transición a la democracia", in *Transition, Démocratie et Élections* (Madrid: Les Cahiers du Colegio de España, 2004), pp.23–33.
39. Javier Tusell, "No hubo un 'Pacto del Silencio'", *Clío* 45 (2002), p.18, and "La reconciliación española", *Claves de razón práctica* 132 (2003), pp.32–39.
40. Isabel Durán and Carlos Dávila, *La gran revancha. La deformada memoria histórica de Zapatero* (Madrid: Temas de Hoy, 2006).
41. James Fentriss and Chris Wickham, *Social Memory* (Oxford: Oxford University Press, 1992).
42. Anton Pelinka, "Taboos and Self-Deception: The Second Republic's Reconstruction of History", in Bischof and Pelinka (eds) (note 17), p.99.
43. Tony Judt, "The Past is Another Country: Myth and Memory in Postwar Europe", *Daedalus* 121/4 (1992), pp.83–118.

44. Henri Rousso (note 9), p.8.
45. Richard J. Golsan, *Memory, the Holocaust, and French Justice: The Bousquet and Touvier Affairs* (Hanover, NH: University Press of New England, 1996).
46. Steven A. Hoffmann, "Japan: Foreign Occupation and Domestic Transition", in Fisher (ed.) (note 25), pp.115–48.
47. Anatoly M. Khazanov, "What went wrong? Post-communist Transformations in Comparative Perspective", in Yitzhak Brudny, Jonathan Frankel and Stefani Hoffman (eds), *Restructuring Post-communist Russia* (Cambridge: Cambridge University Press, 2004), pp.21–51.
48. John Borneman, *Settling Accounts. Violence, Justice, and Accountability in Postsocialist Europe* (Princeton, NJ: Princeton University Press, 1997), p.x.

Index

For Product Safety Concerns and Information please contact our EU representative GPSR@taylorandfrancis.com Taylor & Francis Verlag GmbH, Kaufingerstraße 24, 80331 München, Germany

T - #0175 - 270225 - C0 - 246/174/16 - PB - 9780415850247 - Gloss Lamination